FRIENDLY FIRE

FRIENDLY FIRE

NUCLEAR POLITICS & THE COLLAPSE OF ANZUS, 1984–1987

GERALD HENSLEY

AUCKLAND
UNIVERSITY
PRESS

First published 2013

Auckland University Press
University of Auckland
Private Bag 92019
Auckland 1142
New Zealand
www.press.auckland.ac.nz

© Gerald Hensley, 2013

ISBN 978 1 86940 741 4

Publication is kindly assisted by

National Library of New Zealand Cataloguing-in-Publication Data
Hensley, G. C. (Gerald Christopher)
Friendly fire : nuclear politics and the collapse of ANZUS,
1984-1987 / Gerald Hensley.
Includes bibliographical references and index.
ISBN 978-1-86940-741-4
1. Australia. Treaties, etc. 1951 Sept. 1. 2. New Zealand—
Foreign relations—United States. 3. United States—
Foreign relations—New Zealand. 4. New Zealand—
Politics and government—1984- I. Title.
327.93073—dc 23

This book is copyright. Apart from fair dealing for the purpose of private study, research, criticism or review, as permitted under the Copyright Act, no part may be reproduced by any process without prior permission of the publisher.

Cover design: Jason Gabbert
Book design: Katrina Duncan

Printed in China through Asia Pacific Offset Limited

In memory of my grandson, Geoffrey Peren, 1991–2011

Contents

	Preface	ix
	Cast of Characters	xvi
ONE	New Zealand Adrift	1
TWO	The Government Changes	25
THREE	Growing Concerns	45
FOUR	The Search for a Solution	66
FIVE	Access Denied	91
SIX	The Aftershocks	116
SEVEN	The Excommunication	139
EIGHT	The Oxford Union Debate	158
NINE	The Palmer Mission	185
TEN	The British Step In	215
ELEVEN	We Part Company	241
TWELVE	The End of the Argument	268
	Epilogue	296
	Select Bibliography	308
	Index	309

Preface

This is a strange story. It gives an account of the dispute which arose in 1984 between New Zealand and the United States over the visits of warships possibly carrying nuclear weapons and which ended in New Zealand's suspension from the ANZUS alliance in 1986. These bare facts conceal a bigger story, of a major change in New Zealand's outlook on the world and the boldest revolution its foreign policy has ever undergone.

When a country's centre of gravity moves like this, even if only for a time, there are questions to be answered. The story tries to shed light on why New Zealand, which had fought throughout the Second World War in defence of Western democratic values and emerged with strongly internationalist ideals, lost confidence in this course and veered off on a more lonely path. Not just America and Australia as allies but other long-standing friends in Asia and Europe were baffled at the way in which a country, hitherto so reliable and steady, seemed abruptly to act in a way that was outside its character and history.

The most important clue to this puzzle is nationalism. New Zealand was struggling for a clearer sense of itself, and a new and more congenial sense of national identity was sought in a battle over foreign policy. A new identity could have been built on economic and social policies, as it had been decades before, but in 1984 the activists on Labour's Left abandoned economics to the free-market reformers and concentrated instead on the country's international relationships through the ANZUS quarrel.

As often in a quarrel, the two sides saw different ends of the disagreement. New Zealanders were puzzled why Washington could not see their desire to be nuclear-free as reasonable and their sovereign right. The Americans were puzzled that a country which had welcomed its ships without question for 50 years should suddenly and without consultation exclude them. They did not contest New Zealand's independent right to leave the ANZUS alliance if it chose. They were baffled because it would not choose and insisted on staying in the alliance while refusing to allow its partner's ships to visit.

The waves made by the dispute spread much wider than the United States. The other ANZUS partner, Australia, saw the alliance as crucial to its security and feared that the differences could end in the treaty's destruction. Countries like Japan, the ASEAN members, Germany and the other states of Western Europe were puzzled by what New Zealand wanted. They were in the nuclear firing line, New Zealand was not, and it was hard for them to understand why a remote and non-nuclear country in the South Pacific would become so concerned.

For several, like Japan, their own non-nuclear status depended on delicate understandings which could not stand too much daylight. Europe had just come through a crisis over the deployment of further nuclear weapons. German and other leaders had faced down considerable popular agitation over this issue and wondered why, in the interests of Western solidarity, New Zealand's leaders could not do the same. All were alarmed at the possibility that the country might be about to lead a crusade for unilateral disarmament and upset the fragile balance on which their security had come to depend.

PREFACE

The story of the dispute and how it was managed revolves around the large and ambiguous figure of David Lange. He directed its course and became recognised the world over as an eloquent opponent of the arms race. He was a natural orator with a ready mind and great charm. He had a big heart, which was important for leading the Labour Party, and above all he had that priceless political asset, the gift of compelling attention.

Because of his dominance in the ANZUS affair it is important to keep in mind that this is not a full or rounded biography of the Prime Minister. He emerges from the flow of the narrative looking much less tidy than when he went in. If he was trapped in a devil's bargain with the Left to protect his government's economic reforms, as Bob Hawke believed, he never had any real flexibility, even supposing he wanted it, to seek a compromise over ship visits. No one shows their best side in managing such tight circumstances.

His great gifts were those of an entertainer (a role which he took up in retirement), and so he loved his own press conferences, giving more than any Prime Minister before or since. He conducted a large part of his foreign policy, including the ANZUS crisis, through those press conferences and claimed to be surprised that his quips were closely scrutinised in foreign capitals for signs of what he might do next. His ambassador in Washington, Bill Rowling, came to dread the Monday press conferences.

He was obliged by his political circumstances to reassure his supporters that the anti-nuclear stance would never be compromised, while attempting to persuade the Americans and others to accept that New Zealand could make an equally valuable contribution to the alliance by other means. This was too big a stretch for the Americans who had their network of other alliances to protect. Lange found himself pursuing a two-handed diplomacy, telling the Americans, British and Australians that he was anxious to negotiate, while insisting to the public that his policy was non-negotiable. When this was understood, the Americans lost confidence, deciding that the Prime Minister was simply playing them on a line until they got tired.

Stapleton Roy, coming into a senior post at the State Department, reviewed the negotiating record at the end of 1986 and noted 'the absence of evidence that the government had actively tried to move in the direction in which it had assured the Administration that it wanted to go'.* The Americans came to a sharp conclusion: 'Your Prime Minister could not keep his word,' said George Shultz, the Secretary of State.†

Everyone who worked with David Lange was familiar with the story-telling amid bursts of laughter, with the embroidering or rearrangement of facts to avoid trouble, conciliate the hearer, or make a funnier anecdote. It was part of his charm. Even so it was surprising and saddening to discover that he had told his colleagues that he had known nothing of the proposed visit by the USS *Buchanan* until the end of January 1985, despite having sent the Chief of Defence Staff to Honolulu the previous November to choose it and having discussed it at length with his advisers and with the American ambassador thereafter. His evasiveness is the least comfortable aspect of Lange but it is far from the whole man.

He presided over one of the brightest and most energetic governments the country has known with a brilliance and generosity of spirit that have left an enduring mark. Throughout the twists of the ANZUS dispute the Prime Minister was also overseeing a programme of major and exacting economic change. Running a government is a hugely demanding task and David Lange was not built for the long haul. He was uncomfortable with the relentless pressure of government and could become impatient or impulsive when challenged. When he learnt of the *Buchanan* disclaimer, his friend and colleague Mike Moore was as troubled as I was. He concluded, he said, that there was a good David and a bad David.‡ This story often shows the

---

* Talking to the Washington embassy, 6 November 1986, PM 111/3/3/1 Part 54, ANZ.
† To Denis McLean, ambassador in Washington, in 1991. Margaret Clark (ed.), *For the Record: Lange and the Fourth Labour Government*, Dunmore Press, 2005, p. 149.
‡ A last comment to me in Washington as I left for the airport, 2 October 2011.

PREFACE

lesser David but it needs to be kept in mind that there was another David as well.

In acknowledging the help I have received in writing this account, the first place must therefore go to David Lange whose wit, restlessness and outspoken moments have (I hope) helped relieve the tedium that can shadow diplomatic history. The narrative records a major change in New Zealand's international outlook and how this affected relations with its traditional partners and friends. Michael Bassett's history of the Lange administration, *Working With David*, is an indispensable background and he was the pioneer in trying to unravel the mysteries of the first attempt at a ship visit. The book is not a history of the peace movement that worked to bring about the anti-nuclear policy – Kevin Clements in *Back from the Brink* writes a good memoir of his experiences in the movement. The rise of anti-nuclear feeling in the country from 1945 is comprehensively covered in *Standing Upright Here* by Malcolm Templeton. David Lange's own books, especially *Nuclear Free: The New Zealand Way*, give a cheerful account of varying reliability.*

A full account of this dispute requires access to as much as possible of the records of the countries involved and this is not always readily available, even when a generation has gone by. I am grateful to the Ministry of Foreign Affairs and Trade, and especially to Neil Robertson, for providing all the files I needed, and to Archives New Zealand for their usual helpfulness. It took two years but the State Department released such a flood of material under the Freedom of Information Act that I had to buy a suitcase to bring it all home. Professor Patrick Salmon, Chief Historian of the Foreign and Commonwealth Office in London, went to great trouble to provide everything I wanted to see and a room for six weeks in which to read it. In Canberra I was fortunate to be given good access to the material

---

* Bill Hayden, Australia's Foreign Minister at the time, described it as 'a work which is less sustainable as history than as entertainment'. *Hayden: An Autobiography*, Angus & Robertson, 1996, p. 459.

held by both the Department of Foreign Affairs and Trade and the National Archives of Australia.

A point learnt quickly by the historian of contemporary affairs is that the records though indispensable are also insufficient. As Julian Barnes put it, history is 'that certainty produced at the point where the imperfections of memory meet the inadequacies of documentation'.* Memories are famously inaccurate and need to be checked against the written record, but that record is equally deficient in the feel of things, of the human uncertainties and responses that shape events. I talked with six of the surviving members of the Lange Cabinet, with Sir Geoffrey Palmer, Mike Moore, Richard Prebble, Russell Marshall, Michael Bassett and David Caygill, and with Margaret Wilson, then President of the Labour Party. Among members of the Foreign Ministry, I was helped by Merv Norrish, then Secretary; by the recollections of John Wood and Simon Murdoch who were in the Washington embassy at the time; by Tony Browne, Gordon Shroff and Adrian Macey who were with the Prime Minister on his Tokelau trip; and by Bruce Brown and Derek Leask who were in the party at the Oxford Union debate. In addition I had discussions with Sir Ewan Jamieson, then Chief of Defence Staff; Denis McLean, then Secretary of Defence, and with Ross Vintiner, the Prime Minister's Chief Press Secretary. Of all the significant participants, only Margaret Pope was unwilling to talk and Helen Clark did not reply to two requests.

In the United States I was able to talk with the former Secretary of State, George Shultz, and his then Under Secretary, Michael Armacost, at Stanford University; and in Washington with Paul Wolfowitz, Morton Abramowitz and Bill Brown of the State Department, Richard Armitage and Jim Kelly of the Pentagon and David Laux and Karl Jackson of the National Security Council. Paul Cleveland, ambassador for the last part of the period, and Richard Teare, Deputy Chief of Mission for most of it, went to considerable

---

* *The Sense of an Ending*, Alfred A. Knopf, 2011, p. 18.

PREFACE

trouble to check points for me and Peter Watson was tirelessly kind in his help.

In London, Lord Howe, then Foreign Secretary, gave up a morning to talk and Roland Rudd, the former President of the Oxford Union, remembered the great debate. Among the Australians consulted, Bob Hawke gave the uncompromising views set out in Chapter Three and Kim Beazley, then Defence Minister, was equally helpful if a little less colourful.

Accuracy is critical when history is still being argued over, and so I am ever grateful to my wife, Juliet, for her thorough scrutiny of the text, hoping that she has been as frank with the author as she has been tactful. I am also in debt to my son, Gerald, who (twice) arranged accommodation in Washington and escorted me to Stanford and to the Ronald Reagan Presidential Library on its bare Californian hilltop. The Ministry of Culture and Heritage supported my research with a kind and generous grant; I am grateful again to the Auckland University Press and to its director, Sam Elworthy, for his suggestions; and to Mike Wagg for his thoughtfulness as editor. I can only hope that these underpinnings will support the writer in the only real test, when the result is read.

Gerald Hensley
Kahu Vineyard, Martinborough

Cast of Characters

NEW ZEALAND
David Lange, Leader of the Opposition 1983–84, Prime Minister 1984–89
Sir Geoffrey Palmer, Deputy Prime Minister and Attorney-General
Michael Bassett, Minister of Health
David Caygill, Minister of Trade and Industry, later Minister of Finance
Helen Clark, Chair of the Parliamentary Select Committee on Foreign Affairs and Trade 1984–87, Minister of Health 1987–90
Russell Marshall, Minister of Education 1984–87, Foreign Minister 1987–90
Mike Moore, Minister of Overseas Trade
Frank O'Flynn, Minister of Defence
Richard Prebble, Minister of Transport and Railways to 1987, Minister for State-Owned Enterprises and other portfolios thereafter
Fran Wilde, Associate Minister of Foreign Affairs

Jim Anderton, President of the New Zealand Labour Party to 1983, Member of Parliament thereafter and founder of the New Labour Party 1989
Bruce Brown, Deputy High Commissioner in London
Frank Corner, Chair of the Defence Committee of Enquiry
H. H. (Tim) Francis, Deputy Secretary of Foreign Affairs
W. Bryce Harland, Foreign Service officer, Permanent Representative at the United Nations, 1981–85, High Commissioner in London 1985–91
Gerald Hensley, Head of the Prime Minister's Department 1980–87, Coordinator of Domestic and External Security 1987–89
Air Marshal Sir Ewan Jamieson, Chief of Defence Staff
Denis McLean, Secretary of Defence
Simon Murdoch, Foreign Service officer, Counsellor at the Washington Embassy
Merwyn Norrish, Secretary of Foreign Affairs
Margaret Pope, Lange's speechwriter and married to him in 1992
W. E. (Bill) Rowling, Ambassador to the United States January 1985–88
Ross Vintiner, Chief Press Secretary to David Lange to 1988
Joe Walding, former Minister of Trade, High Commissioner in London 1984–85
Margaret Wilson, President of the New Zealand Labour Party
John Wood, Foreign Service officer, Deputy at the Washington Embassy

CAST OF CHARACTERS

UNITED STATES
Ronald Reagan, President
Morton J. Abramowitz, Director of the Bureau of Intelligence and Research, State Department
Michael Armacost, Under Secretary of State for Political Affairs
Richard Armitage, Assistant Secretary of Defense for International Affairs, Department of Defense
William A. Brown, Principal Deputy Assistant Secretary of State for East Asian and Pacific Affairs, State Department
Paul Cleveland, Monroe Browne's successor, 1986–89
Jon Glassman, Country Director, Australia and New Zealand, State Department
James Kelly, Armitage's deputy at the Department of Defense
Alphonse La Porta, Teare's successor in 1986
David Laux, Asian Affairs Directorate, National Security Council
James Lilley, Brown's successor in 1985
H. Monroe Browne, US Ambassador in New Zealand, 1981–85
George P. Shultz, Secretary of State in the Reagan Administration
Gaston Sigur, Wolfowitz's successor in 1986
Richard W. Teare, Deputy Chief of Mission at the US embassy
Caspar Weinberger, Secretary of Defense
Paul Wolfowitz, Assistant Secretary of State for East Asian and Pacific Affairs

GREAT BRITAIN
Margaret Thatcher, Prime Minister
Admiral Sir John Fieldhouse, Chief of Defence Staff
Sir Geoffrey Howe, Foreign Secretary
Terence O'Leary, British High Commissioner in Wellington
John Stanley, Minister of State for the Armed Forces
Baroness (Janet) Young, Minister of State at the Foreign Office

AUSTRALIA
Bob Hawke, Prime Minister
Kim Beazley, Minister of Defence
Bill Hayden, Foreign Minister

INSTITUTIONS, DEPARTMENTS AND ARCHIVES
Archives New Zealand (ANZ)
Australian High Commission (AHC)
Australian Labor Party (ALP)
British High Commission (BHC)
Department of Foreign Affairs and Trade, Canberra (DFAT)
Department of Prime Minister and Cabinet (DPMC)
Foreign and Commonwealth Office (FCO)
Ministry of Foreign Affairs and Trade, Wellington (MFAT)
National Archives Australia (NAA)

Chapter One
New Zealand Adrift

Alliances, said General de Gaulle, are like flowers and pretty girls: they last while they last. In 1984 the ANZUS alliance had reached the age, perilous at least for pretty girls, of thirty-three. For half of its life the alliance, linking the United States, Australia and New Zealand in a common defence, had attracted little notice. It was an insurance policy against the risk of an aggression which never became real and so could rest quietly in a bottom drawer.

The instability in South East Asia which culminated in the Vietnam War changed this, emphasising to all three countries that they had a common interest in the region's security which fell well short of an attack on their territories. The ANZUS treaty did not cover this situation and though it was the risks in South East Asia which brought the three countries closer together, it was the treaty which became the symbol of this tighter relationship and, when some disillusion set in, the target of complaint. In Australia a newly elected Labor Government responded to party restlessness in 1983 with a review of the treaty but concluded there was no reason to seek any change. In New Zealand, though, the two major parties were more deeply divided over the treaty's value, and its future there hung on the swing of the electoral pendulum.

The treaty itself was a legacy of the Second World War which Australia and New Zealand had tenaciously sought for six years after the war's end. In 1941 both countries had sweated over their defenceless state in the Pacific. While Japan clearly intended to drive south, Britain with its back to the wall at home was in no state to help its Pacific dominions. The United States was the only hope but it was determinedly neutral and there was no certainty that it would intervene if any British territories were attacked. The Japanese settled these worries by attacking Pearl Harbor as well as Hong Kong and Malaya, but for a few anxious weeks with much of its Pacific Fleet destroyed it was not clear that the United States could provide any more immediate protection for the two southern countries than Britain. In Washington there was talk of pulling back to a defensive perimeter around Hawaii and abandoning everything else for the time being. Admiral King, the head of the navy and no Anglophile, squashed this decisively: 'We cannot in honour let Australia and New Zealand down. They are our brothers, and we must not allow them to be overrun by Japan.'*

The resulting wartime alliance worked well but when peace came something of the old anxiety returned. The hopes cherished in Wellington of a global collective security system run by the United Nations were quickly dashed, and though New Zealand still had nostalgic longings for the old imperial defence arrangements it was clear that security in the Pacific now depended on the United States. Washington, however, seemed no more ready to assume the burden of defending Australia and New Zealand than it had in 1941. The Truman Administration was engrossed in the need to stabilise Western Europe, which culminated in the formation of NATO in

---

* Samuel Morison, *History of United States Naval Operations in World War II*, Little, Brown and Company, 1947–62, Vol. IV, p. 246.

1949, and had little interest in Asia and none in any further security guarantees.

This outlook changed, partly because of the fall of China to the Communists that year, but most of all because of the attack on South Korea in 1950. Clearly the United States could no longer ignore the momentous changes under way in Asia. More practically, since Japan was the main base from which to fight the Korean War, a peace treaty with Japan was now urgently needed. Australia and New Zealand had been dragging their feet on a settlement for years. They were genuinely afraid of a renewal of Japanese militarism (as German militarism had revived after the earlier war) and were fearful that it would be encouraged by the growing Soviet–American rivalry. They wanted to see Japan disarmed rather than free. At one discussion the New Zealand delegate put it bluntly: 'The substance of physical disarmament should not be sacrificed for the shadow of hypothetical democratic reform.'*

The Americans wisely saw that the most generous peace settlement was also likely to be the most lasting, but the urgency of their need gave Australia and New Zealand their chance. Quite simply, they would only agree to the settlement with Japan if the United States would also conclude a treaty guaranteeing their own security. Both treaties were signed at a formal ceremony in San Francisco in September 1951, with the New Zealand signatory, Sir Carl Berendsen, telling his government that the wording of the new treaty was surpassed only by the NATO treaty in the firmness of the guarantee given by the United States.

The text of eleven articles was commendably brief – so brief indeed as later to vex the lawyers in the Lange Cabinet who felt it should have been more prescriptive as to what was and was not included. It did not name Japan or anyone else and simply gave an open guarantee that the three parties would support one another if

---

* Quoted in W. B. Harland, 'New Zealand, the United States and Asia: The Background to the Anzus Treaty', in P. Munz (ed.), *The Feel of Truth*, A. H. & A. W. Reed, 1969, p. 186.

attacked. After obeisance to the United Nations and expressing the hope (still to be met) that the treaty would in time be replaced by a comprehensive system of security in the Pacific, it laid down that in the event of a threat to any one of them the parties would consult, and in the event of an armed attack each would 'act to meet the common danger in accordance with its constitutional processes'. The only machinery established was an annual meeting of Ministers – significantly Foreign rather than Defence Ministers, for the treaty was political rather than directly military in its purposes.

The agreement was purely defensive; it guaranteed only the homelands of the parties and was deliberately unclear about how far the boundaries might extend. What attracted unfavourable comment at home was not the commitment to the United States but the exclusion of Britain. The New Zealand Prime Minister had to claim that its purpose was 'to bolt the back door', leaving the country free to help Britain elsewhere. An exchange of letters in 1963 agreed that it did not necessarily cover the armed forces or overseas territories of the parties, but then in the only known occasion when the treaty was invoked the American Secretary of State, Dean Rusk, warned the Indonesian Foreign Minister in 1964 that an attack on the Australian or New Zealand forces in Malaysia risked bringing in the United States.[*]

As the nuclear stalemate turned attention to regional uncertainties and away from the Third World War widely expected in the late 1940s, New Zealand's guarantee sat quietly in its drawer. The new societies emerging in South East Asia were all threatened by Communist takeovers or insurgencies because for many of the youthful overseas Chinese the new China of Mao Zedong seemed a more convincing path to the future than parliamentary democracy. So New Zealand and Australia went back to working with Britain to counter the Malayan insurgency and help bring Malaya and Singapore to a stable independence. This effort, which entailed the longest military deployment

---

[*] Revealed by Lee Kuan Yew in a speech on 8 August 1969, PM 58/455/1, ANZ.

in New Zealand's history, did not involve the new alliance with the United States which remained largely invisible.

That began to change in the 1960s as the United States increasingly became embroiled in Vietnam. It looked for other allies in the region who shared its concern for a non-Communist South Vietnam and especially at Australia and New Zealand. Wellington was distinctly unenthusiastic about involvement in a war to defend South Vietnam because it was doubtful of the chances of success. But the United States was the guarantor of New Zealand's security and, in the words of Sir Alister McIntosh, the Secretary of External Affairs, it was necessary to pay the insurance premium.

It was not that New Zealand's security was ever directly threatened; it was that the United States had become the only credible guarantor of a stable and non-Communist South East Asia. In 1965 this was a considerable worry in Wellington. The aftermath of war and decolonisation had left new governments struggling to establish themselves. Thailand, Malaysia and the Philippines all faced insurgencies; Indonesia had weathered one attempted Communist coup and was about to have another; and Singapore's future was still fragile. To many it looked as if the dominoes were poised to fall. Chairman Mao certainly thought so, telling the Secretary of the Vietnamese Workers' Party in 1964 that one by one the countries to the south would fall to Communism.*

The British, who had laid the foundations for Malaysia and Singapore, were economically exhausted and about to withdraw. Australia and New Zealand would face the coming turmoil in South East Asia alone unless the interest of the United States could be maintained. If a down payment on the insurance could encourage this, then it would be a bargain. So an artillery battery and later an infantry company joined the American forces in South Vietnam and ANZUS became a closer and more active alliance. Australia and

---

* Quoted by Chin Peng, Secretary-General of the Malayan Communist Party, in *My Side of History*, Media Masters, 2003, p. 440.

New Zealand gained a special status in Washington, their wider access and influence reinforced by the reluctance of the other members of the wartime club – Britain and Canada – to join the war.

The war, fought with an army of young men drafted into the ranks, became increasingly unpopular in America; and in a pattern that was to become familiar, American protest spilled over to the two southern countries where activist techniques like the Committees on Vietnam and teach-ins were easily assimilated. Though the protesters were energetic and highly motivated, their number fluctuated and they were far from a majority. The number of committed activists was estimated by the official war historian as in the 'low hundreds'.* Their protests had no effect on New Zealand's part in the war; the combat troops were withdrawn along with most of the remaining American forces in 1971. They left however an enduring legacy, a lasting suspicion of the ANZUS alliance among the young and on the Left.

This distrust was reinforced by growing worries about nuclear weapons. As early as 1975 the American embassy noted that the word 'nuclear' 'still starts New Zealand blood churning'.† The problem then was not so much weapons as nuclear propulsion. Conventionally powered American warships came and went in the years of the Labour Government – a total of at least 22 in the years 1972 to 1975 – and what weapons they carried was never questioned. The immediate difficulty was over public fears of nuclear-powered ships and the dangers of their spreading or leaking radioactivity. In 1969 the Holyoake Government had banned such visits pending US acceptance of absolute liability in the case of an accident. The embargo was satisfactorily settled five years later but the Rowling Government, still nervous, put off allowing a nuclear-powered warship to visit until after the impending election. By then it was clear the issue was broadening beyond fears of propulsion. In June 1975 the Ministry of

---

* Roberto Rabel, *New Zealand and the Vietnam War*, Auckland University Press, 2005, p. 189.
† Cable of 15 January 1975, State Department Papers.

Foreign Affairs was already warning that there would be a growing problem with visits by ships capable of carrying nuclear weapons.*

Opposition to nuclear weapons had much longer and deeper roots in the feelings of New Zealanders than the war in Vietnam, but it inevitably became entwined with doubts about the direction of American policy, doubts assiduously fed by the hard Left which argued that the alliance entangled the country in American nuclear-war-fighting strategies and thus risked New Zealand's own safety. There were fears about whether the US might become reckless in wielding its nuclear deterrent, and worries about whether Washington was in earnest in wishing to make progress in the stuttering talks on nuclear disarmament. But most people simply felt a horror of nuclear weapons and the enormous destruction they were capable of. Mutually Assured Destruction might be the doctrine which underpinned an uneasy security but its implied acceptance of a universal holocaust was repellent when looked at in the cold light of day. The security of the West, in other words, rested on a paradox: a doctrine that was acceptable only if it stayed out of sight.

In their dislike of nuclear weapons and the uncertain stalemate called peace, New Zealanders were no different from most other people, but there was a strange twist. The inhabitants of three remote islands in the South Pacific were by any yardstick among the least likely to suffer a nuclear attack, yet they often seemed more concerned than those in Europe and North America who were undeniably in the firing line. There were explanations for this: the British and American tests in the Pacific, one of which the young David Lange saw from an Auckland balcony; the French atmospheric tests in the South Pacific from which some fallout drifted over New Zealand and put radioactive strontium-90 in the nation's milk and which led Norman Kirk, the Prime Minister, to send a frigate to the test area in protest; and the continuing tests underground at

---

* Foreign Affairs cable of 24 June 1975, seeking information on how Norway and Denmark handled this situation, PM 59/8/2 Part 8, ANZ.

Mururoa long after the other nuclear powers had retreated to their own countries.*

But the strength of New Zealand's distaste was probably reinforced by distance. Where most in the West (and in the East no one had any voice) reluctantly accepted being defended by these weapons as a necessary evil, some New Zealanders felt that their country in its remoteness could perhaps dissociate itself entirely from this evil, and in doing so give a lead which might help the world to come to its senses on disarmament. A dissenting missionary zeal was never far below the country's consciousness, and the hope of setting a moral example and leading the world to better things was beguiling.

New Zealand had long been a non-nuclear country by law. It had been one of the first countries to sign and ratify the Nuclear Non-Proliferation Treaty in 1968 and in doing so had pledged among other things not to hold nuclear weapons on its territory. The only loophole, for the anti-nuclear campaigners, was that this commitment did not cover ships or aircraft in transit. Norway, also opposed to the entry of nuclear weapons, met this difficulty by making a distinction between 'stationing' and 'transit' of the weapons, placing a limit of five days on visits by warships which might be carrying them. Most other countries, including New Zealand, did not, but since almost all nuclear-capable visits were by American warships, this was the point at which the anti-Americanism ignited by Vietnam and the larger worries about nuclear weapons came together and gained critical mass.

So from the early 1970s the bipartisan consensus about the value of the alliance began to fray. The treaty, it was argued, dragged New Zealand into wars which were not its concern and worse, wars that were in support of American 'imperialism' and global dominance. By its uncritical acceptance of American ships New Zealand risked becoming a target for Soviet missiles. The country should

---

* David Lange's account is given in *Nuclear Free: The New Zealand Way*, Penguin, 1990, pp. 10–11.

think for itself and not be content to tag along as a dependent and junior partner, forever condemned to say nothing more than 'me too'. It should, in the words of an anti-war paper, stop looking at the world 'through spectacles of United States manufacture'. There was increasing talk of the need to follow an 'independent' foreign policy, a phrase never clearly defined but which was usually shorthand for views that ran counter to those of the United States and even in some cases of the West in general.

The pugnacious Prime Minister, Robert Muldoon, reacted with the policy of confrontation always congenial to him. He was uneasy that the United States, under the impact of Watergate and Vietnam, might lose interest in New Zealand, and publicly cited this as a reason for welcoming nuclear-propelled warships (NPWs). Since he did nothing by halves he was suspected of pressing for more ship visits than Washington would have liked. An article in the *Wall Street Journal* quoted 'a former New Zealand diplomat' as saying that he had requested ship visits whenever it suited him domestically, such as on the eve of a conference of his political opponents. The Ministry of Foreign Affairs said it had no material on its files suggesting that the timing of visits 'has been determined by other than naval operational requirements'.* But the sequence of NPW visits which began in 1976 had the effect, intended or not, of further polarising opinion.

The accident in 1979 at the Three Mile Island nuclear power station did nothing to calm fears of nuclear propulsion. Senior Labour figures began to refer ambiguously to banning 'nuclear ships', and the party leader, Bill Rowling, said in Washington that nuclear ship visits seemed 'more of a convenience than a necessity' and he did not think that a ban would disturb relations in other areas.† In 1982, when the cruiser USS *Truxtun* visited, a Heylen poll suggested that 53 per cent of Aucklanders would still accept visits by ships carrying nuclear weapons, but Rowling could describe the visit as America 'thumbing

---

* *Wall Street Journal*, 24 September 1984.
† US Embassy report of 20 April 1979, State Department Papers.

its nose at a large body of New Zealand people'. By then the American embassy was reporting that a significant minority of New Zealanders had begun to question their country's close ties with the United States: 'These New Zealanders are wary of what they see as cultural and political dominance by the United States, and they believe that New Zealand's interests would be best served by a rejection of traditional alliances, with the hope that such a neutral stance would spare the country from involvement in any future super-power conflict.'*

Then outside events took a hand, seeming to confirm these views. Western Europe was plunged into an upheaval of anti-nuclear agitation over proposals for the deployment of more American missiles. In the late 1970s the Russians took a surprising gamble: they began replacing obsolete, liquid-fuelled missiles targeting Western Europe with the hugely more powerful SS-20 missiles, solid-fuelled, quick to fire and carrying multiple nuclear warheads. It is still not clear why they did so. It may have been, as they said, that removing obsolete weapons inevitably meant more effective replacements, but governments in the West saw it as a blatant bid to shift the balance of power in Europe. These were 'theatre' missiles and could not reach the United States. By threatening Western Europe alone they raised doubts whether America would be willing to imperil its own cities in the defence of Europe, leading to a possible loss of confidence in the United States and perhaps in time to that long-held Soviet hope, a neutral Europe.

These calculations brought a vigorous response from NATO: the Soviet Union could either remove the new deployments or accept that they would be countered by a matching deployment in Europe of American cruise and Pershing II missiles. Moscow decided to do neither but instead to rely on another gamble – that public opinion in the countries where the new missiles would be based, West Germany, Britain, Italy, Belgium and the Netherlands, would force their governments to back down and refuse the deployments. The gamble nearly

---

* Cable from US Embassy of 28 May 1982, State Department Papers.

succeeded. There were huge demonstrations in Germany – 400,000 took part in one in Berlin; the Greenham Common women took up residence in the British countryside; and the fate of the Dutch and Belgian governments teetered in the storm. Protests against the 'arms race' surged back and forth for months, and though 'European peace movements scarcely required Soviet encouragement to mount protest campaigns' the KGB was estimated by a knowledgeable authority to have spent large sums doing just that.*

In the end, though, after some wavering Western governments and their electorates held firm against the threat, the Soviet gamble failed and the American deployments went ahead. It might indeed have been a last throw of the dice for the Soviet Union which, discouraged by the failure and staggering under the burden of the arms race, began to turn its thoughts to serious negotiations with the Reagan Administration. It was helped to do so because in the process of frightening Europe it had managed to frighten itself.

From 1981 the belligerent speeches of the early Reagan Administration began to persuade Moscow that the West was actually planning a nuclear attack. These fears came close to panic in November 1983 when the Soviet leaders became convinced that a NATO exercise, code-named *Able Archer*, was the cover behind which a real attack would be launched. KGB residencies were asked to count how long into the night windows in the British Ministry of Defence were lit; whether the price of blood was rising (it never occurred to them that in the West people *donated* blood); and whether, as it assumed would be the case in capitalist societies, church leaders and top bankers had been tipped off by the government. Despite these absurd touches, and though the danger was unknown in the West at the time, the Soviet panic – at one point it was believed in Moscow that war was only five to seven days away – brought the world closer to nuclear war than at any time since the Cuban missile crisis 21 years earlier.

---

* Christopher Andrew and Oleg Gordievsky, *KGB: The Inside Story*, Hodder & Stoughton, 1990, pp. 491–2.

With *Able Archer* safely out of the way and protests dying away in Western Europe, the nuclear issue seemed likely to become dormant. But the wash of that upheaval, travelling like a seismic wave across the globe, came to rest in New Zealand. The emotions, arguments and techniques of the campaign and above all the example of widespread popular action were invigorating for the New Zealand peace workers. They needed no more encouragement from the Soviet Union than their European counterparts but the Soviet Union, still smarting from failure in Europe, saw some compensatory hopes in the Antipodes. New Zealand was not Germany, but if it could be detached from the Western alliance that would be at least a consolation prize and might lead to further defections. Oleg Gordievsky, a former rising star in the KGB who had at one stage overseen Australian and New Zealand affairs, was asked in 1986 how much his old service might have spent on a New Zealand campaign. He was cautious, saying that money was not always the answer. 'You must remember', he said, 'that we in the KGB know the Left. We know the buttons to push.'[*]

Despite its growing reluctance to accept nuclear ships, the Labour Party leadership, mindful of broader backing for the alliance, had continued to hold on to its traditional support for ANZUS but as the pressure mounted in the early 1980s it began to hedge. In the face of party calls for withdrawal from all military alliances the leadership asserted that the treaty as it stood was 'out of time' and 'no longer acceptable in its present form'. These criticisms were more in tune with the party mood and indeed with a party which had changed considerably over the previous decade. Its traditional working-class origins had faded with the shifts in New Zealand society and it was increasingly becoming a party of intellectuals – university lecturers, teachers and lawyers, 'a Left of comfortable middle class circumstances rather than a proletarian hard Left'.[†] Middle-class radicals

---

[*] Comment to the author.
[†] Richard W. Teare in *Frontline Diplomacy*, Foreign Affairs Oral History Collection, Washington.

with safe jobs were interested in issues like the arms race rather than the country's economic problems, and though they would occasionally express ritual disapproval of both the superpowers, in practice they concentrated their fire on the United States as closer to hand and more susceptible to influence. Congressman Stephen Solarz said he was told by Margaret Wilson, then President of the Labour Party, that nuclear weapons were immoral and his country should give up its nuclear weapons unilaterally; she did not think the Soviet Union would take advantage of the resulting imbalance.[*]

David Lange, who had taken over the party leadership in February 1983, had earlier told the Americans he foresaw no insuperable problems in working with them in ANZUS, but the man he replaced, Bill Rowling, was more doubtful and more active in the party.[†] He circulated a memorandum which called on the party 'to stick by its principles and not be swayed by the current state of public opinion. Instead Labour should seek to educate the public into an anti-ANZUS position.' The treaty should be renegotiated to replace 'a sterile military obligation' with a greater emphasis on economic development. Above all, it should become a truly equal partnership with 'absolutely no surrender of national sovereignty'.

If the Americans resisted this, then any blame would rest on them, Rowling argued, in words which were something of an embarrassment when he later became ambassador to Washington: 'In the unlikely event that the US makes it clear that the price of maintaining ANZUS is US nuclear ship visits, then a Labour Government could argue that it is the US which has made the cost of ANZUS prohibitive.'[‡] At its conference in September 1983 the party overwhelmingly agreed with Rowling's proposal that in power Labour would renegotiate the ANZUS treaty to take account of 'New Zealand's unequivocal anti-nuclear position'. David Lange, though party leader,

---

[*] Cable of 24 January 1986, State Department Papers.
[†] US embassy report of a discussion with him, 23 December 1982, State Department Papers.
[‡] Memorandum for the Labour Policy Council, 13 May 1983.

did not speak in the discussion. After that conference the party battle lines were drawn and the future of ANZUS rested with the voters.

Something as fundamental as a country's security does not normally become a matter of partisan argument, unless there has been a significant change in its security situation. This was true in the case of New Zealand. Although it was sensed rather than articulated by New Zealanders, the country's security outlook had radically improved after the mid-1970s and the end of the Vietnamese war. It was rather obscured by the agitation against the war and America's humiliating exit from Saigon, but the South East Asian policy which New Zealand and its bigger allies had been doggedly following for a decade turned out to have been an unexpected success.

The fact was that the US effort in Vietnam, though a tactical failure, was a very large strategic success for the rest of South East Asia. In the course of the ten-year war, the region south of Indochina had been transformed. Sheltering behind the wall of American military power deployed in Indochina, it had made good use of the enormous sums spent on the war and of the generous access to the American market available for exports of electronic and other consumer goods. Where in 1965 there had been weak governments racked by political dissension and of doubtful durability, the end of the fighting revealed five stable and self-confident countries, bound together in ASEAN as a counter to Vietnamese power and rapidly growing in wealth. The gloom felt by New Zealand and others as they contemplated a troubled region had been swept away by the war. As Lee Kuan Yew said gratefully to the Americans: 'You did what you were supposed to do, you gave us time for us to get our own houses in order....'[*]

---

[*] Quoted by John H. Holdridge in *Frontline Diplomacy*, Foreign Affairs Oral History Collection, Washington.

Success in South East Asia, however, raised another question. Instability in the region had been New Zealand's only security worry for 20 years. If this had now gone, did New Zealand really need a security alliance with its irksome obligations and attendant risks? A similar thought had occurred to the American colonists two centuries earlier. The British victory in the Seven Years' War had removed the French threat to the New England colonies, leaving them free to concentrate on resenting their ties with London. As the end of their South East Asian worries seeped into the consciousness of a growing number of New Zealanders, they became increasingly doubtful about their country's ties to Washington and the old assumptions underpinning its foreign policy began to seem less convincing. Given that there was no foreseeable threat to New Zealand the only effect of the alliance might be to drag the country into other American wars. The foundations were being laid for another revolution, a revolution in foreign policy.

This was the more easily accepted because the rising generation of New Zealanders were already in what the President of the Labour Party, Margaret Wilson, later called a 'quasi-revolutionary mood'.[*] The country hung on the brink of perhaps the most marked generational change in its history. Government dropped by a generation when the Lange Government came to power. Most of its front bench were in their early forties, all except Mike Moore (who didn't need one) had university degrees, and only a handful had experience of being in government before.[†]

They were the voice of the baby-boomers, members of the large post-war generation who were more than ready and indeed impatient to take over from their returned-servicemen fathers. The low birth rates of the Depression and the war years meant that the successor generation was both larger and more bunched in time. They had grown up in security and prosperity and had not inherited the

---
[*] Interview with Wilson, 4 August 2011.
[†] Lange memorably described Mike Moore's mind as 'a pinball machine put together by a colour-blind electrician'.

reluctance to take risks which marked their parents. The boomers often had an uneasy relationship with their dads. A hundred thousand men had been absent overseas during the war; when they returned, their children had a cooler view of the paternal bonds. They developed a deep distrust of the 'traditional', a word which became almost a term of abuse in the time of the Lange Government. There was a sense of frustration at the returned soldiers' long grip on power and a general repudiation of their fathers' views on society, politics and most other things around which families could argue.

Britain's entry into the Common Market in 1973 had triggered a long-delayed decolonisation in New Zealand which found itself psychologically a little adrift. The gap was filled by a more assertive nationalism, its more emphatic declarations about the importance of the New Zealand identity revealing the underlying insecurity which is often a mark of such nationalist claims. A new isolationism and edginess about foreign influence accompanied this shift. An older generation had grown up in the Empire and the wartime alliance from which they, and especially the Labour Party, had derived a firmly international outlook. The baby-boomers were less interested in the outside world, and Labour Party conferences began to call for a withdrawal from *all* alliances and from most of New Zealand's activities overseas. The Secretary of Foreign Affairs, Merwyn Norrish, told an American visitor in 1983 that the threat of isolationism would require management by the government.*

Isolationism may be the inevitable concomitant of growing nationalism in a small country. Building a new national identity may require a battle against foreign influences. In any case, nationalism, one of Europe's more doubtful inventions, defines itself most satisfyingly by opposition to others. In this case the United States was a barn-door target. Anti-Americanism, once the preserve of the red-faced elderly complaining about American television and food, now shifted to the younger end of society. They cared nothing about Americanisms in

---

* Talking to Paul Wolfowitz, 4 May 1983, State Department Papers.

speech or in food and happily adopted both. They felt the weight of America's international influence; New Zealand should cease to be a humble follower and strike out for itself in pursuit of a better world. Foreign policy became part of the tussle for a new national identity. A Canterbury University psychologist, only half in jest, described the difference between Australian and New Zealand nationalism in parental terms. Australia, which cut its nationalist teeth on a perennially edgy relationship with Britain, had no trouble working with the United States. New Zealand, which never exchanged a cross word with the Mother Country, had to assert its adulthood by quarrelling with Uncle Sam.

What distinguished many of the baby-boomers was that they wanted to change the world and they wanted to get rich – a double vision embodied both in David Lange and in the curious dualism of his government, which combined radical opposition to nuclear weapons with an eagerness to experiment with sweeping economic reform.* The kind of egalitarian and comfortable society which had so appealed to their returning fathers and which they found stifling could in any case no longer be sustained, despite Muldoon's determined efforts to do so. By 1984 New Zealand was drifting dangerously close to the economic reefs: 'Welcome to Yugoslavia' was Lange's greeting to the Singapore Minister of Finance two months before the election. The incoming political generation was more consumer-oriented and wanted greater economic freedom. Along with the traditional foreign policy they wanted an end to the traditional economic policies to which their parents had clung since 1935.

These views were by no means confined to young men. The radical effects of the pill had begun to make even deeper social changes. What grumpy men might call the feminisation of New Zealand society was remaking home life and employment patterns. Women had increasingly influential views on everything from shopping hours to

---

* The same point is made by Paul Moon in *New Zealand in the Twentieth Century*, HarperCollins, 2011, pp. 539–40.

what risks they thought should be accepted in foreign policy. The anti-nuclear campaigner Helen Caldicott toured the country in 1983 and drew admiring female audiences, emphasising the congenial theme that men and their machismo made wars, but that women skilled in conflict resolution would do away with the nuclear threat.

There were other strands in the restlessness which overtook New Zealand society in the 1980s. The environmental movement laid down a challenge to New Zealanders' lazy assumption that there was no need for any effort to preserve their beautiful landscape and was sharply opposed to any suggestion that nuclear power might need to be used to generate electricity in future years. The sacred cause of rugby football found itself painfully entangled in the unlovely issue of apartheid in South Africa. The Maori renaissance brought bicultural concerns into mainstream New Zealand politics. The country began to struggle seriously with the post-colonial debt it owed to Maori and the effort strengthened the focus on internal problems and diminished interest in the wider concerns of the Western community.

These currents surging back and forth made for some very choppy seas; they were, in the words of a sympathetic journalist, 'very weird and paranoid times'.* Tradition seemed to the newly educated young to be worse than no guide at all. Everything was up for challenge and re-examination by a generation which felt materially secure and freed from the old constraints which thrift, conservatism and the desire to behave politely at home and abroad had imposed on their parents. They were impatient for political power but had little experience in using it.

Floating on these currents was the usual froth that accompanies major social change. There were New Age prophets, crystals and the healing arts, and the University of Canterbury appointed its first witch.† There was a fizz of equally unorthodox activity. Losing faith in the patriarchal justice system a group of women kidnapped

---

* Bill Ralston, *Evening Post*, 3 August 1994.
† Or so Yolanda Wisewitch announced.

the playwright Mervyn Thompson, tied him to a tree and threatened to mutilate him. As the pre-eminent symbol of tradition, the Queen suffered more than most. Young women bared their bottoms to display the wobbly message 'Honour the Treaty' as she entered the Christchurch Botanic Gardens, and two others threw eggs at her, adding to Maori rights a call for Britain to get out of Ulster and the Falklands. Back on the Royal Yacht, Prince Philip suggested that New Zealand had more eccentrics to the square foot than any other country he knew.*

As the dispute over ANZUS deepened, the excitement at the boldness of this small country taking on the United States showed signs of paranoia. Fears that the US would take action against the Labour Party were the subject of intense discussion in at least three top-level party meetings.† There was talk of plots to destabilise the government or its currency and television programmes showed close-ups of an Auckland building in which the CIA was claimed to have established a headquarters for subverting the government. There was speculation that the United States was behind a loans scam, in which a naive Maori Affairs Department attempted to borrow $600 million from Middle Eastern fraudsters. And David Lange, meeting a colleague in his office one morning, seated him carefully behind a concrete pillar to avoid, he said, being listened to by the Americans.‡ To the bafflement of overseas observers, New Zealand, praised by Singapore's Foreign Minister as a country that 'did not jump about', suddenly seemed bent on doing just that.

Chosen by 'a sort of divine roulette' (his own words) to preside over this still chaotic new order was the restless, anarchic figure of David Lange, an orator of formidable power who had never been in government.§ Like other baby-boomers, he too had difficult relations

---

* Talking to Denis McLean, the Secretary of Defence.
† Margaret Wilson to the Australian High Commissioner, 20 March 1985, 250/11/18 Part 18, NAA.
‡ Michael Bassett was the colleague, in early 1985.
§ Audrey Young interview, *New Zealand Herald*, 3 July 2004.

with a parent, in his case with his mother who on one occasion told the media she wished he had never been born. He had the warmth, wit and human sympathies of a great politician but no interest in the bruising battles which normally strew the path to the top. A lot of his wit arose from his desire to fend off people and trouble; his colleagues and the head of his department complained that meetings with him often never got beyond the jokes, good humour and flowing talk. Russell Marshall, the Education Minister, found him unable to have a serious conversation and hence to discuss and work through an issue. He could take decisions easily, but did not have the patience to plough through the detail or consult to form a consensus. As a result he was prone to policy by blurt, making off-the-cuff pronouncements which then had to be explained or qualified.* Norrish, his Secretary of Foreign Affairs and Trade, put it tactfully, saying he had an unfortunate tendency to give public utterance to his 'private contingency planning'. Congressman Eckhart from upstate New York was less sympathetic, calling the Prime Minister a 'smart ass who was carried along by the sound of his own voice'.†

He became Prime Minister not through his own ambition but that of his colleagues. 'Most people have to fight their way to the top,' said Mike Moore, the Trade Minister, 'but we carried him to the top. And so he didn't have the scars.'‡ He said himself that he became leader of the Labour Party with none of the usual background, but he had a prime asset in what had become the new frontline of politics – 'the ability on television to convey confidence and assurance without saying anything. And that is very important.'§

However, without trade union or grassroots party experience, not having risen through the ranks and gained the allies that can be accumulated along the way, he never had control of his own party organisation, about which he was prone to grumble. He did not

---

* Interview with Marshall, 19 August 2011.
† Talking in both cases to the Australians, 250/11/18 Part 25 and 370/1/20 Part 48, NAA.
‡ Interview with Moore, 27 September 2011.
§ Audrey Young interview.

enjoy the routine of party meetings, let alone have the patience to sit through them, and it showed. At meetings of the Policy Council he would restlessly pace up and down and often leave before they finished – something his predecessors would never have done. David Lange never saw an organisation that he liked. From the Commonwealth to the Methodist Church, from Federated Farmers to the Federation of Labour, every institution was the subject of complaint and mockery.* This was true even of his own government which he did not so much run as comment on as it passed by. His Cabinet he chaired with wit and brilliance, starting meetings with a monologue which was both penetrating and very funny: 'Lange would then get through a significant part of the agenda with the Cabinet recovering from a good laugh.'† But he preferred to work alone, keeping his inner thoughts and often his next moves to himself. There was no Lange group or faction in the Cabinet, the caucus or the party as a whole, and he had no close friends: he 'could be intimate with ten thousand people, but could not be intimate with one'.‡

This showed clearly in the ferment over the nuclear issue about which when Leader of the Opposition he showed some ambivalence. His trial balloon, suggesting that nuclear propulsion might be more acceptable than nuclear weapons, was promptly shot down by the then party President, Jim Anderton. Most parliamentary leaders are disinclined to accept rebukes of this sort and Russell Marshall, then strongly anti-nuclear, thinks that if Lange had chosen he could have fought the party on this issue and won. But he did not have a support base, could not take even the most sympathetic of his colleagues into his confidence, and his views on nuclear matters were ambivalent and still forming. Above all, he hated trouble and often would rather avoid any issue that might be uncomfortable or displease those with whom he was dealing.

---

* Rally New Zealand, the motorsport body, may have been the only exception.
† Comment by Richard Prebble, 18 September 2011.
‡ Interview with Mike Moore.

So he was reluctant to be closely associated with the nuclear policy for the rest of his eighteen months in opposition, and continued in private to hint at the possibility of change. On becoming leader of the party he told the American embassy that he did not want to see a major dispute over ship visits and indicated that 'he would be willing to finesse the key issue of US disclosure of the presence of nuclear weapons on American warships if the appropriate rhetorical formula could be found'.*

In April 1983 Air Marshal Ewan Jamieson paid the customary call of a newly appointed Chief of Defence Staff. There were others present in the office during his call but when it was over Lange walked him to the lift in Parliament Buildings, making it clear that he wanted to speak privately. He said that he had met the Australian Prime Minister, Bob Hawke, on a recent visit to Sydney and had asked him how he had dealt with 'the loony leftwing of his party' on the ANZUS question. Hawke replied, he said, 'When we were in opposition I played along with them, but once we won the election I kicked the bastards in the crutch.' Lange paused briefly, laughed and then said, 'And that's what I'm going to do' and strode back to his office.†

The following month, influenced (the embassy thought) by his visit to Sydney and Hawke's 'rough and ready ways', he told the American ambassador that he needed to appeal to ANZUS supporters and capture middle-of-the-road voters, like those who had contributed to Hawke's victory. He believed that the force of his rhetoric and his standing as the only person who could lead Labour to victory would enable him to set policy on this issue. The embassy was unconvinced: 'He has shown himself incapable of organising support for his position on this and other issues. Whether he is being disingenuous – only telling US officials what he thinks they want to hear – or has seriously under-estimated the opposition to any change

---

* Cables of 9 February and 21 April 1983, State Department Papers.
† Article by Jamieson in the *Dominion*, 23 August 1994. Hawke does not recall a meeting and flatly denies saying this (interview of 20 December 2011).

within the party is unclear. It appears most likely the answer is a combination of the two.'*

When he visited Washington in January 1984 he told the Acting Secretary of State, Kenneth Dam, that he was in much the same situation as when Hawke took office in Australia. He was obliged to represent publicly his party's policy on this issue and could not say on the record that it would change, but it was possible to see a new administration redirecting policy once it was in power, as President Reagan had done over the strongly pro-Taiwan platform on which he had been elected.†

He gave a similar indication on that visit to Richard Armitage, Assistant Secretary of Defense at the Pentagon. Armitage said that New Zealand's position was not particularly important in itself but it mattered in the face of the enormous Soviet effort to detach Japan and others from the Western alliance. When he said that any change in New Zealand's policy could thus have disastrous consequences, Lange replied, 'Mr Armitage, you don't have to worry about that.' Armitage has since pondered over what he meant (often a problem with Lange pronouncements). Could it have been 'That's for me, not you, to worry about'? He came to a crisp conclusion: 'Lange lied to me.'‡

All these comments were made in private and Washington was cautious about the risk of over-interpreting them. They were characteristically unspecific and gave no hint of any detailed plans. There was no lack of other Lange statements of unshakeable opposition to nuclear weapons and propulsion and the Americans were aware that part of the Lange charm consisted in giving people the impression that he shared their views.

Though the issue was pushed underground, the Labour Party activists were well aware of their leader's ambivalence. ANZUS

---

* US Embassy cable of 26 May 1983, State Department Papers.
† Note by the NZ Embassy in Washington, PM 59/8/5 Part 8, ANZ.
‡ Interview with Richard L. Armitage, 26 September 2011. The words are corroborated by the embassy's defence head who was with Lange.

became the focus for the mutual suspicions between the party organisation and its leader. It was an issue on which Lange had neither the backing nor the temperament to fight and win. So the Labour Party, led by a man who disliked its hierarchy and a hierarchy that did not trust its leader, moved towards the election that would settle the shape of the impending revolution. There was a last irony. Revolutions are famously touched off by the unexpected. The Boston Tea Party which signalled the start of the American Revolution was the result of a *lowering* of the duty on tea. In New Zealand the ANZUS crisis was precipitated by the proposed visit of the most unambiguously non-nuclear ship in two decades.

Chapter Two
The Government Changes

The drama began on the night of 14 June 1984 when the Prime Minister, Sir Robert Muldoon, unexpectedly went to Government House to seek an early election. Legend had it that he was drunk. That is doubtful, but if he was not drunk at the start of the evening he certainly was by its end. His condition was not helped by being served two hefty whiskies while waiting in the study of the Governor-General who was in the delicate position of giving a dinner for newspaper editors and some members of the Opposition and could not get away immediately. Muldoon was, however, quite clear about what he was doing. His caucus was increasingly restive about the wage and price freeze he had imposed and he had earlier told the British Foreign Secretary, Lord Carrington, that he might have to go to the country in March or April. He held on but with his slender majority in Parliament threatened he asked his department in May for advice on the shortest possible interval between a dissolution and the consequent General Election.

In May the Labour Party Executive had released its international affairs policy. In power it would legislate to make New Zealand and its territorial waters nuclear-free and would prohibit visits by warships either nuclear-armed or -powered. It would actively seek the establishment of a South Pacific Nuclear Weapons-free Zone and end the dumping of nuclear wastes and testing of nuclear weapons in the Pacific.

On ANZUS it promised to renegotiate 'the terms of our association with Australia and the United States for the purpose of ensuring the economic, social and political stability of the South East Asian and Pacific regions'. In such an updated agreement the other parties would have to accept New Zealand's unconditional anti-nuclear stance, as well as an 'absolutely equal partnership' and unanimous agreement on all decisions taken by the partners, and for good measure 'an absolute guarantee of the complete integrity of New Zealand's sovereignty'.

The policy's tone had a party activist feel to it, revealing both a considerable unfamiliarity with the working of international agreements, including ANZUS, and also a lack of confidence in the country's ability to look after its own interests. The British Foreign Office noted that it contained no indication of alignment with the West while the American embassy, in a less clear-sighted moment, thought that the shift to a more independent foreign policy that this signalled would be more rhetorical than substantive.

When the policy was released Rowling said he was doubtful the ANZUS treaty could be rewritten; instead it should be abandoned and replaced by an agreement concentrating, not on military matters, but on economic cooperation in the Asia/Pacific region. He repeated in print his themes of the year before: 'Our friends have got to recognise us as partners, not acolytes' and if they did not it would be them and not New Zealand who would be frustrating any agreement for progress and peace.[*]

---

[*] Article in *International Review*, May/June 1984.

THE GOVERNMENT CHANGES

The conference of the Federation of Labour, heavily influenced by the hard Left, contributed to the momentum that month, passing remits calling for a nuclear-free Pacific, withdrawal from ANZUS and a general condemnation of US actions in the Caribbean and Central America. Throughout the proceedings the fraternal delegate from the Soviet Union had a seat of honour on the platform with the Executive while the American and Australian delegates had to be content with places in the hall. There was no controversy or even discussion over the ANZUS remits which were simply pushed through; the only lively moment came when a remit against pornographic displays in the workplace was opposed by the Auckland Engineers' Union, on the grounds that all men were voyeurs and women exhibitionists.

Two weeks later a Bill to enact Labour's anti-nuclear policy was introduced into Parliament by a Labour frontbencher, Richard Prebble. The government argued that it was in breach of the whole spirit of ANZUS and said, rather desperately, that if passed it would not be forwarded to the Governor-General for assent because it would affect the rights of the Crown.* In the end the Nuclear Free New Zealand Bill was defeated, but by the narrowest of margins: 40–39. Two National Party members crossed the floor to vote for the Bill, and the government was saved only because two Labour members moved in the opposite direction. Such tidy symmetry was unlikely to last. Muldoon's mind was made up. Always something of a fatalist, after the vote on 12 June he decided to fight it out at once rather than be nibbled to death trying to stay in power.

After that, the 'Beyond ANZUS' conference arranged for 16 to 18 June in the Wellington Town Hall instead found itself part of the election campaign. Upwards of a thousand attended with almost forty speakers from the anti-war and anti-nuclear movements. There was a seminar on the role of the 'political police' in the United States, Australia and New Zealand, and another on the 'problems

---

* Cable from the British High Commissioner of 15 June 1984, FCO Papers. The government's view was based solely on an obscure British precedent that had not been invoked since 1935.

endured by Asian nations under US influence, and the part played by New Zealand and Australia in supporting American objectives in Asia'. To underline the need for an independent foreign policy Tim Shadbolt, the Mayor of Waitemata, spoke on 'national assertiveness'.

The snap election caught everyone by surprise. The National Party had not even completed its selection of candidates, the party organisation was in some disarray, and after nine years in office National found it hard to find something new to say. Muldoon was exhausted and disheartened and (as Lange was to do) had left his party behind him. The party officials took their revenge with full-page campaign advertisements that said with unexpected frankness, 'Who Needs This Man?', and then dropped him from their message completely.*

Labour was in much better shape. It had selected its candidates and was lifted by the long electoral swell that energises party workers and signals to them that the time has come. Its foreign policy was clear but the outlines of its economic policy were still being hard fought. The right-wing, free-market reformers, led by Roger Douglas, were confident of prevailing over the advocates of more familiar Labour policies. Over his nine years in office Muldoon had stolen many of the Left's traditional policies on state investment (the showy projects known as 'Think Big'), price and wage controls and government subsidies, and their failure had winded the Left as well as Muldoon. The centre of the caucus was moving over to reform but the snap election meant that instead of further debates a quick manifesto would have to be put out. Geoffrey Palmer, Lange's deputy, and Margaret Wilson cobbled something together, with contributions from both sides. What emerged was a compromise which took refuge in generalities, saying it was impossible to be specific without more information. In Wilson's words: 'What was adopted did not tell the full truth, but it told no lies.'† It certainly gave few hints of the tide of economic change that was to come.

---

* Among unhappy campaign slogans, this is equalled only by 'Nixon's the One'.
† Interview with Margaret Wilson, 4 August 2011.

The question of whether there was a deal or non-aggression pact between those who wanted an anti-nuclear foreign policy and those who wanted radical economic reform has been much debated. Those close to the issue have given differing views. Sir Geoffrey Palmer doubts there was any conscious trade-off; Moore knows of no evidence of any bargain and Prebble agrees: many on the Left had no interest in economic policy – 'they could not balance their cheque books' – but were actively opposed to American foreign policy. 'The fact that the Left was preoccupied by the issue was of benefit to us but there was never a grand or even a small bargain.'*

Others saw a trade-off at least in practice. Roger Douglas, the Minister of Finance, thought so but warned against overplaying it. Simon Walker, in charge of the party's publicity, said at the outset that 'Lange wants to win his economic battles in the Cabinet and he won't be able to do this if he's fighting battles on the foreign policy front'.†

This was confirmed by weighty testimony from those even closer. In Lange's first meeting with Hawke as Prime Minister his explanation of the anti-nuclear policy was unconvincing. When questioned by Hawke he agreed that he was himself unconvinced. He explained that when he came to power a deal had been made with the Left to accept their position on nuclear weapons and ship visits in return for him and Douglas having a free hand on economic policy. He said the deal was not done in writing but was something he regarded as binding.‡ He seemed to the Australians to be resigned rather than keen about it. Bill Hayden, Hawke's Foreign Minister, recalled later: 'For some of us who dealt with him privately it was clear that, initially anyway, he held the tiller on the set course with a slack and unenthusiastic hand.'§

---

* Comments by Richard Prebble, 24 August 2011.
† Douglas interview in *Euromoney*, October 1985, and Simon Walker to AHC, 3 August 1984, 250/11/18 Part 14, NAA.
‡ Interview with Bob Hawke, 20 December 2011.
§ *Hayden: An Autobiography*, Angus & Robertson, 1996, p. 457.

When he was in Wellington for the ANZUS Council with US Secretary of State George Shultz, David Laux from the National Security Council was told at a lunch in the Beehive that Lange did not really care about the nuclear issue – what mattered most was his economic reforms which meant that he might have to give way on the nuclear policy.* The American embassy also believed there was a deal whereby Lange had accepted some extreme planks on foreign affairs in exchange for a more radical economic charter. 'In the early days of the Labour Ministry, he will concentrate his fire on economic issues, seeking to avoid confrontation with the Left of his party on some of these sticky international issues.'†

Some years later, Helen Clark, generally regarded as leading the anti-nuclear lobby, was said to have confirmed this. When asked by a Wisconsin Congressman why she had accepted Douglas's policies when she disliked them, she said bluntly that there had been a trade-off by which they gained the anti-nuclear ship policy in return for going along with economic reform.‡ Margaret Wilson thinks this was clearly understood, though never in a formal way. Both factions concentrated on their own concerns and, whether or not it was consciously considered by the reformers, opposing the anti-nuclear policy would have brought all the formidable fire of the Left on to the government's economic policy.

Nothing of this appeared in the election campaign. Lange had been cautious about the Nuclear Free New Zealand Bill (he wanted to leave out nuclear propulsion), and it was agreed that he would keep a low profile in the debate on it. 'Lange in Opposition was very careful of the nuclear issue' was Richard Prebble's judgement. He seemed ambivalent and gave no sign that this was a personal priority. He did not want to campaign on it during the election and the campaign committee agreed. Geoffrey Palmer told the Australian High

---

* Interview with David Laux, 4 October 2011.
† Embassy cable of 25 July 1984, State Department Papers.
‡ Interview with Paul Cleveland, 29 September 2011. Cleveland led a Congressional delegation which met with Clark, then Prime Minister, in the mid-1990s.

THE GOVERNMENT CHANGES

Commissioner that the Labour Party had very deliberately chosen not to make it an election issue and his colleague Prebble concurred: 'We wanted to campaign on the economy and ran the line that the nuclear Bill was just an excuse for an election as Muldoon could not balance the books.' So Prebble was later 'a little surprised when Lange made himself an anti-nuclear hero'.*

One enlivening aspect of the campaign was an unexpected intervention by the United States. Washington had become increasingly apprehensive about the way in which ANZUS, in the guise of ship visits, had become an election issue. Lange had earlier told Paul Wolfowitz, the Assistant Secretary of State for East Asia and the Pacific, that isolationist feeling in the Labour Party, which he did not share, ran deep and was impenetrable to argument. It certainly ran deep: opposition to war and its weapons, as Mike Moore was later to point out, was part of Labour's DNA going back to the First World War. After a visit to Wellington in April, during which he talked to Lange and senior Labour Members of Parliament, the American Commander in Chief, Pacific (CINCPAC), Admiral Crowe, was half-persuaded that it was not going to be possible to work with them in managing the practical operations of the alliance.

The US began to see the uncomfortable outlines of its dilemma: to speak out would look like bullying a small country, but to stay silent would be to risk any understanding of its position going by default. Inaction might set off wider tremors. New Zealand had been an active participant in world affairs and had an influence far beyond its size – 'whatever New Zealand decided to do in the future would have a long carry'. Wolfowitz and his colleagues saw it as a symbol of wider significance: isolationism in New Zealand could encourage it in Europe and elsewhere and lead to 'unravelling' in Australia.

And it was not just a small country; it was a close ally, with all the emotional and other ties that implied. To those in Washington who

---

* AHC cable of 3 October 1984, 370/1/20 Part 23, NAA, and interview with Prebble, 23 August 2011.

argued that New Zealand was no different from other small countries like Uruguay, Wolfowitz had a blunt retort: 'If New Zealand was Uruguay we certainly would not be sitting on all this butter' – American dairy surplus which the Administration felt unable to sell overseas because of the damage this would do to New Zealand's butter market. So it was decided that the importance of what was at stake for the alliance overrode the usual rules and required a statement of Washington's own view on ANZUS and ship visits.[*]

This was to invite controversy and the outcome suggested that it was unwise. The Administration spent much time considering the advisability and drafting the message which was cleared at the top by the Vice President, George H. W. Bush. But it concluded that the need to counter some of the claims being made in New Zealand justified the risk of becoming involved in someone else's election. In particular it was felt necessary to stress that the United States attached 'critical importance' to port visits which were seen as part of Australia's and New Zealand's contribution to ANZUS, and to correct claims (by Rowling among others) that New Zealand had excluded nuclear ships in 1972–75 without calling the ANZUS relationship into question.[†]

The ambassador, Monroe Browne, was given discretion as to whether and how to use this material but Washington's concern, and the fact that the statement was based on a major speech by Wolfowitz, left him in practice with little option.[‡] He put out a press statement stressing the importance of joint exercises and ship visits in maintaining the credibility of the alliance. He was also anxious to emphasise, 'as we approach problems in any one area, we must be careful to see them in the perspective of the entire relationship', making it clear that any change in the security ties would affect the wider association.

---

[*] Report by NZ Embassy Washington, 29 June 1984, PM 59/8/5 Part 1, ANZ.
[†] It had only excluded nuclear-*powered* warships. The State Department calculated that at least 22 other US warships had visited.
[‡] Laux Papers, Box 90658, Reagan Presidential Library.

THE GOVERNMENT CHANGES

The Wolfowitz speech, given at the Australian Studies Center at Pennsylvania State University, was carefully considered, drafted and redrafted. It was wholeheartedly welcomed in Australia as conveying the strongest US commitment to ANZUS since the treaty was signed, but it was much less persuasive to New Zealanders. The Americans had failed to understand how statements which seemed to be plain matters of fact in Washington became amplified and reverberated in the heated atmosphere of a small nation. Lange dismissed it as a venture into the country's internal debate which was 'absolutely improper' and the British High Commission thought its release had significant repercussions. It came just before the first television debate and so ANZUS was the first question put to the leaders. After watching this, the Acting British High Commissioner concluded that Lange could no longer manage 'the review of ANZUS in such a way as to permit ship visits to continue'.

The campaign in general posed few problems for Lange whose easy appeal fully justified his party's choice of him as leader. His opening speech concentrated on the themes of bringing the country together and the need for better management of the economy. There were no difficulties as he toured the country; speaking in sweeping generalities came easily to him and the crowds enjoyed the entertainment as well as the confidence of his speeches. His colleagues provided a little coaching for television. Moore played Muldoon in preparing him for the debates. When he snarled, 'You're just a fat man who has talked his way to the top', Lange was temporarily at a loss. But the preparation worked. Muldoon the veteran came across as dispirited while Lange effortlessly talked his way to the top with the convincing promise of a fresh start.

The election result was a triumph for Labour and a rejection of the Muldoon policies.[*] It was also a clear victory for anti-nuclear views. Three of the four parties who fought the election opposed nuclear

---

[*] Labour received 43% of the vote, National 36%, the New Zealand Party 12.4% and Social Credit 8%.

weapons in New Zealand; together they gained 64 per cent of the vote. The Social Credit Party advocated armed neutrality, though apparently without totting up the cost. The New Zealand Party, a one-off party which gathered in disaffected National voters, seemed to lean rather to an unarmed neutrality, on the grounds that since no one was likely to attack the country, defence spending was a waste of money. Labour, which won a comfortable majority, was explicitly anti-nuclear, but even so it was doubtful whether many of the voters knew precisely what to expect. After the 1936 Presidential election a wise commentator remarked: 'The people have spoken and Mr Roosevelt will tell us what they have said.' Now New Zealand had spoken and, with varying degrees of apprehension, both the Right and the Left waited for Mr Lange to tell them what they had chosen.

The immediate result was a constitutional crisis. Helped by some hints from Roger Douglas (who was Labour's finance spokesman), there had been an accelerating run on the New Zealand dollar in the course of the election campaign and it was clear that Labour in government would have to devalue. Because of the formalities involved in certifying the returns, however, the new government could not take office for twelve days after the vote. The well-established convention was that if any major decision had to be made the outgoing ministry would act on the advice of the incoming one. Muldoon, who was no respecter of conventions and had almost a phobia about devaluations, refused to act, and his officials had to close the foreign exchange markets. For the next two days the Prime Minister resisted all pressure to devalue until persuaded by his deputy, Jim McLay, that if he did not, the Governor-General might have to dismiss the dying government. He then telephoned the ambassador in Washington to ask how to get on the lecture circuit in the United States.[*]

Wellington in the midst of this turmoil was not the most suitable place for an international meeting but the snap election had coincided with long-scheduled arrangements for the ANZUS Council's

---

[*] Interview with John Wood, 11 August 2011.

THE GOVERNMENT CHANGES

annual meeting. Both Australian and American officials had expected the gathering to be postponed, perhaps until December. Officials in Canberra were 'astounded' that the meeting was being held in the interregnum between two administrations, and Assistant Secretary of Defense Armitage at the Pentagon could see only difficulties if it went ahead. Norrish had suggested after the election date was announced that the meeting might be shifted to Canberra, but his then Minister rejected this as suggesting that his government expected to lose the election.

Perhaps for this reason, or perhaps from sheer stubbornness, Muldoon dug in his toes and insisted in going ahead with what Lange described as a meeting of the American Secretary of State and the Australian Foreign Minister with a backbench MP (Warren Cooper, the outgoing Foreign Minister). Lange was invited by Muldoon to attend but wisely declined; two governments could hardly represent New Zealand at the Council table, especially when they differed so markedly on the subject at issue. So despite the unreal atmosphere the talks went ahead. What with this, the crisis over devaluation and the excitement of the 'Beyond ANZUS' conference, Wolfowitz watching the television news one evening was moved to ask, 'Is it always like this here?'[*]

On his way to Wellington, the American Secretary of State, who had been attending an ASEAN meeting in Indonesia, stopped for a night in Canberra to talk to Hawke. They were old friends with considerable respect for one another and Shultz among other things wanted to get Hawke's view on what course his fellow Labour Party colleague was likely to take in New Zealand. As soon as his aircraft landed he drove to The Lodge where they talked in private and then over dinner with others present.[†] Hawke made it clear that giving in to New Zealand would put him in an untenable position with his own party. Neither of them, though, wanted to prejudge events or take a

---

[*] Interview with Richard W. Teare, 19 September 2011.
[†] Interview with James Kelly, 2 October 2011.

strong line. At the end of the discussion Shultz had an understanding with Hawke on how to handle the issue – to hold firm but give Lange some time. Afterwards they put in a convivial telephone call to the East Mangere Town Hall to congratulate Lange on his thumping victory – a call that Hawke later complained Lange had viewed as an attempt to heavy him over his nuclear policy.*

A howling southerly storm greeted the American delegation on their arrival in New Zealand and the American aircrew's unfamiliarity with the difficult landing conditions at Wellington meant they made the final stage of the journey in a Royal New Zealand Air Force plane. The caution was justified: Mrs Shultz was almost blown over as she emerged from the plane and David Laux's glasses came off and went bowling away across the tarmac. But waiting for them inside was a warm welcome from Lange who, acting on a happy impulse, had flown down from Auckland to greet the party. Shultz was impressed by this 'very unusual and much appreciated gesture', and perhaps even more by the Prime Minister-elect's statement to the waiting press that he 'wanted to tell Mr Shultz that ANZUS was fundamental to our economic and defence way of life'.†

That evening the senior officials from the three delegations met to consider what sort of communiqué might issue from this strange meeting. In the way of international meetings one had already been drafted and circulated. Norrish now suggested that a new draft should be considered, one that better reflected the changed situation. The New Zealanders had prepared one and the Australians too had ideas for an 'anodyne' communiqué. The Americans, however, had decided in advance to treat the meeting as business-as-usual. They realised that the communiqué sentence on the importance of port visits would seem provocative to the incoming government but argued that constitutionally they were dealing with the existing Muldoon Government

---

* *The Hawke Memoirs*, William Heinemann Australia, 1994, p. 280. Lange, in *Nuclear Free: The New Zealand Way*, p. 54, talks of an 'ominous edge' and a 'frisson of apprehension' over the call.
† Laux Papers, Box 90659, Reagan Presidential Library.

THE GOVERNMENT CHANGES

and should hold to the communiqué previously agreed. Underneath this constitutional propriety was the issue of French nuclear testing at an underground site in French Polynesia. In any new draft Australia and New Zealand would want language condemning these tests which the United States was reluctant to accept. The original communiqué survived the tussle, and was stillborn.

The next morning the American delegation met in Shultz's room at the James Cook Hotel. Its eight members covered all the main players, from State Department, Pentagon and National Security Council, and because of this the decisions taken that morning set the tone for Washington's subsequent management of the dispute. In the course of the discussion some argued that, if what they feared came to pass, Lange needed to know that the cost would be serious, including sanctions on trade. Shultz halted this by saying that when he was first issued with a rifle in the Marines he was told: 'Never point this at someone unless you are willing to pull the trigger.' He said flatly that he was not going to mingle defence and trade – they should be kept separate.* Not everyone in the room agreed, but he used his subsequent press conference to lay this down as a marker.

Years later he said that it was his fixed intention from the start not to make an enemy of New Zealand – 'we were too close for that' – and so he was resolved to ensure that any retaliation was confined to the security field where the dispute arose. There was periodic pressure from some of his angry colleagues and from the Congress but 'I won that battle'. He was helped in this by his strong relationship with President Reagan. He had private meetings bi-weekly with him, the only Cabinet member who did, and at one of these he discussed the matter with the President who totally supported his approach.† Indeed, a week after the Wellington meeting, the President confirmed at a televised press conference that he did not see the problems with port access affecting trade with New Zealand.

---

* Interview with William A. Brown, 21 September 2011.
† Interview with George P. Shultz, 2 November 2011.

This did not stop other voices being raised from time to time but the Administration's stance on sanctions never shifted from the position laid down by Shultz at the delegation meeting in Wellington.

When the Council meeting was over both Shultz and Hayden spoke to the press, and in doing so made clear the basic lines of each country's attitude to the gathering controversy. Asked about whether port access was essential to the treaty, Shultz was blunt: 'What kind of alliance is this if the military forces of the countries involved are not able to be in contact with each other?' He contrasted this with the situation after the Vietnam War when people worried that the US was losing interest in the Pacific and fretted that its military presence was not more visible.

He firmly dismissed any trade implications: 'The ANZUS alliance is a security and military alliance and that's what we are discussing here.' This led him equally firmly to brush aside Labour's aspirations to broaden the scope of the agreement: 'ANZUS is not an economic agreement in any sense and that is the extent of it.'

Bill Hayden, the Australian Foreign Minister, said that Australia was making clear its concerns about port access and the future of ANZUS but was putting no pressure on the New Zealand Government which had just won an election in which the issue was extensively debated. However, he also took the opportunity to give a hint to the incoming administration. He rejected the frequently repeated claim that the Labor leadership in Australia had walked away from its earlier policy on the treaty. Before the election it had promised a review of the treaty and had duly carried this out when it came to power. 'What happened was that with the experience that we had in Government, there was a consolidation of our commitment to ANZUS.'[*]

Another meeting that afternoon turned out to be much more important in shaping the future course of the dispute. Before they left for Honolulu, Shultz and Wolfowitz called on Lange in the Leader of the Opposition's office (once the wartime office of Peter Fraser) in

---

[*] Joint press conference, 17 July 1984.

THE GOVERNMENT CHANGES

Parliament Buildings. Lange had only Norrish with him and there was perhaps no reason to foresee that a quiet talk among four people would later lead to such sharp recriminations. That may be why no written record has turned up on either side and each had to fall back on their differing recollections of what had been said.*

Unsurprisingly, the difference turned on what that ambiguous figure, David Lange, was thought to have promised. The Americans believed that Lange had said that if he was given six months he would bring about some change in his party's stand on ship visits. When he was leaving at the end of his term, in October 1985, the embittered ambassador, Monroe Browne, said in a television interview that Lange had asked for time to establish with his people the importance of ANZUS in the relationship and that port visits were important to the US. 'It was our impression that he seriously meant to implement ANZUS as we had understood it and so, yes, we did agree that time might be of importance to him.'†

Lange indignantly denied this, calling the ambassador's account 'a sad swan-song of self-justification'. More convincingly, Norrish did not agree with it either. In his recollection, Lange did not promise that he would fix the problem. He did say 'Give me six months' during which he would be going round the various regional conferences and party gatherings. It might have been inferred from this that he would be making the case for ship visits but he did not say so. Norrish thought, though, that the tenor of the conversation would not have given the Americans any apprehensions about the future of ANZUS.‡

Closer examination suggests that the misapprehension, though serious, was neither as wide nor as clear-cut as the ambassador and others in Washington came to believe. It seems unlikely that Lange

---

* Norrish has looked for a record in vain and now thinks he did not make one. Wolfowitz believes he did but so far it has not been found.
† Speaking on *Eyewitness News*, TVNZ, 31 October 1985.
‡ Interview with Merv Norrish, 26 October 2010. He gives a similar account in Margaret Clark (ed.), *For the Record: Lange and the Fourth Labour Government*, Dunmore Press, 2005. Lange pointed out that he could not have promised to go round the regional party conferences over the next six months as these did not meet until March/April.

would have promised to change Labour's policy within six months – he had after all just been elected on a platform that was quite explicit about this. Wolfowitz said that Lange spoke about public opinion in New Zealand: a strong majority was pro-American but also had anti-nuclear sentiments, while a minority was simply anti-American. He talked about the existing Labour Party policy 'to which he said he remained committed until it is changed' and referred vaguely to the 'Norwegian formula' as perhaps opening the way for ship visits. There was no discussion of renegotiating ANZUS or reviewing the prominence of defence and security issues in the treaty, as was included in Labour's policy.[*]

He did say that he needed a breathing space of six months to work on his party and Shultz was happy to agree that the US would not ask for a ship visit in that time. In Lange's own account, Shultz pointed out that there were going to be difficulties but he was not prepared to make a snap decision; New Zealand and the US would have to sit down and talk through their differences.[†] John Hughes, the State Department spokesman, later said that there was 'certainly no commitment' but the American side came away with the feeling that Lange would try to work things out.

These points seem unexceptionable enough to have caused such distrust but they came wrapped in the exuberant Lange rhetoric which may have left impressions not supported by his words. Everyone who ever worked with Lange was familiar with his manner when uneasy. The reassurances and the jokes tumbled out, the sub-clauses billowed like spinnakers and the hearer was submerged in a rush of friendliness and charm. His long-standing friend Richard Prebble called him 'a chronic body language liar' who would lead people to believe he was agreeing when he was not. He tells the story

---

[*] Wolfowitz's account given to his State Department colleagues on his return, 25 July 1984, PM 111/3/3/1 Part 22, ANZ. The Norwegian example would not work for New Zealand because it accepted ambiguity about the exact status of a visiting American warship.
[†] Vernon Wright interview, 5 December 1986, Lange Papers, Box 1, ANZ. The Hughes statement was made on Radio New Zealand, 7 May 1985.

of a fellow Minister who came away from an interview convinced that he had the Prime Minister's backing, only to find when he wrote out the words that Lange had not said anything of the sort. 'It was partly that Lange hated conflict. He just would not confront people if it would cause conflict.'[*] When dealing with a troublesome issue his precise meaning was usually chosen with the care of a lawyer, but the surge of comforting words and the non-verbal body language could give a very different impression.

In public Shultz took an optimistic view of the meeting, telling the American press on the plane going home that Lange was bright and energetic and 'it was an excellent meeting on a personal and substantive level and in any way you want to characterize it'. He thought it a good harbinger for the future and laid the basis for a good across-the-board, cooperative relationship. In private the tough-minded former Marine was far from being carried away. Despite Wolfowitz's later view that there was probably 'excessive hope' that Lange was another Hawke who understood the benefits of staying with the alliance, Shultz was quite clear that for all the friendly words there was no suggestion of a breakthrough. There was still a big problem ahead but he felt that an encouraging start had been made, and he told Hayden after the meeting that he felt a little more relaxed.[†] In the end, Lange's summary of the result for his deputy Geoffrey Palmer – 'US expecting the NZ Government to find a way through, and that we would try' – was probably as accurate as any.[‡]

In any case there was little time for any undue optimism. Within three days of taking office the new Prime Minister was on television vividly reaffirming his party's election policy. He was, as he sometimes said himself, always liable to be carried away by these occasions and he was still on a high after the excitement of the election, the devaluation crisis and taking office: 'I tell you, there's something about a crisis which is exhilarating... that sort of testing that people

---

[*] Interview with Prebble, 13 September 2011.
[†] Bernard Gewertzman, *New York Times*, 17 July 1984.
[‡] Interview with Sir Geoffrey Palmer, 15 July 2011.

who are physical do.' He confirmed that the government would renegotiate the treaty unless its anti-nuclear policy could be honoured. There would be no 'buckling' or (in the interviewer's words) 'no welshing on a commitment' as the Australian Government had done. He accepted that there was a disagreement with Shultz but the treaty was more than a code-word for nuclear ships: 'This government is not going to walk away from ANZUS.' At the close he said a visit by a US warship would be unlikely before the next election: 'and I don't think that will mean the end of ANZUS either'.*

Washington was alarmed 'by the manner in which Prime Minister Lange is painting himself into a corner'. These comments were far from the tone of his conversation with Shultz. Talking off-the-cuff on television did not make for measured pronouncements but the State Department saw a hardening pattern which did not augur well for 'a future quiet dialogue' on the issues. The ambassador was asked to see the Prime Minister to emphasise that the relationship was better served by private discussion than by publicly asserting the non-negotiability of New Zealand's position – or 'are we operating on erroneous assumptions?'

Armed with this directive, Monroe Browne went to the Beehive the same day. Lange said he hoped the US realised that anti-nuclear feelings in New Zealand went much wider than the radical fringe of the Labour Party and were held by good, solid church people as in the US. But he stressed that he was serious in wanting to work through the problem with the US – a solution had to be found, for the nuclear issue was linked to broader ones, including nuclear disarmament, relations with Australia, and the effect of New Zealand's actions on Western security arrangements in other parts of the world: 'My people will have to consider all this.' At the end he promised to try to keep the matter out of public discussion and hoped the Americans would do the same.†

---

* *Sunday*, TVNZ, 29 July 1984.
† Washington's cable of 2 August 1984, State Department Papers, and Wellington's report of the same day, PM 59/8/2 Part 22, ANZ.

THE GOVERNMENT CHANGES

The occasion was smoothed over diplomatically with Lange agreeing to another meeting with Shultz in New York when the UN General Assembly met in September. But the first hints of disillusion had entered the relationship between the two and the Administration began to display a certain wariness. The Australians in Washington were told that whereas a month ago nobody on the National Security Council had heard of New Zealand, it was now on the agenda of every morning meeting.* The American embassy in Wellington reported that the Prime Minister's economic moves had proved popular but 'after two weeks in office he has been somewhat erratic in foreign affairs matters'. In what would become a recurrent theme, it noted that Lange had difficulty reining himself in and then put its finger on the nub of Washington's worry: 'Though claiming in private conversations with the embassy that he desires to change the Labour Party's policy, he has publicly strongly supported the party's anti-nuclear policy, thereby making it extremely difficult for him eventually to reverse himself.'†

This dualism, the contrast between what Lange declared in public and said in private, dogged the dispute throughout. Though his advisers made the point to him several times, the Prime Minister did not seem able or willing to accept that anything he said, even on the spur of the moment, to an audience in New Zealand would be scrutinised minutely in Washington. He seemed to regard his speeches as the business only of New Zealanders and was irritated by American interest in his press conferences: 'They pored over the transcripts with the intensity of scholars on the Dead Sea Scrolls, in order to get the mind-set of this guy Lange.'‡ It left him open to the suspicion of double-dealing which for the Americans gradually hardened into certainty.

His hope was to establish in the minds of New Zealanders and Americans a distinction between the ANZUS alliance and what he

---

* Australian embassy, Washington, 12 September 1984, 221/1/4/4 Part 3, DFAT.
† Assessment of 10 August 1984, State Department Papers.
‡ Vernon Wright interview, 4 February 1987.

argued was the purely operational question of ship visits. Acceptance of nuclear weapons, it was argued, was neither a historical nor an essential part of the treaty, and his government was determined to uphold New Zealand's membership of the treaty. His view, repeated many times to the Americans, was that a departure from ANZUS would be politically very damaging for him, but that New Zealanders did not want nuclear weapons as part of it.* The polls consistently bore him out: around three-quarters of those polled firmly supported ANZUS and were equally firmly opposed to nuclear weapons in New Zealand harbours.

What might in the diplomatic jargon of the day have been called Lange's 'two-track strategy' led his harsher critics in Washington and elsewhere to regard him as a liar. Those who were more familiar with his ways might have seen it as a clear if dangerous example of his tendency to fend off trouble by adopting the views of whoever he was talking to at the time. But the double-dealing may in Lange's mind have been simply the difference between his private views and the public support to which he felt committed by his deal with the Left. On one occasion, when talking over the problem with his advisers, he broke off, fell silent for a moment and then abruptly said, 'Take what you want, said God, and pay for it.' In quoting the Spanish proverb he was clearly following a train of thought, but whether he was musing on the dangers of alienating the Left or the Americans was never clear to his hearers. What happened, though, was that as he strongly and regularly reaffirmed the unbending nature of his government's anti-nuclear policy he gradually became locked into his public position.

---

* Bill Hayden confirms this about the risk of leaving ANZUS: 'There was frank acknowledgment among some senior parliamentarians that were that to happen the government would become a one-term government.' *Hayden: An Autobiography*, p. 457.

Chapter Three
Growing Concerns

The first person to dismiss the hope that Lange might prove to be another Hawke was Bob Hawke. The two met, barely two weeks after the Lange Government had taken office, at a regional Commonwealth meeting in Port Moresby. Australian officials were already worried that New Zealand's ban on port access would make ANZUS unworkable, but in briefing the Australian press they emphasised that at the meeting Hawke would merely probe and seek more information about Lange's thinking: 'He will not go in heavy-handedly.'[*]

He did not, but the impression he formed in the first few minutes of their meeting played an important part in the course of the dispute. Lange came to Hawke's hotel room at the Travelodge for an early breakfast. One of Hawke's economic advisers showed him in and Hawke introduced him. Lange said breezily that he had an economic adviser too but did not think he had met him yet. Successful politicians

---

[*] The *Australian*, 7 August 1984. The *Sydney Morning Herald* quoted the same phrase, revealing a common background briefing.

are in the habit of making snap assessments of the people they meet and Hawke made his now: 'I felt I was dealing with a buffoon.'

Time was short (less than an hour) and they immediately got down to work as well as breakfast. Hawke's starting point was that 'defence, these days, has to be nuclear; everything follows from that'. He emphasised the importance of the ANZUS alliance, especially when the Soviet Union was working to expand its influence in the Pacific, and argued that ANZUS and ship visits could not be separated; the one required the other. Australia had worked through its problems over ship visits and he asked how the New Zealand Prime Minister saw the issue.*

Lange launched into a wordy explanation of the anti-nuclear policy but did not seem to believe it. The more he spoke, the stronger this impression became. When Hawke said, 'David, you don't seem really convinced by what you are saying', Lange simply said, 'That's right'. The nuclear-free policy had been fashioned by the Left and accepted by the party and there was little he could do about it. 'I told Lange I was angered by this and didn't understand how he could possibly conduct foreign policy in the best interests of New Zealand on the basis of such a compact. He shrugged resignedly and said that unfortunately that was the way it was.' Hawke thought to himself, 'What sort of fucking fellow is this?' and when Lange was nominated for the Nobel Peace Prize he considered writing to the committee to say so (presumably in less Australian language).†

The New Zealand leader seemed embarrassed by his position, the captive of other people's doctrine, and Hawke judged him to be weak rather than anti-American. But the brief meeting settled Australia's position. Though privately angry over what it saw as New Zealand's irresponsibility, it would stay on the sidelines of the dispute and not attempt to mediate. The poor chemistry between the two leaders offered no chance of doing more. Hawke felt he had no basis with

---

* Hawke's annotated briefing notes, 221/1/4/4 Part 3, DFAT.
† Interview with Bob Hawke, 20 December 2011, and *The Hawke Memoirs*, William Heinemann Australia, 1994, p. 281.

Lange to help sort things out: 'As far as I was concerned, Lange had made a pact with the devil and had to live with it.'

He passed on his impressions to the Americans, saying that he had no respect for Lange – and indeed a 'contempt' – but would try to maintain a good professional relationship with New Zealand. He told Shultz that they should do everything possible to keep New Zealand in the loop and avoid retaliatory actions, and urged both him and President Reagan to give as much help to New Zealand as was possible in the circumstances. He did not ever believe that Lange would deliver on a ship visit – 'he was very damaging and very duplicitous' – and Shultz never gave him the impression that he had much hope either, despite the encouraging impression conveyed by Lange at their July meeting.[*]

The two breakfasters managed to convey their differing impressions of one another at their subsequent press briefings. Lange (whom I remember coming back from the meeting a little subdued) said that Hawke outlined his government's view of ANZUS responsibilities 'in a careful, non-threatening way', and suggested that these applied also to New Zealand. Still rather nervous from the thunderclouds that hung over their meeting, he felt compelled to say at least three times that Hawke did not threaten or try to coerce him: 'We simply talked.' He reaffirmed both that the port access policy was non-negotiable and that his government had no intention of withdrawing from ANZUS. He also hinted that if the issue of port access could not be resolved before the next naval exercise in March, then that exercise might have to be called off. There were, he said to the New Zealand journalists with him, a number of ways of fixing the problem, but he declined to be drawn on what they were beyond giving his grandmother's view that there were more ways to kill a pig than by choking it with butter.

---

[*] On the other hand, Hawke liked Geoffrey Palmer whom he thought decent and straightforward. Interview, 20 December 2011.

Hawke's comment to his own press following was briefer and bleaker. There might have to be a reappraisal of ANZUS if New Zealand could not reach an accommodation with the United States, but he did not think it helpful to speculate about this or how it might affect New Zealand. He made little effort to disguise his first unfavourable impression of Lange. When asked what had emerged from the breakfast meeting, he said: 'That he's got a bigger appetite than I have.'

They met again, just over two weeks later, at the South Pacific Forum held on one of the handful of coral atolls which had become independent as Tuvalu. Lange found Hawke tense and irritable, but denied the press's impression that they did not get on well – it was purely their difference over ship visits, 'that's all it is'. One of the topics for discussion was the proposal for a Nuclear-Free Zone in the South Pacific. It had originally been an Australian initiative and was making its leisurely way through successive Forum meetings. Officials in Canberra had done a considerable amount of work in the preceding months with the aim of getting the zone adopted at the next Forum. Lange's suggestion that he and others might promote a resolution endorsing this at the United Nations General Assembly was therefore rather resented by Hawke. When asked how he found working alongside Lange, he said: 'I didn't work alongside him. He was at the other end of the table. I found it fairly congenial.'*

On his way home Hawke decided to be more explicit about his misgivings. At a welcoming ceremony in Suva he showed his displeasure, departing from his prepared text to make the point more clearly. Hawke's sponsorship of the Nuclear-Free Zone, which was aspirational and did not affect either port visits or the passage of weapons on the high seas, was a gesture to his own Left. The journalists thought he was anxious to banish any impression that Lange, in his new enthusiasm for the zone, might be seen to be doing more

---

* Lange was more ingeniously positive about the Polynesian festivities, saying that 'anyone who can do a dance with the same man two nights in a row hasn't fallen out'. Ian Templeton in *The Bulletin*, 12 September 1984.

for disarmament than he was.* He may also have wished to reassure the Reagan Administration that his support for the zone in no way affected his view that the alliance was central to the region's security.

He said that American ship visits under ANZUS had worked to the Pacific's advantage for nearly four decades and it was vital to keep this in mind. The smaller Pacific nations, he believed, had been reassured by Australia's recommitment to ANZUS. 'It would be easy to take the soft option, selectively to adopt a passive attitude to those obligations of the treaty which might be difficult to shoulder. We will not do so.'† In the light of their earlier meeting it was clear that he thought the man with a passive attitude was his New Zealand counterpart. Lange got his retaliation in a few weeks later: 'The Government of Australia elected to pursue a different policy from that which it articulated before the election. I respect that.'‡

Next to Australia, Japan was the Pacific country which was probably the most worried about the direction New Zealand was taking. Whatever difficulties Hawke had with the left wing of his Australian Labor Party paled when compared to the delicacy of the Japanese position on port access. Japan, the only country to have suffered from the use of nuclear weapons, had an understandable phobia about them. There was unyielding political antipathy to the presence of these weapons on Japanese soil, and in 1967 the Japanese Diet (Parliament) adopted a resolution spelling out the three non-nuclear principles which had been official policy ever since: Japan would not manufacture, possess or permit nuclear weapons on its soil. This, however, had in some way to be reconciled with the presence of American bases in Japan. The following year the resolution was 'clarified' to specify that support for the three principles depended on continuance of the American security guarantee embodied in the Mutual Security Treaty agreed by the two countries in 1960. It was quietly made clear, in one instance by a paper prepared by

---

* That at least was the *Australian*'s view, 30 August 1984.
† Speaking in Suva, 29 August 1984, CBA 50/8/5 Part 1, MFAT.
‡ Speaking at a UN press conference, 27 September 1984, PM 111/3/3/1 Part 24, ANZ.

the Foreign Ministry, that if this guarantee failed or was withdrawn Japan would acquire nuclear weapons of its own, and it was only on this understanding that Japan signed the Nuclear Non-Proliferation Treaty in 1970 and, with some reluctance, ratified it six years later.

As part of the arrangements under the Mutual Security Treaty, much of the US Seventh Fleet was based in Japanese ports. Since this included large aircraft carriers, guided missile cruisers and submarines, it was a considerable test of faith to believe that none of these were nuclear-armed. Japan's situation, in the North East Asian triangle where the interests of four major powers converged, required this faith. The alternative to turning a blind eye to the armaments of the Seventh Fleet was an end to the Mutual Security Treaty and an 'independent' Japanese foreign policy backed by the acquisition of nuclear weapons.

The security of the Pacific rested on the American–Japanese alliance and neither the Chinese nor anyone else wished to see it disturbed. Indeed, the Chinese, worried about the Soviet Union, wanted the continuing stability of all alliances in the Pacific, including ANZUS (a point they apparently made to the young Lange in 1981).[*] A conspiracy of silence about the weaponry of the US ships in Japanese ports was therefore a necessity and was universally observed.

Now both Tokyo and Washington were agitated by the thought that an inexperienced government in New Zealand, propelled by supporters whose overriding interest was opposition to nuclear weapons, might ignore the convention of silence and ignite an anti-nuclear movement in Japan which could have unforeseeable consequences. Wolfowitz said anxiously that any linking of New Zealand to the Japanese formula 'caused the Japan desk in State to leave the ground'.[†] Lange was occasionally tempted to comment on the difference between New Zealand's policy and Japan's which he said seemed to be one of 'heroic ignores', but warned on

---

[*] Colin James interview, *Far Eastern Economic Review*, 2 August 1984.
[†] Lange–Shultz meeting in New York, 24 September 1984, PM 59/8/5 Part 1, MFAT.

various occasions by his officials he largely avoided the trap. Some of his supporters, however, were less restrained, and were prone to contrast the honest and open stance of New Zealand with the murky and discreditable one of Japan. Perhaps Japan would be inspired by New Zealand's lead and no one gave any thought to the likely consequences of the end of the Japanese–American alliance. This is the peril of single-issue politics: if one aim is made absolute and pursued at all costs, then other desirable aims are ignored and become part of the costs. As Margaret Wilson said of her party members: 'They did not in fact think much about the foreign policy implications – that was "not our world".'[*]

So an apprehensive Tokyo was anxious to get the measure of New Zealand's new leader. Soon after the government took office, the *Japan Times* said that '[r]igid application of non-nuclear doctrines would not contribute to the security of free world nations' and hoped a little nervously that the Lange Government would 'demonstrate realism'.[†] Hints about the need to step carefully were relayed by the New Zealand embassy in Tokyo. Then, meeting Lange at the United Nations in September, the Japanese Foreign Minister spelled out his country's non-nuclear principles and underlined the moral: 'He said the reality of the world today was that the balance of power is maintained by nuclear weaponry. It was important for Western countries to maintain unity among themselves.' He afterwards told the Japanese press that the New Zealand Prime Minister hoped to avoid any dramatic disruption, but when asked how, he said that Mr Lange had not elaborated.[‡]

Then chance, or rather the assassination of Mrs Gandhi, offered the Japanese Prime Minister, Yasuhiro Nakasone, the opportunity to make his own assessment. There was a large gathering of leaders in New Delhi for the funeral and a member of Nakasone's staff approached me to say that his Prime Minister would like a meeting.

---

[*] Interview with Margaret Wilson, 4 August 2011.
[†] *Japan Times*, 20 July 1984.
[‡] PM 111/3/3/1 Part 24, ANZ.

This was easily arranged, though it became clear that, rather against the normal protocol, we were being summoned to meet him. Nakasone sat aloof in his hotel room listening with eyes half-closed to Lange's explanation of his policy. Lange was nervous and his volubility was increased by Nakasone's unblinking regard and disinclination to say anything. When we left the room I did not think the assessment was favourable.

It was not. When Nakasone was about to visit New Zealand in January 1985, President Reagan and Shultz asked him to carry a message to Lange, seeking to break the stalemate on ship visits. The Japanese Prime Minister was reluctant to get more deeply involved beyond explaining Japan's non-nuclear principles. He may not have done even this. Lange's hopes of a serious conversation with him on a car journey through the Waikato were thwarted by Nakasone resolutely falling asleep in the back seat of the elderly Rolls. 'He went to sleep when we left and woke up again for lunch. When we left Ruakura he slept until we got back to Auckland.'* But Nakasone's attack of narcolepsy was diplomatic; the Canadian embassy reported from Tokyo that he had feigned sleep to avoid any discussion of the nuclear problem.

The British position was less sensitive since, as the Foreign Office pointed out somewhat haughtily, they were not party to the ANZUS treaty.† However, though distance and the end of Empire made visits by the Royal Navy less frequent than formerly, it was the only nuclear-armed navy apart from that of the United States likely to come to New Zealand. More important were the traditional links between the two countries, links which at the level of sentiment were probably even closer than those with Australia. As Mrs Thatcher's brief cable to Muldoon on his election defeat said: 'We were particularly grateful for your staunch support for our endeavours in the South Atlantic, and have been happy to argue New Zealand's case within the European

---

* David Lange, *My Life*, Viking, 2005, p. 203.
† When the treaty was signed Britain was aggrieved at being excluded.

community.' London was therefore an involuntary party to the dispute; the ties of feeling were such that at various times both the United States and New Zealand sought its help as a go-between.

The Foreign Office's first instinct was 'to lie doggo', recognising that the Americans might well ask them to join in protests to the new government.* Their presentiment was right; in mid-August, Washington asked its embassy in London to find out whether the British might be willing to help. The US and Australia, it said, were seeking a quiet dialogue and opportunities to convince New Zealand to reverse its policy. Given its special relationship, some quiet words by Britain could be particularly useful. Would the Foreign Office be willing to stress the broader implications of a New Zealand ban on ship visits? This would need to be done carefully; it was important that the US not be seen as orchestrating a diplomatic offensive given (in the words of another message) 'the unique ability of New Zealanders to perceive "heavying"', but there might be helpful opportunities, such as a meeting at the UN or a Lange visit to London, when something could be done.†

This overture encouraged the British to dip a cautious toe into the water. Three weeks later the High Commissioner in Wellington handed over an 'informal memorandum' warning that if New Zealand went beyond general statements about the undesirability of nuclear weapons to doing something about them, visits by the Royal Navy would be ruled out. A ban on port visits would be destabilising and would not bring peaceful disarmament any closer. It would in fact 'affect Western unity and would undoubtedly please the Russians'.‡

When Lange called at Downing Street at the end of September, Mrs Thatcher held to this line. She was in gentle mood, wanting like Hawke and Nakasone to make her own appraisal of the new Prime Minister, and British governments had a lengthy experience

---

* FCO Minute of 16 July 1984, FCO Papers.
† Washington cable of 17 August 1984, State Department Papers. The comment on 'heavying' came in a lengthy think-piece by Washington, 21 November 1984.
‡ Memo of 10 September 1984, PM 59/8/2 Part 22, ANZ.

of being indulgent towards New Zealand. The crisis was a worry but had not yet come to a head and until it did Britain was largely content to watch. Its High Commissioner in Wellington, married to a New Zealander, was optimistic, telling London at the end of the year: 'In defence, I have no doubt that New Zealand will continue as a reliable partner both in ANZUS and in the overall Western Alliance.'[*]

The ASEAN countries also wondered about the new government's intentions. New Zealand, like Australia, had made a helpful contribution to their security over the three previous decades and it still maintained a battalion in Singapore. Any immediate threat was long gone but Singapore preferred to retain the battalion in the meantime, arguing (and Lange agreed) that a withdrawal would give the wrong signal while Vietnamese ambitions were still unclear. In this situation New Zealand's membership of ANZUS was regarded, at least by Malaysia and Singapore, as a useful reinforcement. South East Asia had historically been a cockpit of great-power rivalry and its member states understood that their independence could best be preserved by maintaining a careful balance between the West and the rising power of China. While New Zealand was a member of ANZUS its battalion provided a tripwire for possible American involvement without risking the delicate balance which made it inadvisable for Malaysia and Singapore to have any direct security links with the United States.

Thailand was reported to be uneasy about any threat to ANZUS, and the Malaysian Prime Minister, Mahathir Mohamad, said that ANZUS was important enough for his country to want it to continue – it was 'an arrangement that hurts nobody but gives a lot of benefit to the participants'.[†] Since Mrs Thatcher was due to visit Singapore and Malaysia, London was told that both would like to discuss 'ANZUS and the advent of Mr Lange as Prime Minister'.[‡]

However, Lange himself was the first to visit, coming to Singapore on his way home from London in early October and urged by his

---

[*] Despatch by the High Commissioner, Terence O'Leary, 29 November 1984, FCO Papers.
[†] 13 August 1984, PM 50/8/5 Part 1, ANZ.
[‡] British cables of 13 and 16 August 1984, FCO Papers.

officials to spend some time with the Prime Minister, Lee Kuan Yew. This was something of a punt given their very different temperaments and backgrounds but it turned out to be a success. Lange said he had come to sit at Lee's feet and Lee replied, to Lange's delight, that this was rather a large bundle. Lee, long accustomed to dealing with the British Labour Party, deployed a silky charm which quite won over the New Zealander who told his subsequent press conference: 'I was probably far more impressed with him than he was with me.' Two years later Lange was still impressed, saying: 'I suppose he's the closest thing that I have to an adopted political father.'[*]

The two went gently over their differences on security policy after Lange had told him that the US relationship had exploded in a way he should have foreseen. Lee talked about the responsibility to maintain the balance of power in the world; Lange said New Zealand was firmly part of the Western alliance which could hardly be subverted by the absence of an occasional port visit, asserting (wrongly) that there had been none in 1972–75.

Then Lee hardened his tone and spoke more bluntly. It was essential to maintain US resolve, and he asked Lange to imagine the situation if the Americans were not in South East Asia. Everyone including New Zealanders had to realise how rapid air travel had changed the old world we had grown up in: 'In the present world there is no such thing as opting out.' Lange retorted that countries do not always have to opt in; Singapore did not have nuclear weapons there. Lee flashed out, 'Don't we?' and pointed to the nuclear-armed ships and submarines that regularly passed through the Johore Strait which was less than a mile wide. That was a risk but he preferred that to insecurity. The meeting ended amiably, with Lee suggesting that new Labour Prime Ministers should avoid foreign policy during their honeymoon period and take advantage of it to get unpleasant domestic tasks done.[†]

---

[*] Vernon Wright interview, 5 December 1986, Lange Papers, Box 1, ANZ.
[†] Meeting at the Istana, Singapore, 5 October 1984, PM 58/455/1 Part 8, ANZ.

The new government's foreign policy laid particular emphasis on the South Pacific as New Zealand's primary concern, in a sense (though no one would have used the term) its sphere of influence. The influence, though, came under strain from the anti-nuclear policy. At the Port Moresby meeting the Commonwealth Secretary-General, Shridath Ramphal, described the policy as a positive step which would ultimately have an effect worldwide. Encouraged by this the Papua New Guinea Prime Minister, Michael Somare, praised Lange for giving the region a strong lead in banning nuclear-powered visits. Three weeks later when he (or others) had thought further he issued a statement saying that PNG relied for its security on the ANZUS treaty and expected the treaty to remain in its present form for some time. 'How can we defend ourselves if there is no common agreement between the big countries like America, Australia and New Zealand?'

Apart from Somare's first thoughts, only Vanuatu, which had already declared itself to be nuclear-free, supported the New Zealand policy. Fiji and Tonga said they would not change their views on ship visits; Samoa said it would continue to welcome all friendly warships – 'It is not for us to question which are nuclear ships.' Tuvalu and Kiribati already had treaties allowing American use of their ports and the Cook Islands described ANZUS as 'the cornerstone of defence in our region'.*

In fact the only country that warmly welcomed the anti-nuclear policy was the Soviet Union. New Zealand was small and remote but it was causing trouble to the United States and opened up the possibility of similar movements in Australia and Japan. The KGB's work plan for 1982–85 had made the Pacific a major priority for the first time but the main target was Japan. The election of the Lange Government led to an increase of KGB activity in both Australia and New Zealand. The KGB Centre in Moscow 'was jubilant at Lange's election and told the London residency that it attached "huge importance" to organising European support for his decision to ban U.S.

---

* These views were variously reported in PM 50/8/5 Part 1 and PM 111/3/3/1 Part 23, ANZ.

ships carrying nuclear weapons from New Zealand ports and for his anti-nuclear policies in general'.*

The British embassy reported that the Russian press had 'squeezed as much mileage as possible from the Labour Party's victory'. Lange's pledge on nuclear weapons and the embarrassment caused to Washington by this 'insubordination' had been much stressed, and there were calls for resistance to American economic blackmail.† More provocatively, Tass pointed out that if the US failed to force New Zealand to concede, the Left of the Australian Labor Party at its next conference would be able to commit the party to banning American ship visits and call for the removal of American bases.

Even Kim Philby, the British traitor now a major-general in the KGB, did his bit. Asked to name the world leader he most admired, he said David Lange: 'He had the courage to ban nuclear ships from New Zealand waters. Now we have no reason to target New Zealand with our intercontinental missiles and indeed we have ceased to do so. I am sorry I cannot say the same about Australia.'‡

This was an embarrassment for Lange who was no admirer of the Soviet Union and for whom unwanted advances from the Russian bear were not helpful to his claims of unwavering support for ANZUS and the Western alliance. He later called in the Soviet ambassador, Vladimir Bykov, to complain about misreporting by Tass and others and to give him, 'short but sharp', the message that New Zealand was not anti-American but anti-nuclear. The ambassador said he was recommending patience and objectivity to the Soviet press and for a time there was a lull. Four years later, however, Lange still felt that it would not be politically wise for him to accept an invitation to visit the Soviet Union and Palmer went in his place.§

---

* Oleg Gordievsky in *KGB: The Inside Story*, Hodder & Stoughton, 1990, p. 513.
† For example, commentary by V. Tarasov in *Izvestia*, 18 July 1984, FCO Papers. The Tass view was published on 2 January 1985.
‡ Quoted in Philip Knightley, *Philby: KGB Masterspy*, Andre Deutsch Limited, 1988, p. 257.
§ Raymond Richards, *Palmer: The Parliamentary Years*, Canterbury University Press, 2010, pp. 332–3. Bykov was summoned on 25 February 1985.

Moscow was aware that, whatever Lange's views, other and perhaps more active members of his party were sympathetic. Their concerns were with American imperialism and the wars they believed this caused and they tended to dismiss worries about Soviet adventurism as Western propaganda. It was unlikely that many on the Left, apart from the small Socialist United Party, Soviet-aligned and financed, had great affection for the Soviet system. Some perhaps still saw hovering over this decaying tyranny the spectral dream of a socialist society but for most who had a deeply felt dislike of the capitalist United States the Soviet Union was a welcome counterbalance to the American superpower. Frank O'Flynn, a genial lawyer who had reluctantly become Minister of Defence and was liked by everyone except those who worked for him, told a surprised Shultz in 1985 that since all the contentious alliance issues in Europe had been resolved in America's favour, 'some non-acceptance of US leadership was needed to provide a kind of balance'.*

None of this eased US concerns for it simply underlined the ability of New Zealand to make wider and worse trouble in the Pacific. Shultz's misgivings began to accumulate. There was no decisive moment, just a growing conviction as the reports came in that Lange was unwilling or unable to deliver.† He began to think that 'it was in the nature of the man'; he did not want to solve the problem, perhaps enjoying more the celebrity it brought him.‡

And even for the diminishing number of the hopeful there were no signs of any favourable turn in New Zealand public opinion. In August the US Information Agency reported that a large majority (7 in 10) approved a ban on the entry of nuclear weapons into the country and one almost as large (6 in 10) supported a renegotiation of the ANZUS treaty. A month later its review of the polls was even more explicit. Opposition to US ship visits was widespread, based on

---

* Meeting in Kuala Lumpur, 13 July 1985, State Department Papers.
† The Australian embassy in Washington reported 'a deep scepticism that Lange will be able to deliver' on 29 August 1984. 250/11/18 Part 14, NAA.
‡ Interview with George Shultz, 2 November 2011.

fear of accidents or of being targeted in a nuclear war. The belief that the US was the main beneficiary of ANZUS had risen and there was a relatively limited acceptance of the need to maintain the strength of the Western alliance if progress was to be made on arms control. The greatest opposition was to be found among the younger generation, women and the political Left. 'These same groups are most likely to favour withdrawal from ANZUS.'*

Gloomily contemplating these indicators, Washington looked in vain for any sign that Lange was taking any steps to counter them. They believed that he had undertaken to work on public opinion; he had certainly more than once promised to make the case for ANZUS and to explain why it was important for New Zealand to remain in the alliance. His speaking style was not given to careful expositions and in any case he preferred to communicate with the public mainly through press conferences. He often gave two a week, after Cabinet and caucus, and they were highly effective; with his quick, teasing wit he held most journalists in the hollow of his hand. He did not use any of them to explain how the alliance worked and why its membership of ANZUS reinforced New Zealand's standing in the region.

The difficulty with such freewheeling occasions was that they did not lend themselves to methodical explanation. He could get carried away in reaching for a witticism and sometimes said too much, as he would ruefully acknowledge.† Given this ever-present risk the Americans wondered why he needed to give so many. Palmer put this down to their not understanding New Zealand political practice, but in fact no Prime Minister has been as addicted to the press conference as Lange. He was good at them and loved the chance to shine; when he later reminisced about his travels he liked to talk about the excitement of his press conferences as much as the occasions that led to them.

---

* USIA Research Reports, Laux Papers, Box 90659, Reagan Presidential Library.
† As when he commented, on the loss of the cruise ship *Mikhail Lermontov* in the Marlborough Sounds, that New Zealand was the only member of the Western alliance to have sunk a Soviet ship.

As the weeks went by, Washington regularly erupted in a steaming cloud of anxiety over a succession of his press comments. In late August he was interviewed by the correspondent of *Asahi Shimbun* in Wellington. He was on his best behaviour, declining any comparison with Japan on the grounds that every country's situation was different, and arguing that since ship visits were only part of the treaty relationship it should be possible to talk it through and he expected the Americans then to honour New Zealand's policy. If, 'after our negotiations and talking with them the policy is accepted then I certainly won't be clambering around on board their ships to check their word'. This did not help because it implied an expectation that New Zealand's policy would in time be accepted by the US. If it ever was, Armitage pointed out, the consequences would not be confined to Japan.*

Then the Labour Party conference put on a spectacular display at its victory meeting. It was the biggest conference ever, with over 800 delegates, and the radical Left controlled the floor – the government members were silent except for the economic debate. The excited delegates were in withdrawal mode, urging withdrawal from a lengthy list that ran from beauty contests to ANZUS. The Prime Minister's warning not to turn the foreign policy debate into a witch-hunt against the United States was simply disregarded, and O'Flynn's proposal to hold it behind closed doors to avoid sending the wrong message to world capitals was dismissed as 'gutless'. There was no effort to hide the suspicion that their leader would betray them on ANZUS as he was doing on market forces; in the words of the US embassy: 'They were watching Lange like a hawk, with an E.'†

In quick succession the conference called by large majorities for New Zealand to break all ties with 'nuclear powers'; pull out of ANZUS; close the American Antarctic support base at Christchurch; withdraw the battalion from Singapore; end participation in the Five

---

* *Asahi Shimbun*, 23 August 1984. The comment was made to Norrish by Armitage, 7 September 1984, PM 59/8/5 Part 1, MFAT.
† Cable of 12 September 1984, State Department Papers.

Power Arrangements for the defence of Singapore and Malaysia; withdraw the New Zealand contingent from the observer force in the Sinai; disband the rapid deployment force; and use the armed forces primarily for civil relief work. On a slightly less isolationist note it strongly condemned the 'invasion' of Grenada, and the Falklands War; pledged support for the miners in Britain; called for a review of diplomatic ties with the Philippines in favour of closer ties with Vietnam; and endorsed the 'overwhelming popularity' of the Sandinista government in Nicaragua. To complete the surreal atmosphere, the Prime Minister assured the conference in his closing speech that his administration would not allow the economy to be governed by free-market forces.

All this could be dismissed by Lange as 'party romps' and 'political jollities' but they attracted considerable interest from countries trying to understand where New Zealand was heading. Most grasped that these remits were not Labour Party policy but it was not unreasonable to assume that on past form they were likely to have an important influence on the party's direction. Margaret Wilson, who was elected President at this conference, certainly hoped so: 'the party's role is to foreshadow the future direction of policy through conference remits'.* The Foreign Office therefore found 'the litany of the Left's enthusiasms in the defence field' depressing. The *Australian* decided that the earlier fears were justified. ANZUS was now in extreme jeopardy and 'Australia must act quickly to distance itself from New Zealand's dangerous isolationist tendencies'. The US embassy concluded that Lange was 'unlikely to diverge too obviously from party policy on foreign policy questions lest he provide his opposition with another issue to use against him'.†

The political temperature in New Zealand stayed high. Five hundred anti-nuclear protesters demonstrated at the Tangimoana

---

* Margaret Wilson, 'The Non-Nuclear Policy', in *Labour in Government, 1984–1987*, Allen & Unwin/Port Nicholson Press, 1989, p. 62.
† FCO minute, 12 September; the *Australian*, 10 September; and the US embassy report, 12 September 1984.

defence station, despite Palmer, as Acting Prime Minister, pointing out that it had no nuclear connections whatever (it did however have links to the United States). Three hundred women protested near the American hangars at Christchurch airport and the first 'annual' Nuclear Weapons-free Zone conference met in Wellington. There was a drumbeat of concern that it was close to midnight on the atomic clock and some viewers complained of a surfeit of doom-laden nuclear documentaries on television. It all showed, said a bright journalist, that New Zealanders 'will not take that kind of ship from anyone'.[*]

The United States had confined its discussions and protests to Lange as leader of the government and Foreign Minister. Some American officials ruminated afterwards that they had perhaps confused Cabinet government with the Presidential system they were used to. But New Zealand had had something close to a Presidential system with the previous Prime Minister and the approach was a natural one; Washington could hardly negotiate with the whole Cabinet. But the doubts as to how far the Prime Minister was in control kept resurfacing. When he was in New York telling the United Nations General Assembly that ANZUS was central to his government's policy, Rowling in Wellington was saying that the alliance was no longer relevant and would have to be replaced. ANZUS, he said, was all about defending the country from Japan and the US was now urging the Japanese to rearm. 'If ever there was a denial of ANZUS, that's it.'[†]

Australian distrust deepened. The *Sydney Morning Herald* asked: 'Is ANZUS finished?' Hawke, fending off a call to consider alternatives, told Parliament: 'I express the hope – although there may not be much basis for the hope – I express the hope that they [New Zealand and the United States] will be able to work that out.'[‡] At home the *New Zealand Herald* believed that 'the ride is about to become bumpy', and the *Press* concluded that ANZUS was almost

---

[*] Denis Welch in the *New Zealand Listener*, 20 October 1984.
[†] 26 September 1984. It had been announced that Rowling would be the next ambassador to Washington.
[‡] In the House of Representatives, Canberra, 5 October 1984.

dead and was baffled by the Prime Minister's tactics: 'This policy has been long in the making yet no serious thought has been given to the alternatives.'*

Three weeks later, after further statements to the media by Lange, senior officials in the State Department set down their complaints in a cable which with diplomatic delicacy they decided not to send (that would be a formal protest) but handed over anyway to alert Wellington to their feelings. The main objections were to the Prime Minister's statement that he had 'iron-clad assurances' from Shultz and the White House that the Administration would prevent any moves against trade; this was 'factually incorrect', for though the Administration had made it clear it would oppose any economic retaliation, it could not necessarily control action by the Congress. Lange had also talked of his hopes of resolving the nuclear propulsion question so they were disturbed by his statement to Radio New Zealand that this could not be done within a three-year term. And lastly, they were 'distressed' by another comment made to the *Australian Financial Review* which seemed at least by implication to rule out any restoration of port access.†

Norrish did his best. American officials seemed to be going out of their way 'to examine everything the PM says under a microscope'. If Lange took several steps forward and an occasional half-step back, it was the overall trend that mattered and 'surely State can see that the trend line is up'. Pondering this response in Washington, the State Department's Bill Brown concluded a little reluctantly that the Prime Minister's assurances had to be taken at face value and respected; the US would 'just have to swallow hard over public statements'.‡

In democratic politics, though, it is the public statements that matter. The only trend that was going up was the reassurances Lange and his officials were giving in private. It was obvious that the public trend

---

* *New Zealand Herald*, 27 September and *Press*, 1 October 1984.
† Report by NZ embassy, 31 October, and Norrish's response, 5 November 1984, PM 59/8/5 Part 1, MFAT.
‡ Brown to John Wood, NZ embassy, 6 November 1984, PM 59/8/5 Part 1, MFAT.

was going firmly in the opposite direction. Whatever he signalled in private, his public statements in these weeks were unqualified reiterations of the anti-nuclear policy. It was non-negotiable, he said, and nuclear weapons would never come into New Zealand's ports while he was Prime Minister. There was no sign of any preparation of public opinion for a settlement and no sign of the debate which he had promised to encourage over the value of ANZUS. He simply declared that New Zealand had no intention of withdrawing from the treaty, leaving open the possibility that others might force such a withdrawal if New Zealand's non-negotiable policy could not be accommodated.

In November a senior State Department official came to see for himself. Morton Abramowitz was an observer not a government representative but he passed his views back to Washington. They were pessimistic; he saw little chance of a negotiated outcome. He thought Lange was weak and out of his depth and his civil service advisers were not strong enough to stand against the trend.[*] Indeed he was surprised by the hopes of a deal that buoyed officials, saying to me two months later, 'I thought you guys must have been smoking pot.' He felt that New Zealanders did not understand the depth of Washington's feeling on the issue.

Wolfowitz confessed his worries to the embassy in Washington. Abramowitz was only one of the influential Americans who had come back saying there was no widespread understanding in New Zealand that time was running out for reaching a solution on ship visits. On the contrary, the general view seemed to be that New Zealand could 'get away with' denying port access to US ships and maintain the rest of the relationship unimpaired. He appreciated that the Prime Minister and a handful of senior officials were working on an accommodation but was daunted by what he now understood to be the immensity of the task in New Zealand's political atmosphere.[†]

---

[*] Interview with Morton Abramowitz, 26 September 2011.
[†] Talking to John Wood, Deputy at the New Zealand Embassy, 29 November 1984, PM 59/8/5 Part 1, MFAT.

In an end-of-year interview on television and a press conference the following day, the Prime Minister seemed to confirm this view, implying at least to American eyes that New Zealand's policy had been successful for the past five months and would continue to be acceptable. He gave a categorical assurance that no nuclear-powered warship would visit in his term as Prime Minister and said several times that the US would not seek permission for a visit by a nuclear-armed warship because it knew it would be rebuffed. These comments caused 'consternation' within the State Department, two of whose officials were described as shaken and unnerved, and a 'violent' reaction in the other agencies (Defense and the National Security Council). Worst of all from Washington's point of view, Lange was thought to have claimed that his government would draw on American intelligence sources to determine a ship's armaments, thus implying that the US was prepared to breach its neither-confirm-nor-deny policy for New Zealand. Admiral Crowe in Honolulu was so concerned that he got Armitage out of bed near midnight to make sure that Caspar Weinberger, the Secretary of Defense, was told.

After Weinberger and his assistant had gone back to bed there was some sense that all this might have been an overreaction, particularly when there was a plausible ambiguity over Lange's use of the word 'intelligence' which Wellington argued he had used in the more old-fashioned sense of information or knowledge – it was hard to believe that he would publicly declare that New Zealand would use secret American intelligence. Nonetheless, the embassy in Washington reported that the atmosphere was very bad.* Only their private knowledge that the Prime Minister and his advisers were working on an accommodation had prevented a more serious boil-over. Everything now hung on whether the ship visit which had been under consideration for the past month would be politically achievable.

---

* NZ embassy, 17 December 1984, PM 59/8/5 Part 2, MFAT.

Chapter Four
The Search for a Solution

In the course of these months the differing positions of the two countries, and the arguments used to back them, had become forbiddingly clear. New Zealand hoped to establish that there was a distinction between membership of ANZUS and the acceptance of nuclear weapons. The Prime Minister made repeated declarations that his country was determined to play a full part in the alliance, but with conventional weapons only, and he said even more frequently that nuclear weapons would never enter the country while he was Prime Minister. The exclusion of these weapons was party policy but the periodic pledges to remain in ANZUS were practical politics. Successive polls invariably showed that New Zealanders wanted to keep their alliance cake but could not swallow the possible presence of nuclear arms. Up to three-quarters of those polled supported both keeping the country anti-nuclear and staying in the alliance. When they were pressed to choose, a small but clear majority preferred the alliance even at the cost of admitting nuclear weapons. Though his private views were more ambivalent, Lange was determined not to get on the wrong side of this political fence.

To do so he had to put forward some novel arguments and did so with the assurance of his earlier experience in court. His main submission was that ANZUS had not been a nuclear alliance when first established. New Zealand had therefore never agreed to accept these weapons as part of its alliance obligations and it would be unjust to compel the country to do so now. Its insistence on the non-nuclear character of the alliance was in no way an attempt to evade its share of the common burden. He could point to the battalion in Singapore, annual exercises under the Five Power Arrangements in South East Asia, the helicopter force helping police the Egyptian–Israeli border in the Sinai, and other peacekeeping responsibilities as compelling evidence that New Zealand was seeking no 'free ride' on security. To emphasise the point he raised the 1985 defence budget and increased the Air Force's maritime surveillance capability.

This was a policy of hope: a hope that he and his country's views on being firm members of the alliance while opposing visits by its ships would not be seen as incompatible; a hope that he could convince the United States that New Zealand could be accepted as a reliable partner solely with conventional weapons. As if attempting to reconcile these conflicting views was not difficult enough, he had also to carry the left wing of the party with him, and his proclamations of support for the alliance only stirred their ever-present suspicions. For the party activists ANZUS was the real target and opposition to ship visits offered the best means of reaching it.

The chances of his approach working were not great. For a start it required a distinctly shaky reading of history. The United States had possessed nuclear weapons when the treaty was signed and the agreement's brief wording had never excluded nuclear arms or specified what kinds of armaments were acceptable for defending it. In over 30 years no New Zealand government had ever claimed that the treaty excluded nuclear weapons or raised objections to them. The 1969–75 hiatus in the visits of nuclear-powered ships was purely over the issue of liability for any accident; 22 other American warships visited without any challenge to their weapons.

The past though did not necessarily have the final say. The Prime Minister's hopes might have been accepted if the relationship with New Zealand was all that the United States had to consider. Armitage thought that Shultz and Weinberger, 'though they could not agree on what to have for breakfast', shared a romantic, perhaps sentimental, view of New Zealand which stemmed from the Pacific War. That view might have been able to withstand even a disagreement over ship visits. The country was a long-standing ally that had stood with the US in all its subsequent Asian wars and had a reputation for steadiness and good judgement fostered by a succession of able ambassadors in Washington. 'New Zealand views were valued. It could speak truth to power and offer candid views that carried some weight because New Zealanders were seen less as players than as smart observers', was the view of a former Defense Department official.[*]

Ship visits to ports in the remote South Pacific were not essential. Apart from being inescapably part of Australia's defence, New Zealand's location had no especial strategic significance; hence the jokes about its being a dagger pointed at the heart of Antarctica. Visits were expensive and the US Navy had no particular need to make them other than to underline the alliance partnership. General Chain, in charge of politico-military affairs at the State Department, put the difficulty bluntly in September: if the issue was just bilateral, 'perhaps we could do something. But it isn't – and we can't.'[†]

The US could not, because the alliance with New Zealand did not stand alone but was part of its network of global alliances. If the country were isolated and cut off from the rest of the West, as the more devoted activists seemed to hope, the number of American visits could certainly have been reduced and perhaps ended altogether. But even a small tear in the global web would affect everyone else and,

---

[*] Interview with James Kelly, 2 October 2011.
[†] Talking to Norrish, 7 September 1984, PM 59/8/5 Part 1, MFAT.

THE SEARCH FOR A SOLUTION

as American officials said apologetically, if a choice had to be made, the risks for Australia and Japan were more important than the relationship with New Zealand. NATO members like Norway, Denmark and Spain had anti-nuclear policies comparable to New Zealand's but were careful to reconcile them with their alliance obligations on port access. If New Zealand was made an exception all these delicate arrangements would come into question and might start to unravel.

Even if the understandings with Japan and NATO could be safeguarded, and the New Zealand alliance could be given a special status, the trust that underlay it would be diminished. As Shultz said more than once, what kind of alliance would it be if navies did not have free access to one another's ports? The US could not use different weapons to defend different alliances. It had to be ready to use whatever force was necessary, and defence in the second half of the twentieth century started with the nuclear option. Since a potential enemy might not be willing to accept the same limits, alliances had to be defended not by specified or restricted means but by whatever would be effective.

It all boiled down to one issue: whether the country was willing to accept the naval doctrine known as 'neither confirm nor deny' (NCND for short) on which both the US and British navies based their operational effectiveness. Both cruised far from home and carrying nuclear weapons on long voyages was not welcomed by either navy. They were costly to embark, required elaborate command-and-control arrangements, and took up an excessive amount of space. They were an expensive nuisance and unless required by the threat level captains preferred not to carry them.

The answer to this was NCND. By refusing to acknowledge what their ships might have on board navies could conceal, not the presence of nuclear weapons, but their absence. This was much more useful; the number of weapons actually carried could be greatly reduced since a possible adversary had no way of knowing, at least from a distance, whether a warship was nuclear-armed. There was a political advantage also to NCND. Shultz argued that the ambiguity protected both host and guest when the ships called, since the possible presence of the weapons was never revealed. This of course meant accepting a residual uncertainty. Japan, Australia and the NATO members could live with this uncertainty as the price of their alliance, but from the beginning it was doubtful that the Labour Party activists would be willing to accept the ambiguity which was the purpose of NCND. The party policy insisted on absolute certainty about the absence of nuclear arms in any visiting ship.

The NCND rule for visits was unyielding. In retirement Admiral Crowe, who as CINCPAC in Honolulu played an important part in the search for a settlement, described it as 'a pretty high-handed policy. What amazed me the most about it is that so much of the world accepted it.'* Lange was not one of them. He equivocated; since Washington was unmoveable he often reiterated his understanding of the policy, but never fully accepted it. He called it on one occasion 'outmoded and militarily irrelevant', though without explaining why. More substantively, all his proposals to allow ship visits involved some form of public declaration that the ships were not nuclear-armed and this, for the purists in Washington, would have been a breach of NCND. The insistence on making such a judgement was what distinguished New Zealand from the other anti-nuclear nations and explains why Japan and Australia among others were privately urging the US to stand firm. Their policies were based on the ambiguity which NCND shielded and statements of the kind Lange was proposing would make their position untenable.

In the lunar landscape of nuclear deterrence what concerned a wider group of countries, especially in Western Europe, was that New Zealand might set off a worldwide movement and thus disturb and perhaps even upset the delicate nuclear balance on which their security depended. New Zealand, drinking at the bar of world opinion, might grow expansive and order anti-nuclear refreshment for everyone. For all Wellington's denials of any such intentions, Lange

---

* Interview by Michael Bassett with Admiral William Crowe, 5 December 2002, kindly made available by Dr Bassett.

was a wayward figure and his policy made in the excitement of press conferences could seem alarmingly impulsive.

Some, like the West German Chancellor, worried that New Zealand might end up undermining the Western alliance. Shutting warships out of Wellington or Auckland was hardly a worry but European governments which had just emerged from a hard-fought battle over missile deployments were nervous of the possibility of a renewed campaign on the evils of nuclear weapons. If a respectable, English-speaking democracy were to start a crusade against the stockpiling of these weapons the West's and indeed the world's settled security system might be shaken.

Concerned for the future of humanity, this was indeed what the anti-nuclear enthusiasts hoped to do. The enticing prospect for many at the Labour Party conference was that New Zealand could 'lead the world' and start a global retreat from what seemed to be an ever-swelling number of deadly weapons. The country might be a small weight in the strategic balance but perhaps a cry from the South Pacific could awaken a world immobilised by its nightmare of Mutually Assured Destruction and revive the hope of ending the nuclear arms race.

This appealing dream, as so often, fell victim to harsher realities. If New Zealand's policy was for export, if it was promoted as a template or example for other democracies, these nations might see it as threatening their own security, and the reactions in Asia, Europe and North America could change from disapproval to active hostility. The country relied on exports for its continuing prosperity. If unilateral nuclear disarmament became one of them, its international relationships could be damaged and the country's trade might well be vulnerable to retaliation.

Trade was politically sacred and the Lange administration stepped back. The Prime Minister declared his support for nuclear deterrence and said that if he were the German Chancellor he too would want to maintain the nuclear balance. So the anti-nuclear policy was affirmed to be for New Zealand alone and was not for export. It did not aim to save the world. It was declared to reflect only the fact that

New Zealanders had such an abhorrence of nuclear weapons that they wanted nothing to do with them. This was only half-believed by those diplomats who had followed the party conference. An anti-nuclear policy may have made emotional sense to those whose feelings were outraged by the weapons, but if confined solely to New Zealand it did not make any other sense. The country had no pieces on the nuclear chess board. It had long been a member of the Nuclear Non-Proliferation Treaty; it had no nuclear weapons and did not intend to acquire them. Forswearing the weapons once again may have demonstrated admirable sentiments but it did not diminish the global stockpile by a millirad.

To many outsider observers it looked as if New Zealand was attempting to opt out of the world, to bury its head in its own farmland and to ignore the fact that the threat of nuclear weapons was global, not national. Declarations would not shield New Zealand from the consequences of a nuclear war; as Lange himself pointed out, the southern hemisphere was no longer immune. Western governments believed that the risk of a disastrous war was best managed by standing together on deterrence, not by individual countries wandering away to show their impatience with the deadlock. Whatever the wider dangers, the immediate effect of the New Zealand stand could be to encourage the Russians to stay away from the arms control negotiations in Geneva while they waited to see whether further Western disunity might give them a better deal.

If the policy was not for export then its only justification was that it made New Zealanders feel better about themselves. That was by no means irrelevant in a democracy; the country was thinking for itself and standing up for a principle. It was enough for many who disliked the weapons but were nervous of making wider trouble. Conscious of these limits, the anti-nuclear movement was only half-hearted about pressing the government to be a missionary to the world.[*] The

---

[*] Helen Clark told viewers in Australia that if other small countries took similar stands nuclear disarmament might come to something but New Zealand's move was only 'the beginning of that tide'. Geraldine Doogue interview, National TV, 10 September 1984.

question the Prime Minister and his foreign policy advisers had to ponder in these early months was whether this reluctant acceptance that the policy was not for export would extend to some flexibility on imports; would the public accept visiting warships that would neither confirm nor deny the nature of their armaments?

The omens did not look good. There was a daunting gap between Labour policy which barred ships which might be nuclear-armed or -powered from the country's territorial waters, and American policy which declined to acknowledge the possible presence of nuclear weapons or to make choices among its fleet to suit another country's preference. Bridging gaps is what the art of diplomacy is supposed to be about, though in this case the task was more in the nature of squaring a circle. On the plane coming back from Port Moresby in the second week of August the Prime Minister authorised Norrish to start a search for a way through. He assembled a group of the senior officials involved including Ewan Jamieson, the Chief of Defence Staff; Denis McLean, the Secretary of Defence; and myself as Head of the Prime Minister's Department. This group met informally over the next six months to consider and discuss with the Prime Minister possible ways of reconciling the New Zealand and American positions.

The first approach was based on a variant of the 'don't ask, don't tell' policy which had been adopted by other Western countries and which was in fact the only one which had successfully matched anti-nuclear policies with alliance membership for others. The group sketched out a statement which it hoped might be accepted by Washington. The wording varied as the drafters played with it, but in essence it was a declaration that the two governments agreed that the South Pacific was not a region where direct conflict between the great powers was probable, and therefore that the likelihood of visiting naval vessels carrying nuclear weapons was low. The statement would reaffirm that New Zealand did not wish to have these weapons in its ports, and also that it understood and accepted the doctrine of NCND. To put it baldly, the US would acknowledge that in the absence of any strategic rivalry in the South Pacific it had no reason to carry nuclear arms when cruising there and New Zealand, understanding this, would declare that the status of any visiting US ships would not be challenged.

The issue of nuclear propulsion could not be wrapped up so tidily. Over a third of the US fleet was so powered, a proportion which it was then assumed would steadily increase. That assumption and the fears of many New Zealanders that the maritime nuclear power plants might somehow explode and scatter deadly radiation were both proved wrong over the subsequent decades, but at the time they made nuclear propulsion a sticking point for each side. The Wellington drafters proposed stating that nuclear-powered ships would require further consideration. An enquiry into their safety by a reputable scientific body – the Royal Society was suggested – would be needed and this would take time. In the meantime any visiting warships would have to be conventionally powered.

The plan together with the 'guidelines' to be tried out on the Americans was agreed after two discussions the working group had with the Prime Minister at the end of August. He was anxious that this preliminary exploration be held as tightly as possible. At the beginning of September, Merv Norrish, the Secretary of Foreign Affairs, went to Washington to see whether the guidelines might be acceptable to the Reagan Administration. If its first reactions were favourable, then Lange and Shultz could approve them at their next meeting, with a view to issuing a joint statement before the next ship visit.

In Washington it quickly became apparent that the Americans were not much interested in any statement of the kind Norrish was proposing. In a rough equivalent of the working group in Wellington, policy on New Zealand was in the hands of the 'Inter-Agency Group' chaired by Wolfowitz and bringing together the State Department, the Pentagon and the National Security Council. In Norrish's round of calls all of its members were discouraging. The outlook, they said, was 'grim'. Time was slipping by but they saw no sign of the promise to work on public opinion. The Prime Minister seemed to be digging himself in rather than advocating a change, frequently reaffirming

THE SEARCH FOR A SOLUTION

the unmodified anti-nuclear policy in his press conferences rather than talking of reconciling it with his country's alliance obligations.

When Wellington's South Pacific formula was raised, Michael Armacost, the Under Secretary of State for Political Affairs, said 'we would like to help you' but the Administration was losing confidence in Lange's assurances. There was no sign of any game plan or timetable for defusing the danger. Norrish's plea for more time was sceptically received. Why, his hearers asked, did he think that the situation could be resolved more easily by delay? The passing of time was deepening the difficulty for the US; its continuing restraint could be interpreted as tacit acceptance of a new form of alliance. There should, said Wolfowitz bluntly, be no illusions about any easing of the American attitude, it had too much at stake with its other allies. There had to be ship visits or 'there won't be much left of the alliance'.

The atmosphere was one of courteous but undisguised mistrust. Norrish found himself on the defensive and in the awkward position of having to give reassurances about the intentions of a Prime Minister whom he barely knew. He was unable to explain why New Zealand believed it needed more time, saying it was up to Lange when they next met to convince Shultz that the time would be used to positive effect. When asked about Lange's willingness to go round the regional Labour Party conferences, he could only state that he was 'reasonably confident' that Lange intended to broaden the debate within his party. He could not enlighten them on Lange's 'game plan', only agree that it was a fair question and that he would tell the Prime Minister that he would have to give specifics when he next talked with Shultz. At the end of this unhappy round, Norrish was well aware of the increasing American scepticism but found little interest in pursuing Wellington's proposal for a jointly agreed statement.*

After this, hopes rested on the Shultz–Lange meeting scheduled to take place when the UN General Assembly met. In late September it

---

* His report is in PM 59/8/5 Part 1, MFAT.

was customary for leaders and their Foreign Ministers to congregate in New York for the opening of the Assembly. In his thank-you letter after their July meeting Shultz had proposed this as a convenient time to reconvene, with the unstated thought that the hubbub around the General Assembly would keep it inconspicuous. The Americans would have two weeks to think further about Norrish's proposal and a talk with the Secretary of State might reveal a more encouraging view. It would at least settle the issue. Either way, getting together offered a chance to revive the comparative warmth of their earlier meeting and clear up some of the misunderstandings. Possibly (as indeed turned out to be the case) it could open up another line of approach.

Before they could meet, however, it was probably inevitable that the growing frustration in Washington should touch off another if minor explosion. The Minister of Defence, Frank O'Flynn, made one of his stream-of-consciousness speeches in Parliament, so much his style that it passed largely unnoticed in official Wellington. If a theme could be discerned it was that New Zealand should stand alone in its defence. In its desire for a collective defence arrangement the country had become 'a kind of United States protectorate' and in doing so had made itself a target. It had no enemies of its own and it made no sense to take over the enemies of the US and Britain. If New Zealand was ever attacked its forces could use the tremendous advantages of the terrain, 'cutting bridges and tunnels, and so on'.[*] These musings on guerrilla warfare had little effect except to cause the next speaker to speculate that the Minister would come to be regarded as the disaster of the fourth Labour Government, an unkind thought but not entirely without merit, in the eyes of the Prime Minister at least.

I was in my office two days later, unaware of any of this, when the American Chargé d'Affaires, Richard Teare, arrived in the late

---

[*] *New Zealand Parliamentary Debates*, vol. 457, 19 September 1984, pp. 304–5. O'Flynn had flown American Catalinas in the war and had the fingers, or lack of them, to prove it.

afternoon, hot with haste and agitation. He delivered a peremptory note from Washington complaining that O'Flynn's 'offensive remarks' amounted to a repudiation of the security commitment in ANZUS. If New Zealand was serious it should make 'an immediate public refutation'.*

This was weighty, occurring on the eve of the meeting in New York which, if the Americans continued in this mood, might be called off. It was even plainer that no Prime Minister was ever likely to repudiate the views of one of his Ministers in public, whatever he thought of them privately. I sucked in my breath and argued that the New York discussion was our main aim and we should keep our eyes fixed firmly on that. 'From both countries' points of view anything else is secondary and talk of public refutations only risks souring the atmosphere.' Washington took the point and let the matter drop.

The press was displeased with O'Flynn and the *Evening Post* tutted: 'If New Zealand has only words and moral purpose in its arsenal then let all of us, including government ministers, choose our words with care.'† He himself was upset over Washington's choice of words in its protest note. Bothered by its use of the word 'offensive', he wrote to the American Chargé to say that he would have preferred 'injudicious' or even 'irresponsible'.‡ When they met in New York, Lange gently complained that the O'Flynn speech had 'run amok' round Washington. Shultz said that if anything like that had been said in Washington, they would either have a new Defense chief or his policy would be adopted. The Prime Minister said it was not like that in New Zealand, telling the baffled Americans that 'The Minister of Defence was not the definitive spokesman'.

The meeting was held on the afternoon of 24 September at the UN Plaza Hotel, with ten people crowded into Lange's rather small sitting room.§ The Prime Minister had set the stage a little earlier at

---

* Note of 21 September 1984, DPMC, Box 53.
† *Evening Post*, 21 September 1984.
‡ O'Flynn to Teare, 1 November 1984.
§ Lange, Norrish, Bryce Harland (Permanent Representative to the UN), John Wood (Deputy

lunch with the Foreign Policy Association: 'We want to have nothing to do with nuclear weapons. I don't believe that any apology need be made for that. Our alliance with the United States is a factor in any assessment of our interests. It will take time to work out exactly what our interests require. We are a firm ally. We shall remain a firm ally. We shall continue to support Western positions in the East/West conflict. I commit my Government to that.'

Shultz opened by referring to their earlier discussion in Wellington. Lange had indicated there were some difficult issues to work through with his colleagues, and he had said he understood that these matters took time. Two months had gone by since then but the Americans had not heard of much progress.

Lange conceded there had been some slippage in tackling the issues – he was 'trying to introduce stability into a rather heady atmosphere'. (The Americans might have deduced this from the O'Flynn speech but they may not have grasped how much of Lange's time was also taken up with the sweeping economic reforms his government was planning.) The Prime Minister then went on to spell out the limits within which he had to work and his tone was cool. A solution would not come unless he could give 'a credible assurance to the vociferous' that the US would be accommodating on nuclear weapons. The Australian compromise would not work; the New Zealand Labour Party was not like its Australian counterpart. There had to be some prospect of a change in US policy or it would be 'curtains for ANZUS' and they would have to ask what lay ahead for the US/NZ relationship.

Shultz was equally cool about the prospects for a solution. Whatever happened over ANZUS, the United States would continue to like New Zealand, a friendly country with similar values. An amicable relationship was one thing but a country with an explicit alliance with the US was in a different position. An alliance in which the military forces of the partners could not interact was not credible.

---

in the Washington embassy) and Michael Green on the NZ side; Shultz, Monroe Browne, Armacost, Wolfowitz and Bill Brown on the US side.

THE SEARCH FOR A SOLUTION

Nuclear weapons were an essential part of the strategy of maintaining peace by deterrence. There was no reason to station them in New Zealand but it was part of deterrence to arm some ships with them and the ambiguity of NCND was essential to this strategy.

In a prearranged exploration of the New Zealand position, Shultz talked about how other countries handled the issue and invited Wolfowitz to set out the Norwegian policy which put a limit on the length of a warship's stay, drawing a line between the possible 'transit' of weapons and their being 'stationed' on Norwegian territory. The US, they said, could live with this; the right of transit was the critical element. They clearly hoped that this approach might catch the attention of the New Zealanders. Lange, however, did not respond and his silence ruled it out. It was not in fact compatible with the government's policy. He had said on several occasions that his government could not accept nuclear arms in the country's harbours and the heart of the Norwegian approach, as with all other countries which were anti-nuclear, was that it accepted the possibility of nuclear arms on the ships even if they could stay for only five days.

Then the meeting took an unscripted turn and came to life. Shultz said that Washington had deliberately held back from seeking any ship visits. In the past it had been customary to consult about this in early December. Not to do so now would send an unwelcome signal; how did Lange see this being managed? The Prime Minister's brief urged him to play for time and seek an assurance that the Americans would not force the issue for some months, preferably not before the next ANZUS Council meeting in July 1985. But 'to the visible surprise of his delegation' he disregarded this and invited the Americans to put in a request for a ship visit.

He did so in the characteristic Lange way, saying it would be useful to have the normal request 'so that the Labour Party would have something to talk about'. There was, he said, no point in putting off the issue; with something specific to work on, both sides could see how things developed. Thinking it over more than two years later, he said he had concluded that the situation could not be allowed to drift;

there had to be a test or otherwise the new policy would become established by the simple passage of time.[*] Although he hoped it might lead to 'more positive signals' he did not suggest any undue optimism, telling Shultz that 'whatever the outcome, New Zealand would be in a position, in broad terms, of supporting the United States and Western position in international diplomacy . . .'. But he showed that he meant business by telling a press conference that afternoon that towards the end of the year the US would put in a request for ship visits 'as they normally do'.

The Prime Minister had always in his mind the fear of economic retaliation if things went wrong. Before the meeting ended he sought renewed assurances that the Administration would resist economic 'sanctions', instancing recent talk by several Congressmen about possible measures against imports. This was giving New Zealanders the impression that the US would apply pressure on the country's trade. Shultz said that the Administration's stance had not changed but added discouragingly that there was 'a grain of truth' in some of this talk. In the past the Administration had intervened to say that a particular proposal would hurt a good ally – it had done so over both lamb and dairy imports from New Zealand (and, Lange gratefully added, casein as well). But there was no reason to intervene for a country which was not an ally and much less leverage on members of Congress if it did.[†]

The hour-long meeting also made it clear that the earlier proposal for a joint statement on the South Pacific was not going to work. Lange told Hayden two days later that he had tried the idea on Shultz but 'ecstasy never registered on his face'.[‡] The Americans were wary of participating because it might lead to pressure from other regions for a similar declaration. They would probably not have objected to

---

[*] Vernon Wright interview, 13 January 1987, Lange Papers, Box 1, ANZ.
[†] These accounts of the meeting on 24 September are based on PM 59/8/5 Part 1, MFAT, on the State Department Papers, and on interviews with Norrish (26 October 2010) and Wood (11 August 2011).
[‡] Lange to Hayden, 26 September 1984, 370/1/20 Part 21, NAA.

such a statement made by Wellington, but Lange made it clear that a unilateral declaration would not work for him. Instead he set a new course, inviting a ship visit much sooner than his briefers had envisaged. The most likely time would be in early March 1985 at the end of the exercise 'Sea Eagle' which would be held in the Tasman Sea and involve the three ANZUS navies. The clock had been set running and a way would have to be found in that time to devise a visit that would be compatible with New Zealand's policy.

The news caused the working group in Wellington to swallow hard. Bringing the issue to a head like this was a high-risk strategy. If mishandled the attempt at a ship visit could mark the end of the country's ANZUS membership. But it also offered an encouraging possibility. A successful visit could put the problem to sleep for a year or two. With the principle of ship visits upheld and demonstrated to the world, it might be possible to reach a quiet understanding that no further and perhaps more contentious visits would be sought until tempers had cooled and the time was more opportune.

In Washington there was also some swallowing. After the New York meeting the Americans saw that they would have to adjust their aim. Until then Shultz and his officials had believed that the issue was simply one of getting things back to where they had been, restoring New Zealand's long-standing position on ship visits within a few months. Port calls would resume, with the Prime Minister smoothing over the ambiguity enjoined by NCND by stating that the country's special circumstances made it unlikely that nuclear arms would be brought there by American ships. At the UN Plaza Hotel, however, Lange had told them that such a reversal of policy was not politically possible for him and added that any arrangement would have to be consistent with his own deeply held convictions. Washington saw with dismay that it could no longer look for 'full interoperability' as in the past and that none of the solutions found by other allies was going to fit.[*]

---

[*] Wood to Norrish, 12 November 1984, gives a very perceptive analysis, PM 59/8/5 Part 1, MFAT.

The State Department had earlier been surprised by Norrish's forecast that the best outcome of the negotiations would be 'a pretty full partnership' under ANZUS. Officials had pondered for several days before reporting this diminished view of the alliance up the line to Wolfowitz and Shultz. While there were still those who doubted that the US could live with a partial resumption of port access, especially if New Zealand were to proclaim this as a 'victory', most accepted that a return to the former position was no longer a practical possibility. The best that could now be managed would be to start some sort of evolutionary process, with the prospect of a full resumption held open as the future goal.[*]

The key to this was Admiral Crowe in Honolulu. The nature of any evolutionary process would have to be acceptable to America's other Pacific allies: the Philippines, Japan, and above all Australia. If Hawke were to say that an arrangement with New Zealand presented him with insuperable difficulties, the US would probably back away. All these countries came within Crowe's responsibilities as CINCPAC and his standing in Washington (his next post would be Chairman of the Joint Chiefs of Staff) was such that his view would be decisive. If he judged he could discharge his obligations under any plan worked out with New Zealand no one was likely to second-guess him.

So it was essential to talk to him. He and Air Marshal Jamieson, the Chief of Defence Staff, knew and respected one another. It was decided that when the Minister of Defence visited Honolulu in mid-October Jamieson would go a day earlier and open a discussion about ship visits.

Crowe told Jamieson of Shultz's disappointment that the Prime Minister had not outlined any game plan in New York. Because of that Washington was inclined to force the issue by submitting a list of ships in December. The suspicion was that Lange was playing for

---

[*] Discussion with Jon Glassman, Country Director State Department, 21 November 1984, PM 59/8/5 Part 1, MFAT.

time with which to prepare the public for a collapse of ANZUS; if so there was an inclination to take prompt action to bring the issue to a head. Jamieson convinced him after a prolonged discussion that this would be premature and almost certainly disastrous; instead the admiral agreed to advise Washington that they should work to find ships that might be acceptable to New Zealand.

The stay in Honolulu was somewhat complicated by O'Flynn having a heated row with the equally incensed admiral over the contribution of ANZUS to the security of the West. The Prime Minister had said nothing to him about these delicate negotiations; he later told his colleagues that he knew 'something was going on, but I didn't know what it was'.* Before Jamieson left it was agreed that he would return in mid-November. In the meantime Crowe would reflect on how to organise a voyage which might square New Zealand's position with his own.†

On the day of Jamieson's return to Hawaii, the American ambassador called on Lange to get a more definite reading on the Prime Minister's intentions. When he came away the ambassador was not sure that he had achieved this, but the lengthy discussion helped bring a little more shape to Wellington's thinking. It was a formal occasion, with Lange flanked by his advisers (Norrish, McLean and Hensley), and Ambassador Monroe Browne (increasingly deaf and out of his depth in coping with the agile and jokey Lange) supported by his deputy, Teare.

The Prime Minister again spelt out the message he had conveyed in New York. It was summed up afterwards by Norrish as 'perhaps a slow curve, but definitely not a U-turn'. He would not push for a showdown as this would deliver the wrong result for both countries. The central issue was nuclear arms and any room for manoeuvre would have to be around this. New Zealand wanted to stay in ANZUS and maintain naval cooperation with its allies and 'if we can

---

* Sir Kerry Burke, then in Cabinet, in Margaret Clark (ed.), *For the Record: Lange and the Fourth Labour Government*, Dunmore Press, 2005, p. 47.
† Jamieson's report of the meetings, 15–20 October 1984, Jamieson Papers.

reach some understanding on weaponry, you can litter our ports with ships'. He said he had bought into the concept of deterrence after hearing Reagan at the United Nations and getting a lecture from Lee Kuan Yew, and he accepted the centrality of NCND for the US. The principal problem was to reconcile this with New Zealand's conditions for a visit. The Americans should not think that his caution was a delaying tactic. It was (and Jamieson would tell Crowe this) simply that New Zealand was looking for a way of broaching the issue in a politically feasible and therefore gradual way. He would like to start discussion on specific visits before the end of the year.

With Lange's encouragement Norrish then elaborated on 'a challenge to the professionals'. They hoped that Jamieson's second meeting with CINCPAC in two days' time would produce a list of ships to which the Prime Minister could grant access on assurances from his officials, in particular Jamieson as head of the Defence Force, that such visits met government policy. How this might be done was fleshed out in a discussion among the New Zealand side. Approval to visit would depend on the nature of each ship's visit, and the port from which it deployed. A ship coming from Honolulu on a cruise of the South Pacific would be more palatable than one returning from a deployment in the Indian Ocean. Lange noted that Jamieson's advice would only be as good as the circumstances of each ship. Approvals would therefore be given on a case-by-case basis rather than the blanket acceptance of the past.

An industrial dispute at the Marsden Point oil refinery then called the Prime Minister away. After he left, his officials spent some minutes giving their interpretation of the conversation and, in the embassy's view, 'trying to find grounds for optimism in it'. It thought there had been 'a good deal of thinking aloud' in the course of the meeting but the officials explained that this was their first opportunity to discuss some aspects with Lange and they were 'not confident that they fully understand his thinking even now'. This accounted for the tentative tone of much of the session; they said that they needed

THE SEARCH FOR A SOLUTION

further meetings among themselves and with the Prime Minister to clarify some points.

This left the embassy a little wary – the 'conversation can hardly be described as encouraging'. Lange was holding to his anti-nuclear declarations while hoping to restore port access with arrangements he and his officials had yet to work out. It was not clear that assurances by Jamieson and other officials about visiting warships would stand up 'when bounced off our NCND doctrine'. And when Lange was asked when he might lay this proposition before the public, he seemed to have no firm plans except to say, 'I can con caucus into not having legislation for some months more.'[*]

Washington's own view, in a lengthy telegram signed by Shultz's deputy, was realistic. The objective now had to be the restoration of an acceptable level of port access no later than the next ANZUS Council, expected to be in July 1985, and 'we have decided that we have no better alternative at this time other than to accept at face value Prime Minister Lange's commitment to try to achieve this'. It understood from the ambassador's conversation that any initial ship visits would have to be of a kind which allowed New Zealand to avoid breaching NCND while saying, with credibility, that the vessel was unlikely to have nuclear armament. The US could accept this as a first step to restoring full access but not as a final position. And if the exclusion of nuclear weapons was central for New Zealand, the protection of NCND was central for the US. There would therefore need to be careful consultation over the wording of any announcement to avoid causing trouble with other countries and to make it clear that any judgement on a vessel's nuclear status was the view of New Zealand and not of the United States.[†]

This caution, after five months of the Lange style, was understandable but a plan was taking shape, if Jamieson could persuade Crowe to cooperate. He stayed as Crowe's house guest for three days in

---

[*] Wellington cable to Ottawa (for Jamieson) and Washington, 15 November 1984, PM 59/8/5 Part 1, MFAT, and US embassy cable of the same date, State Department Papers.
[†] Cable from Acting Secretary of State, 21 November 1984, State Department Papers.

mid-November and they were able to talk over the difficulties frankly and comfortably. Crowe by background was a diplomatic rather than a fighting admiral and understood what was at stake, saying: 'We must do everything possible to save the relationship. Achievement of a breakthrough which <u>might</u> lead to a completely satisfactory outcome is worth a major effort.'*

Washington, concerned about election pressures on Hawke and being urged by the American ambassador in Tokyo to settle the issue before there was trouble in Japan, was in tougher mood and inclined to bring things to a head. It instructed the admiral to tell Air Marshal Jamieson that clearance would be sought for a visit by a conventionally powered combatant after Sea Eagle in early March, with the expectation that a second and similar ship would call in May or June. If New Zealand rejected the first visit the US Navy would withdraw from the exercise 'with a flourish', making it clear that there could be no effective working relationship if one partner imposed restrictions.

Crowe was unhappy with these instructions which he felt made it more difficult to get the outcome he was seeking. In the best Nelsonian tradition he disregarded them, saying that he would make every effort to find a warship which would give the least difficulty. He assembled three possibilities from which Jamieson was invited to choose. All were elderly destroyers which did not carry nuclear weapons unless deployed on operational missions (because of the onerous daily inspection and reporting regimes they required). The ships carried anti-submarine missiles (ASROCs) but not the nuclear-tipped version which would endanger them because of their age and slower speeds. He did not offer any FFG-7s because as the most modern and operationally capable frigates they were committed to higher-priority tasks.

Of the three destroyers Jamieson chose USS *Buchanan*, partly because it was the oldest but mainly because it would be coming

---

* Quoted in Jamieson's briefing notes for the Prime Minister when he returned from Honolulu, 20 November 1984, Jamieson Papers.

from Japan and be making a visit solely for the exercise and visit to New Zealand. It had in fact visited New Zealand before, making a port call at Auckland in 1979. Crowe was punctilious about NCND and gave no hint that the ship would be nuclear-free but the circumstances and the care he was taking to arrange it were clearer evidence than any verbal assurance. It was not in America's interests any more than New Zealand's to have any such weapons on *Buchanan* and the US Navy's actions confirmed this. It would be cutting across its normal procedures and going to considerable expense to send the ship all the way down to the South Pacific at a time when a more modern, conventionally powered destroyer would be passing through the Tasman Sea on its way back to Pearl Harbor.*

Jamieson briefed the Prime Minister on his choice of *Buchanan* immediately he returned and the working group began to feel that the first hurdle had been crossed. If a ship like that could come and go in March, Washington's scepticism would be softened and the next steps could be discussed in an easier atmosphere. Norrish drafted a Cabinet paper so that Lange could brief Ministers 'at least partially' on the progress that was being made. The Prime Minister, however, gave it back to him, saying that he would inform his colleagues in his own way. His own way turned out to be not to tell them anything – neither his deputy Palmer nor anyone else in the Cabinet was aware of the negotiations he was conducting about a major plank of the government's platform.

Nonetheless he seemed comfortable with the plan, though on one occasion he disconcerted his advisers by looking out the window and musing almost to himself, 'I could probably sell getting out of ANZUS to the public more easily than this.' It was only a flash but it stayed on the retina; both Jamieson and I were chilled by the brief glimpse that the Prime Minister we were working for might be playing a double game.

---

* Jamieson's briefing notes, 20 November 1984. For fear of leaks the name of the ship was not committed to paper.

Otherwise the plans for a visit proceeded smoothly. The choice of *Buchanan* was very tightly held in both capitals. Norrish told Hayden in Canberra that he was more confident that something could be worked out with the Americans.* The Prime Minister talked of possible visits at his press conference after Cabinet on 3 December, but did not go into any details. He did so in the flippant, faintly jeering tone which so upset the Americans. When asked how the ships' nuclear status could be assessed, he said that proof was not required from the US Government; New Zealand would make its own judgement based on advice from Defence. Then came one of his memorable lines: 'If New Zealand's assessment is favourable, not only can they come but I will be on the poop.'†

First, though, there was the dance of the clearances to be completed. In the past the US had sought only a blanket clearance, submitting a request each December which covered all ship visits for the following year. This was no longer practicable when each visit would need to be scrutinised on its anti-nuclear merits, but Washington still wished to maintain the practice which would enable it to set out its formal position on port access. The Inter-Agency Group itself laboured over the wording. The ambassador called on Lange on 12 December to go over the draft with him. The note reiterated that there could be no exceptions to NCND and that restoration of 'normal port access' was essential to the continued effectiveness of the ANZUS alliance.‡

The Prime Minister read over the draft, querying only the reference to the restoration of normal access which the ambassador suggested could be countered in New Zealand's reply. Overall, Lange saw no difficulty and suggested that the note be submitted the next day. New Zealand's response a week later was also discussed in draft

---

* On 3 December 1984, though Hayden responded that New Zealand was not 'behaving wisely'. 370/1/20 Part 25, NAA.
† Press conference, 3 December 1984.
‡ Meeting of 12 December (my note in the records of the Prime Minister's Department) and Lange's to Norrish, 13 December 1984, PM 59/8/5 Part 2, MFAT.

with the Americans and some amendments made at their request. It stated that it welcomed visits from its ANZUS partners and wished 'to ensure access of United States naval ships within the framework of its policies on visiting warships',[*] but the restatement of its policy and the tone of Lange's latest press conference still caused some hesitations in Washington.

The discussion of blanket clearances was pure formality, however, since they were no longer relevant to New Zealand's policy. What the Prime Minister said next was of much greater significance to the Americans. After disposing of the blanket request he went on to suggest that a note seeking specific clearance for the *Buchanan* be submitted without delay, so that it could be considered at the first Cabinet of the New Year. The ambassador left with the clear impression that under the Prime Minister's eye approval of the *Buchanan* visit could be assumed, as the next step in the plan worked out with Crowe.

In accordance with this understanding, Teare (in place of Monroe Browne who had gone home for Christmas) called on Norrish a few days later with a note seeking clearance for the destroyer. This posed an unexpected problem; leaving the ship's name lying around in the Beehive over the Christmas holidays would be to risk it leaking. Norrish asked that the American embassy hold it instead and two days later Washington agreed to resubmit the request in the New Year.[†]

It now seemed clear that the Americans would go along with the approach that Wellington had been developing and Norrish told heads of mission that though there were still some hurdles to be faced, he was personally optimistic. As they departed for the Christmas holidays the members of the working group (still the only group apart from the Prime Minister who knew the identity of the proposed ship) were much more relaxed. It looked as if diplomacy

---

[*] PM 59/8/5 Part 2, MFAT.
[†] Teare's appointments diary. His first call was on 17 December and he returned with Washington's agreement on 19 December. Courtesy of Richard W. Teare. Because of the holiday period the note was not resubmitted until 17 January and the proposed Cabinet consideration slipped to 28 January.

had met the challenge and that the risk of a major explosion which had hung over the country's foreign policy since July had been defused. It was to be sure only the first step, but as was said of St Denis who walked a long distance after having his head cut off, in such a situation it was the first step that counted. As Rowling departed to be ambassador in Washington, Norrish felt able to assure him that whatever else might come up, he would not have to worry about ship visits.

Chapter Five
Access Denied

As the decisive moment approached, the Labour Left was, in the American phrase, loaded for bear, their guns primed and charged to fight off any challenge to the purity of their policy. Their vigilance was partly the suspicion, consecrated in the mythology of the radical Left, that parliamentary leaders always sold out at some stage, as Hawke was held to have done; and partly because they knew their Lange, and his tendency to assume the shape of whoever had sat on him firmly, better than his colleagues, his officials or indeed the country as a whole.*

It was common knowledge that the Americans had agreed to hold off seeking a ship visit for several months – that had been agreed when Shultz and Lange first met in Parliament Buildings. As the year came to a close it seemed likely to the peace movement that this period of grace must be expiring. The leader of the anti-nuclear group in the

---

* Michael Bassett, *Working With David: Inside The Lange Cabinet*, Hodder Moa, 2008, p. 108.

caucus, Helen Clark, decided to visit the US to find out. Although she then chaired the parliamentary Select Committee on Foreign Affairs and Trade, her visit was not an official one, but was organised with the help of leaders of the American anti-nuclear movement, especially Congresswomen Pat Schroeder and Cora Weiss.

Schroeder was a long-standing representative from Colorado who became the first woman to serve on the House Armed Services Committee. Weiss was a lifetime stalwart of the peace movement and her anti-war credentials were impeccable. As an opponent of the Vietnam War she had travelled to Hanoi several times, was an early member of 'Women Strike for Peace', President of the Hague Appeal for Peace, and attended women's disarmament 'summits' in Moscow. These and other contacts, like the somewhat offbeat Rear Admiral Eugene Carroll who headed the Center for Defense Information, were as good sources of information in leaky Washington as could be found, short of penetrating the State Department or the Pentagon.

Clark gave interviews to the media and a press conference at the National Press Club. Shultz's insistence on the obligation of an ally to accept visits was dismissed as something that had worked only with the previous government. New Zealand, she said, had no intention of leaving the alliance provided the US accepted the 'non-negotiable non-nuclear policy' and gave equal decision-making weight to New Zealand. She repeated two misleading statements that were to gain great currency when the lobbying effort ramped up in January: that NATO members like Norway, Denmark and Spain were comfortably able to combine a ban on nuclear weapons with membership of their alliance; and that, given the prohibition on nuclear propulsion from 1972 to 1975, the Labour Government's stance was not a whim or a fantasy but a long-standing policy.[*]

---

[*] The *Washington Post*, 10 December 1984, which reported the press conference, corrected the statement about the NATO members, pointing out that US Navy ships could visit these countries without disclosing their weapons. The Labour Government in 1972–75 continued an earlier ban on nuclear propulsion (imposed by the Holyoake Government in 1969 pending

Though they did not uncover its name, she and Margaret Wilson, now President of the Labour Party, returned home before Christmas with the news that the Americans were about to propose a ship visit. Washington, they reported, did not appear to understand the dynamic behind the party's policy and, more cryptically, that the Americans were being led up the garden path. Clark telephoned Kevin Clements and said 'Push the button' to mobilise the anti-nuclear network in Christchurch.[*] Across the country the machinery of protest was set in motion: the telephone trees, networks, the haunting of newsrooms and demonstrations that distinguished the Left when energised by a hot issue. The Coalition against Nuclear Warships (CANWAR) and Peace Movement Aotearoa arranged for people to bombard the Cabinet with messages protesting against any American ship visit, and the backbench anti-nuclear group, led by Helen Clark, Fran Wilde and Jim Anderton (the previous party President), mobilised support within the caucus. To make sure that the government did not backslide as soon as this pressure was lifted, the party decided to renew its efforts to have the ban on ships cemented into legislation.[†]

When the New Year turned, a brilliant public relations campaign caught the government unprepared. Radio and television news carried a drumbeat of statements about the dangers of nuclear weapons, the imminence of nuclear war and the risk of being targeted by Soviet missiles if American warships were admitted. The public was told that there was no risk to ANZUS, with reassuring if untrue references to the NATO members which excluded nuclear weapons. In an inspired moment it was announced that Lange had been nominated for the Nobel Peace Prize for his crusade against

---

clarification of liability in case of an accident) but raised no objection to nuclear weapons on visiting ships. The State Department and the American embassy issued statements more than once pointing out that 22 US warships visited New Zealand in this period without any questions being asked about their armament.

[*] Kevin Clements, *Back from the Brink: The Creation of a Nuclear-Free New Zealand*, Allen & Unwin/Port Nicholson Press, 1988, p. 134, note 29.

[†] Margaret Wilson, 'The Non-Nuclear Policy', in *Labour in Government, 1984–1987*, Allen & Unwin/Port Nicholson Press, 1989, p. 64.

nuclear arms. It was never clear who made the nomination. Anyone in New Zealand could, simply by writing to the Norwegian committee, but the statement made New Zealanders feel that the eyes of the world were on them.*

In the midst of the summer holiday season and with Ministers unaware of the Prime Minister's plans, the government did not find it easy to mount an effective response. Lange went on television on New Year's Day to insist that no nuclear-armed ship would come and to restate his rather old-fashioned picture of naval vessels: 'If my Defence people could tell me "look, this is not nuclear-armed" I would be on the poop to welcome the thing.'† He devoted most of the traditional New Year 'State of the Nation' speech to the economy but was reassuring about ANZUS: 'The extent of that common interest is so overwhelming that the difference between us over nuclear weapons can be resolved within the ANZUS framework.'‡

The growing excitement caused the other ANZUS partners to feel that some stiffening was needed. Shultz sent General Chain to brief Lange on the latest round of arms control talks in Geneva, but added in his letter of introduction that he believed that the Soviet return to the table had much to do with their perception of Western resilience and unity. He then pointed to the moral: at a sensitive moment like this, 'You can help by doing everything in your power to maintain this sense of Western unity and strength.'§

Hawke wrote what turned out to be a much more celebrated letter two days later. He said he had no desire to act as an emissary but since he was going to Washington where the prospects for ANZUS would be discussed 'in some depth' he would like to know Lange's thinking. With the prospect of a ship visit being considered, however, his main purpose was to set out Australia's concerns about the

---

* David Lange was one of a record 99 nominations that year. The Peace Prize went to the International Physicians for the Prevention of Nuclear War.
† *Today Tonight*, TVNZ, 1 January 1985.
‡ Speech to the Whakatane Rotary, 7 January 1985.
§ Shultz to Lange, 8 January 1985, PM 59/8/5 Part 2, ANZ.

dispute. His country, he said, had important interests at stake – the future of ANZUS and two of its most important bilateral relationships – and it had to protect those interests. A special arrangement for New Zealand would damage them: 'We could not accept as a permanent arrangement that the ANZUS alliance has a different meaning, and entails different obligations, for different members.'*

The letter was polite but frank about the risks for him of a more favourable deal for New Zealand after he had faced down pressure from his own Left in 1983. Hawke was dismayed at the way Lange had painted himself into a corner and was very worried about the repercussions in Australia. The adviser who helped draft it told the British that he could not see how Lange could agree to the coming ship visit because his judgement that it was not nuclear would not be credible to New Zealanders. He and other officials in Canberra saw the New Zealand policy as threatening the future of the whole ANZUS alliance, and they let their view be known that 'Mr Lange makes things worse every time he opens his mouth and simply helps dig his Labour Party ever deeper into a hole it cannot get out of'. They speculated that the New Zealand Government's drastic economic measures were forcing it to play up the only popular element in its platform, but the trans-Tasman aspect involved required plain speaking by Australia.†

Though delivered by the Australian High Commissioner in double envelopes with, according to Lange, no less than four seals and to be opened by him alone, it was perhaps inevitable that the letter would leak. Two weeks later it did, probably in Canberra, though Hawke is adamant it would not have been from his own office. The British there were told by someone in the New Zealand High Commission that it 'may' have been given to the *National Times* by a New Zealand Minister 'who saw it as a means of rallying public opinion behind Mr Lange's stand'. The Americans understood that the editor of the

---

* Hawke to Lange, 10 January 1985, and comments from BHC, Canberra, FCO Papers.
† *Sydney Morning Herald*, 18 January, openly reflecting a briefing from 'Canberra sources'.

National Times had carried the letter to Washington in his pocket, so that it could be datelined from there rather than Canberra.

Geoffrey Palmer also thought it was leaked by the Australians in Washington, perhaps at the behest of the Americans. Whoever was responsible, it put New Zealand's nationalist pride on the line: 'I just thought that you couldn't possibly have the Australians telling us what to do.'* Perhaps, as the British High Commission in Wellington thought, Hawke should have conveyed his views more subtly. The terms of the letter were a reasonable statement of Australia's concerns but in the overheated climate in New Zealand the leak went off like a pipe-bomb. Fortune once again favoured the energetic and the letter was a gift to those who were orchestrating the public relations campaign. Lange would now appear to be bowing to overseas demands. The recipient himself saw 'that we were being portrayed as going to make this cataclysmic backdown' and it was not only the British who concluded that the leak had badly damaged the prospects for approval of a ship visit.†

There were stirrings of anxiety in Japan, with two newspapers discussing what Nakasone might have said to Lange, and Japanese diplomats calling at the State Department to express their concern and be kept abreast of developments. In the Norwegian Parliament, a small radical party was invoking the 'New Zealand example' in calling for a withdrawal from NATO. Soviet propaganda was also interested in the coming challenge. Tass caught the right nationalist angle, saying that 'Washington now attempts to twist the arms of a disobedient country' and citing claims by Gerald O'Brien, a former Labour MP now a member of the World Peace Council, that the CIA had been involved in the 'removal' of Labour governments of both Australia and New Zealand in the 1970s.‡

---

* Vernon Wright interview with Geoffrey Palmer, 8 February 1987, Lange Papers, Box 1, ANZ.
† Vernon Wright interview of 5 December 1986, Lange Papers, Box 1, ANZ, and cable of 28 January 1985 from BHC, Wellington, FCO Papers.
‡ Tass, 13 January 1985. O'Brien represented the Island Bay electorate in Wellington from 1969 until his defeat in 1978.

In this charged atmosphere the American embassy, as agreed with the Prime Minister before Christmas, resubmitted the request for a visit by the destroyer *Buchanan* on 17 January 1985. Norrish showed the note to the Prime Minister before Lange left for Auckland the following day.* Telling the Australian High Commission this a week later (though he did not mention the ship's name), Norrish was confident that Lange would 'take on the Left' and approve the visit. He said that Rowling, on his way to Washington, thought it would satisfy 'all but the anti-ANZUS element'.†

Equally inevitably, the American request leaked two days later. It surfaced in Sydney but where it originated is as murky as for most leaks, but more likely from Washington rather than Wellington. Lange's chief press secretary, Ross Vintiner, was rung by a Sydney reporter early on the morning of Saturday 19 January with the news, said to be from their Washington bureau, that a ship visit had been requested. He immediately telephoned Palmer, who had just taken over as Acting Prime Minister but had not been taken into Lange's confidence, and he had never heard of *Buchanan* either.

The Prime Minister had chosen this moment to leave for an eight-day visit to Tokelau, New Zealand's remotest dependency consisting of three atolls just below the equator. They could be reached only by a sea voyage from Samoa and Lange was about to leave Auckland and fly to Apia. The atolls had only the most primitive wireless links through Apia, as did the elderly island trader, the *Avondale*, which Lange had preferred to take instead of the frigate which the Navy offered. With the frigate he would have had secure communications with Palmer and his Cabinet throughout, though the battered *Avondale* with its captain in an ancient Hawaiian shirt was more his style than the formalities of naval quarters. It meant, though, that for all practical purposes the Prime Minister and architect of the proposed visit of *Buchanan* was out of reach for the next eight days.

---

* Malcolm Templeton, *Standing Upright Here*, Victoria University Press/NZIIA, 2006, p. 407.
† Norrish to AHC, 24 and 26 January 1985, 250/11/18 Part 18, NAA.

Then and later there was a widespread view that the Prime Minister had fled to escape the gathering storm. That was not strictly correct. Some Tokelauan elders, newly elected as leaders of their islands, called on him in early November, and suggested a visit which would be the first by a Prime Minister. It was the kind of easy, undemanding occasion he loved – Polynesian warmth, feasting, and on one island a policeman who stood with a large New Zealand flag outside the lavatory whenever the Prime Minister was inside. He accepted at once and decided to bring his two sons in the summer holidays. Though not exactly foreseeable then, the timing could not have been more awkward and, even at the cost of disappointing the Tokelauans and the boys, he should have cancelled or postponed the visit. The unfortunate Palmer, on whom all the trouble devolved, said years later that if he could replay the crisis, he would ensure that the Prime Minister was in the country when it broke.[*]

On the day of the leak Palmer was alarmed and angry. Lange later privately described Palmer's efforts as 'headless chookery'. 'I mean Geoff was in an unenviable position. He couldn't communicate with me. He was beset, I'm sure, by party activists. He was not familiar with the Establishment he was operating with, Foreign Affairs or Defence, and there was, I understand, a vague air of panic and confusion . . . .'[†] This was true but unkind given that he had never mentioned the forthcoming *Buchanan* visit to Palmer. He had briefly mentioned to the Cabinet in December that a request would be coming from the Americans but went into no detail, even with his deputy, saying later and rather lamely that he had intended to brief Palmer when he returned from Tokelau.[‡]

Later that morning a hasty briefing was arranged by officials from Foreign Affairs and Defence. Palmer complained that he had been kept in the dark by them – which was also unkind since briefing Cabinet was the Prime Minister's constitutional responsibility.

---

[*] Interview with Sir Geoffrey Palmer, 15 July 2011.
[†] Vernon Wright interview, 5 December 1986.
[‡] He mentioned it so briefly in December that Bassett took no note of it. Bassett, 16 March 2012.

It was clear that with the story running hot some kind of statement would have to be put out quickly to hold the situation until Palmer and his colleagues could form a more settled view. A simple release confirmed that the government had received a request for a ship visit after Sea Eagle: 'We are now preparing to answer this request in accordance with our established procedures – New Zealand will make its own, independent assessment.'[*]

It was not possible to communicate with Lange, now rolling through the blue Pacific. There was a radio-telephone on the bridge of *Avondale* but the attempt to use it only caused exasperation at both ends, with much shouting and crackling but no understanding, and it had to be abandoned. In the end a short message warning of the problem was sent by Palmer through Apia to the island of Nukunonu. Tapped out one letter at a time, it took two hours. When complete the text was brought by Tony Browne, the Tokelau Administrator, to the Prime Minister who read it, said, 'He's a bigger bloody fool than I thought he was', and stuffed it in his pocket.[†]

Unable to communicate even by insecure means with Lange, the Acting Prime Minister had to decide what to do about the American request. In the hectic week that followed he was beset by lobbying and advice from the anti-nuclear group while most of his ministerial colleagues were still at the beach. His first reaction, following his briefings, was to hold to the official position as it had evolved over the previous weeks. On 23 January he said that the government would not be hurried into a decision on the American request, but New Zealand had excellent sources in the External Intelligence Bureau (EIB) and the 'highly expert' Defence Department and 'we have no difficulty in arriving at an independent assessment of our own'.

Though commendably non-committal, this sounded to the Left suspiciously like laying the groundwork for an acceptance. By

---

[*] Released on Monday 21 January.
[†] Information supplied by A. P. F. Browne and Gordon Shroff who were with the Prime Minister on the visit, 16 December 2010. Adrian Macey who was also there remembers an outburst as 'Geoffrey Palmer has NO political sense', 20 April 2012.

coincidence the Labour Party Executive Council was about to hold its first meeting for the year on the following Thursday, 24 January, and it became the focus for the discontent of backbenchers. They were already seething over the economic reforms; any backtracking on the cherished anti-nuclear policy was likely to cause a revolt.

The insurgents were led by Clark and Anderton who, by now thoroughly discontented with the Lange Government, described Palmer as 'duplicitous and politically inept'. They gathered urgently that day in the office of Fran Wilde. Margaret Wilson (Lange would occasionally refer to her and Clark as 'the coven'[*]) telephoned the Acting Prime Minister from the meeting to argue vehemently against the visit of this still-unnamed ship. Palmer argued equally firmly for the need for an independent assessment.

When it seemed that he could not be shifted the meeting decided to step up the campaign, mobilising the trade unions, key Labour Party people, peace activists in all three alliance countries, and the media. That night Anderton said he telephoned Palmer with a clear threat: if he went ahead with a favourable recommendation to Cabinet, Anderton would make his opposition public and gather as much support as he could. He predicted that half the caucus 'would be on the wharf with him' to protest the visit and the government would be split wide open.[†]

The issue also dominated the meeting of the Party Executive that day. The members were grumpy about the government's economic policy but the nuclear issue was one on which they would not compromise – the party would fracture instead. The constant feedback they were getting, supported by the growing strength of the environmental movement, was for a firm stand against nuclearism. There was no discussion or even allusion to the possible impact on New Zealand's relationships with the US, Australia and other partners. The Executive's mental horizons stopped at the

---

[*] Margaret Pope, *At the Turning Point: My Political Life with David Lange*, AM Publishing New Zealand, 2011, p. 61.
[†] Vernon Wright interview with Jim Anderton, 5 March 1987, Lange Papers, Box 1, ANZ.

country's territorial limits. Since no one trusted the US to observe the ban on arms, they rejected the NCND doctrine. In the gathering momentum the distinction between 'nuclear-armed' and merely 'nuclear-capable' began to blur. No particular decision was taken but the fundamentalist mood now suggested that even 'nuclear-capable' ships would be unacceptable, whether carrying nuclear arms or not.[*]

The next day (Friday 25 January) the party's general secretary wrote to Palmer with a formal account of the Executive's decisions. It had considered at length, he said, the problems if a ship visit was approved. Uppermost in the view of members was the need to ensure that there was no deviation from party policy and that the credibility of the party remained intact with its members. It did not see NCND as a problem for New Zealand: 'there is no need to accommodate the American point of view'. So, 'to help strengthen the government's hand', it had unanimously resolved to urge it 'to admit no vessel to New Zealand ports unless either there is publicly available and credible evidence that the vessel is neither nuclear-powered and/or armed or a declaration is filed by the US Government with the New Zealand Government certifying that the vessel is neither nuclear-powered or armed'.[†]

The meeting, he said, did not have the benefit of either Lange's or Palmer's presence 'to appreciate the resolve of the Executive on this matter' but he proposed a meeting on the following Monday in the hope of resolving the issue speedily and without public comment. The letter and the thinking behind it were a vivid illustration of the limitations of single-issue politics. As the philosopher Isaiah Berlin pointed out, in a messy world even absolute principles have to be balanced and tempered by the demands of other desirables.[‡] Other anti-nuclear countries, like Denmark or Spain, had decided that

---

[*] Interview with Margaret Wilson, 4 August 2011.
[†] John Wybrow to Palmer, 25 January 1985. This line had been discussed at the party conference the previous September. PM 59/8/5 Part 2, MFAT.
[‡] Isaiah Berlin, 'Two Concepts of Liberty', in Henry Hardy and Roger Hausheer (eds), *The Proper Study of Mankind*, Farrar, Straus and Giroux, 1997, p. 241.

the importance of their alliance made it worthwhile to accept an occasional few days of uncertainty about the temporary presence of nuclear weapons in their harbours. This 'compromise' of principle was not acceptable to the Labour Party Executive Council. Although the nature of the ship and its possible armament was still unknown, the absolute purity of the nuclear policy overrode all other considerations, including any thought of the effect on New Zealand's friends and partners and indeed on Western solidarity.

Lange was the crucial link who might have widened this narrow horizon. He was the only political figure who knew the effort that had gone into selecting *Buchanan* and why it was most improbable that it would be nuclear-armed, and as 'New Zealand's first political pop star' he was the only person who could have persuaded his party.[*] But like Macavity the cat he was not there; the link never went live.

No one quite knew where he was as his creaking ship turned for home. It was a journey he remembered with considerable irritation. A delay in loading meant the vessel could not get away on time from the last island, Atafu; it developed a problem with its driveshaft and could travel only at a reduced speed – 'that bloody ageing hulk that went 4.6 knots and most of them sideways';[†] and it ran out of water. As a result it was a day late reaching Pago Pago in American Samoa and this delay may also have affected the course of history. Instead of returning on 27 January, as scheduled, the Prime Minister was only able to get back the following day, when Cabinet was halfway through its meeting.

In the meantime Palmer's views had hardened. He talked with Wilson, Clark and other MPs who flooded into his office, and he read the 'Cabinet bundle', the collection of papers put together by

---

[*] The phrase is Ross Vintiner's.
[†] Vernon Wright interview, 5 December 1986.

departments as background for the projected Cabinet consideration on 28 January. The Cabinet bundle, like the earlier briefing paper offered by Norrish, was in fact never given to Cabinet or even circulated to Ministers who as a consequence knew nothing about the arrangements for a ship visit.

The main paper, which had been drafted by Foreign Affairs in December, signalled that a clearance was being sought for a visit after Sea Eagle but did not name the ship. Cabinet was not asked to agree to the clearance (though that was implicit in consulting Ministers) but to understand the process by which Lange in consultation with the Defence authorities could make a reliable assessment. Absolute certainty was acknowledged to be impossible, but smaller vessels which had no strategic role could be judged on such matters as their recent operational history and the purpose of the current voyage. It concluded, with words the Prime Minister was never to use: 'I am convinced that we can make such a judgment.'*

The bundle included two papers from EIB which analysed the circumstances in which nuclear weapons might be deployed, noted in passing that the Oliver Hazard Perry class of frigates were 'most unlikely' to be fitted with nuclear delivery systems, and agreed with Foreign Affairs that experienced service officers could reach 'a reasoned judgment' on the probability of the weapons being carried. There was also a draft press statement announcing the visit of *Buchanan*, saying that the government had made a considered judgement that the ship conformed to its policy and was to be welcomed; a factual paper on its characteristics for publication; and a memo from Defence on the naval exercises in which *Buchanan* might take part.

The key element was a paper, signed by the Chief of Defence Staff, Air Marshal Jamieson, on 24 January, to be given to the Prime Minister on his return. It went through *Buchanan*'s armaments in some detail, noting that its only nuclear-capable system was the

---

* Cabinet paper drafted 20 December 1984, PM 59/8/2 Part 23, MFAT.

ASROC anti-submarine missile (of 20,000 missiles produced, only 850 had nuclear warheads), and that the ship's obsolescent status made it less likely to be held at a high state of readiness. 'I can give no absolute guarantee that the ship does not carry any nuclear warheads for that purpose but after careful consideration ... I believe it most unlikely.' The last sentence was a matter of some debate among the working group. None had any personal doubt that the ship was 'clean' but short of making a careful inspection it was not possible to give any flat assurance.[*]

After being heavily lobbied Palmer now thought this advice 'unsophisticated' and not politically saleable. 'I approached the question actually as a lawyer with the burden of proof at the criminal standard of beyond reasonable doubt.' His conclusion was based on the wording of the party's policy. As his colleague Richard Prebble said: 'Palmer regarded the decision to decline as if it was a question of statutory interpretation and not involving any judgement by him as to the merit of his decision.'[†] Palmer later thought his advice was 'a bit cautious'; it was certainly the first time that a criminal standard had been applied to a visiting warship.[‡]

Having reassured the party that there would be no compromise on its policy, he decided on the Thursday that Vintiner should fly to Pago Pago and brief the Prime Minister on the media and party storm that had erupted. An Air Force Boeing 727 was laid on, and Vintiner travelled up the following Sunday, the day Lange was due to arrive in American Samoa. Radio contact with the ship was sufficient to let Lange know that his press secretary would meet him, but not enough apparently to respond that mechanical trouble meant that the ship would be a day late. Vintiner carried with him a brief note which Palmer had typed himself, the Cabinet bundle, and a

---

[*] PM 59/8/2 Part 23, MFAT.
[†] Interview with Sir Geoffrey Palmer, 15 July 2011, and comment by Prebble, 16 September 2011.
[‡] Both these comments are from his Wright interview, 8 February 1987, Lange Papers, Box 1, ANZ.

range of media coverage together with letters opposing the visit from some backbenchers (one from Anderton threatening to resign prompted Lange to say that it was the best argument for having the ship). He did not carry any list or assessment of the caucus numbers – the Prime Minister knew enough to work this out for himself.

Palmer's note, dated '1.30pm Sunday', reported 'massive developments on this front in your absence'. Australian pressure had been very hot; the Australian embassy in Washington was 'leaking against us' and sources there had leaked the ship visit request as well as both the Shultz and Hawke letters. The evidence about nuclear weapons had been assessed by officials and was enclosed. 'I have not yet seen it' but O'Flynn thought it was not sufficient to convince the public and the request should be refused. The Executive had passed a resolution and several members were strongly opposed – 'Anderton says he will break with us if we do' – and some members with marginal seats were worried about being targeted by activists if the request was allowed. 'The Peace groups are still with us but will demonstrate if we let the ship in.'

He recommended that when Lange arrived home he should say nothing until after Cabinet; that body should discuss the issue but make no decision; nothing should be announced until after caucus. His own view was that everything depended on 'the strength of the case we can develop publicly that the ship is not carrying nuclear weapons'. Twenty-six years later he remembered the note as saying in essence 'politically we could not do this'.[*] He was right; the battle for the *Buchanan* was lost by default in the week the Prime Minister was absent.

Vintiner arrived in Pago Pago to find that the *Avondale* was not now expected until the next morning. There was a party on the ship that night as the Tokelau tour came to a close and Lange was thought to have drunk about a bottle of wine. Since he was not known to drink then, this perhaps was a sign of the Prime Minister's edginess about

---

[*] Interview with Palmer, 15 July 2011.

which Vintiner was warned when he greeted the party coming off the ship.

Lange was in 'avoidance mode' when Vintiner spoke to him. He would not engage in conversation and they were an hour into the flight home before he would relax and begin to talk. Ross then gave him the package of papers with Palmer's note. He read the note, stood up and walked down to the back of the plane. When he walked back, he and Vintiner had a 'fairly robust' discussion about what it all meant. His view was still that the ship could come. His wife, Naomi, who had come up on a commercial flight to meet him and the boys, said that given the media coverage the decision was simple; Ross, who felt that the government's credibility was on the line, warned that he and Lange's personal staff might well resign if the visit went ahead.

The Prime Minister read the media coverage intently and then paused. He looked up at Ross, closed the folder and said, 'That's fine.' The decision was taken and he said nothing more about it for the rest of the flight; but as the plane approached New Zealand, Vintiner thought he became a different person – the Pacific mode was gone and he walked off the plane with the step of someone who had made up his mind.

Cabinet had begun its sitting that morning in his absence. Without a record, recollections years later of what happened (or rather did *not* happen) are rather vague since no one understood the importance of the issue for New Zealand's foreign policy. No Ministers had been briefed and no Ministers had any papers on the request. Palmer spoke before lunch. He said he had tried unsuccessfully to get in touch with Lange and then set out his view that the ship could not be accepted. He realised that the US would not be happy with this but his greater concern was to avoid a fracture in the party. Jamieson's advice would inevitably become public and it would be difficult to defend to the party. Neither he nor any of his colleagues could recall any disagreement with this assessment, or even any real discussion. Prebble's later memory was that 'there was not much point in a reaction to Palmer – he had made the decision and we felt sympathy for the position Lange had put him in even if, in my case, I felt he could have handled it differently'. *

Some Ministers did, however, complain that he had consulted with Margaret Wilson, his house guest, about the requirements of the manifesto and not with any of his Cabinet colleagues about the implications for the country. Prebble felt this strongly and 'expressed my view that the manifesto was capable of a different reading. Indeed, I was incredulous that Geoffrey should regard a major defence and foreign policy decision as being decided by the President's reading of the manifesto.' Russell Marshall thought: 'This was the biggest foreign policy issue to face the country in decades and Cabinet should have been totally informed and prepared' – instead he had no recollection of any discussion. If there had been one, he thought the *Buchanan* visit would have been approved by Cabinet, though he himself would have opposed it. His later conclusion was that a young and inexperienced government 'did not do care and delicacy' and did not try hard enough to find a way around the standoff that was looming.†

Mike Moore, who like all his colleagues knew nothing of Lange's arrangements for the ship, saw no point in questioning what had already been decided. Years later, however, he thought that he and his colleagues had let the side down over the collective responsibility of Cabinet for important decisions. The pace of change in the new government was such that everyone was engrossed in their own portfolios – 'I was flat out and having the time of my life' – and no one thought to insist on a proper Cabinet discussion.‡

Cabinet is, in the words of the Cabinet Manual, the central decision-making body. 'Cabinet Government is based on teamwork

---

* Interview with Palmer, 15 July 2011, and Prebble, 18 September 2011.
† Interview with Russell Marshall, 19 August 2011 and his article in the *New Zealand International Review*, July/August 2011.
‡ Interview with Mike Moore, 27 September 2011.

– it is not and should never become presidential government.'* In this case the methodical Cabinet processes – circulation of papers, Cabinet committee consideration and decision in Cabinet itself – were bypassed in the panic over party unity. On a major matter this is never a good sign in government. It means either that a Prime Minister has achieved a presidential domination of his Cabinet, as with Muldoon when he imposed the wage-price freeze in 1982, or that a smaller group has taken control and blocked off wider discussion, as happened in Britain with the decision in 2003 to go to war with Iraq.

When Lange reached the Cabinet room in mid-afternoon he realised as soon as he took his seat that Palmer had in effect already taken the decision. Reminiscing later, he said that from the papers he had seen on the plane it was perfectly plain to him that the ship could not come. His memory was that when he joined his colleagues: 'The Cabinet had already examined the material, and having announced my decision they said, yes, that was theirs. And that was it.'†

Lange once said that his political life could not be explained by an orderly progression but 'as a series of situations'.‡ This was one of them. A new situation had arisen and his quick mind had already worked out a response: to ask for another and perhaps more easily acceptable ship. He mentioned this to Cabinet briefly and without going into any detail, so quickly that Michael Bassett, who always jotted down a brief record, failed to note it – by the time he had scribbled something on the previous item the ship issue had been disposed of. All Bassett caught (and this was more than several other Ministers did) was a vague statement from the Prime Minister that *Buchanan* was not acceptable and he intended to seek from the

---

* Geoffrey Palmer and Matthew Palmer, *Bridled Power: New Zealand Government under MMP*, 3rd edition, Auckland: Oxford University Press, 1997, p. 64.
† Vernon Wright interview, 4 February 1987, and again at the end of the next paragraph. Both these are recollections by Lange two years later and should not be regarded as accurate. He did not announce his decision to have it confirmed by Cabinet and he was certainly there for longer than a quarter of an hour. Bassett, 16 March 2012.
‡ Audrey Young interview, *New Zealand Herald*, 3 July 2004.

Americans another ship that was – possibly an Oliver Hazard Perry class frigate (FFG-7). Lange later claimed that this was all he had to do: 'I was in the Cabinet room for about a quarter of an hour. Then I went and had a shower.'

He gave me a different version that evening: 'You've no idea how difficult it was in Cabinet, Gerald. I was in a minority of one.' At the time I was surprised that a popular Prime Minister could ever be in a minority of one; I was later even more surprised to learn that there had been no discussion at all in Cabinet. I finally came to the view that this was Lange-speak for the fact that the *Buchanan* plan had disintegrated during his week away and there was nothing he could do about it. His friend, Mike Moore, said that Lange often liked to give the impression that he had fought for something in Cabinet when he had not.*

At a lengthy press conference after Cabinet, Lange confirmed that a request for a ship had been received and said that Cabinet had decided it needed more information. He reaffirmed that nuclear weapons would never come into New Zealand while his government was in office, and to make this even clearer he said that a Bill to enshrine the anti-nuclear policy in law would be brought in sooner than planned. It was a small sign of his desire to conciliate the peace movement; at the beginning of the month he had dismissed the push for early legislation, saying that the anti-nuclear groups had got their cake, eaten it, and that he didn't intend to give them the icing.

Ambassador Monroe Browne was called in the following afternoon to meet the Prime Minister who had his advisers with him. He was told that Cabinet had 'considerable reservations' about the current request. Lange blamed the furore of nationalistic feelings on the leak of the Hawke letter. Another ship was needed that could confidently be said to be nuclear-free, and after some hedging he said that a FFG-7 frigate would be 'nearer to filling the bill'. The frigate was said by bodies as different as EIB and CANWAR not to

---

* Interview with Mike Moore, 27 September 2011.

be nuclear-capable, and Jamieson explained to the meeting that the important point was that these vessels were not fitted with the dual-purpose ASROC. Lange said that with a new ship 'I'll go to the line with Cabinet, Caucus and the people of New Zealand'.[*]

The ambassador 'then unloaded on Lange'. What had changed except opposition, which was only to be expected? It was hard to believe that the Hawke letter had made a decisive difference. The scenario for the *Buchanan* visit had been worked out in a series of discussions; the US had gone along with it and had expected it would be followed in good faith. Lange, who the Americans thought looked distinctly uncomfortable, 'explicitly acknowledged at several points that he had broken faith with us over the timing and even substance of the game plan'. He kept coming back to his predicament: Palmer had examined Jamieson's conclusion on *Buchanan* and found it less than adequate. Could the US make another exception and request a ship less difficult to accept?

In the end Monroe Browne said he would pass the proposal to Washington but made it clear 'he considered it most unpromising and practically a betrayal on Lange's part'. Lange said he had been careful in Cabinet not to refer to *Buchanan* by name and its identity was known only to those in the room. As the meeting broke up it was agreed that 'absolute secrecy must be maintained' over the Prime Minister's request for a substitute ship.[†]

Both Norrish and I had earlier warned the Prime Minister that the US Navy would not allow anyone to pick and choose among its fleet but Jamieson was sent off from the meeting to telephone Crowe in Honolulu. The admiral was wrathful, making it clear that he had done his best and did not want 'some fat Prime Minister' telling him what ships he could send.[‡] That was a later reaction but when he heard the news from Jamieson he was 'dumbfounded and very angry', because of the trouble he had taken over *Buchanan*, pushing

---
[*] Note of meeting by Tim Francis of Foreign Affairs, 29 January 1985, PM 59/8/5 Part 2, MFAT.
[†] Embassy report, 29 January 1985, State Department Papers.
[‡] Interview with Bassett, 5 December 2002.

NCND to its limits. He said there were no FFG-7s available and in any case he was not disposed to provide a vessel which could be seen as getting round the NCND policy, and so set a pattern which would be impossible to break in future and have repercussions in both Europe and Asia. Indeed, from the moment the peace movement claimed that the FFG-7s were nuclear-free, sending one would have been hailed as a breach of NCND as a result of New Zealand's pressure.[*]

Early next morning I was woken by a phone call from Norrish: had I seen the morning paper? It carried an Agence France-Presse (AFP) report, from Hong Kong but datelined 'Wellington', which quoted a 'government source' as saying New Zealand had asked for a substitute warship after being unable to confirm that the vessel proposed for a March visit was nuclear-free. 'Sources here' said the new request was for an Oliver Hazard Perry class guided-missile frigate.

Now it was our turn to be dumbfounded; the leak settled whatever lingering chance there might have been of Washington meeting our request. The list of possible leakers was short – only those who had been at the previous day's meeting. The two Americans had no obvious motive to talk to the press, and Lange's advisers had certainly not done so. It came back to an old truth: that unusual vessel, the ship of state, leaks from the top. Lange, briefing the parliamentary press gallery with his customary ebullience the previous night, had been drawn into giving more hints than he realised and bright journalists with handy reference books had done the rest.[†] Lange did not admit this and instead had his office swept for bugs.

The affair of the *Buchanan* now played out its predictable last stages. The Americans concluded that patience and a flexible response were no longer possible. The AFP leak had astounded people and the reverberations 'rumbled round Washington all day'. The State Department complained to the British embassy that the ship had been proposed only after careful informal consultation and

---

[*] Interview with Sir Ewan Jamieson, 13 December 2011.
[†] The *New Zealand Herald*, 12 March 1985, devoted an article to explaining how journalists were able to piece the story together from Lange's comments.

they believed the New Zealanders had said they would accept it.* In an unprecedented move the Joint Chiefs of Staff met to consider the US response and the President himself was consulted. It was seen as the end of the line; too many months had gone by without visible progress on the issue.

The Reagan Administration believed that access for ships was essential for an alliance that was predominantly maritime; without it the alliance could not function. Although Washington continued to blame Lange for 'insufficient political preparation of public and party opinion in New Zealand which might have permitted an accommodation', it also sensed that there had now been a shift in public opinion. The embassy reported that 8000 protesters had marched through Auckland, describing the US and Soviet Union as equal threats to peace, and New Zealand as a world leader of the peace movement. The *Washington Post* saw perceptively that this was not just the European combination of anti-nuclear and leftist elements. 'The cause appears genuinely popular and nationalistic: a small country making its special contribution to the harnessing of the world's nuclear furies.' New Zealand retained its sovereign right to decide whether the United States still served its national needs, but once the question divided the two main political parties, the ANZUS alliance looked doubtful: 'an alliance only in the even-numbered years is not an alliance'.†

Working behind the scenes with Lange was no longer the key to a solution. The Prime Minister had lost control of events and the issue had become part of a widening internal debate. Having failed to prepare the ground over the previous three months, having neglected to brief his Ministers or have a proper Cabinet deliberation, he had now left the initiative to his opponents in the caucus and on the street. In his press conference after the Cabinet meeting on 28 January he appealed for trust in his judgement. 'If they

---

* British embassy, Washington, 30 January 1985, FCO Papers.
† *Washington Post* leader, 24 January 1985.

don't trust me I'm gone. If they do, we don't have nuclear weapons in New Zealand.' But his calls to 'trust me' went unheard; by this stage no one trusted him, neither the anti-nuclear movement nor the Americans. For all his cheery manner, he was by temperament a loner. He had worked on the *Buchanan* project on his own, without telling any of his colleagues, and now he had to deal with its collapse on his own.

Washington's reply on 3 February to his appeal for a frigate was unyielding. It simply reaffirmed that the request as before was for *Buchanan* to visit. With his caucus unanimously supporting a refusal, Lange wrote back the following day to say that the government did not have enough information to provide the assurance it needed. 'We regret that in this instance we must decline.'*

The *Buchanan* plan had been sunk.† Palmer's decision was very popular with the party and, it quickly became clear, with public opinion. Whatever misgivings some Ministers had were submerged by the reception it received. The issue was settled and busy Ministers like Moore saw no point in arguing and neither did Prebble: 'We could recognise that there had been a shift in public opinion. No point in fighting a lost cause and to be frank we were pleased with the public support and over the PM getting such good polling numbers.' So the complaints about the lack of consultation with Cabinet were not pressed. 'The Cabinet was also careful never to let on what a shambles the decision-making had been. We were aware that any hint that it was a cock-up would be politically very damaging.'‡

There was, however, a last surprise in this strange month. Lange walked away from the crash claiming he had not been at the wheel. He told his colleagues that he had not known about the request for *Buchanan* until he got back from Tokelau. He made disparaging

---

* Monroe Browne to Lange, 3 February, and Lange to Monroe Browne, 4 February 1985, PM 111/3/3/1 Part 27, ANZ.
† The ship itself was decommissioned in 1991 and sunk for target practice in 2000, off Hawaii.
‡ Interviews with Prebble, 24 August and 18 September 2011.

remarks about Defence and Foreign Affairs being more concerned about the relationship with America than with Labour policy and in his allusive way left them with the impression that these officials had arranged for the request. Prebble remembers Lange being more explicit, telling him 'he believed his officials, namely Hensley and Jamieson, had been jacking up the visit without his knowledge or approval'. No one seems to have thought it improper or even odd that senior officials had taken it on themselves to force the elected government's hand. The Prime Minister's denial of any foreknowledge made sense to Moore since Palmer, his deputy, was clearly unaware of the request.

Lange was careful never to make this claim in public and neither his officials nor the Americans knew of it at the time. It was not until several years later that Prebble was told in Washington that the US Navy would never have gone to such lengths to find a ship if Lange had not asked for it, and realised for the first time that the Prime Minister had known about *Buchanan* beforehand.

Lange skirted around the subject in his books and later recollections, but in 1994 he described a television documentary which showed him agreeing to the *Buchanan* visit after Jamieson had reported on his discussion in Honolulu as 'fantasy'. Margaret Pope, by now his wife, said in a letter to the editor of the *Dominion*, '[Jamieson's] report of his visit wasn't received until after the travellers returned from the Tokelaus'.[*] In the newspaper article which triggered these exchanges she described the documentary's claim that Lange had invited *Buchanan* to come to New Zealand and then forgot to tell Cabinet as 'most extravagant'. 'He didn't tell his colleagues about the Buchanan because, like them, he'd never heard of it.'[†]

These denials were risky, even in the small circle in which they were first made, but they were part of Lange's repositioning of himself after the debacle. Losing a battle may be less painful if you claim

---

[*] Lange's letter of 11 August 1994 and Ms Pope's undated letter kindly made available by Richard Long who was then editor.
[†] Margaret Pope, the *Dominion*, 3 August 1994.

you never fought it in the first place. Disclaiming any knowledge was an instinctive move, diverting attention away from his failure and enabling him to reassert his control over the issue. Though he continued to insist on the importance of ANZUS and the Western alliance for New Zealand, events were moving him inexorably into the role of the world's nuke-buster, a standing confirmed by his triumph in the Oxford Union debate a month later.

Chapter Six
The Aftershocks

Lange said some months later: 'I don't think that anyone should think for a moment that what happened after the beginning of 1985 took me by surprise.'* Whatever the truth of this claim, it was certainly not true of the Reagan Administration, which was stunned. There had all along been a persistent undercurrent of scepticism about whether the Prime Minister would deliver, but no one could quite believe that New Zealand, the steady, long-standing ally, would refuse entry to an American ship. The shock was more that this comfortable view of the country had been up-ended than that the growing doubts about Lange had turned out to be true. Even then, though, the Prime Minister's encouraging remarks to Monroe Browne on 12 December and the more cheerful demeanour of his advisers had all reinforced the belief that *Buchanan* would be admitted. When there was confusion over the Cabinet decision on 28 January, John Wood, the Deputy

---

* Press conference, 17 July 1985, PM 111/3/3/1 Part 37, ANZ.

in the Washington embassy, was told by Tim Francis, the Deputy Secretary of Foreign Affairs in Wellington, to assure the Americans that it was merely a 'hiccup' in the Cabinet process. He did so (Bill Brown in the State Department was 'surprised but relieved') and was made to look a fool.*

The surprise made the resulting anger more personal and more intense. Administration officials felt aggrieved. They had bent over backwards to try to meet New Zealand's demands. The Lange Government had been invited to choose the timing and even the ship that was to visit, only to publicly reject its own arrangement. The Americans felt they had been deceived and duped. Against the background of the vocal anti-Americanism of Labour Party conferences, largely overlooked by officials in Wellington but never in Washington, it looked as if the New Zealand Government had gone through the motions of a ship visit with the aim of insulting and humiliating the United States.

The professionals in the State Department kept cooler heads, believing that the country had made a fundamental mistake but that the relationship would somehow have to be repaired or at least kept going. President Reagan was as calm as ever, lunching with Hawke on 7 February and telling his diary, 'We are both upset about New Zealand – refusing to allow our destroyer to use the port.' He wondered briefly how Bill Rowling's presentation of credentials as the new ambassador would go – 'That could have been a little touchy but it wasn't.'† His remarks throughout this month continued to be the mild comments of a man who was not much interested. He ruled out any trade retaliation and simply expressed his 'deepest hope' that the traditional cooperation between the two countries would be restored.

At the Cabinet level, though, the disappointment was deep and lasting. The sentimental liking for New Zealand cherished by Shultz and Weinberger turned, as sentimental feelings often do, into the

---

* Interview with Wood, 11 August 2011.
† *The Reagan Diaries*, ed. Douglas Brinkley, Harper Perennial, 2005.

anger of disillusion. Shultz was a man of common sense and firm principles who was liked and respected by everyone who had any dealings with him, ranging from the Russians to the New Zealanders. Even Lange paid tribute to him: 'there is no one who I have met internationally who is so absolutely literally straight up and down on an assurance or a pledge or a position'.[*] This regard was not reciprocated. 'Your Prime Minister could not keep his word' were Shultz's only words to the New Zealand ambassador, Denis McLean, in December 1991 and he turned and walked away.[†] His sense of betrayal was reinforced by the fact that he had sufficiently relaxed his scepticism about Lange towards the end of the year to tell the President that a solution was in sight.

The ambassador in New Zealand, Monroe Browne, also felt betrayed, and was reported by his British colleague to be 'deeply depressed'. He was a political appointment, a devout Republican from California with an interest in horse racing (he bred and raced horses in New Zealand with some success).[‡] He had no experience in the winding paths of diplomacy, which did not matter for his unruffled three years with the Muldoon Government, but which left him sadly baffled and out of touch when the crisis arose. He never mastered his relationship with Lange, alternating uneasily between 'Mr Prime Minister, sir' and 'David', and was haunted by the suspicion that the Prime Minister might be making fun of him.[§] His bitterness over the rejection of the ship visit clouded his last year as ambassador – he left towards the end of 1985 – and unlike his successor he never managed to be other than a messenger in the dispute. The Administration which had appointed him was well aware of his shortcomings. Admiral Crowe indicated to Jamieson that Washington preferred to minimise the ambassador's role in sensitive

---

[*] Vernon Wright interview, 5 December 1986, Lange Papers, Box 1, ANZ.
[†] Margaret Clark (ed.), *For the Record: Lange and the Fourth Labour Government*, Dunmore Press, 2005, p. 149.
[‡] Lange once said that he was the only ambassador to have a horse, Lacka Reason, named after his country's foreign policy.
[§] He was, doing imitations of the ambassador cupping his ear and saying 'Pardon? Pardon?'

discussions but 'he must be expected to play a part'. With the help of his deputy, Richard Teare, he did, and neither his deafness nor occasional incomprehension seems to have affected the negotiations.

The shock passed and the anger subsided into a permanent suspicion about the perils of dealing with New Zealand, but the central concern for the United States was the possible effect on its delicate network of global alliances. The breadth and durability of such a network, as Shultz liked to point out, was unique in the history of alliances. Its longevity rested on lasting fears in Europe and elsewhere of the Soviet Union's intentions, but the lengthening stalemate began to provoke questions about how expansionist those intentions were, and whether the grim discipline of nuclear deterrence was the only way of dealing with them. There was a restlessness about nuclear weapons in both Europe and Japan. Despite all the fuss over occasional ship visits, New Zealand had no nuclear weapons on its territory and unlike Australia, with its joint installations, or Japan, a major base for the Seventh Fleet, it was not crucial to the web of containment. It might, however, be crucial to its continuance. If New Zealand made even a small break in the net it was not easy to know how far it might run.

The immediate reaction of the State Department's spokesman, therefore, was to describe the rejection of *Buchanan* as 'a matter of grave concern, which goes to the core of our mutual obligations as allies'. Allies, he said required equitable burden-sharing and the interaction of military forces. Some Western countries had anti-nuclear movements which sought to diminish defence cooperation among the allied states. 'We would hope that our response to New Zealand would signal that the course these movements advocate would not be cost-free in terms of the security relationship with the United States.'[*]

In the corridors of the State Department and National Security Council, officials were angered by what they saw as Lange's broken

---
[*] Press statement by Bernard Kalb, 5 February 1985.

promise to deal with the issue of ship visits before it reached crisis proportions. Some thought that this information should be released to embarrass Lange, but Shultz forbade it. The Prime Minister saw Washington's reticence from a different angle. When the departing Monroe Browne accused him of bad faith, Lange said that Shultz's silence showed there had never been such a promise – if there had been, Washington would have leaked it and 'he would have been done like a turkey'.*

The Under Secretary of State for Political Affairs, Michael Armacost, told the British that the United States had to call a halt: the American position was being eroded by its efforts to accommodate New Zealand. The Administration had no wish to be vindictive towards the country. There would be no retaliation such as economic sanctions, only some steps in the defence and security relationship to signal that alliance obligations were reciprocal. The risk of repercussions elsewhere, in countries like Japan, Greece and Belgium, would be the main driver of the US response. Washington had to make it clear to its allies that they could not expect American protection if they preferred to pick and choose, taking an 'à la carte' view of their own responsibilities.

Such a carefully measured approach was not so congenial to others, such as columnists and Congressmen, whose profession inclined them to be less reticent. New Zealand, said William Buckley, could start a War of Jenkins' Ear, triggering a sweeping unilateralism that could take in Australia, the Low Countries and West Germany which would mean the end of the Western alliance system.†

The chairman of the Senate Foreign Relations Committee, the moderate Senator Lugar, said he was shocked that a country hitherto regarded as a close ally and loyal friend should take actions so inimical to American interests. If the Administration was not prepared

---

* Report of UK/US Planning Talks, 25–26 February 1985, FCO Papers, and Lange press conference, 4 November 1985.
† *Washington Post*, 19 February 1985. The loss by Captain Jenkins of an ear was said to have led to the outbreak of war between Britain and Spain in 1739.

to take firm action then the Congress should. He announced on 12 February that his committee would review America's commitments and obligations under the ANZUS treaty. Admiral Crowe, now thoroughly angry, joined in to tell the Senate Armed Services Committee, 'It boggles my mind, how New Zealand can expect the United States to carry out its defence obligations' after the decision it had made.

Senator Cohen of Maine (and later President Clinton's Defense Secretary) wrote to the President even before the final rejection of *Buchanan* to urge a firm response. 'No nation has a moral corner or monopoly on the fear of nuclear war. But to be aware and fearful of nuclear war is not enough.' He was not in favour of being 'delicate and diplomatic' and suggested the US should now look at a bilateral security treaty with Australia and shut New Zealand out of its defence activities.* When the White House said cautiously, 'Your thoughts are being carefully reviewed', he incorporated these thoughts into a 'sense of the Senate' resolution which by the end of the month had attracted 53 signatories (including Joe Biden, the future Vice President, and John Glenn, the astronaut), a majority of the Senate.

The House, as tradition suggested, was less inhibited. Prodded by their industry lobby groups, representatives from meat and dairy districts seized the moment to call for an end to the preferential treatment of New Zealand lamb, wool and casein imports, and there were calls for the Administration to release surplus American butter and other dairy products onto the world market. Congressman Dick Cheney from Wyoming took this even further by introducing a Bill to ban both New Zealand and Australian products (including uranium). The inclusion of Australia was a surprise, but then Wyoming, a mining state, was also a big beef producer. Cheney, having shown his farmer voters that his heart was in the right place, then said the Bill 'was a statement in itself' and he would not be taking it further.

The House itself had an hour's debate on a motion of Representative Molinari to discuss ANZUS. Eleven members spoke in support,

---

* Cohen to Reagan, 31 January 1985, Laux Papers, Box 90658, Reagan Presidential Library.

expressing concern at the ripple effects of New Zealand's action, the importance of the Western democracies hanging together, and the possibility of economic sanctions. More seriously, the chairman of the House Agricultural Committee said that 'the ANZUS issue would make it very difficult for New Zealand's friends in Congress to be as helpful' as in the past. Stephen Solarz, a bright and energetic member of the House Foreign Affairs Committee, planned hearings on ANZUS by his East Asia and the Pacific Subcommittee. All this sound and fury did not necessarily signify much, and Wolfowitz and others pointed out more than once that Congress was not the Administration, which would continue to oppose any economic retaliation. But to New Zealanders, familiar only with parliamentary government, it looked as if the whole machinery of the American government was being wheeled out against them.

There were scattered signs of consumer resistance to New Zealand products. Sales of Steinlager in the military bases in Hawaii dropped by half in February – the distributor in South Carolina said 'if New Zealand pulls out of ANZUS you can take your beer with you'; and sales of New Zealand ice cream in California were hit (it was winter). The Corbans export manager said the issue was raised wherever he went and wine sales dropped. The *Martinsburg Journal* of West Virginia said 'if they don't want any more visits from our Navy, we don't want any more of their mutton'. Anti-nuclear women, however, attempted to organise a 'girlcott' to buy New Zealand goods where they could find them. All these efforts were scrappy, uncoordinated and had little effect. New Zealand exports were not especially visible in the huge American market and the American shopper was not particularly concerned, if she was even aware, about the importance of port access. Over the following year American tourism and imports from New Zealand actually increased.

More awkward was that New Zealand was arranging one of its regular borrowings on the New York money market. As they did the rounds of the banking houses to promote the bond issue, Roger Douglas, the Minister of Finance, and Bernard Galvin, the Treasury

Secretary, were regularly questioned about the alliance. On their way back to their hotel at the end of the day Galvin commented that the ANZUS issue was much bigger than he had thought. 'Yes,' said Douglas. 'Thank God it's not in my department.'* But their New York legal advisers insisted on the inclusion of a paragraph about ANZUS in the prospectus in case the regulatory authority felt there had not been full disclosure.

The main worry, and it was still only that, was that the US Government agencies that had worked hard in the past to fend off protectionist threats from Congress might now sit back on their oars. Sometimes described as New Zealand's Washington constituency, the backing of these agencies was a source of both envy and irritation to others less well-placed: 'You guys had more influence than Wisconsin.' At Agriculture and Commerce the embassy was assured that it was still business as usual but there was a noticeable weakening of enthusiasm. The Office of the US Trade Representative (USTR) said they wanted to be helpful but their room for manoeuvre had been narrowed: 'We want you to understand that it is going to be extremely difficult.' If, for example, the casein lobbyists seized their chance to attack New Zealand imports (and casein constituted 21 per cent of New Zealand's trade), the Administration could no longer bolster its general opposition to protectionism by adding the more potent argument of damage to an alliance partner.

The reaction to all this in New Zealand was an upsurge of nationalist sentiment. Since the public were unaware of the American feelings of betrayal over the *Buchanan* visit, the US response seemed haughty and unreasonable. New Zealand, after all, was simply asserting its right to its own foreign policy and its stance was an admirable gesture against the nuclear arms race. The American reaction looked like bullying, the reaction of a big power that had been put in its place. This was inevitable in any dispute between two nations of such

---

* Galvin to the author at the time.

disparate size and power. Comparisons of David and Goliath were unavoidable, not at all hindered by the Prime Minister's first name.

The stakes for America's global interests were such that Washington felt it had to press ahead anyhow. But the power of nationalism, which had overcome liberalism in the nineteenth century and Communism in the twentieth, was more than a match for Congressional disapproval or the Administration's handful of measures. Far from encouraging New Zealanders to reconsider their nuclear restrictions, as the Americans somewhat naively hoped, the response hardened the country's resolve, even to the point where businessmen and establishment figures who disapproved of the anti-nuclear policy found themselves defending it as patriotic citizens.

New Zealand's emerging nationalism had at last found a cause around which it could rally. Keith Jackson, professor of political science at the University of Canterbury, could even call rejection of the ship visit the country's 'Declaration of Independence'. For the baby-boom generation, though less so for their elders, the country had struck out on its own and become truly independent; there could be no better evidence of its independence than quarrelling with all its friends. Editorialists such as the *New Zealand Herald* thought that the country was in danger of forgetting that the letter of the treaty was less important than the willingness of its partners to make it work: 'Far too many people seem to be putting wishbone where backbone ought to be.'[*] Public opinion, however, or at least the vocal expression of it, leant the other way. Pride in the uniqueness of New Zealand was reflected in relish at its bold stand. Reproving the great powers appealed to the moralistic streak in some. Those less interested in the substance were gratified that their little country was causing an international stir.

Television, still a young medium in staffing and attitude, took enthusiastically to the nationalist cause. *Eyewitness News* thought that, if not an outright declaration of war, the American response was

---

[*] *New Zealand Herald*, 4 February 1985.

as close to it as diplomatically possible. Officials in Washington were reported to be staggered by the decision: 'They simply don't believe the tiny South Pacific nation would stand up to the might of a superpower.' TV *News* talked to a shivering woman outside the White House who prayed that other leaders would follow New Zealand, 'but across the road in the White House, her pleas and ours fall on deaf ears'. For several nights there were interviews with Admiral Larocque, another maverick but obligingly anti-nuclear admiral, who offered to argue New Zealand's case to the Congress and who predicted that the United States would ultimately back off 'because we do not want to break up the ANZUS treaty'.[*]

Underneath the excited proclamations that the country would no longer defer to the views of others, that it thought proudly for itself and would hold unshakeably to the results, was a reassuring safety net. The cost was not great. Loss of access in Washington and defence and intelligence benefits was a worry only for the professionals, and ANZUS had never gripped the public imagination except as a symbol of the relationship with the United States. The *San Francisco Chronicle* in a leader entitled 'A Sad Goodbye' said sharply, 'New Zealand is allowed to take a pious stance because it is a no-risk stance' – as long as the US Navy dominated the Pacific, New Zealand was secure.[†] Loss of trade might have been a different matter but the Administration had wisely ruled that out; it had no interest in an alliance maintained by compulsion. Trade was the one pressure point which could change New Zealanders' minds, as France proved two years later when it secured the release of the *Rainbow Warrior* prisoners by holding up $200 million worth of New Zealand imports. The Prime Minister understood this and regularly sought reassurance from Washington that it was not about to change its mind on trade.

In a survey released on 22 February the United States Information Agency confirmed the point. Drawing on a recent poll by the *Dominion*

---

[*] *Eyewitness News*, TVNZ, 19 February 1985.
[†] *San Francisco Chronicle*, 22 February 1985.

newspaper, it reported strong opposition, 56 per cent to 29 per cent, to visits by nuclear-armed ships. A narrower majority, 48 per cent to 42 per cent, favoured the government's ban on actual ship visits such as the *Buchanan*. 'However, support for the government's ban drops off considerably when damage to New Zealand's exports or exclusion from ANZUS are raised as possible consequences of this policy.' A later survey showed that a small majority thought the US had not treated New Zealand fairly following the ban on *Buchanan* and did not believe that the ban was contrary to the country's ANZUS responsibilities. Continued membership of ANZUS was overwhelmingly endorsed, with 78 per cent in favour and only 12 per cent opposed.*

Balancing these conflicting views, the Prime Minister declared that New Zealand had an unshakeable commitment both to exclude nuclear-armed ships and to remain a firm and loyal member of ANZUS. The future of ANZUS was now of increasing concern, but the weight of his public appeal was more to the anti-nuclear spirit. In a radio interview he compared *Buchanan*'s armaments with those of *Truxtun*, the nuclear-powered cruiser whose visit to Wellington in 1982 had aroused protest and which had since become something of a symbol of the opposition to nuclear ships. New Zealand had invited the US to send a ship which would not be nuclear-armed but it had 'now twice declined to do that'.† He appealed to other half-buried emotions over the Springbok tour riots four years earlier, asserting that the country could be a good member of the alliance without having to accept nuclear weapons: 'just because you decide not to use a long [police] baton doesn't mean giving up fighting crime'.

His first press conference veered between the flippant – any intelligence cuts would mean less reading – and the agitated, when he called Weinberger's remark that New Zealanders would greatly damage themselves 'a straightforward threat'. Some claims sounded like the last-ditch efforts of a trial lawyer, as when he argued that if the

---

* USIA Research Reports of 22 February and 3 April, Laux Papers, Box 90659, Reagan Presidential Library, and *Dominion* poll of 18 February 1985.
† Radio New Zealand *Morning Report*, 5 February, and press conference of 6 February 1985.

Americans made port access a condition of staying in ANZUS, then it would be they who had unilaterally withdrawn from the treaty.

In private, both governments agreed on the need for what Lange called 'a period of quiet reflection'. Whether the first attempt at a ship visit had been defeated by the unfortunate leaks (as Lange and Rowling argued) or by insufficient preparation of public and party opinion (as Wolfowitz said), there was now a new situation to be thought through. With hopes of port access effectively dashed, unless the Americans could be persuaded to modify their NCND stance, New Zealand policy was left balancing on one leg with no option but to keep stressing its unaltered adherence to ANZUS. This meant having to dismiss occasional port visits as only a minor aspect of the relationship. Lange emphasised that New Zealand would continue to pull its weight in the alliance, as it always had done, and if necessary would even increase its defence spending. He told *Asiaweek* that there was no need to renegotiate the treaty but it should be a dynamic partnership and able to adapt and change as he said it had in the past. He asserted that there was 'no way' the ships ban could end in his country's exclusion from ANZUS.*

In Washington, Rowling, just arrived and yet to present his credentials, found himself confronted by a crisis which he had been assured would not occur. He said ruefully some months later that 'he would never again be party to a promise before it had been fully endorsed by Cabinet'. He blamed Lange for the fiasco, saying it was no wonder the Americans felt they had been misled since there had been an agreement on the *Buchanan* visit clearly understood by both sides, but New Zealand had not lived up to it: 'When it had come to the crunch, however, Lange had been unable to deliver.'†

---

* *Asiaweek*, 13 February 1985.
† Talking to the Australian Consul-General, Honolulu, 11 December 1985, 370/1/20 Part 49, NAA.

At a first lunch on 4 February, Wolfowitz and Rowling peered into the crater left by the explosion. Wolfowitz was still shaken. He complained that he and his colleagues had been engaged with their New Zealand counterparts for several months, with Lange's blessing they assumed, in an effort to find a way through. Until ten days ago he had believed they were in sight of success. Over the months they had taken 'their very senior people' with them but New Zealand had made no public effort to match the private assurances that were being given. Now his own credibility had been eroded and those in the Administration who had argued against an attempt at compromise were in the ascendant and saying 'I told you so'.

He thought it would be months or longer before relations could improve. The best course was to allow time for anger to calm and the dust to settle. There was a fundamental contradiction between New Zealand's strong anti-nuclear convictions and its equally strongly expressed commitment to the alliance. That was a circle which could not be squared by the New Zealand Government alone; it required the agreement of the other two ANZUS partners which would not be forthcoming. New Zealand, he said bluntly, was faced with a choice: it would have to take the initiative and offer a compromise or accept that ANZUS was not sustainable as a tripartite partnership.

Rowling, as a good ambassador, kept his private irritation to himself, but agreed that he too had been taken aback by the events. He passed Wolfowitz's views to Wellington and the Prime Minister circulated the discussion to Cabinet, the first paper it had ever received on the issue. Lange's only comment was brief: 'Having taken the momentous decision on ship visits we must now follow a consistent line on continued cooperation in ANZUS and more widely with our Western partners. To do anything else could have very damaging consequences.'

At the same time he told Rowling that going back to the pre-*Buchanan* situation was 'patently not possible'. The government's policy on ship visits was about as firmly established as any policy could be: 'There is no alternative but to look ahead from that base.' He flatly disagreed that ANZUS was no longer sustainable in its present form. With time New Zealand should be able to prove its point about the permanence of their common interests to both its Australian and American partners. It might even be possible to resume ship visits: 'It makes no sense for U. S. navy ships to be totally absent from our ports.' The key was to maintain a period of calm and restraint. He would rein in his own comments and hoped that the American reaction would also be carefully controlled; any disproportionate measures could provoke a public response in New Zealand which would be difficult to control.*

For the moment all the two sides could agree on was that they should stay as quiet as possible, but even this could not be maintained. As with any divorce, the two partners started with intentions of calm discussion and civilised behaviour, only for their accumulated resentments to burst out and turn conversations into angry exchanges. The Prime Minister meant what he said about the need for a time of quiet reflection but, in the words of his speechwriter and later wife, 'his love of performance needed an audience'.† Like other good performers, he was most himself in front of an audience and was stimulated to further flights by the response of his listeners. On these occasions he could no more restrain the flow of his wit and ridicule than stop breathing, and so, despite his periodic pledges of restraint, his press conferences continued to entertain the journalists and irritate the Americans.‡

The Reagan Administration was hardly better placed when it came to cooling the atmosphere. Senior officials were still seething with anger over the *Buchanan* rejection. Rowling complained about charges that New Zealand wanted a free ride, and about loose talk of

---

* Exchange of cables between Rowling and Lange, 4 and 7 February 1985, Cabinet Paper CS (85) 52.
† Margaret Pope, *At the Turning Point: My Political Life with David Lange*, AM Publishing New Zealand, 2011, p. 193.
‡ As a result Rowling became apprehensive about the Prime Minister's Monday press conferences. He told Ross Tanner, then Economic Counsellor at the embassy, that he was uncomfortable having to defend impromptu comments made to journalists in Wellington. Ross Tanner, 29 October 2012.

retribution – 'the dogs had been let loose'. He hoped for a continuation of naval cooperation and, as soon as politically possible, 'an easy ship visit or visits'. But Wolfowitz insisted there would have to be consequences; to ignore what had happened would leave a question mark 'over our whole defence cooperation'.* He was vague about what they might be but it was obvious that deciding on the consequences would take skill and some judgement. They had to be noticeable or the US's global partners might not take note, but if too severe they might provoke a nationalist reaction in New Zealand and destroy any lingering hopes of nudging the country into a compromise.

Australia, as the other partner, would clearly have a say in deciding what the consequences should be, but Lange's hopes were Hawke's fears. The ANZUS row could hardly have come at a worse time for the Australian Prime Minister. The Americans wished to test a new missile – given the experimental name MX. Its flight would end in the Tasman Sea and the Australians agreed to provide airfields and other facilities to assist the Americans in monitoring the test. The arrangement had been very closely held in Canberra but it became known in early February when Hawke was visiting Brussels. There was a sharp domestic reaction, and disaffection in the Australian Labor Party spread beyond the Left and threatened Hawke's leadership.

He was forced to announce the withdrawal of Australian cooperation and flew to Washington to see Shultz and seek American help. Years later he was still grateful. The MX problem was fixed in a day, with the Americans withdrawing their request for Australian facilities and accepting the greater expense of monitoring the test at sea. When he got home, though, he was still required to make a public act of contrition and promise better consultation with his Ministers in future. Rowling took the opportunity to complain that rules were being bent for Australia but not for New Zealand. Wolfowitz demurred. The MX test was a one-off affair; Washington did not need its partners' assistance in developing its nuclear deterrent but denial

---

* Rowling's report, 8 February 1985, PM 59/8/5 Part 3, MFAT.

of port access had worldwide consequences for their conventional as well as nuclear fleet.

The affair was a sharp reminder to Hawke of the need to keep a neutral stance between the US and New Zealand. It brought ANZUS back to the centre of political debate and damaged Hawke's standing domestically. He went on television to declare 'I won't be a Prime Minister of this country' if issues of central importance to its security, such as port access, were put at risk. In the face of this firmness a lengthy Cabinet discussion of his handling of the affair ended up amicably. But, as his Foreign Minister put it, the government was reminded that it had still not succeeded in weaning the Left away from 'the politics of gesture'. The MX discontent was a warning to step carefully. The US was seen by many in Australia as attempting to bully New Zealand. If the government in Canberra was thought to be encouraging it, the reaction across the Australian political spectrum might be enough to blow the government's present policy off course.[*]

Nonetheless, the government felt it had been let down by Lange. The head of Hawke's department told a British visitor that after the election Lange had made it clear to the Australians that he personally favoured the continuation of ship visits, but needed time to win over those people in his party who were strongly opposed. But after four or so months it became clear from his public remarks that far from trying to persuade such people to change their minds, he was himself taking a hard line. It was an extraordinary situation when a Labour government in Australia wished to see a Labour government in New Zealand replaced, but though Ministers could not say so aloud, 'that was in fact their view'.[†]

Public opinion in Australia did not agree with New Zealand either. When Lange said on Australian television that New Zealand was not prepared to burn for either friend or foe, this did not strike his listeners as sounding like the staunch support of an alliance partner or even

---

[*] Reports by BHC, Canberra, 13 February and 7 March 1985, FCO Papers.
[†] Sir Geoffrey Yeend to David Wilson, 13 March 1985, FCO Papers.

a friend if Australia were ever to face trouble.[*] A poll by the *Australian* newspaper on 9 February revealed that 76 per cent of those asked considered that New Zealand's recent action had either greatly or partially damaged the ANZUS alliance. Although there was an active peace movement (half a million voted for the Nuclear Disarmament Party in December), most Australians were concerned about their defence. The official view held that there was no identifiable threat to Australia but most people continued to feel themselves to be threatened, though the source of concern varied over the years, with China, the Soviet Union and Indonesia all sharing the honour at different periods. It may be that a continent has an inbuilt sense of menace.

Editorial comment was uniformly critical, with New Zealand's policy being variously described as misguided, isolationist and detrimental to Australia's security interests. The *Australian* argued that nuclear arms were part of the world's reality and control of them could only be negotiated if some sort of balance was maintained between the two superpowers. Most, however, endorsed Hawke's intention of staying out of the dispute. Both the *Sydney Morning Herald* and the *Canberra Times* warned that any display of heavy-handedness by the US could darken public opinion in Australia as well as New Zealand.

The Premier of Queensland, Joh Bjelke-Petersen (a New Zealander by birth), took a sterner view. He announced that his state would ban New Zealand chocolates and beer. He backed down the next day, partly because he had no such power and partly because Queensland sugar growers pointed out that the chocolates were made with their sugar. He explained that the imports had only been 'held up' because of incorrect packaging but went on to denounce the anti-nuclear policy anyhow. Steinlager beer got the best of it, running advertisements proclaiming 'it's not a beer for your average Joh'.

In London the Foreign Office was in a dilemma. Not being a party to the treaty Britain was not formally involved, but it had close ties

---

[*] 18 February 1985, PM 111/3/3/1 Part 28, ANZ.

with all three members and had nuclear-capable warships that occasionally visited New Zealand. It did not wish to be thought to be acting for the United States but knew that Washington would seek its help. In any case, its relations with both countries were such that it hoped to avoid as long as possible having to choose. Understandably, therefore, its first thought was to play for time: 'We might argue that the debate be less public and left to confidential discussions between the two governments involved.' A more robust diplomat wrote in the margin, 'Looks pretty unrealistic to me', and it was.

If it was not possible to lower the temperature, someone else wondered whether there could be a special non-nuclear status for New Zealand within ANZUS – 'a lower premium, less cover'. This was in fact the core of Lange's argument. But it was unlikely to appeal to the Americans or even to meet the more pressing concerns of British Ministers. They were worried about the effect on NATO and on their own situation. The domestic nuclear debate had revived, with fresh demonstrations at Molesworth where the next flight of cruise missiles would be based under the NATO plan, and the peace movement was already pointing to the example being set by New Zealand. Ministers were more likely to agree with another thought expressed in the round of minutes: 'If New Zealand gets away with its existing line, the rot can be guaranteed to spread. This we must prevent: we cannot seek the role of a neutral intermediary.'*

It was clear to everyone that the Americans would feel obliged to send a global message about alliance obligations. The need was not merely diplomatic, to strengthen alliance cohesion, it was seen as essential to defend the US's strategic posture. A Pentagon paper argued the effect on the US's naval strategy if the New Zealand example were to spread. The Soviet Navy operated primarily from its home waters and the few countries where it did make port calls – such as Vietnam, Libya and Albania – were unaffected by peace

---

* This was the outcome of an internal debate in the Foreign Office, 8 February 1985, FCO Papers.

movements. In the absence of any agreement with the Soviet Union on nuclear arms control, New Zealand's ban was 'most serious' because if it spread a widespread denial of access would severely downgrade the effectiveness of US forces while leaving the Soviets essentially unaffected.*

This concern was reflected not only in the views of Britain and Canada but in the reactions of a number of countries in Asia and Europe. The messages were politely and cautiously phrased but they all revealed an anxiety that New Zealand's actions might disturb the current strategic balance.

Japan tiptoed carefully around the issue, fearful that the New Zealand example might focus attention on their own situation and encourage the thought, as the Canadian embassy in Tokyo put it, that its own ban on nuclear warships 'should be honoured in practice as well as in principle'. After the first few weeks, though, Japanese officials became more confident. They had long experience in handling the inconsistencies in Japan's non-nuclear policy and the lack of public interest gradually gave them confidence that they could deal with any calls to follow the Lange policy.

In South East Asia several countries were worried that, as the Thais put it, New Zealand had rocked their security boat. The Thais were not unsympathetic to the aim and were appreciative of New Zealand's contribution to the region's security over the years but complained that its present stand risked damaging that security. Helpful though its support for Malaysia and Singapore was through the Five Power Defence Arrangements, the larger if unspoken benefit New Zealand had brought to South East Asia was its links with the United States through ANZUS. This was a general view among ASEAN members, concerned to maintain a counterweight to Soviet and Chinese influence. The Indonesian Foreign Minister, in a quick consultation at Jakarta airport, told Lange that New Zealand was

---

* 'Implications of the "Nuclear Free" Movement on the U. S. Worldwide Military Posture', 26 February 1985, PM 111/3/3/1 Part 30, ANZ.

right and the Americans were overreacting, but editorial comment there reflected some unease at the disturbance of established security arrangements in the region.

The Malaysian Foreign Minister expressed 'sadness' over the crisis and the cancellation of Sea Eagle: 'We want these exercises to carry on because they are also for the benefit of South East Asia.' When Lange stopped for a day in early March, the Malaysian Prime Minister, Mahathir, hoped that what had happened was a passing phenomenon and agreement would ultimately be achievable. In Singapore Lange got a lecture from the Foreign Minister, Dhanabalan, who said that 'New Zealand had underrated its impact and influence in the world' and its actions would have a ripple effect on others. This made Lange apprehensive when he went off to dinner with Lee Kuan Yew, but the tactful Lee said he would probably welcome a respite and made it a relaxing evening. He did however warn of the dangers to Western solidarity and marvelled at the way in which what had seemed to be a sideshow when they met in October had become a major issue: 'Was it all worth it – the balls would bounce the same way in the end.' Lange remembered Lee's earlier advice to stick to domestic affairs for the first eighteen months, and said he now wished he had taken it.[*]

NATO members in Europe were if anything sharper about the dangers to them. They were shaken by the anti-nuclear agitation of the past few years and Belgium and the Netherlands had still to give final approval for the stationing of 48 cruise missiles on their territories. Any divisions in the West could flow on to the arms control negotiations in Geneva which were teetering back and forth, seemingly dependent on Moscow's moods. Canada, whose Atlantic outlook had made it an active NATO member, sympathised with New Zealand's situation and was as helpful in practice as it could manage. But its Prime Minister, Mulroney, emphasised that support for alliances was 'an important signal of solidarity to send out'. Denmark, too, was

---

[*] Singapore and Kuala Lumpur meetings, 7 and 8 March 1985, PM 111/3/3/1 Part 31, ANZ.

sympathetic, having spent much time and effort getting its partners to accept its anti-nuclear views. It suggested that New Zealand had made its point about weapons and needed now to 'de-dramatise' the situation and allow time for reflection.

The Belgians, still coping with anti-nuclear demonstrations, said that global security was indivisible: 'Small members of alliances had to realise that their actions could impact upon other members of that alliance or even other alliances.' Norway pointed out that it shared a border with the Soviet Union. If they applied the New Zealand policy, naval cooperation would be impossible and the Russians would have a free hand in the north. The Italians disagreed with the New Zealand view that world security could be enhanced by seeking to keep one region free of strategic confrontation; the best hope of enhancing security was through negotiated reductions in arms which, by implication, New Zealand's action was not helping. The Germans, too, thought the Russians would try to exploit the ANZUS troubles and that difficulties might arise within NATO.

In the European Parliament a group of largely British Conservative MPs tabled a resolution criticising New Zealand action on American ship visits and said this would have serious consequences for New Zealand's trade relations. It was never pressed to a vote and a second group then issued a statement supporting New Zealand, but Lange was nervous enough to put out a press release saying that he had 'firm assurances' that the British Government would continue to help New Zealand with its access to the European market.[*]

The only lighter note was the French who complained (to the British, not New Zealand) that if New Zealand's stand was copied by others in the Pacific they would have serious logistical problems 'in addition to the criticism which they already face'.[†]

Amid this chorus of diplomatic disapproval, Soviet support was predictable though unwanted. It focused at first on the difficulties

---

[*] 15 February 1985.
[†] The various reports are in PM 111/3/3/1 Parts 30–32, ANZ.

for ANZUS, with a front-page cartoon in *Pravda*, and made some play with the possibility of trade sanctions. Then the emphasis shifted to the more sensitive subject of the 'nuclear allergy' which it suggested Belgium, the Netherlands and Japan might now catch from New Zealand. After the Prime Minister's complaint to the Soviet ambassador, Tass carried his statement on New Zealand's continuing commitment to the Western alliance and the New Zealand embassy in Moscow thought that articles thereafter at least for a time were more sober in tone.

More surprisingly, a Chinese commentator in the *People's Daily*, which had not previously commented on New Zealand's nuclear policy, said that the New Zealand stand was completely legitimate and for the US to press for a visit 'is both a kind of probe and an exertion of pressure'. This puzzled the New Zealand embassy; Beijing was not normally keen on any moves which might weaken resistance to Soviet expansion in the South Pacific. When the United States complained about the article, the Chinese Foreign Office said apologetically, with perhaps the hint of a smile, that it was not possible to control the press.*

International organisations also made supportive statements. The Commonwealth Secretary-General, Shridath Ramphal, again praised New Zealand for 'striving to assert its sovereignty despite its smallness'. On a visit to Wellington, the Secretary-General of the United Nations, Pérez de Cuéllar, said that New Zealand's anti-nuclear policies were also the UN's and praised the country for its consistent campaign against the arms race. The strong-minded Jean Kirkpatrick, American Permanent Representative at the UN, went to remonstrate with him. The Secretary-General agreed that his remarks might have been incautious and perhaps hindered by his poor English but he was far from contrite: he had a responsibility, he said, to reflect the UN's position on an issue as important as disarmament.

---

* *People's Daily*, 31 January 1985, PM 111/3/3/1 Part 26, ANZ.

When they surveyed the international reactions, those that favoured New Zealand as well as those that were critical, the Americans were confirmed in the need to take some action. Officials considering the Administration's response were aware, as they gloomily confessed to the embassy in Washington, that they were going to look like bullies, attempting to heavy a small and thoroughly worthy little country. This, they concluded, had to be worn. New Zealand as a sovereign country had every right to decide what it wanted to do on ship visits and anything else, but as long as it wished to be an alliance partner it could not take unilateral decisions that affected the other partners and changed the nature of the alliance. This was a point which was crucial for other and more important alliances than ANZUS. Some NATO countries, as well as Japan and Australia, were anxiously awaiting and indeed pressing the Americans for some public reassurance that all alliance members had to share the burden of security and that New Zealand would not be allowed to become an exception.

Even as the destroyer *Buchanan* was making a consolation tour of South Pacific ports, planning had started in Washington to decide on the measures the Administration would impose.

Chapter Seven
The Excommunication

The Reagan Administration had always made it clear that there would be a cost to any denial of port access but it had never spelt out, even to itself, what this cost would be. Since New Zealand in its view had breached its defence and security commitments under the alliance, any response would logically focus on limiting the US's own commitments in these fields. Although some in Congress and business uttered occasional menacing comments about trade, arousing corresponding fears in New Zealand, the Administration had from the earliest days ruled out the possibility of economic sanctions. Defence and intelligence cooperation would clearly be the target – to think otherwise, Wolfowitz told the ambassador, would be 'living in a dream world'.* There was as yet no 'menu' but the three departments in the Inter-Agency Group began work on a detailed review, drawing up a list of measures which would be promulgated in a directive signed by the President.

---

* Wolfowitz to Rowling, 8 February 1985, PM 59/8/5 Part 3, MFAT.

Britain was quick to discover that a review was under way and was the first to try to influence it. London's main concern was to protect the five-nation intelligence community. This close partnership had grown up among the English-speaking allies during the Second World War when Britain was the senior member, and Canada, Australia and New Zealand were naturally included. Britain had long since lost its dominant position to the United States but it worried about the precedent that would be set if even the most junior partner New Zealand was expelled. 'We would not wish to see a prominent breach in US/NZ relations, least of all in the intelligence field, where we have a strong community of interest', was an early reaction by the British embassy.[*] At the beginning of February, Sir Anthony Duff, Mrs Thatcher's intelligence adviser and about to become head of MI5, went to Washington to urge restraint. His message was that it was for the US to decide on its bilateral relationship with New Zealand but the five-nation intelligence cooperation was so close that it was in effect multilateral and in everyone's interests that it should not be lightly disturbed.

Both Mrs Thatcher and the Foreign Secretary, Sir Geoffrey Howe, came to Washington in the third week of February and they also urged the Administration not to take any precipitate action beforehand. Shultz seemed to agree with this, but the British ambassador was cautious: 'as so often in this town, when a war like this breaks out, the air is filled with a vast amount of distracting static', with interested parties enthusiastically leaking and worst-case scenarios inevitably attracting the most notice. Making the case for not 'monkeying about' with the intelligence relationship was important, but if Britain was to have any influence on US decisions 'we will need to demonstrate that our objective – like theirs – is to work for a change in New Zealand's policy, not just to shield the New Zealanders from the consequences of their present one'.[†]

---

[*] British embassy cable, 11 February 1985, FCO Papers. Duff was in Washington 6 February.
[†] Ambassador's briefing before Mrs Thatcher's visit, 13 February 1985, FCO Papers.

Signs that the Americans were already taking unilateral action deepened British fears. Canada and Britain were both annoyed when the Pentagon abruptly cancelled a naval exercise in which New Zealand would have participated. It was not an ANZUS exercise and the two countries felt they should at least have been consulted. Neither had alliance obligations but both had a relationship with New Zealand that was older and broader than any treaty. From Wellington, High Commissioner Terence O'Leary was reporting that the New Zealand Government's 'Anglo-Saxon obstinacy' and the US's impulsive response were likely to make the dispute worse. Britain should not stand aside. The memory of New Zealand's support in the Falklands War was still fresh and as the High Commissioner pointed out: 'We owe New Zealand an historic debt of blood and honour and patience and should not too readily accept a hasty and short-sighted American judgment of how best to deal with New Zealand.'[*]

So when he got to Washington, Howe made a point of 'agreeing' with Shultz that a friend should not be turned into an enemy and stressing the hope that the US would consult its allies before taking further steps against New Zealand. He argued against any cutback in intelligence cooperation, saying this would become public and would be unhelpful on broader grounds. Britain would find it difficult to work a two-tier relationship in sharing information. 'The best bet for influencing Lange's policies was the effect of isolation and lack of security on public opinion in New Zealand.'[†] The Americans did not find this especially persuasive. No one in New Zealand seemed too worried about isolation and it was far from clear that the country's long years of security would be shaken by the loss of the alliance.

Mrs Thatcher told the President that she supported a firm approach by the Administration and had no intention of modifying Britain's NCND policy. The US and Britain could not 'put their defence policies in little boxes – nuclear here, non-nuclear there'.

---

[*] BHC, Wellington, cable, 21 February 1985, FCO Papers.
[†] Howe to Shultz, 21 February 1985, FCO Papers.

But she too urged the President not to interfere with the existing intelligence cooperation with New Zealand. President Reagan was non-committal – he simply 'noted' the thought. Talking to Secretary Shultz, she commented that Lange had impaled himself on an electoral hook. She had earlier thought that he would be able to get off it. Shultz said he had thought so too, but Lange seemed to have made little effort and had progressively become more rather than less difficult. His tone was ominous. New Zealand had removed itself from the ranks of those protecting freedom and would feel the effect; it would lose the special consideration it had enjoyed through its participation in the common defence.

The Australians had no disagreement with Shultz's approach but, consistent with their policy of not becoming involved in the dispute, they did not (at least officially) play any part in the lobbying over the scope of the draft directive. Hayden, the Foreign Minister, urged the Americans to be careful, arguing that isolating New Zealand in defence and intelligence could damage their own interests in the Pacific. The *Sydney Morning Herald* was less sympathetic, saying that New Zealand had run up a debt with the US and was now getting the bill for its actions.[*] Hawke told a British visitor that any dilution by the Americans of their NCND policy would cause serious problems for him and for the Australian Government. He thought that 'the leadership' in New Zealand now had some personal doubts but the structure of the New Zealand Labour Party ruled out any major change in the immediate future. Lange was living in 'cloud cuckoo land' if he imagined he could negotiate his way out of the crisis; New Zealanders would only change their tune when their pockets were touched. He agreed with his visitor that it might be a case of waiting for the next election.[†]

By mid-February both British and Canadian friends let Wellington know that the review of defence and intelligence cooperation was

---

[*] *Sydney Morning Herald*, 1 March 1985.
[†] Hawke to Butler, British Minister of State for Defence Procurement, 27 February 1985, FCO Papers.

Above Friendlier times: American and New Zealand warships moored together in Wellington Harbour in 1981. DOMINION POST COLLECTION, ALEXANDER TURNBULL LIBRARY

Below The American delegation arrives in storm-swept Wellington in July 1984. 'Is it always like this here?' – Paul Wolfowitz. DOMINION POST COLLECTION, ALEXANDER TURNBULL LIBRARY

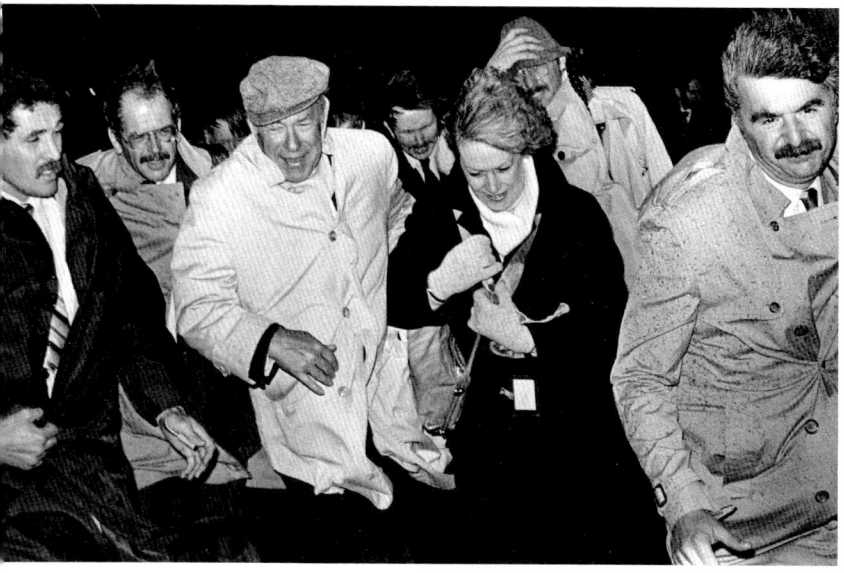

Military chiefs at the last full ANZUS Council meeting in July 1984. From left: General Phillip Bennett (Australia); Air Marshal Ewan Jamieson (New Zealand); and Admiral William Crowe (United States). COURTESY OF SIR EWAN JAMIESON

Australian Prime Minister, Bob Hawke, with David Lange. 'I felt I was dealing with a buffoon' – Hawke. *DOMINION POST* COLLECTION, ALEXANDER TURNBULL LIBRARY

David Lange is greeted by Japanese Prime Minister Yasuhiro Nakasone while in Delhi for the funeral ceremonies of Indira Gandhi, October 1984. *DOMINION POST* COLLECTION, ALEXANDER TURNBULL LIBRARY

'New Zealand Speaks'.
CARTOON BY PATRICK COOK, *NATIONAL TIMES*, CANBERRA, 28 SEPTEMBER–4 OCTOBER 1984; REPRODUCED BY KIND PERMISSION

The President and Secretary of State: George Shultz was the only Cabinet member who had private bi-weekly meetings with President Reagan.
RONALD REAGAN PRESIDENTIAL LIBRARY

Former and future leaders of the Labour Party: Helen Clark leads David Lange out of the Labour caucus room. *DOMINION POST* COLLECTION, ALEXANDER TURNBULL LIBRARY

Left Postcard of USS *Buchanan* sent at the time its visit to New Zealand was declined. COURTESY OF LEE NOLAND

Below David Lange with New Zealand's ambassador to the United States, Sir Wallace (Bill) Rowling. Rowling blamed Lange for the crisis, saying 'there had been an agreement, clearly understood, but New Zealand had not lived up to it'. DOMINION POST COLLECTION, ALEXANDER TURNBULL LIBRARY

Above President Reagan walking the family dog, Lucky, with British Prime Minister Margaret Thatcher in the White House garden on 20 February 1985 – the height of the ANZUS dispute. 'The US and Britain could not put their defence policies in little boxes – nuclear here non-nuclear there' – Thatcher. RONALD REAGAN PRESIDENTIAL LIBRARY

Below 'No Parking between Wars'. CARTOON BY RAY OSRIN, *CLEVELAND PLAIN DEALER*, 25 FEBRUARY 1985; REPRODUCED BY KIND PERMISSION OF THE RAY OSRIN ESTATE

Above The Oxford Union debate. From left: Reverend Jerry Falwell; Roland Rudd, President of the Union; and Prime Minister Lange. AP/WIRE

David Lange calls on Margaret Thatcher after the Oxford Union debate. *DOMINION POST* COLLECTION, ALEXANDER TURNBULL LIBRARY

Above The General Secretary of the Chinese Communist Party, Hu Yaobang, with the Prime Minister in Wellington on 19 April 1985. Defence Minister Frank O'Flynn (second from right) stands behind the Chinese leader. DOMINION POST COLLECTION, ALEXANDER TURNBULL LIBRARY

Below 'Nukebusters': Prime Minister David Lange and Naomi Lange at Victoria Falls on an official visit to Zambia, April 1985. COURTESY OF DOMINION POST

Above left Deputy Prime Minister Geoffrey Palmer. DOMINION POST COLLECTION, ALEXANDER TURNBULL LIBRARY

Above right Richard Armitage. COURTESY OF RICHARD ARMITAGE

Below Queen Elizabeth II with the New Zealand High Commissioner, Bryce Harland, in the Savill Garden, Windsor Great Park. COLLECTION OF THE AUTHOR

Above David Lange with his Cabinet colleagues David Caygill and Mike Moore. DOMINION POST COLLECTION, ALEXANDER TURNBULL LIBRARY

Below Credentials ceremony, Government House, Auckland, January 1986. From left: Prime Minister David Lange; Governor-General Sir Paul Reeves; the newly appointed United States ambassador, Paul Cleveland; the US Consul-General, Gary Posz; and the Deputy Chief of Mission at the US Embassy, Richard W. Teare. COURTESY OF AMBASSADOR PAUL CLEVELAND

Above Michael Armacost with President Reagan and George Shultz.
COURTESY OF MICHAEL ARMACOST

Below Prime Minister Lee Kuan Yew of Singapore is greeted by David Lange at Wellington Airport. 'Was it all worth it – the balls would bounce the same way in the end' – Lee Kuan Yew. *DOMINION POST* COLLECTION, ALEXANDER TURNBULL LIBRARY

Above The co-presidents of the International Physicians for the Prevention of Nuclear War, Bernard Lown (USA) and Evgueni Chazov (Soviet Union), flank David Lange at the organisation's World Congress in Cologne in May 1986. 'Lange was trying to dance at two weddings' – Erich Geiringer. AP/WIRE

Below Britain's Foreign Secretary, Sir Geoffrey Howe, welcomes David Lange to the Foreign and Commonwealth Office in London. DOMINION POST COLLECTION, ALEXANDER TURNBULL LIBRARY

Above David Lange and the Secretary of Foreign Affairs and Trade, Merv Norrish (centre), meet Secretary of State George P. Shultz in Manila in June 1986.
DOMINION POST COLLECTION, ALEXANDER TURNBULL LIBRARY

Below Prime Minister Lange is kicked out of Café ANZUS.
CARTOON BY TOM SCOTT, 5 JULY 1986; REPRODUCED BY KIND PERMISSION

nearing completion. The Prime Minister decided that I should go to Washington at once to see what could be saved. It might still be possible to soften the intelligence restrictions before the concrete hardened but it was not clear what sort of welcome would be offered there. An inter-agency meeting discussed the visit as I crossed the Pacific on 21 February and considered whether only one person should be made available to talk to me. In the end, though, it was agreed that I could put my case to the heads of all the intelligence agencies and to the State Department and National Security Council. A dark, wintry day echoed the mood as Simon Murdoch, the embassy's Intelligence Liaison Officer, worked through the meetings with me. It quickly became clear that in one sense I was too late. The decisions had already been taken by the President and could only be defended, with varying degrees of vigour, by those I spoke to. All that could be done was to emphasise the wisdom of a reconsideration when tempers had cooled, and in the meantime the need for great care in implementing the decisions if the situation was not to be made worse.

I protested that 45 years of cooperation had been swept away without consultation – what conclusion were the other partners, Britain, Canada and Australia, to draw? It made little sense to choose as a mark of American displeasure restrictions which were largely invisible to the public but which damaged our common Western interests. If, as they claimed, New Zealand had retreated into a parochial view of the world, the answer surely was to share more information, not less. The ANZUS alliance had overwhelming support in the country, but with a public debate getting under way, this was a time which called for sensitive management by a large ally. To mishandle it would bring accusations of interference and could provoke an upsurge of anti-American nationalism and even of non-aligned sentiment.

In a series of hour-long meetings around Washington all this was heard courteously enough but with little sign of agreement. Michael Armacost at the State Department complained that the US had looked on the bright side for months but after the rejection of *Buchanan* a painful choice had to be made. To my urging that the US would have to step very carefully, he retorted that it was not the US that was filing for divorce: 'Hell, we're being told we can't come into the bedroom any more.' It was clear, he said, that some members of the Labour Party had no interest in an amicable solution and quoted O'Flynn, 'it is all inconsequential'.

At the CIA my appointment was with the hawkish Director, William Casey, but after a flurry while I waited in his ante-room, I was instead shown in to see his deputy, John McMahon. He seemed uncomfortable and said, 'Do you want the bad news now?' For the first time he spelt out the President's restrictions on intelligence cooperation. He made a proper defence against my opposition but was careful to point out that these were national decisions and not what the Agency itself would have advocated. The same point was made by the head of the National Security Agency who was clearly unhappy; both agencies felt they had been overruled by higher authority on exchanges they would have preferred to maintain.

In the White House basement Admiral Poindexter, the Deputy Secretary of the National Security Council, outlined the restrictions on defence cooperation. He proved to be a devoted listener, laboriously taking down page after page of notes to the point where I felt I should have shortened my presentation to spare his writing arm. He agreed with the importance of careful risk management. The President did not want to go down in history as having 'lost New Zealand' and had directed that the reaction should be controlled and not 'petulant'. No public announcement would be made and the story would be downplayed if it leaked, unless there were any distortions on the New Zealand side. His parting words were, 'We both have to manage it very carefully.'

The winter darkness had descended when we met in the early evening with Morton Abramowitz, the Director of the State Department's Bureau of Intelligence and Research. His message was bleakly frank. He had not been surprised by the *Buchanan* rejection though everyone else had been 'floored'. He had been depressed by his visit to New Zealand in November, finding no real evidence of the government's commitment to ease the port ban and believing that officials were deluding themselves. Instead he had sensed a strong and widely held moral conviction that New Zealand should show the world the way.

He said it was felt in Washington that Lange had misled the US over the *Buchanan* visit in the sense that he had never been prepared to make the public case for it. 'He let events direct his policy' and had no real sense of where he privately claimed he wanted to go. Abramowitz agreed that the new measures would damage the alliance relationship with New Zealand but argued that disadvantage was outweighed by the need to safeguard the US's other alliances. When I asked whether this was a wise way to treat an ally of more than 40 years, he shrugged and said, 'So be it.'

My briefing for the Prime Minister was therefore not very encouraging. Whatever differences of emphasis there were among the agencies, the Administration's overall reaction was strong and unforgiving. Two points were clear. The overriding priority was the other alliances and they were obviously worried about Australia and Japan. New Zealand, however pro-American, could not weigh in the balance against these two. 'Some cold decisions have been made on the US's interests in the Pacific, and New Zealand is not judged to be a vital one.' The second was that the Administration regarded its response as restrained – 'a controlled burn-off'. It could do more, depending on Wellington's actions and statements which they would continue to monitor closely. 'The signal is that they will play it carefully if we do.'*

The next step was to visit our other three partners to check their reactions. In the light of the American reductions in intelligence sharing (still not formally announced to us), they had reluctantly to make some corresponding adjustments. Information received from the Americans could not be passed to New Zealand, and since the huge American system dominated the flow of intelligence this put the other partners to considerable effort and expense in editing

---

* These accounts of the meetings on 22/23 February 1985 are from my notes taken at the time.

material for Wellington. Although Canberra had to make the largest adjustment, the other two were as anxious as possible to be helpful, partly from a slightly exasperated sympathy with New Zealand but mainly to ensure that the five-nation partnership survived in as complete a form as possible.

In Ottawa, Marcel Massé, the head of External Affairs, said there had been some 'testy exchanges' with Washington over the President's directive. They had told the Americans that the measures taken on intelligence were unwise and should be implemented in a way that did least harm to the five-nation intelligence arrangements. It was in Canada's best interests to minimise the short-term damage in the hope of returning as soon as possible to full cooperation. While complying with the American restrictions, they would do their best to help New Zealand and were looking at ways to increase the availability of their own material.

Like the Canadians, the British gently noted the difficulties caused by the ban on ship visits but their immediate concern was for the precedent set by the US response. In Washington I was told 'the British have been all over us' in an effort to limit the damage being done to the last and most durable aspect of the wartime alliance. One relic of that time was the Joint Intelligence Committee which met weekly in London to look at draft assessments and which included representatives of the other partners. It would now be an embarrassment for the British if we continued to attend and we at once made it clear that we would leave. Otherwise the atmosphere was sympathetic, with the British offering to do as much as they could informally, increasing the flow of their own information, where necessary editing out any American-sourced material, and briefing us orally wherever time was too short for editing documents.

In Canberra the Australian attitude was 'entirely proper without being particularly warm'. Unlike the Canadians and British 'they had no criticism to make of either the choice or the severity of the American measures'. But then the greatest burden of helping New Zealand fell on them. As with their programme of defence exercises, they had to split their intelligence sharing into two streams – one for the US and the other partners, and one edited and reworked for New Zealand. New Zealanders seconded to work in their intelligence agencies had to go home but Canberra also promised to do their best to keep up the flow within the letter of the American restrictions.[*]

The Prime Minister arrived in Los Angeles on 25 February, to be met by Rowling, Tim Francis and myself. He was on his way to England to take part in a debate at the Oxford Union but had announced that he would take advantage of his stopover in California to emphasise the continuing importance of ANZUS to New Zealand. In the aftermath of the *Buchanan* it had become a major concern of the government to insist on this. Palmer wrote to Kenneth Dam, his former teacher at Chicago and now Shultz's deputy, to say that he had been heartened by President Reagan's affirmation that ANZUS was very much alive and working: 'We, too, believe that the alliance is basically in good shape.' He wanted to reassure Dam that New Zealand remained a reliable ally, firmly committed to a defence partnership which reflected their common interest.[†]

In the House he ridiculed Opposition claims that New Zealand's ANZUS membership would be ended or suspended, giving a little lecture on American constitutional law to show that ANZUS could only be changed by a two-thirds majority of the Senate.[‡] He and the other lawyers in the government seemed to regard the alliance as akin to a legal contract, the interpretation of which was open to learned argument. General de Gaulle knew better. In the same debate, Lange was characteristically more ambivalent, saying that what had been a conventional alliance was now seen by the present Administration 'as having a part to play in the projection of United

---

[*] My reports to the Prime Minister, 27 February–7 March 1985, PM 59/8/5 Part 3, MFAT.
[†] Palmer to Kenneth Dam, 20 February 1985, PM 111/3/3/1 Part 29, ANZ.
[‡] *New Zealand Parliamentary Debates*, vol. 460, 12 February 1985, pp. 2905–7.

States nuclear power'.* But he too repeated that ANZUS could not fail because 'there is an indivisibility of interest'.†

The United States meanwhile was telling its NATO and other allies of the measures 'curtailing' cooperation with New Zealand. In the hope of encouraging New Zealand to return, it would keep the alliance structure in place and avoid broadly felt damage. For that reason significant elements of defence cooperation would be preserved, including arms sales and logistic support, and some sharing of intelligence. Washington was prepared to accept New Zealand's non-nuclear position on ship visits provided that country in return respected its NCND policy. It did not want to give way to petulance, spoiling the chances of an eventual policy reversal by New Zealand, 'upsetting our far more important relationship with Australia, or encouraging a backlash in third-world countries'.‡

The Prime Minister's stopover provided the State Department with a suitable opportunity to formally pass these measures to him. The President's directive was completed and signed; the question was who could deliver it. The well-regarded Bill Brown, Principal Deputy Assistant Secretary in the hierarchy and Wolfowitz's deputy, was despatched to Los Angeles to pronounce the excommunication. Choosing someone of middle rank might have been thought to convey something of Washington's displeasure (Shultz himself had been in Los Angeles the day before), but Brown said it was purely accidental – he was the only one available to go at short notice.§

The meeting took place on 26 February at the home of the Consul-General, Peter Heenan, in the suburb of Brentwood. Bill Brown encountered Lange in the hotel cafeteria early that morning (the Prime Minister had just appeared on *Good Morning America* at 5 a.m.) and confirmed the arrangements with him. The New Zealand party

---

* Ibid., p. 2900.
† Press conference, 18 February 1985.
‡ Briefing for Britain, Canada, other NATO countries and Australia, 3 March 1985, State Department Papers.
§ Interview with Brown, 21 September 2011.

preferred to meet at the Consul-General's house rather than the Prime Minister's hotel. The Americans thought the change had been made to discourage any press interest so Brown tipped off several reporters in advance. At nine o'clock in the morning everyone gathered around the table in the Consul-General's dining room, with two Americans, Bill Brown and his colleague Jon Glassman from the State Department, on one side and Lange, Rowling, Francis and myself, together with the Consul-General and Margaret Pope, on the other.

In all but bell, book and candle, Brown's manner conveyed the ecclesiastical solemnity of the occasion. But before he could start he was a little taken aback when Lange pointed out that his message had already been leaked in considerable detail that morning in London, Canberra and Honolulu where Admiral Crowe had issued a statement that Brown could only call 'regrettable'. He then set out the backdrop to the Administration's decision. The US had sought to work with New Zealand over the past seven months on the basis of an assurance that Lange would seek to change public and party attitudes in order to ease the issue of ship visits. The ship *Buchanan* and the timing of its visit had been chosen on the advice of New Zealand officials. New Zealand had unexpectedly rejected it and thus became the only allied country to refuse a visit by an American ship. The US had been deeply hurt by this, 'especially as they had been led to believe that the *Buchanan* proposal would go through without a hiccup'. After that the country could not expect to receive the benefits of a good ally. The Administration was not trying to punish the country but it had to respond to the operational changes New Zealand had imposed.

The Prime Minister did not comment on what assurances had been given over the *Buchanan* visit but said he had never backtracked on ship visits and that it was he in September who had urged the US to make a request for a visit rather than delay any further. He repeated New Zealand's view that ANZUS was a conventional alliance which did not bind it on nuclear matters and this view had been endorsed by a general election. The moribund Muldoon administration and its ANZUS Council communiqué had entrenched the divisions between the two governments and there had been inaccurate reporting by the embassy in Wellington. He was, however, determined to maintain his country's commitments to the alliance. He then asked for the list of measures to be outlined.

Brown would not hand over a copy of the list, presumably because the Administration feared the Prime Minister would release it. Stating that the Administration wished to keep the door open and see a review of the policy on port access, he then went through the list in full detail. On intelligence the US would no longer hand over finished assessments. New Zealand diplomats and liaison officers would not receive briefings or be able to attend intelligence conferences hosted by the US. No 'imagery' or intelligence derived from satellites would be made available and New Zealand officers at CINCPAC headquarters in Honolulu and American intelligence agencies would not be replaced at the end of their present terms. Not all was lost: cooperation in electronic 'signals' intelligence would continue on a more restricted basis and the US would continue to provide some information on Soviet activities in the Pacific and on any security threats to New Zealand or its forces overseas. In practice the American intelligence community tried to give New Zealand the benefit of the doubt wherever there was room for a favourable interpretation.

On the military side the thinking was similar. All exercises with New Zealand would be cancelled and the US would try to exclude it from other multinational exercises in which the US was also involved. Existing secondments with both defence forces would not be replaced and all talks, conferences and military exchanges with New Zealand would be postponed indefinitely, except where New Zealand's security interests were threatened. There would be no expansion of the long-standing cooperation on logistical support but it was not cancelled and defence purchasing was not excluded. As with New Zealand's intelligence partners, the Pentagon was quick thereafter to hint at the possibility of building a worthwhile defence relationship 'of some sort'. Military staff were anxious to preserve the 'empty chair' to which they hoped New Zealand might in time return.*

There were one or two modifications to the list as given to the embassy and me in the previous week. In particular, nothing was said about the future of the next ANZUS Council. None of the concessions were major but they did confirm the Administration's assurance that it wanted to peg the relationship where it was at present and not see any further erosion. There was one exception: henceforth the New Zealand ambassador's access to Administration officials would be limited to Wolfowitz's level and below. This was petty. Halting any possibility of the ambassador's talking to the people who mattered most made little sense and caused chronic irritation for years. Some, like Armitage in the Defense Department who liked Rowling, were reduced to having him to an occasional quiet dinner at home.

Lange took notes throughout the presentation – the only time Brown had ever seen a Prime Minister doing so. When Brown had finished reading the lesson, Lange said, 'That's a pretty heavy meal', later continuing the food metaphor by saying to the press, 'but we can digest it'. He seemed almost relieved, welcoming the assurances that the Administration was determined to keep this a controlled and measured response. In an aside to me he whispered, 'Thank God they didn't touch trade.' Brown had indeed emphasised that trade issues would be kept separate and dealt with outside the treaty relationship. New Zealand's exemption from the Gatt Subsidies Code, which gave its lamb exports some protection against complaints from American sheep farmers, would expire at the end of March, but that had been a temporary concession and its expiry had nothing to do with ANZUS.

When Brown said that the Administration continued to hope that the ships ban was reversible, Lange said the answer was a categorical 'no'. New Zealand's position on nuclear weapons was not reversible and he had constantly reiterated this. 'As Prime Minister

---

* Memo by Head of Defence Liaison Staff, Washington embassy, 25 February 1985, PM 59/8/5 Part 3, MFAT.

I am confronted with the choice of either accepting an easy docile relationship with the United States or standing firm on government policy which, given the nationalistic response which any apparent external interference would evoke, would widen the range of political support I receive.' He would not yield to the temptation to enhance his domestic standing but it was hard to see the practical sense of the measures Brown had outlined – they were excessive and an attempt to intervene in the country's internal politics. 'I think it *is* punishment.'

In the subsequent discussion, Brown expressed concern about Russian activities in the Pacific and read parts of a lengthy statement made in Tashkent a day or so earlier by Jim Knox, the New Zealand trade union leader, describing US imperialism as a threat to world peace. Knox's burst of Marxist eloquence gave the Prime Minister some merriment as he pointed out that the statement – in official Sovietese – was highly unlikely to have been Knox's own effort. Lange was well aware of what the Russians were up to in Cam Ranh Bay and New Zealand would continue to play a major part in stopping them from moving into the South Pacific.

Then at the end Lange's tone became sharper. He needed to give the people of New Zealand an assurance that their security would be safeguarded. The measures outlined by Brown were far from being reasonable or moderate and he would have difficulty holding back a vigorous and nationalistic response. Nothing would be easier than for the government to exploit nationalistic feelings but it would not take this path. New Zealand was committed 'to remaining a good ally'. It was not some kind of Central American country and it would be unwise to treat it as if it was another Nicaragua.[*]

The 50-minute meeting ended on this rather sombre note. Brown and Glassman left, with Brown giving a fairly neutral statement to some members of the press waiting in the street (though not 'the hundreds of journos and television crews, pushing each other

---

[*] This account of the meeting has been put together from two reports in PM 59/8/5 Part 3, MFAT, the interview with Brown, the Lange Papers, Box 27, ANZ, and my own notes.

around' remembered two years later by Lange).* The New Zealand party lingered for five or ten minutes to talk over the proceedings. When everyone came out into the sunshine they found the two Americans standing rather forlornly on the pavement. They had come by taxi but in leafy Brentwood there were no cruising cabs to hail. They gratefully accepted the offer of a ride back into town with the New Zealand party, and the journey and its amicable conversation somehow underlined the artificiality of the excommunication which everyone had just attended.

At the end of the morning the Prime Minister was to speak at a lunch given by the 'New Zealand Connection', a gathering of expatriate businessmen and others with an interest in New Zealand. He would clearly be expected to say something about the Brentwood meeting. So while he called on Tom Bradley, the Mayor of Los Angeles, three of us hastily put together a preamble to his speech. In it he confirmed that he had just been given the list of measures which was the Administration's response to New Zealand's desire to keep itself nuclear-free. 'They amount in effect to a drastic scaling down of cooperation with New Zealand' in the areas of intelligence sharing and defence and were serious and to some extent damaging. 'They are not in my view the kind of actions which a great power should take against a small, loyal ally which has stood by it, through thick and thin, in peace and war', but though they might be ill-judged they would in no way undermine New Zealand's total commitment to the Western alliance or to ANZUS.

The Prime Minister's arrival for lunch at the Ambassador Hotel got off to a slightly discomforting start. He was driven into the underground garage and his security detail insisted on leading everyone in through the hotel kitchen where Robert Kennedy had been shot in 1968, a coincidence on which Lange commented with nervous jocularity. He still remembered it years later, saying that the hair had risen on the back of his neck.

---

* Vernon Wright interview, 5 December 1986, Lange Papers, Box 1, ANZ.

His speech had been worked on by Margaret Pope throughout the overnight journey from Auckland, including a stopover in Honolulu in the small hours. It recapitulated the familiar nuclear themes. New Zealand had never been part of a nuclear strategy and did not wish to shelter under America's nuclear capability even as a deterrent to any attacker. In this it did not offer itself as an example to others; its strategic circumstances were unique – 'We are isolated and remote'. His underlying fears about trade came through clearly. New Zealand was very vulnerable and could be hurt by American trade sanctions. But it was a question of what the US really wanted to achieve; the last time it had imposed sanctions was over the Soviet invasion of Afghanistan. Stimulated by the occasion and the morning's excitement, Lange embroidered and extended the text with his finest eloquence and felt it to be one of the best speeches he ever gave.

It was followed by a half-hour session, chaired by the New Zealander Peter Watson (who afterwards served in the George H. W. Bush White House), in which the Prime Minister replied to questions. Everything went smoothly and the meeting with the press also went well. Like any star, Lange liked to remember these occasions: 'There was a marvellous press conference session afterwards with television cameras, 30 or 40 of them set up around the back, journalists all around the place. It was sort of eye-in-the-storm stuff.'[*]

However, for reasons which the New Zealand party never quite understood, the speech gave further offence to the Administration. The State Department claimed it was a 'gross distortion' to say that the US had sought the meeting, though Lange and the rest of his party had all thought that to deliver the list was why Brown had flown to Los Angeles. The press described it as raising the dispute over the ships ban to a new level. According to the *Washington Post*, 'New Zealand Prime Minister David Lange threatened today to reduce South Pacific maritime surveillance and other activities important to the US in retaliation for U.S. sanctions against his nation'. This

---

[*] Vernon Wright interview, 5 December 1986.

was the opposite of the point Lange was trying to make, that any economic retaliation by the US would damage New Zealand's ability to contribute to the security of the South Pacific.

As is usually the case with disputes, talking seemed to make matters worse. It was becoming increasingly hard for both sides to treat the whole issue as simply a difference of interpretation. The Administration believed that rejection of a visit by a US warship was incompatible with membership, or at least full membership, of the alliance. By banning even the possibility of nuclear weapons in its harbours New Zealand was single-handedly attempting to alter the terms of the alliance for its own benefit. Since this was unacceptable to the other two partners Wellington had a choice, either to amend its ban or withdraw from the alliance. The American problem was that New Zealand did not see it as a problem and declined to make such a choice. In fact it was unable to choose. With the public strongly in favour of ANZUS membership and almost equally opposed to the presence of nuclear weapons, the government was transfixed, unable to do more than repeat that both were essential.

Had New Zealand not been an alliance member its nuclear policies would have been its own affair and none of Washington's business. However, the country's insistence on staying in the alliance while restricting its defence cooperation required a corresponding readjustment or scaling down of cooperation by its American partner. In their eyes therefore the restrictions were not 'punishment' for rejecting a ship visit but a logical response to a reduced alliance commitment.

This might have seemed a persuasive argument in departmental conference rooms but it was too fine a distinction to survive in public perceptions. Sir Robert Muldoon liked to contend that for public discussion issues had to be black or white; shades of grey might be necessary for implementing a policy but not for explaining it. This was certainly true of the Administration's list of measures. Days had been spent in carefully calibrating the response in order to signal a changed relationship but not a hostile one, but the distinction was lost as soon as it emerged into the light. When they became public no one thought for a moment that they were simply a logical readjustment of alliance responsibilities. In Congress and among the more populist commentators they were hailed as a well-deserved punchback for New Zealand's abrupt and unfriendly challenge.

Equally inevitably they were seen in that country as a peevish overreaction, the kick of a great power irritated at being defied. The measures fell between two targets: as punishment it was not enough to change people's minds but it was enough to cause New Zealanders to resent that they were being singled out for a stance they had freely chosen. The Foreign Office had thought, 'The Americans would be better to leave well alone, so as to reduce public interest in this issue.'* This was not possible, because New Zealand was still an alliance member and Australia and other allies were pressing for credible evidence that it would not receive special treatment. But the argument by Washington officials that they were simply making a rational response was undercut by the undisguised resentment they displayed. They were human and were deeply angered by having been, as they felt, deceived by the Prime Minister and his officials.

The policy differences had now become a quarrel. In Parliament, Palmer described the US response as an overreaction and 'extremely harsh'. Although they would diminish the operational capabilities of the armed forces the measures would not change the government's policy: '[We] are not going to bend to their will in the matter.'† One or two editorials complained that the country was 'going it alone' and risking more than the temporary goodwill of its friends but their misgivings were lost in a surge of public approval. Once the public had been reassured about the explicit exclusion of trade, the excommunication ceremony in Los Angeles rose above the technical details of intelligence and defence to become a question of national independence and identity. In his Los Angeles speech, Lange had begun to sound the note which became dominant after his appearance at the

---

* Think-piece by the South Pacific Department, 18 February 1985, FCO Papers.
† *New Zealand Parliamentary Debates*, vol. 461, 27 February 1985, p. 3300.

Oxford Union. New Zealand was right to hold to its principles and resist American pressure. The Prime Minister should be seen as 'a practical idealist who puts New Zealand's interests first but has perceived the opportunity to give a moral lead to mankind'.[*] The Leader of the Opposition, Jim McLay, was portrayed as an American lackey and those who queried the logic of the ship visits policy were swept away by the flood of Lange's emotional rhetoric, intimidated by periodic charges that they were 'snuggling up to the bomb' and 'cleaning the Americans' boots with their tongue'.

Underneath the rhetoric, however, there was a need for a fresh look at New Zealand's policy. Assertions that the country remained a full and reliable member of the alliance were not accepted by either of the other two partners and to keep saying so was pointless. If alliance membership was to be reconciled with the nuclear policy another ship visit was required. With the most plausible candidate just rejected it was not clear, while the United States kept a resolute hold on NCND, how another could fare better. Nonetheless, the search for an acceptable ship, or rather a procedure for admitting it which both sides could accept, had to continue. The ingenious possibilities that were devised all suffered from the same disadvantage: they hinged on the Americans putting their trust in the Prime Minister, and after the *Buchanan* affair the Administration had none. Future promises to pay were no longer acceptable tender because New Zealand had no credit left in Washington.

The search dominated the relationship for the next eighteen months but it was to hold decreasing interest for the Prime Minister as we farewelled him that afternoon on the breezy tarmac of Los Angeles airport. Events were propelling him on a new path as an anti-nuclear celebrity. If he had let events dictate his policy, he was supremely good at oratory, and New Zealand's political pop star was about to achieve the greatest triumph of his premiership at the Oxford Union.

---

[*] BHC, Wellington, report, 27 February 1985, FCO Papers.

Chapter Eight
The Oxford Union Debate

The debate which took place in the galleried hall of the Oxford Union had a significance much greater than those who organised it could ever have hoped. It was felt by almost all who were closest to Lange to have been decisive in locking him into his role as anti-nuclear crusader. In the view of Ross Vintiner, his chief press secretary, he had previously taken the opportunistic view that was natural to him, letting the flow of events decide where he would stand. Now he saw the international possibilities and pleasures which were opened up by his eloquence as a spokesman for all those who feared the irrationality of a spiralling nuclear arms race. His deputy, Geoffrey Palmer, agreed. He thought the debate was pivotal; Lange, who did not seem deeply committed before, was afterwards devoted to the cause.[*]

---

[*] Vintiner interview, Bassett Papers, 6 September 2006, and interview with Palmer, 15 July 2011.

That a university debating society should have delivered such consequences was accidental but not surprising. Against the background of considerable concern about nuclear weapons in both Europe and North America, the wide publicity given to the rejection of *Buchanan* would have ensured an audience for Lange wherever he had spoken outside New Zealand. Speaking at the Union was a distinction in itself, but to speak on defence was even more notable because of the reverberations from an earlier and even more famous debate. Around the same February date in 1933 the motion 'That this House will in no circumstances fight for its King and Country' was carried by 275 votes to 153. It was a piece of undergraduate fun and many of those who voted with the majority fought bravely in the subsequent war. There was predictable anger in Britain, and Cambridge threatened to withdraw from the Boat Race. But it also resonated abroad, in Europe and North America, and plausibly encouraged the aggressors of the 1930s: Hitler concluded that Britain's youth would not fight and Mussolini saw Britain as 'a frightened, flabby old woman'.[*]

The year before Lange's appearance there had been another, less resounding, debate. In February 1984 the American Defence Secretary, Caspar Weinberger, and a British anti-nuclear campaigner had debated the motion 'That there is no moral difference between the foreign policies of the USA and USSR'. The evening before the debate Mrs Thatcher telephoned Weinberger to say, 'Are you mad, Cap?' Though she argued that he could not win before such an audience, he went ahead and won by 271 to 232.[†] According to a colleague he won in the last minute with his closing sentence: 'However you feel about this motion, when you go home tonight you will never have to fear a midnight knock on the door.'[‡]

---

[*] Winston Churchill, *The Second World War*, vol. 1, *The Gathering Storm*, Cassell and Co. Ltd, 1948, p. 131.
[†] *Montreal Gazette*, 29 February 1984.
[‡] Interview with Armitage, 26 September 2011.

Towards the end of 1984, Jeya Wilson, a New Zealander of Sri Lankan descent who was treasurer (and later president) of the Union, urged making an effort to get the new and exciting Prime Minister of New Zealand. The President, a tall young man named Roland Rudd, looked at possible topics, decided that nuclear weapons was the obvious one and got in touch with Lange's office. The Prime Minister was attracted by the possibility and gave his early agreement, though the exact motion was left vague and no opponent had yet been found. Wilson and Rudd said they would look for someone close to the Reagan Administration and Billy Graham's name was mentioned.

Early in the New Year, Vintiner, who was making the arrangements on the New Zealand side, was told that Lange would be debating with Jerry Falwell, an undistinguished television evangelist whose Moral Majority had worked hard for President Reagan's re-election the previous November. He was also told that the motion would be 'That the Western nuclear alliance is morally indefensible' which had been approved by Falwell. It was understandable that he would have done so, since he would be able to paint Lange as having no difficulties with the Soviet nuclear alliance, only with the Western one. It was equally unacceptable to the Prime Minister. It would be politically (and economically) disastrous for him to seem to be siding with the Soviet Union against NATO and indeed the whole Western alliance system.[*]

Rudd agreed to consider new wording and Vintiner proposed 'That nuclear weapons are morally indefensible'. He then had considerable difficulty in getting hold of young Mr Rudd to get this confirmed and began to suspect that, having secured Falwell's assent to the earlier version, Rudd feared he would pull out if it were changed. Even after agreement was reached on the new wording and work began on Lange's speech, Vintiner was cautious, believing that both sides may have been led to believe that a different motion was to be debated.[†]

---

[*] This and the following paragraphs draw much on Bruce Brown's excellent account, 'The Great Debate at the Oxford Union', in Margaret Clark (ed.), *For the Record: Lange and the Fourth Labour Government*, Dunmore Press, 2005, pp. 158–67.
[†] Vintiner to the writer, 4 December 2011.

When the Prime Minister reached London at the end of February it was found that the wording of the motion had indeed gone back to the original proposal on the *Western* nuclear alliance. There were already stories in the press including *The Times* that this would be the topic. Rudd was hastily summoned to the Howard Hotel in London the night before the debate and given an ultimatum by Lange: either the motion was the one he had agreed or there would be no debate. This was no bluff. He had told Baroness Young from the Foreign Office that he would otherwise not take part; and he asked the High Commission to find a platform and an audience, if necessary in New Zealand House, where he could give his prepared speech.*

Rudd was upset. He said that Falwell had probably already left the United States, the Union had spent a considerable amount of money, including first-class airfares for both speakers, and if the debate was called off it would be bankrupted. However, he had no choice but to agree and went back to Oxford, a little shaken by his clash with 'the grumpy man in the Howard Hotel'.† Falwell also agreed to the revised topic when he reached London but it was too late to change his prepared speech which suffered accordingly. Much of it was based on the argument that the *Western* nuclear alliance was necessary because of the threat posed by the *Soviet* nuclear alliance.

That, however, was far from being the only difficulty faced by the motion. Lange had accepted the invitation without consulting anyone, and as soon as it was known, he faced a wave of advice to reconsider it. Moore told him it was unbecoming; Margaret Wilson said the issue was settled in the Labour Party and to debate it would be a high risk – did he really need it? He said that he wanted to do it, that it was important to do it, and she was left with the feeling that he was already composing the speech in his head. Russell Marshall thought the speech he gave 'was not a statesman's speech, it was an entertainer's speech' and he should have weighed the adulation

---

* He also apparently tried out on Lady Young his famous line, 'I can smell the uranium on your breath'. She was not amused.
† Interview with Roland Rudd, 2 December 2011.

against the more important reactions in Britain and the US. Even Jeremy Pope, in the Commonwealth Secretariat, rang from London to advise against it. In Wellington the *Evening Post* thought that whether or not Lange triumphed in the debate, 'he and his country have much more to lose than Mr Falwell'.*

The heads of both the Foreign Ministry and the Prime Minister's Department were of the same mind. To argue publicly in another country that the foundation of its defence was immoral was to court trouble, particularly when he himself had several times assured both the British Prime Minister and other Europeans that he accepted their need for the nuclear deterrent and would do the same if New Zealand found itself 'only a bus ride' from Soviet territory. The timing was particularly delicate given New Zealand's regular need to renew access for its butter and lamb to the European market, over which every country in the Community had a veto. Negotiations had been held up for months by the unwillingness of French and Irish Ministers to agree to a continuation of the imports and it required British pressure and the use of their diminishing negotiating coin to get a deal that was crucial to the New Zealand economy. If Mrs Thatcher was annoyed by what was said at Oxford and the British sat on their hands during the next round of negotiations beginning in late 1985, New Zealand had no other leverage to get a satisfactory outcome.

There was indeed considerable concern in London over the possible effects of what the Foreign Secretary referred to in Cabinet as 'this media circus'. A senior Foreign Office official took Bruce Brown, Deputy High Commissioner, to lunch to say that they were surprised that Lange would speak on the motion: 'It would be pretty rum if the Prime Minister of one (very friendly) country argued in another that the policies of its government were morally wrong', and would make discussions between the two PMs difficult. Brown said he was 'equally surprised' – all arrangements for the debate had been made between the Prime Minister's Office and the Union. The Foreign

---

* *Evening Post*, 26 February 1985.

Ministry and High Commission had been bypassed and had to pick up information from people with Labour Party connections like Jeremy Pope. He undertook to seek enlightenment from Wellington and a little later was able to report that Lange had insisted on changing the subject to concentrate not on the Western alliance but on nuclear weapons in general.*

This was an improvement but the Foreign Secretary, Sir Geoffrey Howe, still thought that Brown should be called in to be told 'in suitably undramatic terms' that the motion would be seen as an attack on NATO, would weaken the Western position on arms control, be provocative to the US and other countries, was insensitive to the Pershing and cruise missile deployment difficulties still faced by Belgium and the Netherlands, and would be damaging to the New Zealand cause in the European Economic Community (EEC). A list like this was dramatic enough but there was more: the debate could cause political trouble for the Conservative Government in Britain. As the Foreign Office noted, because of the ANZUS row, anything said by Lange would get great publicity and what he would say went to the heart of a major difference between the Government and the Labour Opposition which advocated unilateral nuclear disarmament.

So the High Commissioner in Wellington was instructed to talk to Lange, but quietly and informally to avoid any attempt to portray London's worries as an attempt to muzzle the Prime Minister. O'Leary reported that the cheerful Lange was not at all affronted by the approach and equally unwilling to suggest that he might pull out of the debate. He said he had deliberately insisted on the 'nuclear weapons are morally indefensible' topic, which was a phrase of President Reagan's he had taken from *Time* magazine, because he intended to use the debate to correct the 'false leftist and unilateralist image' being attributed to the New Zealand Government. He would say nothing that could be construed as an attack on the Western alliance or on the necessity for NATO to maintain a nuclear deterrent

---

* Brown to Norrish, 13 February 1985, PM 111/3/3/1 Part 28, ANZ.

– he was in enough trouble already and was determined not to be miscast as an unreliable Western partner.*

Lange was in high spirits when he arrived in London at the end of the month, later saying that he felt bulletproof and demonstrating this by keeping a packed press conference at the High Commission roaring with laughter. The ANZUS alliance continued, he said with legalistic precision – none of the three parties had given the required twelve months' notice to withdraw. His country faced no grave danger; it was far away and unlike continental Europe did not have an arsenal pointed at it. He was picked up on the similarity of his words to those of the appeasement-minded British Prime Minister, Chamberlain, about Czechoslovakia in 1938 and used it to stress his country's efforts to uphold regional stability – New Zealand unlike Britain had a battalion in Singapore. New Zealand might be anti-nuclear but it 'has never been slow in picking up the tab to preserve the values it believes in'.

Amid the excitement, the wisecracks and the offhand dismissals (information on the armament of American warships would be of no help to the Russians because they weren't coming to New Zealand), his comments in London marked a noticeable change in his rhetoric. Whether it was this sharper tone, or that he simply got carried away, he managed to offend the Americans once again. He said that the cutbacks in cooperation announced in Los Angeles were aimed at destabilising and replacing his government and described the American efforts as 'akin to the very totalitarianism we're supposed to be fighting against'.

Polishing the opening speech for the debate brought some different tensions. Margaret Pope brought a draft with her and was given a room at the High Commission to work on it. After something of a struggle, the Deputy High Commissioner was able to insist on checking the text. Arguing that 'you can't say or imply that the Prime Minister of a friendly country favours an immoral policy', Brown

---

* Exchanges between FCO and BHC, Wellington, 17–18 February 1985, FCO Papers.

was able to make a number of deletions and changes to avoid giving undue offence to the British Government. This involved some tense exchanges with the drafter, but in the end 'Bruce won; Margaret Pope sulked'.* Lange rose above her irritable mood and agreed to the changes: 'There was a delicate path to tread there, and we trod it with some finesse I think.' Then he drove to Oxford and, exhausted by his efforts, fell asleep in the car.

His arrival at the university on 1 March was accompanied by the mysterious disorders that so often gathered around David Lange who could to an extent unique among New Zealand parliamentarians produce the manifestations of a political poltergeist. When he reached the Randolph Hotel it was to find that there was both a bomb and a death threat. They had to wait in the manager's office and then the police advised against using the rooms that had been assigned to them. So the Prime Minister was removed to what he later described as a broom cupboard while Ken Richardson, his Private Secretary, volunteered to take his room and reclined there in great luxury 'while I'm in a monk's cell'.†

Rudd had arranged a dinner before the debate and the interest was such that he had to enlarge it to include MPs, editors and other notables as well as the two principals. He saw a more congenial side of Lange, sociable and lively, greeting and shaking hands with everyone, in contrast to the irritable man of the night before. Lange and Falwell met for the first time over dinner. In talking to the Methodist minister, Lange made the most of his own Methodist background to win his respect and perhaps partially disarm him.

The atmosphere was electric with anticipation when they arrived at the Union. Its Victorian debating hall was packed, even the galleries upstairs. The final voting figures of just over 500 understated the numbers because those in the galleries could not get down to vote.

---

* The two quotations are the recollections of Derek Leask who was Counsellor in the High Commission and was interviewed 14 June and 6 July 2012.
† This and the preceding Lange comment are from the Vernon Wright interview, 5 December 1986, Lange Papers, Box 1, ANZ.

As proposer of the motion Lange led off. The speech was eloquent and well-argued but as always his performance was more compelling than his texts. He spoke for twice the length of his notes.*

The only defence of nuclear weapons, he argued, was that they were a necessary evil, an abhorrent means to a desirable end. But the nature of the weapons was such that their very existence corrupted the best of intentions. The means perverted the ends and had brought the greatest of all perversions – the belief that this evil was necessary. The irrational nature of the weapons meant that they did not enhance the security of those they defended – 'The means of defence terrorise as much as the threat of attack' – and to compensate for that insecurity the world was held to ransom by a perpetual cycle of building and deploying more nuclear weapons.

As often with opponents of the arms race, he seemed to be suggesting that it was the weapons that were the problem, rather than the insecurities and fears of those who built them. Like everyone else, he had little to suggest in the way of practical alternatives, only that the great strength of the West lay not in the force of arms but in its free and democratic systems of government. The weapons ignored this true strength and placed everyone's will to live in hostage. Rejecting them was 'to assert what is human over the evil nature of the weapon'.

These arguments were delivered with all the brio, retorts to hecklers and improvised wit that Lange could command. He held the audience in his hand. A young New Zealander at Cambridge returned the next day 'buoyed with the joy of being a New Zealander, mighty among the nations of the world'.† Rudd's recollection was that everyone was flattered by his presence and by the grace and aplomb with which this practised parliamentarian took interjections from the undergraduates. The most memorable moment, then and since, came when a young American naval officer who was a Rhodes Scholar,

---

* The speaking notes are in the Lange Papers, Box 18, ANZ.
† Letter from Justice Stephen Kos, 16 August 2012, quoted with permission.

THE OXFORD UNION DEBATE

Mark Gronslo, objected to this treatment of America's allies. Lange stood up, put his hands on the despatch box, leant over and said, 'I can smell the uranium on your breath.' There was a roar of laughter and Rudd thought it 'a wonderful piece of theatre'.* But years later there were some in Washington who were still angry that a young man in uniform had been held up to ridicule in this way.

Falwell spoke clearly and well but he stuck closely to his text, which because of the change of motion was not as sharply focused as it might have been, and his seconder, the Conservative MP Julian Amery, was felt to be a more effective debater. The Methodist evangelist seemed to have no very deep knowledge of the subject and was uncomfortable with the noisy atmosphere. A man used to the tranquillity of the pulpit or the television studio, where everything down to the lighting was arranged to his wishes, was thrown by the rowdy conduct of a mock parliament with interjections and points of order.

Lange, on the other hand, relished this and his enjoyment showed. An older Rudd remembered him as 'a phenomenal pro at work'. But Derek Leask thought he gave the impression of holding back, of keeping himself on a tight rein, and did not think he was the inspired orator of legend.† Lange himself had been a little apprehensive, feeling that anyone who could not handle a student debate should not be handling the issue itself: 'If Falwell had got the better of me that night I would have gone very rapidly downhill.' He need not have worried; the motion was carried 298 to 250 – not as large as the King and Country vote but a comfortable endorsement.

Inevitably with David Lange there was an odd tailpiece. Ten days later the *Sunday Express* ran a piece in its gossip column, 'Lady Olga Maitland's Diary', saying that though Lange's first-class airfare had been paid by the Oxford Union he had used it for official business around the world, stopping in Los Angeles and going on to Geneva and Singapore. The source was revealed in a rather murky letter

---

* Interview with Rudd, 2 December 2011.
† Interview with Leask, 6 July 2010.

received by the High Commission from two senior members of the Oxford Union Society at All Souls. In the snide tone of university feuds, it complained that Lange had engaged in political discussions round the world on the £3,700 airfare provided 'by a student society with precarious finances'. The story floated about but young Mr Rudd showed precocious public relations skills in sinking it, telling the *Daily Mail*: 'We made about £5,000 from the TV rights, got massive publicity and enjoyed a first-class debate. Mr Lange did us a world of good.'*

In New Zealand the debate was seen as a triumph, dramatising the anti-nuclear policy and doing so before an international television audience. Lange's performance put the small country where it longed always to be, on the world stage. Palmer on behalf of Cabinet sent a telegram: 'Cabinet congratulates you on your commanding performance at the Oxford Union. It was a great victory for you and for New Zealand.' He himself told a press conference that 'people are now feeling good about being New Zealanders'.† Mike Moore concluded that Lange had been right to go ahead and that history would see it as one of the highlights of his political career.‡ Lange's later verdict was fair: 'It has now become part of some peculiar legend of mine.'§ It had not merely justified New Zealand's position, it became a celebration of it.

Others were predictably more grudging. The *Australian* said that Lange's political pilgrimage would do nothing to compensate New Zealand for the damage his government had done to its military alliances, 'but it does seem to have made him into an unlikely folk hero among unilateral disarmers in far-flung reaches of the globe'. The *Sydney Morning Herald* reported it as 'David Topples Goliath' and treated it light-heartedly, straining for a joke about the

---

* Not surprisingly, Roland Rudd went on to make a fortune in public relations and by 2012 was chairman and co-founder of RLM Finsbury, a large financial communications firm.
† Press conference of 4 March 1985 at which Palmer also quoted Cabinet's telegram.
‡ Interview with Moore, 27 September 2011.
§ Vernon Wright interview, 5 December 1986.

ubiquitous brand of Antipodean shoe shine: 'The Brits might have class but the Kiwis have proved they have polish.'*

Though the canny Union had sold television rights to PBS in the United States, which onsold them to the BBC and Television New Zealand, it was never clear whether screenings around the world were as widespread as legend had it in New Zealand. Howe could tell Cabinet in London that the debate had not been 'the media event we feared' and that coverage had been relatively restrained. Kenelm Digby, who moved the King and Country motion and later settled in New Zealand, said 60 years later about his own effort: 'It was just a debate. I don't know what all the fuss was about.'† After the nuclear weapons debate the Foreign Office was inclined to the same view. To their relief it was not broadcast live in Britain and there was little news coverage, though *The Times* ran a summary of Lange's speech on its centre page. There were no reverberations from the peace movement or the unilateralist wing of the British Labour Party except a message of congratulation from Neil Kinnock, the party leader.

That it was not broadcast live was an unexpected advantage. In the course of his bravura improvisations Lange ad libbed several barbed cracks about Mrs Thatcher which went down with uproarious laughter in the Union but would not have improved the atmosphere in Downing Street when he saw her three days later. In the informal way that the visit had been organised by the Prime Minister's Office, it had not apparently occurred to anyone that Lange should pay at least a courtesy call on the Prime Minister of the country he was visiting. After the Foreign Office gently pointed out how 'unusual' this would be (diplomatic politeness for 'rude'), a call was hastily arranged.

As part of her briefing the Foreign Office asked for a transcript of the debate. This was awkward and it was kept waiting over the weekend while Bruce Brown combed the text and removed the

---

* *Australian*, 2–3 March and *Sydney Morning Herald*, 4 March 1985.
† *Evening Post* obituary by Peter Kitchin, 23 August 2001.

offensive witticisms. Its note for Mrs Thatcher described the Union speech as notable for its care not to offend NATO susceptibilities. She was told that public opinion in New Zealand was running strongly in favour of the ships ban. The Americans were regarded as bullies and resentment had been expressed even by right-wing establishment figures. There was also overwhelming support for ANZUS, but on the basis that New Zealand had the right to determine its own policy on ship visits.

Perhaps because of this background, the call (Lange was always a little nervous on these occasions) went unexpectedly well, described (by the High Commission) as 'friends speaking to friends'. He thanked her for going to battle with the Americans over intelligence cooperation and she said firmly that Britain would continue to fight for New Zealand's interests in the EEC and elsewhere. Even her comments on the nuclear question were mild – she had told the Americans that Britain's ties with New Zealand were such that the people would not understand if she were to make any public criticism. On the Union debate, she contented herself with saying that she could not agree that nuclear weapons were morally indefensible if that meant that conventional weapons, like the thousand-bomber raids on Germany or the flying bombs, were somehow more acceptable. Britain, she said, could not accept any breach of NCND and had an obligation to NATO whose deterrent had kept the peace in Europe for 40 years, a remarkable achievement.

Lange was anxious to please and drew a distinction between New Zealanders' view of Britain and the United States. It was inconceivable that the United Kingdom would fly in the face of New Zealand policy on the nuclear ban and it was politically unacceptable in New Zealand to publicly question its actions. New Zealanders would assume that visiting RN ships would not be carrying nuclear weapons. Mrs Thatcher said she could not accept any statement by Wellington to that effect since NCND could not be challenged. He understood that but after consulting his colleagues at home he thought a formula could be found where each country would have its policy but no questions would be asked of any visiting British ship. 'New Zealand would find a solution for the United Kingdom as Japan had for the United States.'

This was a surprising reversion to the classic 'don't ask, don't tell' policy of the NATO anti-nuclear countries, and perhaps owed something to the influence of the newly arrived High Commissioner, Joe Walding, a stoutly practical former Labour Minister who had a day earlier asked me accusingly how we had let the *Buchanan* fiasco happen. If workable it could have removed even the difficulties with the United States, but Lange's distinction was that New Zealanders would accept an ambiguity with British warships that they would not with American. At the end of his note of the meeting, Mrs Thatcher's Private Secretary, Charles Powell, commented that Lange was showing evident signs of wishing to get off the hook but there was scope for continued misunderstanding and the United Kingdom would have to step very carefully.* He was right; the idea thrown out by Lange was never followed up, though the British continued for several months to enquire about its progress. It was most likely a thought of Walding's which the Prime Minister picked up briefly to get him more comfortably through his hour with Mrs Thatcher.

In the midst of this London visit the logic of the quarrel over ANZUS continued to unfold. The original list of measures to be made known in Los Angeles had included postponement of the next ANZUS Council meeting to be held in Canberra in July. This had been removed in response to the embassy's representations that when cooperation in ANZUS was in deep trouble this was hardly the time to suspend high-level political consultations, but the United States remained unwilling to attend if New Zealand was there. It would

---

* A note of the meeting on 4 March is given in PM 111/3/3/1 Part 31, ANZ, and a franker account in Powell's note of the same date, FCO Papers.

look as if the crisis had subsided and relations were returning to normal.

For the same reason it was important to Lange that the Council meet as usual; it would be a reassuring sign to New Zealanders that the alliance relationship was still functioning. He had gambled that the port access ban could be managed within the framework of ANZUS which the country still overwhelmingly supported, by around 78 per cent according to the polls at that time. Exclusion from the next Council would be an alarming sign that he had lost that gamble.

After the Los Angeles meeting he sent Tim Francis back to Washington to urge the Administration not to toss away the relationship 'over the issue of a couple of ships' and to press in particular for an assurance that the Council would meet in July as usual. Cancellation, Francis said, would be disastrous; dialogue had to be maintained to affirm their common interests. The Americans were unpersuaded, seeing it as an obvious effort by Lange to show the New Zealand public that he still had the situation under control. They were still smarting from barbs in London and Oxford about 'totalitarianism' and had not forgotten his dismissal of the last Council meeting as the 'last gasp of a moribund government'. Armacost said that the loss of evident mutuality in alliance obligations had put ANZUS into abeyance. The best that could be done was to keep 'a light in the window' for New Zealand's possible return.[*]

The Americans had already told Hawke of their unwillingness to attend a Council meeting if New Zealand were present and it was planned to issue a joint statement saying that the meeting had been 'postponed' but that Shultz would come to Canberra in July for bilateral talks. Then Hawke struck unexpected trouble; he could not get his Cabinet to agree. Some members felt that it would cause dissension in the ALP and look as if Australia was abandoning New Zealand

---

[*] Francis's report of 1 March, PM 59/8/5 Part 3, MFAT, and State Department cable of 13 March 1985, State Department Papers.

at the bidding of the US. The story began to leak, helped by an incautiously worded reply by Hawke to a parliamentary question, and Hawke felt he had to make a quick announcement on his own, saying that the serious difficulties between the US and New Zealand made holding a meeting impracticable.

It took Washington by surprise and further irritated his Left, compelling him to say that he did not want to stay as Prime Minister if the alliance was questioned. It was an unwelcome surprise too for Wellington which received only fifteen minutes' warning of the announcement. Palmer, who had a few hours earlier said he was unaware of such a possibility, held up gamely. He would not admit that there was a crisis in New Zealand's foreign policy, only 'a major disagreement', and took issue with Hawke's statement that ANZUS was virtually inoperative. The alliance, he said, had three members and unless one gave the required year's notice of withdrawal the obligations of the treaty remained binding. 'There is no doubt that is correct.'[*]

In London, Lange took a less legal but more irritable approach. He ridiculed Hawke, more than once, for allegedly changing his mind three times over the postponement, though the New Zealand High Commission in Canberra pointed out that this was inaccurate. And he retreated further into a nationalist trench. He told the press that the postponement would only harden New Zealand's position: 'You cannot in the end have a situation where a very large country says to a very small one "Alright, you've had your democracy, you've had your election, you've made your decision, now come on – get into line because we say so."'[†] The dispute risked spiralling out of control. It was time for some quiet thought about where New Zealand was heading rather than press conference outbursts.

The cancellation of the Council meant that New Zealand's membership of ANZUS, for long the centre-post of the country's foreign

---

[*] Palmer press conference, 4 March 1985.
[†] Lange press conference (London), 7 March 1985.

policy, had been in effect declared to be 'inoperative'. There was no point in continuing to quarrel over the *Buchanan* decision and the American response. The more important question was what to do next, especially when most New Zealanders still saw the alliance as essential to their security. Palmer thought that a long-term strategy was needed, suggesting to Lange (who was on his way home) that they would have to look at whether New Zealand was heading towards some sort of 'armed neutrality', whether it would increase its reliance on Australia, and whether it needed other friends – if so, he said pertinently, who might they be?* Norrish took a less wide-ranging view, telling his colleagues that over time it might be possible, not to get back to ANZUS, but gradually to rebuild confidence to the point of being able to resume small-scale cooperation and exercises with the Americans in the South Pacific.† Whatever the remedies favoured, it was clear that how to function outside the alliance framework and how to repair the bilateral relationship had become the most urgent issues for New Zealand's foreign policy.

The answer that emerged was called 'pro-Western regionalism', in the hope of mollifying New Zealand's friends and signalling that the country was not embracing non-alignment. It was described as 'a dramatic shift in emphasis', demonstrating New Zealand's determination to be self-reliant but to continue to support the Western alliance.‡ The country would no longer look at the wider world as an alliance partner but would shrink its horizons to focus on the arc of small South Pacific states to the north. It did not want any part of the West's nuclear strategy in Europe and elsewhere; instead it would make its contribution to Western security in the non-nuclear South Pacific and prove that it was neither neutralist nor seeking a free ride on the efforts of others.

The need to be more self-reliant in defence and security and to assume a greater leadership role in the South Pacific was spelt out in

---

* Palmer to Lange (in Geneva), 5 March 1985, PM 59/8/5 Part 3, MFAT.
† In-house Meeting, 28 March 1985, PM 111/3/3/1 Part 34a, ANZ.
‡ Cabinet paper of 14 March 1985, PM 111/3/3/1 Part 33, ANZ.

two Cabinet papers – the sudden flow of Cabinet discussion perhaps reflecting the methodical nature of Palmer and his growing influence in this delicate situation. The argument was that, though the basic ANZUS guarantee remained, its operational character had changed and the withdrawal of military and intelligence cooperation was irreversible, barring an unlikely backdown by either side. New Zealand would have to do more on its own. By safeguarding its security interests in the immediate neighbourhood, and by ensuring that the South Pacific did not become an area of instability and conflict, New Zealand could display its reliability and in time seek a more stable relationship with both the United States and Australia.

This would cost money. The new strategy meant spending more on defence partly, it was argued, because New Zealand's armed services were designed to fight with other people's forces and did not have an adequate capability for independent action in the South Pacific islands, and partly to demonstrate that the government was in earnest about self-reliance. The changes were not striking: a sixth Orion maritime patrol aircraft was acquired, stocks of spares and munitions were increased, steps were taken to acquire a fleet-support tanker to increase the range of the country's frigates in the wide Pacific Ocean, and the avionics and weapons systems in the Air Force's Skyhawk fighters would be upgraded. The expense was put boldly by Lange at more than \$100 million or at least 'a substantial sum of money which I am not going to disclose'.* New spending was probably not half of that but in another sign of the country's shrinking strategic outlook it was agreed that some of the cost would have to be met from contributions elsewhere. In due course the battalion stationed in Singapore would have to come home but for the time being it and the observer group in the Sinai would stay to discourage any thought that New Zealand was slipping into isolationism.†

---

* It was \$76 million.
† Cabinet Papers of 18 March and 1 April 1985.

The American ambassador was called in on 15 March to have this thinking outlined to him and to hear the Prime Minister's hope that the public exchanges be allowed to die down. Lange saw no early prospect of reviewing the port access issue. He did not think the US would be willing to talk seriously about this until the arms control talks in Geneva had made progress or until the missile deployments in Belgium and the Netherlands had been settled – not perhaps before the end of the year. In the meantime New Zealand was determined to work closely with the US and to play an active role in the South Pacific.

He thought that relations between Wellington and Washington were coming out of the 'immediate turbulence'. The public was turning its attention to other things and he did not want to keep the issue in play. As evidence he pointed out that he had been restrained about the Western alliance in the Union debate and had tried not to 'give succour' to the anti-nuclear groups in Western Europe. Perhaps the two governments could now come back to some sort of normality and 'just weather the thing' for a few months. He himself intended to 'just shut up'.* He explained to a gathering of European ambassadors three days later that he had been taken aback by 'the well of nationalist fervour' he had seen in the US and would call off the rhetoric to prevent things getting further out of hand.†

This virtuous vow of silence was tempting fate, which immediately responded. The same day he felt it necessary to issue a statement accusing Shultz of telling an 'untruth'. Coming back from Moscow the Secretary commented in passing that New Zealand had broken the defence relationship by refusing access to US ships. Lange said this was false. In the sort of argument which is said to give lawyers a bad name, he declared that 'one day we will get it across to the world and to the United States' that New Zealand had never banned American warships, only those which did not conform to its policy.‡

---

* US Embassy report of 15 March 1985, State Department Papers.
† 18 March 1985, PM 111/3/3/1 Part 32, ANZ.
‡ Lange press statement, 18 March 1985.

By now Washington was used to this and the incident passed without comment, another drop in the already deep pool of suspicions about David Lange. The Americans too were ready for a truce, but for different reasons. They were cool about the talk of building a new bilateral relationship. New Zealand could not claim a diplomatic refund for its increased efforts in the South Pacific; that was simply and sensibly in its own interest. The old relationship had gone with the denial of port access and it was not easy to find new links in the absence of alliance cooperation. It was best to allow time for reflection. Wolfowitz told Rowling that the NZ/US relationship had been special because it was based in large part on alliance cooperation. 'New Zealand's access and reception in Washington which was far in excess of its size was based ultimately on the alliance relationship' so now it had to change.[*]

There was another and more immediate reason for not defining the new relationship: the Congress. Four Western European countries (France, the Netherlands, Norway and Italy) and Japan and Singapore had been telling the State Department they did not want a high-profile debate in Congress about their own arrangements for ship visits. They did not want New Zealand to be let off too lightly for fear of the encouragement this would give to anti-nuclear activists in their own countries, but neither did they want New Zealand thrown out of the alliance in case they were eventually compelled to follow the same course.[†]

Interest in Congress seemed at last to be dying down and neither the Administration nor the New Zealand ambassador wanted to do anything to rekindle it. Rowling had gone around almost all the members of the House Subcommittee on East Asia and the Pacific, concluding that at the coming hearings, 'if all we get is a rap over the knuckles and an exhortation to reconsider, we will have done well'.[‡] There were two competing drafts: one by Stephen Solarz, the

---

[*] Wolfowitz to Rowling, 10 April 1985, PM 111/3/3/1 Part 34a, ANZ.
[†] Briefing by Glassman, State Department, 27 March 1985, PM 59/8/5 Part 3, MFAT.
[‡] Rowling cable to Wellington, 15 March 1985, PM 111/3/3/1 Part 32, ANZ.

chairman, called for the Administration to consult with Australia on terminating the treaty; the other, by Representative Leach, the ranking Republican, commended the President for rejecting economic sanctions and proposed that the US would agree to a South Pacific Nuclear Free Zone in return for New Zealand's accepting ship visits.

The Administration preferred the second (though a bargain over the Zone was never practicable) but noted that there seemed to be little desire to push either resolution to a vote. They were more an excuse to hold hearings at which House members could record their views and question Wolfowitz and others at length on their handling of the situation. This was well understood in Washington but Wolfowitz still had a residual concern that one false step in Wellington or a setback in Europe could raise the temperature enough to stimulate the passing of an awkward resolution calling for New Zealand to be expelled.

He stressed this in his six-hour testimony to the Subcommittee. Asked about bullying New Zealand, he said that the Administration was not looking to punish the country. New Zealand was free to choose whether or not it wished to be an ally, but it was not free to choose the benefits of being an ally without bearing its share of the burden. He discouraged the passing of Solarz's resolution, saying that the Administration was still very much in the phase of working for a successful solution, and he was supported by Leach and others who argued that Washington had overreacted and the enduring relationship with New Zealand needed delicate handling.* He managed it so neatly that at the end Solarz summarised his own message for him. The chairman said that he took ANZUS seriously 'as a promissory note on the honour of this country'. The denial of port access meant that this commitment could not be kept but 'we should approach

---

* Eleven liberal Democratic Representatives, headed by Representative Weiss, wrote to the President on 29 April asking him to reconsider the cancellation of defence cooperation with New Zealand.

this question with patience as befits a great power', and Wolfowitz needed only to say 'I agree with every word'.*

Congressional activity, whether in the House or the Senate, remained on hold, but vulnerable to attacks by trade lobbyists or external accidents. The cooling-off period desired by both governments made unsteady progress but with no lessening of suspicions on either side. Lange still hoped for another meeting with Shultz to show that the relationship had not broken down and at the beginning of April, just before he left on a tour of Africa, he wrote to say that it was a pity 'we have not been able over recent months to maintain our close personal contact and exchanges well away from the glare of media publicity'.† Perhaps they could talk at the next ASEAN gathering in Kuala Lumpur and this might open the way for more comprehensive talks in Washington later in the year (on Lange's hope that the arms control outlook might then be more favourable).

This rather jaunty overture was met with profound silence from Washington. While the Prime Minister travelled through Eastern and Southern Africa, falling out with his accompanying journalists and becoming increasingly discontented, efforts by Rowling to arrange the Kuala Lumpur meeting in July were dodged or stonewalled by Wolfowitz and others. It became clear that the State Department was reluctant to arrange a meeting unless there were signs of movement on its principal concern, port access. Without this, they worried that talks would suggest that the two were establishing 'a new version of what is normal'.‡

Wellington too became a little anxious. The Americans were stalling, but if they agreed they might only use the meeting to imply that New Zealand was getting cold feet and looking for a way out. Rather than risk a rebuff, Lange cancelled his request. It did nothing to cool his temperature; he complained at the same time that a visit by the nuclear-powered cruiser *Texas* to the South Pacific was a 'blatant

---

* Hearings on 18 March 1985, PM 111/3/3/1 Part 32, ANZ.
† Lange to Shultz, 1 April 1985, PM 111/3/3/1 Part 34a, ANZ.
‡ Wolfowitz to Rowling, 10 April 1985, PM 111/3/3/1 Part 34a, ANZ.

attempt at pressure tactics' by the US. He was further irritated when the State Department agreed that O'Flynn should have a brief conversation with Shultz at Kuala Lumpur, the Foreign Ministry having carefully reassured them that he would not raise anything of substance. In his large, looped writing the Prime Minister scrawled: 'This is a jack up. Shultz would not see me and now he is changing.'[*]

Then events took a turn which left the Americans dismayed. New Zealand's policy became entangled in their sensitive relationship with China. As part of a carefully planned evolution, two American warships were on their way to Shanghai, to be the first such visit since 1949. The Chinese leader, Hu Yaobang, met Australian and New Zealand journalists in Beijing as a preliminary to his arrival in those two countries. Inevitably he was asked about the understandings behind the Shanghai visit. Whether it was a fault in the translation or a confusion between nuclear-powered and nuclear-armed (the American destroyer and frigate were conventionally powered), Hu replied that Washington had given assurances that the ships were not nuclear-armed.

This set the cables flying and caused something of an international sensation, especially in Japan. The Americans quickly said that there had been no departure from their established NCND policy; the Chinese Foreign Ministry, with face involved after Hu's mistake, called for undertakings that the ships were indeed non-nuclear; and the visit was cancelled with little prospect of being reinstated for a year or more. In American eyes this was the fallout, unintended Rowling said, of New Zealand's policy. Wolfowitz pointed to a 'certain schizophrenia' in the country's attitudes, with its press often claiming that the anti-nuclear policy was intended to be an example to other countries. Was there any way of diminishing the moralism and getting greater realism in the public discussion? China perhaps did not seem a problem but it would hardly be to New Zealand's

---

[*] Cable of 18 April 1984, PM 111/3/3/1 Part 34b, and Lange's minute of 29 May 1985, PM 111/3/3/1 Part 36, ANZ.

advantage if Japan were to back out of the Mutual Security Treaty. Rowling was doubtful about whether much could be done about those who wanted to 'hold the torch up for others' and Wolfowitz accepted his judgement – 'forget I even raised it'.*

Over the weeks in March and April the consequences of New Zealand's 'inoperative' status in ANZUS continued to work through. One by one the well-established military exercises with allies and friends began to fail as the Americans made it clear they would not take part if New Zealand did. The big ANZUS exercise, 'Kangaroo 85', was cancelled, as was a maritime one run by the Canadians and another by the British. The quarterly meetings of American and 'old' Commonwealth military advisers were 'postponed' and New Zealand withdrew from similar gatherings on the intelligence side.

When the American commander suggested that New Zealand be excluded from the South East Asian exercise 'Tiger Balm', Lee Kuan Yew's response was 'no New Zealand, no Tiger Balm'. The New Zealanders had been there a long time and he did not want the current quarrel to affect Singapore's relations with them. This was not to say that he was not concerned at what he saw as Lange's 'naive' approach to strategic issues or the consequent erosion of ANZUS. He told the Australian Foreign Minister that when he first talked to Lange the previous October 'he had not understood that Mr Lange was surf-riding'.† And over lunch with Mrs Thatcher in Singapore he said that 'It was all right to cock a snook at the Americans in some areas of lesser importance where they were prepared to turn a blind eye, and not notice the snook that was being cocked. But this was serious.'‡

The only country with the ability to offset the gradual fraying of New Zealand's defence capabilities was Australia, and its Defence Minister, Kim Beazley, came to Wellington in the second week

---

* British embassy, Beijing, 11 April 1985, FCO Papers, and Washington embassy cable, 23 May 1985, PM 111/3/3/1 Part 36, ANZ.
† On 12 March 1985, 370/1/20 Part 32, NAA.
‡ Note of Lee–Thatcher talks, 8 April 1985, FCO Papers.

of April to see what he could do. There were predictable demonstrations urging 'Go Home Hawke Emissary', and Wellington was covered with posters of him as a gunslinger with bulging holsters coming to lay down the law.[*] He did not find his discussions with the Cabinet much more encouraging, telling an adviser: 'I've just come from a meeting of the Flat Earth Society.'[†] He made it clear, however, that Australia was not prepared to allow New Zealand to become isolated from the Western community. To the extent that was financially possible, it would arrange a parallel set of exercises with names like 'Tasman Link' and 'Tasman Warrior' to replace something of what had been lost.[‡]

His approach was as a firm friend of New Zealand and this was tactful given that lack of other options meant the country had now become much more dependent on its neighbour. Australia could exert pressure on the replacement of the country's ageing frigates; it controlled most of the flow of external intelligence to Wellington; and because of its commitment to help, it could ensure that New Zealand kept up its spending on defence equipment and on intelligence-gathering. In the words of a perceptive reporter, the country's dependence on Australia had increased 'because, in the final analysis, they're the only power in this region with whom we have a cultural affinity'.[§]

Beazley's touch was important in managing this new relationship in which New Zealand had become a loyal ally of Australia. Hawke's view of Lange had not changed and he was overheard in the Australian High Commission making clear to Beazley his displeasure at the Minister's more gentle approach.[¶] Lange visited Canberra on the way home from the unhappy African tour but his time there was no better. His journalists had never seen a prime ministerial visit

---

[*] He was pleased with the posters and one was found for him.
[†] Comment to Paul Dibb, Beazley's adviser and architect of Australia's new defence policy, repeated to the writer.
[‡] Cable to Ottawa and other posts, 9 April 1985, OTT 50/8/2 Part 3, MFAT.
[§] Richard Harman on 'The World This Week', 23 April 1985, Newztel.
[¶] An overheard telephone call from Wellington, 9 April 1985, FCO Papers.

THE OXFORD UNION DEBATE

with such a low profile, with not even a notice in the press gallery to say that he would be in town. The Australian Prime Minister, it appeared, was too busy to see him. Lange bravely denied that there were any difficulties but Hawke's officials briefed against him to the press, portraying him as an amateur who shot from the lip and was inconsistent in his aims.*

The deadlock over ANZUS continued to drag on, with New Zealand insisting that it was a full if purely conventional member, while the United States and Australia were looking to the future as a purely bilateral relationship. Lange, not by temperament a man to hold firmly to long-range goals, began to doubt whether the alliance was worth it. There was a touch of self-pity in an appeal which went to Britain at the end of April. The Americans had failed to recognise that heavy-handed tactics were not the best way of dealing with a small ally. Anything the British, 'with their long history of dealing sensibly and sensitively with Commonwealth associates', could do to encourage the Americans to take a wider view of the Western alliance would be very welcome. But Whitehall was not tempted; its policy laid down by the Defence Secretary was that no sanctions would be applied – it had no security alliance with New Zealand – but equally it would do no favours for a country whose policy was 'thoroughly unhelpful, both to bilateral defence cooperation and to wider Western interests'.†

Small signs hinted that, for lack of encouragement, the Prime Minister's insistence on support for the wider Western alliance was beginning to waver. He was invited to contribute an article to the American quarterly *Foreign Affairs*. A draft was prepared for him by Foreign Affairs but it emerged from his office reworked to reveal a consistent pattern of cuts removing any references to New Zealand as 'essentially pro-Western'. His speech to the University of Otago Foreign Policy School two weeks later revealed a marked distancing

---

* Harman, 23 April 1985.
† Wellington to London, 30 April, LON B 106/4/1 Part 4, MFAT, and Secretary of State for Defence (Heseltine) to Howe, 16 April 1985, FCO Papers.

from ANZUS, asserting that its security guarantee 'has led to a considerable distortion in the conduct of New Zealand's foreign policy'. Norrish complained that the original speech notes had set out the middle-of-the-road positions Lange was thought to desire. The text that emerged from the PM's speechwriter 'suggests very strongly that ANZUS is useless and points to policy positions that are considerably further out'.[*] Or, as Margaret Pope the speechwriter put it to Bruce Brown after the Union debate, 'Time to get out of ANZUS, Bruce.'[†]

---

[*] *Foreign Affairs*, Summer 1985. Drafts of both the article and the Otago speech together with Norrish's note are in PM 111/3/3/1 Part 35, ANZ.
[†] Brown, 'The Great Debate at the Oxford Union', in Clark (ed.), *For the Record*, p. 164.

Chapter Nine
The Palmer Mission

By June 1985 much of the dust had settled over New Zealand's novel status as the 'inoperative' member of ANZUS. Military exercises had been rearranged, intelligence exchanges cut back, and the complaints of other countries had been absorbed. Apart from these rather technical issues, the country did not seem to have suffered much damage from its new stand. As it unrolled, however, the logic of events was likely to require a choice to be made between the country's opposition to ship visits and continued membership of the alliance. The fact that the New Zealand Government was still unwilling to make such a choice became increasingly irksome to the Americans.

As Bill Brown of the State Department said in a speech in Melbourne, the United States was not asking New Zealand to accept nuclear weapons but to accept ship visits without requiring the US to compromise its global policy of NCND. The US had no issue with a friendly or neutral country that would not accept its warships (though none did apart from Vanuatu). The difficulty was with an ally which in their view wanted the benefits of an alliance while being unwilling to accept even a small obligation in return. Other alliance partners who were anti-nuclear, like Norway or Denmark, agreed to accept occasional ship visits as the price of membership. If New Zealand was unwilling to do this, if it wished to exclude the main guarantor of its security, then the Americans felt that the proper course was for it to withdraw from the alliance.

The quick-witted Prime Minister saw sooner than most the incompatibility of the two aims he had tried to pursue since coming into office. He had hoped or perhaps gambled that, faced with New Zealand's determination to hold to its anti-nuclear policy, the US would agree to a purely conventional ANZUS partnership with New Zealand. It was now clear that Washington would not accept a special status for New Zealand in the alliance, if only because to do so would be to lower the bar for all its other partners and greatly complicate its task of global alliance management. So, encouraged by his speechwriter who later became his wife, he began to tone down or omit his earlier declarations of unswerving commitment to the alliance, to raise doubts about the reliability of its security guarantee, and to insist that being inoperative did not matter because if a threat arose the US would still be obliged to defend New Zealand.

Edging away from ANZUS in these grandmother's footsteps was the most that could be risked because the polls continued to indicate that New Zealanders were even more attached to the treaty than to the ban on nuclear weapons. A poll in August showed that while opposition to nuclear visits had risen by 1 per cent over a twelve-month period, to 59 per cent, support for ANZUS had risen by 11 per cent since the previous December to 71 per cent. And while anti-nuclear views were supported by the most vocal part of the population, the split was even, at 45 per cent each way, for those who would or would not accept American ship visits as the price of staying in the alliance.* Seymour Topping, managing editor of the

---

* *New Zealand Herald* poll, 17–21 August 1985.

New York Times, made a tour of New Zealand in July to find out how 'both sides had allowed themselves to stumble into this dispute, through political and diplomatic fumbling'. Travelling around the country he concluded that public support for the anti-nuclear policy was much less clear cut when its adverse implication for relations with the US became apparent.*

Whatever the chances of success – a 'slim hope' was Norrish's view – a continued effort had therefore to be made to square the circle of New Zealand's conflicting desires, even if the only result would be to demonstrate that it could not be done. The Americans, deeply suspicious of Lange and the New Zealand Government after the events of January, sometimes speculated about Wellington's motives in pushing for continued negotiations. At low moments they were seized with fears that New Zealand was simply aiming, as laid out in Rowling's unfortunate memorandum for the Labour Party in 1983, to paint the Americans as high-handed and intransigent and to pin on them the blame for any inability to remain in ANZUS.

This recurring suspicion reflected how little credit New Zealand now had in Washington but it had some substance. Wellington had a political need to pursue the hope of a settlement, however slim. It was essential to demonstrate to the New Zealand public that every possibility had been explored and that in the end the hope of being both anti-nuclear and an active member of ANZUS could not be reconciled. This is indeed what happened. After exhaustive but unsuccessful negotiations an outcome was accepted with resignation by New Zealanders in 1986 who might have been more distressed if it had happened a year earlier.

An opportunity to test the water came in June when Norrish was due to attend one of the regular meetings of the ambassadors and consuls-general who headed posts in North America. There was some delay in settling the dates because (according to Glassman in the State Department) Norrish was determined this time to have

---

* Seymour Topping, 8 July 1985, PM 111/3/3/1 Part 37, ANZ.

a brief directly endorsed by the Prime Minister.* Lange agreed to a series of informal meetings with members of the Inter-Agency Group to deliver the message that obsessing about the point of disagreement was in neither side's interest and should not be allowed to overshadow the much wider relationship. To do so risked weakening support for ANZUS in New Zealand. If the port access issue could be put to one side it might be possible over time to reach an accommodation. In the meantime the Americans could usefully be reminded, by pointing to New Zealand's increased defence spending (up 18 per cent for the 1985/86 year) and efforts to check Soviet influence in the South Pacific and South East Asia, of the range of interests which the two countries continued to share. The road ahead lay in acknowledging these common Western interests and not in concentrating on the deadlock over ship visits.

Norrish did his best to push this message, suggesting to his sceptical hearers that there was more than one way in which a small ally could pull its weight and its actions should by now have allayed any concerns that the country was taking a hard left turn. In fact the PM had told him before departure that support in caucus for non-aligned, anti-defence policies had dwindled to around four to five members who were under tighter discipline, particularly on economic issues. For the time being Lange was feeling more secure about the direction of foreign policy.†

The Americans, still angry over the mismanagement of the *Buchanan* request, were not ready to look at the broader relationship. Instead, James Lilley, Brown's successor in the State Department, complained that they felt the US position had been 'exploited in a jingoistic way' and caricatured with all the talk of the American response as 'totalitarian', the alliance relationship being dismissed as 'a lean-to on the Pentagon' and ANZUS supporters being decried as 'nuke lovers'. The government was surely capable of explaining the

---

* Reported by the Australian embassy, Washington, 24 June 1985, 370/1/20 Part 36, NAA.
† Cable from State Department, 4 July 1985, State Department Papers.

working of the alliance more accurately than that. New Zealand had undercut American interests in Australia, Japan, Western Europe and even Papua New Guinea and there was now a spillover in China. Relations, they had told the British, 'were at a very low ebb'.

Pointing to New Zealand's increased efforts in defence and the Pacific did nothing to soften this resentment. Armitage said the Administration was not going to give New Zealand special credit for doing things in its neighbourhood that were in its own interests. Nor was it impressed by New Zealand's claim that it was giving up on global deterrence and concentrating entirely on South Pacific affairs. Whatever New Zealanders thought, he said, the rest of the world did not see the country as locked away in the South Pacific. 'You cannot change the way the world perceives you that quickly.' All its helpful work there was offset by the fact that when asked to take a minuscule risk over *Buchanan* it had refused and this refusal had set a new path. He summed up the point in a phrase remembered for years in Wellington: 'One "Aw, shit" is worth ten "Atta boys"' – one hesitation undoes decades of support.

Wolfowitz thought bleakly that the best that could be hoped for was to keep things stable and prevent them getting any worse. The State Department was making a sustained effort to hold back Representative Solarz and his Subcommittee; any action by Congress to redefine the US's obligations to New Zealand would set off 'a big downward spiral'. The price of a solution had gone up since *Buchanan*. It would now have to focus not on a single visit as before, but on a *schedule* of visits. It could start at the low end with a FFG-7 or a 'rustbucket' but it would have to be clearly understood that other ships would follow. To take a first step now, the US would have to be able to see further ahead, to know where the process was heading.*

Back home, Norrish told the Prime Minister in a closely held report that the American mood had been tougher than he expected

---

* Norrish met with Lilley, Armitage, Wolfowitz and Armacost, 28–29 June 1985, PM 111/3/3/1 Part 37, ANZ. Two of Lilley's quotes were from Lange, the 'lean-to' was O'Flynn.

and commented to the Australian High Commission that 'he had got the hard line all the time'.* He and Rowling agreed that Washington would not let things stay as they were; inaction by New Zealand for much longer would end in the break-up of ANZUS and serious damage to the wider connection. If both the anti-nuclear policy and the US relationship were to be preserved, New Zealand had to work out an arrangement for ship visits that the US could live with. Despite their unforgiving talk, he believed the Americans would look at ways of reconciling ship visits with the anti-nuclear policy. It would take a serious effort and would have to start soon.

The latest time would be September and would require an emissary who carried weight in both capitals. Geoffrey Palmer, the Deputy Prime Minister, would be speaking at the opening of the UN General Assembly that month and it had earlier been suggested that he might also visit Washington to renew the dialogue. The embassy's first notification to the State Department did not suggest any great freight of expectations: 'While they cannot point to an immediate prospect of progress, my authorities believe it is important that the two governments talk, and are seen to be talking, about the major issue.'† After the Norrish discussions, though, the Palmer visit took on a new significance. As a last chance to discover whether a settlement was possible, the advance notices and talk of major preparations for the visit began to accumulate to the point that there was a distinct risk, once again, of New Zealand over-promising what it could deliver.

In the meantime one of those events occurred which bedevil the hopes of policy-makers working quietly at their desks. The French secret service blew up a Greenpeace vessel, the *Rainbow Warrior*, in Auckland Harbour with the loss of one life by drowning. It was the skilled use of the explosives, one in the ship's side to warn those on board and a few minutes later one placed at the stern to twist the hull

---

* AHC cable of 11 July 1985, 370/1/20 Part 38, NAA.
† Wood (in the absence of Rowling who was on a raft on the Colorado River) to Wolfowitz, 20 June 1985, Laux Papers, Box 90658, Reagan Presidential Library.

against the possibility of its ever being refloated, which suggested to Wellington's Terrorism Committee that it was a professional operation. After that, helped by the arrest of two agents left behind as sweepers, a trail quickly began to unravel which led to Paris and the DGSE, France's external intelligence agency. In one of the strange coincidences that dogged his life the trail went past David Lange. The agents bringing the explosives down from their landing place in the northern tip of the country stayed on three occasions at a motel near Helensville of which he was part-owner.

In the already fevered atmosphere, this covert operation against a ship and its volunteer crew ready to cross the Pacific and demonstrate against continued French nuclear testing under the atoll of Mururoa set the bells shrilling. Television commentaries and the more impressionable journalists were already warning of American attempts to 'destabilise' New Zealand and its government as punishment for locking out its navy. Now here was irrefutable evidence, with the listing hull half under water at its mooring, of another great power willing to attack the country for its anti-nuclear sympathies. Never mind that Britain and the US knew nothing of the operation. In the general excitement they were accused of at least sympathising with the French operation, if not of having secret foreknowledge of it. The ensuing outrage dimmed any hope of stretching Palmer's negotiating brief for Washington to increase the chance of a settlement.

It was clear that the government's manifesto commitment to enshrine the anti-nuclear policy in law would, by cementing in the ban, make a settlement much more difficult. Once again Lange did not help matters by agreeing that the purpose of the law was to make it more difficult for any future government to reverse the anti-nuclear policy – 'not difficult, very difficult' was his airy reply to a press question, marked heavily on the White House copy.[*] The Americans took note of this and saw the plans for legislation as proclaiming New Zealand's lack of interest in a settlement with them.

---

[*] Press conference, 8 July 1985, Laux Papers, Box 90461, Reagan Presidential Library.

The Prime Minister had succeeded in postponing the introduction of the Bill for a year but, pressed by a suspicious Left who had set this as their next goal, he could not do so indefinitely. The prospect of legislation thus set the clock ticking on the time left in which to reach an agreement. Lange said he would consult with the US about the legislation but 'if we can't sort this out before the end of the year, it is not going to be sorted out'.

An ASEAN gathering in Kuala Lumpur gave a further opportunity to test positions. The meeting between Shultz and O'Flynn was confined on Wellington's advice to only fifteen minutes and covered nothing new. O'Flynn, who had told a bemused visitor that negotiating from strength was 'ridiculously illogical', was not allowed to negotiate at all.* Norrish's talk with Wolfowitz did not go any more easily. State Department officials complained that he had not come up with enough convincing detail. They thought he was 'blowing smoke' to cover an essentially negative response from the Prime Minister. Wolfowitz's attitude was cool: without more specifics, there was no point in Palmer coming to Washington. Who he would see if he did come was 'a problem for you'. New Zealand would not want another bare fifteen minutes with Shultz; Palmer's access would hinge on what he had to say.†

Shultz himself went on to Canberra for the meeting with the Australians which had taken the place of the cancelled ANZUS Council. His opening statement in public described New Zealand's stand as 'escapist' and 'isolationist', and though he told the Australians that these remarks were directed as much at the Congress as at New Zealand, there was no doubt that his view of Wellington's motives was hardening. His companions thought he was evolving an increasingly doctrinaire view of the sacredness of burden-sharing in alliances, wondering whether it would be better to have New Zealand cast out, as a useful example of how allies should

---

* At this time a newspaper ranking the performance of Ministers from 'high' to 'low' had to invent a special category for O'Flynn – 'disaster'.
† Embassy briefing from Glassman, 18 July 1985, PM 59/8/5 Part 3, MFAT.

not behave, than to make the American concessions that would be needed for a post-*Buchanan* accommodation. He certainly struck the Australian Foreign Minister as 'very tense' at the prospect of legislation.*

When he asked about the chances of a change in New Zealand's direction the Australians were discouraging. They saw no evidence of it and did not think that the Labour Party's structure was flexible enough to accept any significant modification. They also thought there was little prospect of an electoral change. It did not seem likely that the opposition National Party would win the next election in 1987, but if it did it would probably have difficulty making any major alteration in the anti-nuclear policy.

The Australians themselves were unhappy about the prospect of legislation, worrying that the exclusion of New Zealand might bring down the whole ANZUS treaty, the cornerstone of their defence strategy. A new security treaty with the US was unlikely to be acceptable either to the Congress or the Australian Labor Party. If ANZUS collapsed and Australia's defence position was seriously impaired, 'that's when Canberra will turn on Wellington'.† So for them the main achievement of the Canberra meeting was that it nailed down the continuance of Australian–American cooperation under the ANZUS treaty, whatever happened to New Zealand.

Shultz chose his departing press conference to give a formal warning about the legislation: the US would review its commitments to New Zealand under ANZUS if New Zealand enacted legislation to ban port visits. This was quietly welcomed by the Australians as further confirmation that only the New Zealand commitments would be affected, and not the treaty as a whole. Lange took it as a call for

---

* PM 59/8/5 Part 3, MFAT, and Hayden briefs the New Zealand High Commissioner, 17 July 1985, PM 111/3/3/1 Part 37, ANZ.
† Babbage (Australian Department of Defence) to Commodore Walker, Head of NZ Defence Liaison Staff, 9 July 1985, PM 58/206/2, MFAT.

consultation and responded that legislation 'would be introduced with great care and only after a thorough dialogue with the US'.*

Shultz's mind, however, was running on the philosophical basis of alliances and on his way home he delivered a speech in Honolulu on 'Alliance Responsibility'. He had come to the view that arguing (as Lange was) about the net advantages and costs of an alliance was 'narrow self-interest'. He saw ANZUS like the other post-war alliances as having been founded on the need to defend a common set of political and moral values, and New Zealand as a prime example of an ally which had lost sight of that common interest.

It was a deliberate and carefully thought-out statement, going through at least eight drafts. He introduced it by saying, 'It's a serious speech. It's not interspersed with cheer lines of any kind. It invites you to listen carefully, and I'll read it carefully.' It was intended not just for New Zealand but for all America's allies, but the first part on New Zealand, serving as an illustrative text for his sermon on alliance behaviour, had been redrafted and strengthened on the road to the point where the *New York Times* simply described the speech as 'Shultz, in Honolulu, Denounces New Zealand'.

His complaints about New Zealand's policy were not new but they were made in public and shorn of diplomatic niceties. His essential point was that, in rejecting *Buchanan*, New Zealand had decided that the operational obligations of the treaty did not apply to them. 'In a sense New Zealand walked off the job – the job of working with each other to defend our common security.' New Zealand would remain a friend but 'without access to ports, we could not fulfil our treaty obligations either in peacetime or in a crisis'.

He drew the moral for the whole system of Western alliances. The ability to work together was the real deterrent to aggression. 'By adding a new element of risk and uncertainty, New Zealand has weakened regional stability, one of the most important links in the effort to prevent nuclear war. And the erosion of Western unity only

---

* Press conference, 8 July 1985.

weakens the Western position and the chances for success in arms control.' Without alliance unity the Soviet Union would simply sit back and wait for unilateral concessions.*

This was a trumpet blast at a time when both sides were urging a truce in the war of words. Lange considered a press statement saying that Shultz was making a mountain out of a molehill – whether the US Navy could visit New Zealand was hardly critical in global strategic terms – but wisely did not release it. Instead he made his reply at the annual dinner of the Wellington Regional Labour Party ten days later. He argued that the two countries were drifting apart on ANZUS, claiming that the US saw it as part of its global nuclear strategy whereas New Zealand regarded it as a purely regional alliance and wanted no part of the global nuclear struggle. He went on to suggest that the country could not depend on the treaty's security guarantee. 'We must, for our own security, assume that in a regional disturbance we in the South Pacific are on our own' – a view that rather left Australia out of consideration.†

Looking back over his first year in office, 'one of the most turbulent years in the history of the country', the American embassy thought Lange's anti-nuclear stand had been a political plus, helped by the perceived harsh reaction of the US which aroused a wave of nationalistic feeling that swept away many doubters. Those originally fearful of the consequences had been calmed by his skilful public relations campaign, designed to demonstrate that ANZUS was still intact and there had been no effects on New Zealand's trade. His frequent statements that there was regular contact with the US through the embassy and in discussions with senior American officials seemed to have convinced the public that the 'family squabble' could be worked through.‡

This was what Washington was afraid of, that the sharp edges of the difference would become buried in the drifting sand of a new

---

* Honolulu speech, 17 July 1985, State Department Papers.
† Speech at annual dinner of the Wellington Regional Labour Party, 27 July 1985.
‡ US embassy, 'The Labour Government After A Year', 1 August 1985, State Department Papers.

normality and the situation would slide into a comfortable acceptance that the relationship was working as usual. New ideas were needed from New Zealand but the Administration was pessimistic, telling the British, 'they did not detect the will in Lange himself to do anything'.*

Wolfowitz decided to be more explicit about the price of a deal. He told Rowling that Palmer's visit would be a failure unless he came with a detailed negotiating package. The package would have to include a ship visit programme commencing with, say, a Perry class frigate, but going on to accept more difficult vessels; a willingness to discuss the anti-nuclear legislation; and, desirably, an indication of readiness to hold a public enquiry into all aspects of nuclear propulsion. The Palmer visit was only a few weeks away and if it was to succeed preliminary discussions by officials would have to start very soon. Wolfowitz said he had support for further negotiations but he was 'not going to stick his neck out' unless there was some assurance of movement by New Zealand.†

Work was already under way in Wellington to define Palmer's negotiating position and to ensure that he had a full mandate from Cabinet and caucus. It was interrupted briefly by the Prime Minister's absence at the South Pacific Forum in Rarotonga. At this Lange made a proposal reflecting his government's new concern with the South Pacific. He suggested that a meeting be held in Wellington early in 1986 to discuss security arrangements in the Pacific with the aim of 'enhancing them and giving them more coherence'. But his heart was not in it.‡ He raised it briefly at the private 'retreat' and at the Forum's closing session. Hawke expressed concern (it would have excluded the United States), there was no other comment, and the idea lapsed.

While in Rarotonga he and Hawke also had a brief talk about the ANZUS problem. Hawke asked if there was no way out of the legislation and on getting the expected answer asked if it could

---

* British embassy, Washington, 23 July 1985, FCO Papers.
† Wolfowitz called on Rowling at the residence, 26 July 1985, PM 59/8/5 Part 3, MFAT.
‡ It was never discussed in Cabinet. 370/1/20 Part 55, NAA.

THE PALMER MISSION

be permissive rather than mandatory. If it prohibited visits 'the Americans would go ape', but he thought the Americans might be able to live with a discretionary regime.* The chemistry between them was as bad as ever.

The Forum then adopted the South Pacific Nuclear Free Zone Treaty and eight countries, including New Zealand and Australia, signed at a table under the palm trees. The new treaty did not ban port visits or passage on the high seas and so had little practical effect. The Americans, however, said they would keep an open mind about endorsing it, despite a momentary embarrassment when a State Department spokesman claimed that the draft was expected to arrive by a bottle in the sea.†

By the curse that always seemed to hang over these negotiations at a delicate stage, it was also time for the annual Labour Party conference and it did not disappoint. The British High Commission was shocked by 'the anti-Americanism of the delegates and their readiness to believe ill of New Zealand's friends and well of her enemies'.‡ Members called for a withdrawal from ANZUS and the adoption of a policy of neutrality and non-alignment. They passed the customary extensive set of resolutions calling for the abandonment of the Five Power Defence Arrangements in South East Asia, the withdrawal of New Zealand forces from Singapore and the Sinai, support for the Sandinistas in Nicaragua, and landing rights for Aeroflot. A more precisely aimed resolution, sponsored by Helen Clark and Fran Wilde, specified that no ship should be admitted unless there was publicly available, credible evidence to guarantee that the non-nuclear policy

---

* Lange talks to AHC, 12 March 1986, PM 59/8/5 Part 7, MFAT.
† Anti-nuclear groups claimed to be sending hundreds of bottles back to the spokesman as a rebuke.
‡ BHC, Wellington, 2 September 1985, FCO Papers.

was not breached. Lange was privately very angry but, with an eye on his caucus, had to declare that he could live with this requirement.*

In fact he could not; public evidence that a ship had no nuclear arms would breach the rule of NCND, and neither an American nor a British ship would come in those circumstances, as the resolution presumably intended. Just before this, Air Marshal Jamieson had been quietly despatched to London to sound out the defence chiefs there on the ideas being worked out for Palmer's brief, and the conference remit did not help the credibility of his case. He explained the purpose of the legislation as being to enable the resumption of some ship visits and outlined a 'ladder' of increasingly sensitive visits, starting with the now-traditional FFG-7 but rising to include a British warship from the Task Force that was to cruise the Pacific in 1986, perhaps even the aircraft carrier *Illustrious*, on the Lange theory that a British ship would be more acceptable to anti-nuclear New Zealanders.

British officials, unable to consult Ministers in the time available, gave a cautious but encouraging response. The Foreign Office saw it as 'a genuine attempt by Lange to find a way out of the present impasse'. As it stood, the offer might not be enough, but 'we would want to ensure that the door is not slammed in Lange's face'. There would be greater difficulty with the Americans and there was some anxiety about 'wedge-driving' between the two Atlantic allies; Britain could not go ahead if the US was opposed. With the usual unease of serving officers, the service chiefs Jamieson spoke with declared the issue to be 'political' and the sooner it got back into political channels the better.†

A visit to Wellington a few days later, in early September, gave the British Minister of State for the Armed Forces, John Stanley, the opportunity to do this. His brief said: 'The New Zealand Government's stance on ship visits will inevitably damage both our

---

* US embassy, 18 September 1985, State Department Papers.
† Jamieson to AVM Sutton in London, 30 August, and Sutton's report to the Foreign Secretary, 2 September 1985, FCO Papers.

bilateral defence cooperation and wider Western security interests.' The policy was 'somewhat schizophrenic' and isolationist but Mrs Thatcher had decreed a low-level response and Britain should do what it could to help. One thought, much debated in Whitehall, was that Stanley should take a leaf from Lange at the Oxford Union and make a speech in New Zealand that was critical of its policy. The speech went back and forth between the Defence Ministry and Foreign Office for frequent redrafting in the hope of avoiding giving offence, but the occasion in Wellington was no packed debate, Stanley was no Lange and the speech got little attention.

The Prime Minister did, however, explain to him the approach which the legislation would take on ship visits. It would, he said, be a 'trust me' approach. The Act would give the Prime Minister responsibility for approving visits. Advised by the Chief of Defence Staff (CDS) and the Intelligence Council he would decide whether or not a proposed ship carried nuclear weapons and therefore whether or not it could visit. He told Stanley that being 'nuclear-capable' was no longer an issue, the decision to admit a ship would be solely his to make, and any rejections would be made in confidence.

Stanley raised a point troubling London and Washington. A paper had fluttered out of the Labour Party conference saying that any decision by the Prime Minister would have to be reasonable and would be subject to judicial review. If the admission of a ship could be challenged in court any hope of maintaining confidentiality and therefore NCND would be gone. The paper was denounced by both Lange and Palmer as false and unauthorised but only the latter was probably true.

The problem, Lange said, was to keep the grounds for his judgement on each visit out of the view of the courts 'and as little subject as possible to the collective paranoia of Party and public and the widespread belief that the government in New Zealand was untrustworthy. Any warship visit would cause political trouble. It had to be faced.' His solution was not entirely reassuring. Judicial review would always be a possibility, but he thought a New Zealand court might well hold back if national security were involved. 'This was a somewhat surprising doctrine to Mr Stanley but nevertheless it is what Mr Lange said.'*

Lange told Stanley that he would like a ship visit before the legislation was passed; otherwise the standoff with the US might become irreversible. He thought a FFG-7 frigate would be too much of a climb-down by the US; a *Buchanan*-type destroyer would be too much of a climb-down for New Zealand. Something in between was needed, though where a warship that was neither frigate nor destroyer was to be found he did not say. But the party conference insisted on having the reassurance of the legislation first and the government backed off. It argued instead that legislation was an essential prerequisite for any ship visit; it was now contended that the lack of a firm legal foundation had undermined that of the *Buchanan*.

A methodical approach was taken by Palmer to ensure that his brief for Washington was backed by Ministers and indeed all members of the parliamentary party. There were to be 'no false starts this time'.† The Prime Minister took all ten members of the caucus foreign affairs group to lunch and found them entirely understanding about the need for ministerial discretion in approving visits (though Clark and Anderton had said little). Nonetheless, Lange's note for caucus took a careful and slightly negative tone about the coming discussions: Palmer would make it clear that, while New Zealand sought an improvement in its relationship with the US, the policy on port access was not negotiable.‡

The full position was approved by Cabinet on 26 August. A serious effort was needed to reach a working arrangement with the US. That meant ensuring that the anti-nuclear legislation held open the prospect of ship visits; an absolute ban would cause a complete break with the US. This would have to be followed by the resumption of

---

* BHC report of Stanley's meeting with the Prime Minister, 6 September 1985, FCO Papers.
† Lange to Monroe Browne, 19 August 1985, PM 59/8/5 Part 4, MFAT.
‡ Lange to Monroe Browne, 22 August, State Department Papers, and Note of 21 August 1985, PM 59/8/5 Part 4, MFAT.

some ship visits, perhaps in the first half of 1986 with the visit of a FFG-7 known to be nuclear-free, followed later by a Royal Navy ship. Devising a law which conformed to the anti-nuclear policy but did not breach NCND required the Prime Minister to make a decision on each visit. The legislation would establish a framework and criteria for this, but the exact wording would need to be discussed with the Americans. 'A good working relationship with the United States is of fundamental and enduring importance to New Zealand's broader political, security and economic interests.'*

Everyone in Cabinet declared themselves comfortable with this aim. Rowling, brought home to help, spoke to 18 of the 20 members and found no dissent. But it was not going to be as straightforward as that. Once again Lange sounded a different note at a press conference, giving no hint of the search for a workable compromise. Palmer would not be seeking to make the legislation more palatable to the Americans and New Zealanders could be reassured that 'we are going to remain true to them'.† This reflected the ever-present fears in the party and among the anti-nuclear activists that Lange might dilute or trade away the anti-nuclear policy.

They were already alarmed about the visit. Fran Wilde said that to run a 'trust me' policy would be 'politically insane'. Russell Marshall, then Minister of Education, said the conference should make it clear that no one wanted a 'trust me' approach: 'We have simply to insist that the Prime Minister and the Government only give approval if they are absolutely sure that the criteria have been met.'‡ Suspicion of Lange's intentions prompted a meeting of peace groups in Wellington who announced that they would protest any ship which carried 'missile launchers, aircraft or torpedo tubes equipped for delivering nuclear weapons', and this was widely felt to further limit the government's room for manoeuvre.

---

* Cabinet paper of 26 August 1985, PM 59/8/5 Part 4, MFAT.
† Press conference after caucus, 22 August 1985.
‡ Article by Patricia Herbert in the *Press*, 5 September 1985.

Though Lange said that nothing would satisfy 'these people' and Palmer declared that the government could not allow peace groups to defeat the restoration of good relations with the US, none of this eased the suspicions of the Americans.* The Washington embassy was told there was 'an abundance of scepticism' about the Palmer mission. The New Zealand Country Director in the State Department said: 'There is speculation that the whole visit is a set-up – offering the US something they are bound to reject but which will leave the onus of appearing unreasonable firmly with the Reagan Administration.'† This wariness did not stem wholly from fears of a replay of the *Buchanan* fiasco, fears that New Zealand would make hopeful promises only to renege on them in a tide of anti-Americanism. Administration officials were also divided over whether the US should even try to negotiate a 'New Zealand formula' for access. The gain might be outweighed by the consequent difficulties with other allies, especially if New Zealand's self-assessment of visiting ships amounted to a breach of NCND, a public declaration that the vessel was not nuclear-armed.

The doubts were revealed in a hesitation about Palmer's appointments. The State Department was unwilling to commit to a call on Shultz without knowing whether Palmer would be empowered to discuss a genuine programme of ship visits. It was finally agreed 'on the express understanding that Palmer will be prepared to discuss more than just the general thrust of the legislation'. Conveying this news, Monroe Browne again expressed a worry about raising false expectations. Lange said he totally agreed and would be 'wholly cooperative and positive'. The two governments must work together to bring US Navy ships back into New Zealand and he would not be setting out on this course if he did not intend to persevere.‡

Washington, feeling it had heard all this before, remained sceptical about whether Lange would persevere to the point of restoring

---

* US embassy, 18 September 1985, State Department Papers.
† Glassman, 5 September 1985, PM 50/6/4 Part 11, MFAT.
‡ Monroe Browne meets with Lange, 22 August 1985, State Department Papers.

'normal access' to New Zealand ports. The more hard-line members of the Inter-Agency Group had wanted to insist on 'unfettered access' but Beazley, the Australian Defence Minister, managed to remove this restriction. In a helpful visit to Washington in mid-September he pointed out that the US Navy did not enjoy unfettered access even in Australia. The more flexible notion of 'normal' access became Washington's bottom line.

Even so it remained wary. In an effort to demonstrate that Palmer would come with a full briefcase, Rowling told Armacost that he would talk about the 'implications' of the legislation; would offer three ship visits over the next year or so – the inevitable FFG-7 to break the ice, a nuclear-capable British ship (perhaps an aircraft carrier), and a US ship similar to *Buchanan*; and Cabinet had also agreed to commission a study of nuclear propulsion. This evoked little enthusiasm: Armacost said they could not sell a sequence to the Navy which ended up with a *Buchanan*. That had been the starting point in February and would have to be again.

Wolfowitz noted bleakly that in February a nuclear-capable but modest ship had been more than the New Zealand Government could handle; now it talked of three visits ending up with the same sort of ship. Both he and Armacost repeated their worries about the legislation. It would open port calls to damaging debates – every visit would be made 'a subject of public acrimony' – and it was hard to see how the Prime Minister's assessment of suitability would preserve the necessary ambiguity under NCND. Rowling in turn repeated that public opinion could not accept visits unless there was legislation to provide reassurance.*

The next day Armacost telephoned to relay Shultz's views. The Secretary looked forward to Palmer's arrival but was not encouraging about the outcome. He could not see how legislation could avoid jeopardising NCND and so prevent a 'normal' pattern of visits. The US did not want to play out time and could not embark on a

---

* Rowling to Armacost, 5 September 1985, PM 59/8/5 Part 5, MFAT.

gradual solution without certainty as to what would be achieved. A nuclear-capable ship and not a FFG-7 should be the first to visit; the visit schedule should be compressed in time to achieve normal access within the life of the current government; and normal access should be defined as admission of all the types of warship previously received by New Zealand. The two sides were now in negotiating mode and Shultz's position was perhaps an opening bid, but it also made clear how steep the climb would be if a settlement was to be reached.*

The embassy in Wellington, however, reported that a serious effort was being made. This time the key Cabinet Ministers were on board – Douglas, Caygill, Moore and Prebble – and Margaret Wilson was willing to go along with the initiative. Moore indeed had suggested that it would be easier for Lange if a Cabinet committee made the decision on entry – a 'trust us' formula. The ghost of *Buchanan* could not be driven out, but careful planning had gone into the mission and Lange had worked to lay the political groundwork. The ambassador saw evidence of greater support in 'questionable parts of the government' and so far the Prime Minister had stood his ground, though there were doubts as to how he would stand up to the heavy attack a 'difficult' ship would cause.

This time around Palmer was seen as a major plus. He had volunteered for the mission because of his links with Kenneth Dam, his old teacher at the Chicago Law School who was now Shultz's deputy. Palmer felt that if there was any flexibility in the American position, Dam would reveal it, but he unfortunately left the Administration just before Palmer arrived.† Though Palmer inevitably came under party suspicion as being too pro-American through having lived, studied and taught in America, the American embassy thought he had anti-nuclear credibility after declining *Buchanan*. He could probably deliver some fence-sitters, and by co-opting him, Lange had

---

* Armacost telephones Rowling, 6 September 1985, State Department Papers.
† Interview with Sir Geoffrey Palmer, 15 July 2011.

diminished the risk of a challenge in a crisis over a ship visit. He had found the case for *Buchanan* 'inadequate' but he was now a principal architect of ostensibly new arrangements which he could plausibly sell to the party and the public.*

Palmer arrived on 18 September, accompanied by his wife, John Henderson, Director of the Prime Minister's Office, Tim Francis and two young women from his office, the chief of staff and press secretary. The embassy greeters at the airport were taken aside by Francis to be told that the presence of these two staffers was important for Palmer and they were to be appropriately looked after – a task of some delicacy when on an evening out one of them wanted to present a flower to a policeman on duty.†

That evening everyone gathered at the residence on Observatory Circle for a discussion on how to approach the meetings arranged for the following day. The embassy had in the customary way prepared a brief for the Deputy Prime Minister. Palmer waved it away, saying he had lived in the country for six years and knew Americans well. He had been at the University of Chicago with Wolfowitz and got better marks than he did. He then read out a thick sheaf of the opening remarks he had written in Canada for the meeting with the Inter-Agency Group the next morning.

The opening line (in the recollection of at least one of those present) was: 'We New Zealanders are a uniquely spiritual and caring people.' It went on to argue that the United States and New Zealand, a large and a small democracy, should acknowledge each other's principles. But the US did not recognise New Zealand's; in fact it was being un-American in going against its own principles in the way it was treating its smaller ally. There were frequent references to the American Constitution and other revered texts. The clear message

---

* US embassy, 18 September 1985, State Department Papers.
† Interview with John Wood, 11 August 2011.

seemed to be that 'you have abandoned your own morality and principles'.*

When he finished there was a silence while the embassy considered how to comment. Rowling was initially cautious, saying only that it was important to give the US a clear sense of where the Labour Party stood on the issue. His two younger colleagues then said, as tactfully as they could, that this was not what the Americans were expecting and, after the *Buchanan* failure, might seem provocative. Rowling then joined in expressing the general doubt about this approach: the US was hoping that he would present detailed New Zealand proposals for solving the problem. Palmer, however, preferred to stay with his notes and made only a few drafting changes.

On a grey and rainy morning the first and possibly decisive meeting was held in Wolfowitz's conference room at the State Department, with the full Inter-Agency Group present. Palmer thought his opening statement was 'clear, direct and forceful' and when he finished the Americans 'were absolutely silent'.† This was perhaps because among other things he had said they were talking too much and the speeches coming out of Washington made the Administration's behaviour seem to New Zealanders like George III's towards the American colonies.

Or perhaps their silence was simply thoughtful. His words about New Zealand's uniquely spiritual and caring nature did not win over his hearers. It struck them as clearly implying that the US was not. In the words of Armitage (a practising Catholic who had adopted a number of Vietnamese orphans): 'The discussion was over at that point.'‡ One of the New Zealanders present remembered that the temperature dropped sharply and the talks never recovered from this inauspicious beginning.§

---

* Interview with Simon Murdoch, then Counsellor at the embassy, 21 July 2011.
† His recollection given to Vernon Wright, 8 February 1987, Lange Papers, Box 1, ANZ.
‡ Interview with Armitage, 26 September 2011.
§ Interview with Wood, 11 August 2011.

His speech was not so much the diplomatically worded offer of a deal for which his hearers were waiting as a sustained rebuke to the Americans for not settling on New Zealand's terms. As Queen Victoria complained of Mr Gladstone, he addressed the gathering as if it were a public meeting. He complained that 'a great amount of rhetoric emanating from US sources had made the position of the New Zealand government more difficult'. If the impasse was to be broken the US would have to show more flexibility, and he was there to discover if it existed. So far all New Zealand had seen was an uncompromising hard line that New Zealand had to change its policy as Australia had.

The problem was that the US did not understand New Zealand's political circumstances. The first thing they had to grasp was that the political situation was different in New Zealand. The caucus and party would not tolerate any retreat on the anti-nuclear policy and continued American pressure would drive New Zealand into some sort of neutralist stance. 'Public support for the government depended on its not abandoning the anti-nuclear policy.' The American response to the *Buchanan* affair was an overreaction; the measures were harsh and unreasonable and did not take account of the values and democratic institutions which the two countries shared. It was hard for New Zealanders to understand why all this and the ANZUS relationship had to be jeopardised over port access which had little strategic significance.

Wolfowitz took a deep breath and noted that a 'family dispute' like this was always more fraught than others. He could understand why New Zealand wished to avoid 'entangling alliances', a temptation to which the US had succumbed disastrously in the past. In the Administration they saw the policy as an isolationist move by an ally which affected other allies and fed innate American doubts about the value of alliances. The US was not seeking to involve New Zealand in its strategic deterrence of the Soviet Union – ship visits had nothing to do with that – but New Zealand's actions damaged wider deterrence. As long as the Soviet Union felt that alliance ties could be broken the Western stance was that much weaker; the Russians sensed that they could 'get isolationism working for them'.

Like Palmer he thought philosophical principles were important, but not as important as getting a solution. The accumulated baggage of having failed once weighed on both governments but it had led to 'great diffidence and suspicion' on the US side. It might not be possible to reach agreement at the philosophical level 'but we may agree on ships and that's all we need'. He then got down to specifics: the New Zealand position started too low, moved too slowly and did not reach a point which could be called 'normal port access'. Bringing in legislation, the solemn force of law, would create new inflexibilities where more flexibility was needed. Washington could not accept the public refusal of a ship – 'The Chinese tried that. The US cancelled a ship visit and China wasn't even an ally.' If normal port access was not possible, then the US would have to review its alliance obligations.

Palmer then passed over some of the clauses from the draft Bill but did not open any discussion on the details. He argued that legislation would create greater flexibility, not less, but if normal port access meant going back to the past, and Muldoon's use of visits for political purposes, then his government could not agree. If New Zealanders had to choose between ANZUS and the anti-nuclear policy they would choose their own policy. In the chilly atmosphere the familiar arguments went back and forth but nothing resembling a negotiation got under way.

Armitage was troubled by Palmer's plea that the US should understand his government's difficulties; there did not seem to be any effort to understand the US's problems. He still wondered whether the political will existed to stand up to the fierce criticism which would follow the admission of an American vessel. 'You have to convince people here of that because the US felt itself led down a path on the *Buchanan*.' Laux from the National Security Council compared the New Zealand peace movement with Europe in 1982, but there political leaders had used the unrest not as an excuse but as a means of educating their people in the strategic realities. Stung by all this,

THE PALMER MISSION

Palmer had the last word, pointing out that he was the only elected politician in the room; it was easier for those who were not to talk about changing or influencing public opinion.*

The meeting at the Pentagon with the Secretary of Defense was even less encouraging. Weinberger said Washington needed certainty over ship visits, not 'a virtual lawsuit' each time, and Palmer's brief did not go far enough. 'Your policy must be your policy' but the US would just have to let the alliance go. But when Palmer walked down the Pentagon corridor to see Armitage there was a 'rather promising exchange'.

Armitage certainly described the outlook as bleak. If nothing was done, relations between the US and New Zealand would deteriorate over time – not as a matter of policy but as a fact of life. But after the usual exchange of complaints about each other's policy something more positive appeared. Palmer said that Jamieson was sitting in Wellington with his bags packed, ready to begin discussions on a programme of visits. A formula which envisaged visits in conformity with the policies of both governments might enable the defence chief to do business.

Armitage thought that whatever their form the words had to reflect a concept of port visits understood by both countries and clear to America's other friends and allies. The US was now running into access difficulties with India which had asked the British, citing the New Zealand precedent, to confirm or deny the status of a prospective visit. Palmer suggested for consideration an agreed statement saying 'The New Zealand Chief of Defence Staff will come without delay to discuss in detail the resumption of ship visits in accordance with the firmly held policies of both governments and the spirit of cooperation which has traditionally existed between the United States and New Zealand'. Armitage undertook to discuss this with Wolfowitz but was worried about Lange's willingness to face trouble: if a nuclear-capable ship came into Wellington Harbour

---

* NZ embassy's report of the day's discussions, 19 September 1985, PM 59/8/5 Part 5, MFAT.

'the left wing would go bananas'. Palmer argued that New Zealand had a lot more to lose than the US if a visit went wrong: 'We will have invited you in.'*

If this was the hint of a possible negotiation it withered that afternoon in the face of Shultz's lack of trust. After the unhappy experience of February, 'I formed a poor impression of Mr Lange', and nothing he had heard so far had increased his confidence.† The Secretary was characteristically plain-spoken. He was 'unequivocally' opposed to legislation, though that was for New Zealand to decide. He could not accept an arrangement for visits where the New Zealand Government would carry out research leading to it 'figuring out accurately' what weaponry was on board and then 'discriminating for or against particular ships on that basis'. He added with surprising frankness that 'over a period of time you would have to assume that some of our visiting vessels would carry nuclear arms'. Differences over ship visits would affect the alliance relationship but nevertheless he hoped the two countries would remain firm friends.‡

Shultz had lost confidence in New Zealand's promises and, despite the hopes raised in the talk with Armitage, neither he nor Weinberger (prone to disagree on everything else) believed that Wellington was in earnest about resolving the difference. Palmer had not brought the proposal for a workable accommodation Washington was hoping to hear; instead his message was that the Americans should see the error of *their* ways and be able to live with the legislation. As they smiled and shook hands for the photographers, a New Zealand journalist thought 'it was already clear that Mr Palmer's legal logic was having no impact on a United States Administration with global responsibilities and global policies'.§

So the afternoon ended on a dying note. A meeting had been arranged in the State Department to review the day's talks and agree

---

* Embassy note of the meeting, 19 September 1985, PM 50/6/4 Part 11, MFAT.
† Interview with Shultz, 2 October 2011.
‡ Embassy report, 19 September 1985, PM 59/8/5 Part 5, MFAT.
§ John Bishop, *Eyewitness News*, TVNZ, 1 October 1985.

on a common line for the media. An hour was set aside for this but it was over in five minutes: there was nothing to talk about. Palmer found himself standing on the footpath outside for ten minutes, grimly repeating 'I have no comment to make' to the reporters crowding round him, until the cars could be found.*

The mood soured further when Palmer, back at the embassy, recounted the events of the day at a press conference. Contrary to the usual practice, he gave an account of the American position as well as his own. He complained of the lack of a 'matching flexibility' on the American side and accused the Administration of overreacting. He did not hold out much hope for an agreement; the 'balance of probabilities' suggested that the two positions could not be reconciled. After that it seemed rather inconsistent to add that the two sides should talk through their differences 'rather than sniping through the newspapers'.†

The State Department claimed that the two sides had agreed not to characterise each other's position, regretted that this understanding had been breached, and went on to describe Palmer's account as 'partial and inaccurate'. Behind this chilly diplomatic language there was some anger among senior officials; according to one source, 'the language is not printable'. But Shultz issued a soothing statement the next day, saying that the discussions, though unsuccessful, had been 'thorough and friendly' and the US and New Zealand would remain as friends despite the ANZUS difficulties.‡

That night there were mixed views in the embassy over the report to be sent to the Prime Minister. The embassy people were discouraged, more so than the visiting party. Francis believed Palmer had stood up well and if the Americans did not want New Zealand in the alliance then so be it. Henderson agreed; this was the time to get onto

---

* Interview with Murdoch, 21 July 2011.
† Tom Bridgman, NZPA correspondent in Washington, 21 September 1985.
‡ *New Zealand Herald*, 24 September and Shultz statement, 20 September 1985, PM 50/6/4 Part 11, MFAT.

the front foot, get out of ANZUS and blame it on the Americans. The Prime Minister could go to the country on this and win.

The embassy staff argued against reaching any such conclusion before the visit was even over. Rowling was hastily brought in to speak to Palmer who accepted this. He told the Prime Minister that the position was not quite closed off. There were still some meetings to come in two days' time but it was highly unlikely that the outcome would be any different. If so, he would say that agreement had not been possible but New Zealand would do everything in its power to build a solid relationship with the United States on that basis.*

Both sides seemed gripped by pessimism and it was not surprising that the final talks, on a Saturday morning two days later, did not go well. They ended with lunch at a Texas-style steak restaurant in Georgetown. Meeting Murdoch outside the restaurant, Armitage complained that Francis had kept wanting to 'take the talks down South', towards a break. He said that he and his fellow American officials had stretched their instructions to pursue a solution, only to find a senior New Zealand diplomat trying to close it off. Wood thought this was true. Francis seemed to have set out during the morning's talks to provoke the Americans, disparaging ANZUS and saying some thought his country's interests would be better served by being out of it. Palmer, however, saw Francis's contribution as his 'finest hour', mounting an attack on the Americans as imperialists who were behaving very badly towards a loyal ally.† For Armitage this was the end; he decided New Zealand was not interested in a solution.

So lunch was a rather reserved occasion. Over two hours both sides worked over all the outstanding issues. Palmer was still aggrieved, saying he had come to Washington with a set of proposals and had made no progress; indeed after Shultz's stand they had if anything gone backwards. New Zealand had moved a long way but the US

---

* Palmer to Lange, 19 September 1985, PM 59/8/5 Part 5, MFAT.
† Vernon Wright interview, 8 February 1987.

had not. But Wolfowitz seemed determined to keep hope and the negotiations alive. After some vigorous exchanges about good faith, he said both sides had to keep trying even though the legislation might 'simply be leading us up to the cliff edge'. If they continued to work on the practical issues of nuclear capability and normal access Shultz's mind might yet be changed.*

The outcome was a rather cocky cable to Wellington saying 'At a final meeting today the American officials blinked'. The blinking turned out to be Wolfowitz's determination to keep trying in the hope that 'refinement of the detail of our proposals might conceivably tip the balance'. But there was no suggestion in the cable that further thought in Wellington would help, only the carefree summary that 'I played the straight man, Francis added a song and dance routine which had the Americans speechless, with Rowling delivering the coup de grace'.†

Thus ended what the American side regarded as 'a futile effort'.‡ So did Palmer who privately concluded that a deal was not possible. He later summed up the difference with some accuracy: 'his tendency was to "lawyer a problem through" but the US simply regarded it as a matter of high policy'.§ For Washington, it *was* a matter of high policy, affecting their entire alliance network. The difficulty was that, with no one quite meaning it, the visit had become freighted with a special importance in the weeks before Palmer arrived. The expectations of officials like Wolfowitz and Armitage had been raised by assurances from Rowling that Palmer was not Lange, he was a knowledgeable negotiator who would have a mandate to find a solution.

They were disappointed that after all the advance publicity Palmer had not made a more determined search for a compromise. Having set out his mandate from Cabinet in the first talks, he thereafter offered

---

* This account of the discussions draws mainly on the recollections and notes of embassy staffers John Wood and Simon Murdoch.
† Palmer to Lange, 21 September 1985, PM 59/8/5 Part 5, MFAT.
‡ Interview with James Kelly, 2 October 2011.
§ Interview with Palmer, 15 July 2011.

nothing new, saying his mandate was exhausted. The Americans were perplexed by the suggestion that anyone would come to a negotiation with a set of proposals that could not be modified. The embassy diplomats understood he was authorised to be 'flexible' if he detected any flexibility on the American side. They suggested that someone like Wolfowitz might be told quietly that the New Zealanders had not come empty-handed if his side could reciprocate. This was a familiar negotiating tactic to get both sides beyond reciting their opening positions, but it was ruled out by the visiting party.

So the American disillusion was all the sharper. They judged Palmer to be honest and straightforward but he had not come with any new or substantial offer; his proposals were words and 'lawyering'. They had suspected this from the beginning, feeling that if New Zealand was really anxious to find a workable compromise there would have been more serious signs. Palmer's brief had gone through an elaborate process of clearance, but with no hints of any willingness to rethink the substance of the American objections to the legislation. The make-up of Palmer's delegation did not suggest a readiness to talk in earnest or it would have included Norrish and perhaps Jamieson.

As a result confidence that the Administration could do business with New Zealand was all but snuffed out. Even Lange's staff felt that Palmer had interpreted his brief too inflexibly and not done what he was expected to do.* Wolfowitz alone seemed anxious to keep a light in the window. He had risked Shultz's displeasure and 'gone out on a limb' in order to keep alive the flickering prospect of a negotiated solution.† For the time being, though, there was nothing more that could be done in Washington. Palmer went on to London where after the Stanley visit the British had begun to take an interest, deciding they could no longer 'lie doggo' in the deepening conflict between two of their closest friends.

---

* AHC, Wellington, 9 October 1985, 221/1/4/4 Part 8, DFAT.
† Wolfowitz's complaint to the author, August 1995.

Chapter Ten
The British Step In

Everyone was left winded by the outcome of the Washington talks. The British embassy saw it as a major failure which had further soured the atmosphere. There had been no disposition on either side to reach a fix or a fudge of their differences – both stated their conflicting points of principle with great clarity but got no further. Given that the two parties had different destinations in mind, Shultz had seen no point in exploring different paths. His main aim was normal access to New Zealand ports under NCND and he judged that Palmer's proposal did not offer this. The Americans were surprised that Palmer had come without authority to discuss a phased programme of visits and Shultz now laid down that an acceptable framework for visits must come first.[*]

Behind these judicious words there was considerable anger. New Zealand, it appeared, had once again over-promised and

---

[*] British embassy cables, 21 and 26 September 1985, FCO Papers.

under-delivered. The Americans believed they had been led to expect a serious discussion by a senior member of the government about how ship visits could be restored, but instead of a discussion they had been given a lecture on their shortcomings. There had been no negotiation about the detail of New Zealand's proposed legislation. Indeed, Palmer had never shown them the full draft and had only passed over selected parts. Although Shultz commented that it was still unclear whether the New Zealand government's policy was 'malign' or simply confused, he seemed to have made up his own mind. He believed that Palmer had known in advance that his proposals were unworkable but had wanted to put the blame for the continued deadlock on the United States. The visit 'had not been appreciated' he told the British Foreign Secretary, Sir Geoffrey Howe. 'The real purpose of the Palmer trip was to get a good image in New Zealand.'*

His anger was shared by most members of the Inter-Agency Group who felt they had been deceived about Palmer's aims. Officials in the State Department wondered rather wildly whether the issue could better be dealt with at a technical level and the politicians kept out of it. There had been flickers of a possible solution in the earlier talks with Rowling and his staff but these had been snuffed out by the Palmer visit. Lilley, Wolfowitz's deputy, conceded that the US shared some blame for the mess but he complained to the New Zealand embassy that 'we had been disastrous dissemblers, and had never been honest with ourselves or with the United States. The proposals brought by Mr Palmer had been staggering in their lack of integrity. The government had been prepared to deceive the people in its construction of a "jerry-built structure" to allow ship visits to take place.'†

Palmer too was upset and angered by the way, as he reported to Lange, Shultz had 'brought the blinds down completely' on his hopes. In New York, where he was attending the opening of the UN General Assembly, he poured out his frustrations to Hayden, the Australian

---

* British embassy, Washington, 15 October 1985, FCO Papers.
† File note by John McKinnon, NZ embassy, PM 50/6/4 Part 11, MFAT.

THE BRITISH STEP IN

Foreign Minister. New Zealand, he said, had shown a lot of flexibility and made concessions which had not been matched by the United States. They could not seem to understand that, by providing a lawful framework for the decisions, the legislation would actually assist port visits. Much careful work had gone into its drafting, said the aggrieved lawyer, and Shultz had rejected it out of hand. At one point some possibilities had seemed to be emerging – 'the Americans had blinked' was how he had reported it, he said proudly – but Shultz had brought the shutters down.

He thought that Shultz's attitude had caused some consternation among his officials and wondered if he had read his brief ('pure self-deception' said the marginal note in Canberra). He had told the Americans that they did not understand the political situation in New Zealand. The government could not abandon its anti-nuclear policy; if it had to choose, it would abandon ANZUS. 'The government simply could not afford to see the break-up of the Labour Party.' He could understand American worries about the possible ripple effect on their global network of alliances but if they did not show more flexibility there would be a greater effect from forcing New Zealand out of the ANZUS alliance. Anyhow, there was little more that New Zealand could do; it was up to the Americans to make the next move if they wished.

His complaints went on for seven pages in the record before Hayden could get a word in. When he did it was to ask whether an agreed schedule of visits could in time become 'normal port entry'. When Palmer said no, this would not be possible, Hayden said the US would in that case be accepting a serious curb on its global position: 'He understood, therefore, Mr Shultz's problem.'[*]

This cool response reflected a certain Australian impatience with New Zealand's continuing difficulties. Briefing Hayden for the meeting, Canberra said it was not surprising that New Zealand's proposals were unacceptable. What was surprising and disturbing

---

[*] Palmer to Hayden, 27 September 1985, 111/3/3/1 Part 40, ANZ.

was Palmer's failure to grasp the messages the US gave clearly at all his meetings – that the procedure in his draft still breached NCND and that every subsequent request for a ship visit would be hostage to Lange's political position. It was hard to see how any dialogue could be maintained unless the New Zealanders could bring themselves to admit the nature of the impasse more clearly.*

Kim Beazley, the Australian Minister of Defence, had earlier described Lange to a British caller as not understanding how dangerous his game was; he was like a small boy with a box of matches in an ammunition dump.† After the Palmer mission he too was bothered by the 'chalk and cheese' differences in each side's account of the discussions. Wellington did not seem to grasp that the principal American worry was not the fact of legislation but that the process by which the Prime Minister would approve a ship visit would in itself be a breach of NCND – he would be declaring that the ship did not carry nuclear weapons. This would make trouble for other allies who relied on a universal adherence to NCND for their own political peace. He had seen suggestions that New Zealand's policy was having an effect on countries like China and India, and several NATO members were watching the progress of the legislation carefully. Any procedure by which Wellington made declarations about American warships would greatly worry not just the Administration but its other allies.

So hints from Lange that Australia might now help by intervening with the Americans were rebuffed. Beazley and Hawke talked it over and agreed that even a quiet 'sussing out' of what might be done would be a substantial change of Australian policy, needing careful consideration in Cabinet. The US/NZ disagreement was 'not a fight we particularly want to buy into'; it would cause them considerable political problems with the Opposition and with those in the ALP who were opposed to ship visits.‡

---

* Canberra to Hayden, 26 September 1985, 370/1/20 Parts 43 and 44, NAA.
† BHC, Canberra, 20 August 1985, FCO Papers.
‡ NZHC, Canberra, 30 September 1985, 111/3/3/1 Part 40, ANZ.

THE BRITISH STEP IN

In any case, Canberra saw little hope of achieving anything. Given the box that the New Zealand Government was in domestically, a compromise did not seem possible. It would be unable to go ahead with any legislation that was acceptable to Washington. Behind these thoughts shared with the New Zealanders in Canberra there was a sterner view, reported by the British High Commission: the Australians 'expect and wish' the US to stand firm in its opposition to the legislation and had warned Wellington that pushing the US into reviewing its ANZUS commitments could make it even more difficult for the Australian Government to continue full defence cooperation with New Zealand.[*]

After getting little sympathy from Hayden (who told Palmer he did not think New Zealand was behaving wisely and said publicly on his return that 'the Americans have been patient and forbearing' over the dispute),[†] Palmer took his complaints to the General Assembly. He devoted almost half his speech to nuclear issues, including the French attack on the *Rainbow Warrior*. The tone was tough and, to British ears at least, made tougher by 'his raw Kiwi accent'. New Zealanders, he said, were deeply anti-nuclear and simply wished to run their own affairs in accordance with their own wishes. He noted the work of a former Prime Minister, Peter Fraser, in ensuring that the rights of small nations were protected by the UN Charter. Now by an irony of fate his government was again concerned to protect its independence and sovereign rights 'against the increasingly complex and sophisticated pressures that are generated from large countries within the international community'. As the British report said: 'There could be little doubt amongst his audience as to the two "large countries" he had in mind.'[‡]

He then went on to London where he contrasted the flexibility shown by New Zealand and the distance it had travelled 'at no inconsiderable political expense' with the 'rigid and totally

---

[*] BHC, Canberra, 27 September 1985, FCO Papers.
[†] Press conference, 14 October 1985.
[‡] British Permanent Mission, 26 September 1985, FCO Papers.

uncompromising response' received from Shultz. There too the tone was cool and Palmer concluded that the British line was as hard as the American – Palmer thought that the message given by Stanley, the Minister of State, 'could have been drafted by the Pentagon'. Stanley made it clear that while the legislation contained its 'public intelligence assessment' of the status of a visiting warship, no port call by the Royal Navy would be possible. If New Zealand could shelve the legislation and enter into practical discussions to get an outline of agreed visits, that would be better than enshrining the impasse in law. But Palmer rejected this, saying that it was the absence of legislative support that had led to the rejection of the *Buchanan*.

The Foreign Secretary, Sir Geoffrey Howe, took a gentler approach. He was more concerned about the consequences for the Western alliance and for Britain's own relationship with New Zealand if the dispute dragged on. When Palmer 'argued with some heat' that only New Zealand had been willing to make concessions, he suggested that it might be best to sit tight and allow a period for reflection. Muting the rhetoric would assist an attempt, quietly and in private, to find a way through – though he added that he could not in all honesty see one at the moment. Britain like Australia was reluctant to contemplate involvement in a quarrel which seemed unlikely to be resolved and which might only end in giving offence to one or perhaps both of the disputants. With the failure of the Washington talks, though, and the rising tempers on both sides, the need for a helpful friend became more obvious and the logic pointed to Britain. Howe undertook to think it over.[*]

Concerned about the implications of the dispute but with even less leverage, the Germans took a tactful line with Palmer when he arrived in Bonn. The Foreign Minister, Genscher, pointed out that the Federal Republic and New Zealand though far apart shared common security interests. Regional threats no longer existed, all eventually

---

[*] Palmer's report, 1 October and FCO note of meeting, 30 September 1985, PM 59/8/5 Part 6, MFAT, and FCO Papers.

had global implications. Western states, he said, were like the crew of a boat; some might be sitting on the edge and some in the middle 'but we would all go down if the boat sank'. The Defence Minister, Woerner, said Germany depended for political as well as security reasons on the Western alliance which they saw as worldwide and including ANZUS. 'As long as it does not endanger the alliance or your position in an area where you are so important, we feel reassured by what you have said.'[*]

Back home at Auckland airport, Palmer announced that New Zealand's foreign policies had pushed it to a prominent and respected place in world affairs: 'We have had publicity the like of which you could not buy in these last few months' and David Lange 'had become a leading figure in world politics'.[†] He continued this theme in his report to Cabinet, saying that the anti-nuclear policy was better understood abroad 'as a sane, logical and practical response' to New Zealand's strategic situation, though he gave no examples of this better understanding. The country's stand was hitting the headlines everywhere (there was a temptation to get more but 'I foreswore it'), helped by the 'exaggerated and shrill way' the US had dealt with it. It was important to assure key governments that New Zealand was determined to play a full part in the Western community and 'we are not, as the Americans portray us, a maverick, isolationist and somehow unreliable country'.

He concluded, however, that there was no solution to the ship visit problem. ANZUS was inoperative and in practice no longer of great relevance to New Zealand. Foreign policy should concentrate on essentially New Zealand interests. Cabinet was advised to play the ANZUS question down and convince people that their country was 'sturdy, independent and capable of looking after itself'. A quiet period was needed to get ANZUS and ship visits out of the headlines and allow the underlying and stable relationship with the United States to re-emerge.[‡]

---

[*] Note of meetings in Bonn, 2 October 1985, LONB 106/4/1 Part 6, ANZ.
[†] *New Zealand Times*, 13 October and *New Zealand Herald*, 14 October 1985.
[‡] Report to Cabinet, 7 October 1985, PM 59/8/5 Part 6, MFAT.

For all the indignation in both Wellington and Washington a small group of American diplomats, with the tenacity that marks their profession, had not given up hope. Despite Shultz's disapproval, despite the deep scepticism of the Inter-Agency Group, Wolfowitz and his little group of advisers in the East Asia Pacific (EAP) division of the State Department were still trying to coax a small flame from the grey ashes of the talks. Wolfowitz at the final lunch with Palmer had wondered whether 'creative lawyers' might be able to find a way through. Since his services had scarcely been required during the visit, perhaps Colin Keating, an international lawyer with Palmer, might be called back from New York for 'an informal brainstorming session' on the draft legislation.

Glassman in State did some quick thinking in the days that followed. Perhaps the drafting could make it plainer that the government's intention was to facilitate visits, not exclude them. He seemed to be thinking of a formula which would empower the Prime Minister to invite, in principle at least, all classes of vessel to visit New Zealand ports subject to certain safeguards. With the principle of unfettered access declared, the vessels that actually visited could be worked out and agreed in private, taking the policies of both countries into account. There was no need to fuss about the detail of a visits programme – Glassman thought they 'could get away with' one nuclear-capable visit in 1986.*

For a brief moment hope flared up. Then the inevitable happened: David Lange made a speech. It was not an especially provocative one and indeed was warm about the need for a good relationship with the United States. But his talk to the Canterbury Labour Party Council seemed to be clearly paving the way for a New Zealand no longer in ANZUS. He argued that there was no point in trying to reconcile the irreconcilable. The nuclear deterrent was 'bizarrely inappropriate' for New Zealand's situation and if the ANZUS treaty involved New Zealand in accepting this, then the relationship was irrelevant

---

* NZ embassy cables of 25 and 26 September 1985, PM 111/3/3/1 Part 40, ANZ.

THE BRITISH STEP IN

and dangerous to New Zealand. He suggested that it was 'more important to preserve a good relationship with the US and Australia than to preserve a treaty which causes conflict between friends'.*

Rowling was said to be 'furious' about this speech and Palmer told the American ambassador that it 'was a mistake and I have told David so'.† The Americans read it as a declaration that the Prime Minister was no longer looking for a way to restore ship visits or ANZUS as a working alliance. As often with Lange's speeches, they cast about for a clearer light on what he meant. Armacost spent an hour with Bryce Harland, the Permanent Representative in New York, seeking to know what Lange had in mind in making this speech and more particularly why he had chosen this time when Washington was contemplating another round of informal talks. As equally often with Lange's speeches, there was no convincing answer. It did not help that Radio Moscow praised the speech for its 'firm and realistic policy'. Senior Administration officials concluded that the discussions with Keating would achieve nothing and they were called off.

The two sides were once again back where they had started. It was not the end of attempts to renew the search for a settlement – for all the irritation there was too much at stake in the relationship to do that – but there was a growing disbelief on both sides that any solution was achievable, and on the American side an underlying suspicion of New Zealand's motives that corroded all remaining efforts. Shultz complained to the British Foreign Secretary: 'They are very difficult to deal with. They tend to issue public statements at variance with what had been said in confidential talks.'‡ Others were less polite. A State Department official told the embassy that they had kept full records of all the discussions and meetings on the issue and 'had proof positive in them that the Prime Minister was a liar'.§

---

* Speech of 27 September 1985.
† Norrish to AHC, 3 October 1985. He thought the speech was intended to quash any fears of a compromise on the anti-nuclear policy after Palmer's visit to Washington, 250/11/18 Part 25, NAA.
‡ Shultz–Howe talks in London, 10 December 1985, FCO Papers.
§ PM 50/6/4 Part 11, MFAT.

The stalemate caused tempers to rise in New Zealand too, with outbursts of ministerial anger over minor matters, like a satellite broadcast by Wolfowitz which Palmer chose to interpret as an attempt to reach out to New Zealanders over the heads of their elected government. In this restless atmosphere it was tempting fate for Palmer to call for 'a period of studious silence'. The silence was broken almost immediately by the publication of a letter from seventeen retired defence chiefs which attacked the government's belief that the South Pacific should be regarded as 'uniquely privileged to stand apart and yet secure in a divided world'. Nuclear deterrence had kept the peace for 40 years and they believed that an occasional visit by a friend's nuclear ship was of little consequence 'when compared with the burdens and responsibilities which are being borne on behalf of all by Western friends whose values we claim to share'.*

This was politically awkward; the ageing military leaders were widely respected, several having had distinguished records in World War II. Then a short-tempered Lange made it worse. Caught late at night by a reporter, he was stung into saying, 'These geriatric generals can carry on like this for as long as they like.' He was ruefully aware of the blunder he had made but the 'geriatric generals' affair haunted him for some time and pulled another brick from his public standing. That standing, a towering wall in March when he had felt 'bulletproof', had been crumbling all year. Journalists dated the end of the honeymoon to April when he had made a tour of East and Central Africa wearing his 'Nukebusters' tee-shirt and been laughed at by the press for doing so. According to the polls, though the government remained popular and secure of re-election, his personal standing had steadily declined from 76 per cent in April to only 26 per cent by August. No leader likes losing popularity, but Lange's insecurity and constant need of reassurance made this decline more unpredictable in its manifestations.

It began to show in increasingly erratic and rambling press conferences and his once-cheerful wit took on a darker and more acid

---

* Open letter of 8 October 1985.

THE BRITISH STEP IN

tone. He complained regularly about Washington's silence. 'The President of the United States at Geneva was given a world reception of great admiration when he pledged to keep talking to the Russians ... when it comes to New Zealand the US will not even discuss issues of moment between us.'* There was constant quibbling – the claim that ANZUS was always inoperative, it was designed to be; allegations of 'classic pieces of disinformation' by Washington; fencing with reporters at the level of school playground repartee; abuse of the Opposition as grovelling and licking Washington's boots; and an underlying note of bitterness towards the United States, all summed up in a Foreign Office minute as 'Lange's recent obfuscations'.† On one occasion he declared that 'The justice system of New Zealand is not for sale to France and the New Zealand legislative system is not at the behest of the United States' – an unfortunate comparison given that he later handed over the *Rainbow Warrior* prisoners when the French applied restrictions on New Zealand imports. Asked whether Australia could act as an honest broker he was tempted, he said, to observe that 'they were neither honest nor broker'.‡

Not all press conferences were as uncontrolled as this but there was a growing impression that the Prime Minister was lashing out rather than making considered responses. Behind the signs of strain was a sense of political danger as ANZUS drifted towards the rocks. A clear majority of the public had consistently supported the treaty and a smaller but clear majority also supported the anti-nuclear policy. That support, though portrayed in talks as the overwhelming will of the people, was far from monolithic. All but one of the metropolitan newspapers were opposed to the policy, the *Press* conveying a general editorial gloom that the mess looked like going from bad to worse.§ When a survey in August showed that support for stay-

---

* Press conference, 25 November 1985.
† Minute of 27 September 1985, FCO Papers.
‡ Press conference, 25 November 1985. 'Charming!' was the comment in Canberra alongside the Australian reference.
§ The *Press*, 21 September 1985.

ing in ANZUS had strengthened, the pollsters concluded that there would be 'considerable damage' to the government if it had to choose between the two.*

So the search for a resolution had to continue, or at least be seen to continue. If Washington withdrew its security guarantee when the legislation was passed, in the words of Lange's speechwriter, 'it would be unwise to allow the public to believe something of value had been lost'.† This was why the Prime Minister constantly grumbled that the Administration would not 'pick up the phone' to talk to him. It also explained why his phone did not ring. The Americans suspected that New Zealand's anxiety for continued talks was for show rather than negotiation. In the latest unhappy example, a proposal for the country's top international lawyer, Chris Beeby, to come to Washington for talks was announced first to Reuters rather than to the State Department.‡

The new coolness was not just the aftermath of the Palmer mission; influential members of the Inter-Agency Group still hoped that New Zealand opinion would change when the deadlock became apparent. They understood that the Lange policy was popular but believed that the public was more attached to the alliance and would blame Lange if this and the broader relationship were damaged.§ A stop on normal ministerial contacts – in industrial language a lockout by Washington – might shock people into seeing the need for compromise on port access.

Proposed visits by the Trade and Agriculture Ministers were therefore declined and new restrictions reiterated that the New Zealand ambassador could not talk to people above the rank of Assistant Secretary. The fear was that even such long-established contacts might be portrayed by Lange as 'business as usual'. Wellington was

---

* Heylen poll carried out for Massey University in August 1985.
† Margaret Pope, *At the Turning Point: My Political Life with David Lange*, AM Publishing New Zealand, 2011, p. 131.
‡ An example of what the AHC earlier described as 'the rather haphazard way in which important matters are at times handled in New Zealand', 8 May 1985, 250/11/18 Part 21, NAA.
§ British embassy, Washington, 26 September 1985, FCO Papers.

THE BRITISH STEP IN

nervous and covered up the cancellation of ministerial visits but the policy was a miscalculation, overrating voters' concern about contacts in Washington and underrating the strength of Kiwi nationalism, now thoroughly roused by being told what to do. The restraints lingered on for some time but they were petty and made little practical sense.

Neither side could see how to break the stalemate as October wound on; and for all of Shultz's sternness, neither side was comfortable with it. On his way home Palmer told an Australian Minister in Melbourne that even the opening he had glimpsed at the end of his Washington visit seemed to have gone, chased away by Lange's Canterbury speech. He could now see no legislative formula which could accommodate the two countries' positions. The best that could be done was a 'managed stand-off' in the hope of maintaining the present position as long as possible. His instinct was that when this was no longer possible 'the public would come down on the side of keeping ANZUS'.[*]

The thoughts of both countries now turned to the British as offering a chance of getting things moving again. The Americans hoped that London's greater familiarity might suggest more useful ideas on how to deal with this baffling and moody nation. In the regular series of planning talks between the two countries the Americans poured out their frustrations. They did not, they said, want to bully the New Zealanders. The West was not the Warsaw Pact and New Zealand was a sovereign country. But Wolfowitz told a British official, 'the whole approach was too tricky' – it was without precedent among other allies and the risk of refusals would compromise NCND.[†]

Beneath the Secretary of State, however, and possibly without his knowledge, the State Department had not given up and was still looking for possible legal drafting to try out on the New Zealanders. Their

---

[*] Conversation with Gareth Evans, 12 October 1985, 370/1/20 Part 45, NAA.
[†] Wolfowitz to David Wilson, 7–8 October 1985, FCO Papers.

British counterparts at the planning talks encouraged this; the outcome was not inevitable and they should both look at ways of moving the issue in the right direction.* London was urged on by a passionate appeal from its High Commissioner in Wellington. New Zealand had tried 'an over-clever legal approach' which failed. It was not going to abandon its non-nuclear policy but it was willing to continue to seek a mutually acceptable accommodation. If the Americans continued to refuse to talk, the country might unwillingly drift into non-alignment which was in no one's interests. 'Treating New Zealand as a pariah is ill-advised at this stage (I would say at any stage).' Its propositions are not cut and dried and 'in our own interests we should try to replace them with workable and tolerable ones'.†

This message was being reinforced with characteristic vigour by the incoming New Zealand High Commissioner, Bryce Harland, a career diplomat whom Lange had moved from New York to London in October. The Foreign Office officials had a slightly ambivalent attitude – he had once run off with one of their wives – and occasionally speculated on how closely he represented his Prime Minister's views, but there was no doubt of his energy and persistence. He wasted no time; even in his round of introductory calls, traditionally confined to niceties, he 'plunged straight in' on ship visits, so fervently that Ministers' ears were said to be still ringing.

Mrs Thatcher was in robust form when he called on her. She said that New Zealand had a very special place in British hearts and the fact that it had been the first to offer support in the Falklands campaign had made a great impression. So she was all the more upset now: 'This was the first blot on relations between Britain and New Zealand.' The ship visits policy would have serious long-term effects and 'she doubted whether the New Zealand people understood that their government would be isolating the country and losing fundamental friends'.

---

* US/UK Planning Talks, 2–3 October 1985, FCO Papers.
† O'Leary to London, 18 October 1985, FCO Papers.

THE BRITISH STEP IN

She flared up when Harland commented that American threats of countermeasures made people feel they were being pushed around. That was 'monstrous'; New Zealanders were trying to push others around. Mr Lange had started the dispute by banning ship visits and others had the right to decide their reaction. 'She saw no realistic prospect of a solution along these lines [the legislation], in which case the only thing was to ride out the problem without letting it affect wider relations.' Harland held up better than his predecessor, Joe Walding, who had needed a stiff drink after his call on Mrs Thatcher, saying peaceably 'that he saw some virtue in this'.[*]

Geoffrey Howe again took a more gentle approach, agreeing that he was the soft cop to his Prime Minister's tough policing, though he said this was not deliberate and there was in practice little difference in their views.[†] His manner, though, was more sympathetic, perhaps encouraged by his son's position as press officer for the Campaign for Nuclear Disarmament. He complained that 'the wretched ship question' was drifting because of doubts as to who should take the lead. 'It often happened in a family situation that there was confusion as to who should be speaking to whom.' When Harland said it was Palmer's view that the ball was in the American court, he said more bluntly that the dispute had been started by New Zealand and the ball was in its court. However, he said his impression was that the Americans were willing to try for a way through but were held back by misgivings about New Zealand's seriousness. If Britain could tell them that, regardless of protocol and procedure, New Zealand was prepared to talk, then discussions might be resumed.[‡]

When Harland confirmed this willingness after a quick call home, Howe moved at once, anxious to get something moving before the legislation became firm. Two days later he proposed to Washington that three-way talks be held in London at senior official level. After Palmer's visit the New Zealanders would not wish to risk a second

---
[*] British note of conversation, 22 November 1985, FCO Papers.
[†] Interview with Lord Howe, 5 July 2010.
[‡] Call on Howe, 28 October 1985, LONB 106/4/1 Part 6, ANZ.

rebuff in Washington, and the Americans were most unlikely to want to go to Wellington. While the British disclaimed any desire to mediate, a meeting in London would provide a buffer to absorb the accumulating resentments of the other two. A tentative feeler was put out in Washington – 'We have not yet abandoned hope of resolving the issue' – but the Foreign Office did not want New Zealand to get wind of their interest.

The Americans were still cautious and reluctant to move without a clearer signal that New Zealand was willing to make an effort. The dark shadow of the *Buchanan* still hovered over them. Brigadier-General Drew told the British why: 'To put it quite bluntly, the New Zealand government had lied to the US government last year when they had asked them to submit a request for a ship visit and had assured them it would be approved.'*

They were not keen on the idea of tripartite talks in London, but were attracted to the thought of separate but coordinated approaches by the US and Britain. Did the British have a 'step-ladder' up which a solution might be reached? They did not, but they at once set to work on a scale of possibilities in descending order of attractiveness. In varying forms this 'ladder', a programme of possible Anglo-American naval visits in ascending order of 'difficulty', became the core of the renewed effort to find an answer.

The Foreign Office was well aware there were differences in the two approaches which, if not delicately managed, could cause transatlantic friction. Britain set a lower bar for a solution – 'we take a less absolute view'. Its main concern was to safeguard entry for Royal Navy ships whereas the United States had its wider network of alliances to consider. If, as the Foreign Office acknowledged, New Zealand could move political hearts more easily in Britain, it also meant that from Howe down there was a sympathy for New Zealand's difficulties and a somewhat better understanding of its views. This was constantly underlined by O'Leary who had lived

---

* US–UK talks in London, 23–24 October 1985, FCO Papers.

THE BRITISH STEP IN

in New Zealand before and had a New Zealand family: 'Mr Lange is loquacious and inconsistent but he is not slippery or deliberately dishonest.... He needs our help to get out of a pit which is largely of his own digging before overt US pressure leads him to dig even deeper.'*

These views, and London's pressure, encouraged the State Department to try again. Howe and Shultz were friends who were in regular contact and the Foreign Secretary's attitude was softening Shultz's aversion to further dealings with New Zealand. He had gone so far as to agree that it would be helpful if Howe could 'weigh in with the New Zealanders'. This encouraged Wolfowitz to stretch his mandate for another try. He and Lange met at the fortieth anniversary celebrations for the UN, where Lange was the only small nation representative to be invited to speak. His encounter with Shultz at the main reception lasted only a few minutes but a longer talk with Wolfowitz – later described by Lange as 'a very hard worker, a person of, I think, very high probity' – started the stalled negotiations moving again.†

Wolfowitz said, with an impressive disdain for the record, that Shultz's comments to Palmer should not be interpreted as either final or unduly negative. He at least did not see the negotiating process as being played out. The legislation did not have to be a breaking point if they could agree on a practical programme of port visits on terms acceptable to both sides. This had been recognised for some time in the State Department but Wolfowitz's approach was not official policy and was opposed by the rest of the Inter-Agency Group, the Pentagon and National Security Council, which still felt that US interests would be best preserved by toughing it out. Wolfowitz's subordinates found themselves engaged in a retrospective effort to get approval in Washington for the course which he had proposed to Lange in New York.

When after two attempts they finally secured agreement to test what level of access might in practice be permitted by the legislation,

---

* BHC, Wellington, 21 November 1985, FCO Papers.
† Vernon Wright interview, 13 January 1987, Lange Papers, Box 1, ANZ.

the submission sat in Shultz's in-tray for over a week and approval when it came still trailed clouds of suspicion. It acquired the unhappy name of 'the carrot and stick policy'. The 'carrot' was Washington's readiness to talk about the legislation, provided Wellington agreed to allow ship visits on the old pattern. The 'stick' was that in the absence of such agreement, the Administration would proceed to review its security guarantee and make it clear that the broader relationship would suffer serious damage.

This was the sort of offer that only a reluctant committee would design; neither stick nor carrot looked persuasive. The only new feature was American willingness to discuss the legislation which was merely common sense given that much of the dispute revolved round the proposed wording of the law. Otherwise the policy was simply what Washington had been saying for months: the alliance relationship would be ended if normal port access was not allowed. The British were uneasy. If the Americans made new threats, Howe thought, 'it will not be possible to contain Mr Lange'. He had hoped that nothing would be said in public about the consequences of failure to find a solution, but this was apparently an essential part of the strategy as approved by Shultz. The Administration said it had no wish to throw down the gauntlet but, while the New Zealand Government continued to maintain that the issue did not threaten the wider relationship with the US, it had to say plainly that there would be serious long-term difficulties if no solution could be found.[*]

While making up his mind on this strategy, Shultz cast about for other means of influencing Wellington. He urged Howe to intervene again in support of the restoration of normal port access: 'The Kiwis pay close attention to your views.'[†] And he sent Philip Habib, a distinguished retired ambassador, to take soundings with Lange.

Habib's first posting, years earlier, had been in Wellington, and as often with diplomats he had a special sympathy for the capital

---

[*] Cables between FCO and British embassy, Washington, 15 and 19 November 1985, FCO Papers.
[†] Shultz to Howe, 20 November 1985: 'I believe it would be a propitious moment for you to convey your concerns once again to the government of New Zealand.' FCO Papers.

THE BRITISH STEP IN

where his career had begun. He came privately 'as an old friend of New Zealand' and was hurried through the underground garage of the Beehive up to Lange's office on a Saturday morning. The US and New Zealand, he said, had both made mistakes in handling the issue and he wanted to see how the relationship could be returned to a more sensible and normal footing. He was convinced that if the legislation went ahead, the Administration would not only suspend the alliance but, more importantly, the special relationship between the United States and New Zealand would be permanently impaired.

The Prime Minister's response broke no new ground. New Zealand had gone a long way to meet the main American concerns but had not met with any flexibility from Washington. He had removed from the draft any elements which he thought might have compromised NCND. 'What else could New Zealand do – other than give up the legislation which, as Mr Habib should know, was not on.'* Habib returned to California and told Shultz he saw no sign of flexibility.†

In the meantime the 'new' strategy made its appearance on 22 November when Lilley made a formal presentation to Rowling and handed over a 'non-paper'. A non-paper was the diplomatic equivalent of a stage whisper; it could be read, understood and discussed but did not officially exist and could not be referred to in public. This one was stern in tone and showed the extent of American exasperation. It did acknowledge that there was no prospect of Wellington giving up the legislation – that, said Lilley in less formal language, 'would be pissing into the wind' – but was unyielding in its other demands.

The Palmer approach was 'totally unacceptable' because it involved a judgement and in effect a declaration by the Prime Minister about the armament carried by an American warship. The Administration was still looking for an assurance by the New Zealand Government that normal port access under NCND could be attained within the present parliamentary term. The enactment of the legislation in its

---

* Notes of the conversation on 23 November 1985 in PM 111/3/3/1 Part 43, ANZ.
† Interview with Shultz, 2 November 2011.

current form would lead the US to redefine its treaty obligations to New Zealand and effectively to terminate the alliance relationship. In the meantime visits to Washington had been misrepresented by Wellington to convey an unwarranted impression of business as usual. If Lange wished to pass possible redrafts of the legislation, he could do it through the American embassy in Wellington.*

This unpromising document, described by Glassman as 'a pile of manure', was handed to Rowling in the presence of the Inter-Agency Group whose acrimonious discussions had produced it. But beneath the pack ice a warmer current flowed. When Lilley had cleared the room and the vigilance of his colleagues from the other agencies had been removed, he disclosed a more encouraging message. If New Zealand could give a 'positive assurance' that it wished to restore port access, then a dialogue could begin on a practical programme of visits and perhaps on the wording of the legislation itself.

The language was wary and the offer conditional, and it was still far from clear that it had the backing of the whole Administration. But it signalled that Washington had come out of the sulk which had followed the Palmer mission and, however cautiously, was willing to try again. Wellington was gratified if also wary, and at once suggested that the next step might be for David Caygill, the Minister of Trade and Industry, who would be visiting Los Angeles in December, to meet there with Lilley. 'Though it is late in the day [the legislation would be introduced into Parliament before Christmas] there is still an opportunity, if the Americans care to seize it, to get a constructive process of consultation under way.'†

Lilley was now in a delicate position. He had to be careful not to get too far ahead of his seniors in the State Department and in the Inter-Agency Group. There was still a deep distrust of New Zealand's motives and Lilley could only get authority for the meeting if it was kept entirely secret and if Caygill came with an unequivocal readiness

---

* State Department report of 23 November 1985, State Department Papers.
† Cable to Rowling, 25 November 1985, PM 59/8/5 Part 6, MFAT.

to discuss a plan for ship visits. Anything more qualified would only strengthen the hand of those in the Administration who wanted to deliver a very hard response when the legislation was tabled.

The opening was also hostage to the unpredictable public statements of the Prime Minister. There was a sharp intake of breath in the State Department when he was reported as telling the Auckland Chamber of Commerce that 'everything was still wonderful' in trade with the United States. This was true – exports were up 49 per cent and record numbers of American tourists visited New Zealand – but emphasising the fact might be seen as provocative by those in the Administration who wanted to punish the country. More seriously, they worried about the overall drift of Lange's and Palmer's press conferences, finding it difficult to square the sweeping reiterations of the anti-nuclear policy with the government's private assurances that it was serious about re-establishing port access.

Wellington, however, was making an effort to respond, and after lengthy discussion in both Cabinet and caucus some helpful changes to the legislation were agreed. The entry of foreign warships was no longer prohibited and the carriage of nuclear weapons was no longer an offence in New Zealand law – 'Now you do not have to make the choice between observing the law and compromising the NCND doctrine'. The requirement for the Prime Minister to be advised by the CDS and Intelligence Council in approving visits was dropped, in case it was assumed that these two were relying on secret American information. Court proceedings querying the Prime Minister's decision could only be started with the consent of the Attorney-General (in New Zealand a member of Cabinet), and though nuclear-propelled warships were excluded 'at the moment' this could be changed by an authoritative scientific review.[*]

One non-paper deserved another, and as the hasty arrangements for the meeting firmed up, Caygill was equipped by the Prime Minister with one which set out New Zealand's terms more

---

[*] US embassy, Wellington, 3 December 1985, State Department Papers.

forthrightly and in more detail than had previously been managed. It gave the required assurance that the government looked for a resumption of port visits by 'some US Navy ships' which made an important point rather obliquely – the legislation was a way of having *some* ship visits, not a way of having ship visits. It was prepared to discuss immediately a programme of visits which could be accepted and described publicly as 'normal access in accordance with the policies of both governments'. Frigates and destroyers were possible candidates, though cruisers were more politically difficult. Attack submarines which were nuclear-powered might be possible over time since there could be flexibility over propulsion if its safety could be demonstrated.

The spirits of the EAP branch of the State Department began to lift. Lilley had already been warned by Shultz's office that his idea of going to Los Angeles to talk to Caygill was a risky one and that he was to give nothing away to the New Zealanders. Now it looked as if a real negotiation might be in prospect. There was still some way to go and the exclusion of cruisers would not be acceptable to the Defense Department. Glassman suggested injecting a little drama into the talks, breaking off to telephone Lange and perhaps asking Lilley and himself to delay their return to Washington. With a little induced excitement it might be possible to get the Pentagon to accept that, though no class of ship was banned in principle, cruisers were 'bloody difficult' partly because of their putative armament and partly because of their prominent presence in New Zealand harbours. If a programme of visits was agreed annually, the possibility of a cruiser could be held over to be discussed at the next round.

New Zealand's ability to keep the negotiations secret would be the test of its good faith. There was a strong desire within the Administration not to allow Lange to claim a political victory by renewing contact when he was about to table the legislation. The ingenious Glassman thought this over and telephoned the embassy to propose a strong public statement in New Zealand that normal port access under both countries' policies was the goal and that the legislation did not

THE BRITISH STEP IN

exclude any ship or class. Instead the actual visits of ships would be worked out by mutual agreement at regular scheduling conferences.*

Caygill and Rowling met for two hours with Lilley and Glassman, once again at the house of the Consul-General in Los Angeles. This time the talks around that unpropitious dining table went well, and in accordance with Shultz's stern injunction that they take place through diplomatic channels 'rather than at press conferences' they stayed confidential.

Caygill explained that only the Prime Minister and Palmer were aware of the talks and his 'non-paper' had not been endorsed by Cabinet. His approach, though, was sympathetic. He said that two of the four demands in the US non-paper – resumption of normal port access, with no class of vessels being explicitly excluded – were accepted by New Zealand. Nuclear propulsion was more difficult but could perhaps be managed over time. The last requirement – no breach explicit or implicit of NCND – was the hardest to meet. He acknowledged frankly that he could not see any amendment that would not undermine the credibility of the law.†

Lilley sought a commitment to restore normal port access within the life of the present government, and asked for an indication of when the first ship other than a FFG-7 might be received. Caygill saw no difficulty with frigates or destroyers but larger warships like cruisers would still be a step too far. When Lilley pointed out that cruisers had visited New Zealand in five of the last ten years, Caygill repeated that the premature inclusion of cruisers would shake public confidence in the decision-making process. When pressed about a date for the first ship visit he said that it would be unwise to have one before the legislation was in place. Without the backing of the law the Prime Minister would be forced to provide greater public justification for his decision. With the Act in force he could simply say, 'We are aware of the law and, beyond that, we are not prepared to comment.'

---

* Record of discussion by John Wood, 3 December 1985, Caygill Papers.
† Caygill's report to the Prime Minister, 11 December 1985, Caygill Papers.

Overall, Lilley felt that Caygill was interested in 'problem-solving' and not as with Palmer in 'moralising'. He seemed to understand that the United States had to look beyond New Zealand at the other governments who would be pressed to emulate any port entry regime brought in by New Zealand, and said that with its relationship with the United States at stake his country did not want to 'posture on the world stage'. The discussion left the impression that the obstacles to visiting ships – even cruisers and nuclear-powered submarines – were not insuperable and that agreement on a programme of visits 'in accordance with the policies of both governments' might well be possible.

The unyielding blockage was the legislation. Lilley did not query the political need for it, and did not mention the Administration's willingness to seek visits only for ships deployed 'in connection with alliance defence requirements' (i.e. mainly for exercises), if the New Zealand Government shelved the legislation. But, as he emphasised to Caygill, Washington remained highly sceptical that the proposed law could be made compatible with normal access. No matter how secret his deliberations, if the Prime Minister was given the right to refuse access based on his determination as to whether or not nuclear weapons were on board, this could only be seen as a breach of NCND. The obligation to legislate, and the almost complete loss of confidence in New Zealand's trustworthiness, doomed the Caygill mission, though it was the most promising of Wellington's efforts to heal the breach.[*]

Three days later the legislation was introduced into the House. 'Depressing news' said the Foreign Office, making it harder than ever to get amendments and risking a strongly critical outburst from the Americans, 'thus compounding all our difficulties'. Even Mr Harland,

---

[*] The Caygill Papers contain Lilley's talking points; the New Zealand record in a cable of 7 December is contained in PM 59/8/5 Part 6, MFAT, and the American record in a cable of 11 December in the State Department Papers; there are additional comments in reports by the British embassy, Washington, of 7 and 9 December 1985, FCO Papers.

they said, seemed dispirited.* The British, however, were made of stern stuff. Their Cabinet was told: 'Even if we cannot change the legislation to allow resumed visits, it is worth keeping up the pressure on New Zealand to make it less of a bad precedent for others to follow.'

When Howe met Shultz in London on 10 December, the day the legislation was tabled, he argued that though it was hard to see how the opposing positions could be reconciled they should keep trying. They needed to tap the affinity that still existed in New Zealand for Britain and the United States and 'he thought the US too inclined merely to condemn them if they did not fall into line'. Lange might be 'muddle-headed' on nuclear issues but Howe thought New Zealanders would regret the end of naval visits and an approach that gently made this clear might have a chance. 'He was not optimistic however.'†

To the astonishment of his staff, Shultz went along with this approach, though still stressing that he was not prepared to accept a 'half-baked solution' which compromised NCND. The Foreign Office went back to work at once, seeking the closest correspondence with Washington in working for changes to the New Zealand Bill. The State Department was more wary, preferring parallel approaches. Given their obligations under ANZUS they felt obliged to keep their own dialogue going, but they felt barred from proposing changes to a Bill which they disliked in principle, and in any case their interests were not the same as the British; their global concerns meant the price for any deal would be higher.

So work began in London on yet another 'piece of paper', setting out revised drafting formulations which the Foreign Office felt might meet their own and the American objections. By now there was not even a gleam of optimism: 'We have no illusion about the likelihood of resolving the problem but feel that the issues at stake remain sufficiently serious that we should continue to try.'‡ As always in diplomatic deadlocks, the paper multiplied as the chances of agreement

---

* Note of 10 December 1985, FCO Papers.
† Howe–Shultz talks, 10 December 1985, FCO Papers.
‡ FCO to Washington embassy, 20 December 1985, FCO Papers.

diminished. Progress can be summarised on the back of an envelope; failure fills many files.

The Americans no longer had any hope that the square peg of their policy could be fitted into the round hole of New Zealand's. They saw no sign that Lange was preparing public opinion for any resumption of ship visits, or that the legislation was intended to get ships in rather than keep them out. A State Department desk officer who visited New Zealand at this time reported that his expectation of overwhelming support for the anti-nuclear policy was not borne out, but he believed that if a nuclear-capable visit was proposed there would be a 'pretty major confrontation' in the government caucus.[*]

Lange's popularity and therefore his influence seemed to be on the wane. The government's radical economic policies were causing increasing unrest in the Labour Party and, whatever the status of his deal with the Left, he could not afford to challenge the anti-nuclear activists or afford to split the party. A new American ambassador was about to arrive in Wellington but Shultz did not think he could do more than improve the atmosphere.

With his mind made up, he was content to let the British try. Though not emphasised at the time, there was an outer limit for these diplomatic endeavours. The Australian Government was nervous about the more restless members of the ALP and secured a promise from Lange that the legislation would not be passed until after the ALP conference the following July. Shultz took note of this date. At some point the United States would have to end its ANZUS obligations to New Zealand but he was willing to hold off until then.

---

[*] Bernie Oppel to the NZ embassy, 19 December 1985, PM 59/8/5 Part 6, MFAT.

Chapter Eleven
We Part Company

The new American ambassador arrived at the beginning of January 1986. Paul Cleveland was a professional diplomat, the first the Americans had sent since 1949, and he was able to establish an easier relationship with Lange. Given the widening gap in the relationship between the two countries it was not close. Cleveland found him 'unreliable if not duplicitous' and on the few occasions when port access was discussed gained little of real substance. Nonetheless he went regularly to see the Prime Minister because it was a requirement of the job and he enjoyed the meetings. Most of their conversation was about domestic politics in New Zealand and on this subject Lange was charming and very funny, with frank comments and amusing stories about his colleagues. Cleveland felt he was a quick study but had no ability to sustain a serious conversation – speaking in staccato bursts and often seeming a little ill at ease, 'he flicked from flower to flower' but was never other than entertaining.[*]

---

[*] Interview with Paul Cleveland, 29 September 2011.

Just before the new ambassador left Washington he was called to a half-hour meeting with the Secretary (an unusual procedure for most departing ambassadors). When Shultz asked him what he hoped to achieve, Cleveland said he would try to persuade the New Zealand Government not to enact its ships policy as legislation, and to point out the difficulties this would cause in the relationship with the US. Shultz, a taciturn man, said, 'You can try but I don't think you will succeed' and suggested that there was not much time left. Along with this discouraging observation, he gave two instructions for the ambassador to keep in mind. The first was that economics and politics should not be mixed. He did not want to use economic measures to threaten or punish New Zealand if a break came over ANZUS. And the second was: 'Whatever you do or plan to do, first check with the Australians.'

Cleveland's presentation of credentials was hastily arranged – the Governor-General, Sir Paul Reeves, was not pleased at having to come in from his beach cottage – because Representative Stephen Solarz was about to arrive. It was the traditional season for visits to the southern hemisphere, with Congress in recess and Washington in the snowy grip of winter, and there was something of a procession ranging from the House Armed Services Committee to a clutch of Senators. The Armed Services Committee chairman managed to annoy everyone, including his ambassador, by saying that New Zealand should be expelled from ANZUS and claiming that Beazley in Australia agreed with him. The Senators, well briefed by the Administration, probed the points of difference but kept silent.

The most serious of these visitors was Solarz, chairman of the House Subcommittee on East Asia and the Pacific. He had been interested in the New Zealand problem since the *Buchanan* affair, had visited Japan and Australia to get their views before coming to Wellington, and wanted to try out some ideas of his own. He was regarded by his colleagues in the House as 'lightweight and impulsive' and was not viewed with any favour by the Reagan Administration, but he was bright and energetic, and his Subcommittee could influence the reactions of Congress as a whole.

He had in mind a Congressional resolution which would pay tribute to the values and sacrifices shared by the two countries, note that the US could not now fulfil its ANZUS commitments to New Zealand, and conclude that these commitments should be suspended until they could be renewed. Hayden discouraged this as likely to cause further debate in Australia which, with the ALP conference coming up in July, 'we would prefer not to have'. Any Solarz resolution, though, was unlikely; while it had some support among Democrats it would be opposed by the Administration.

The indefatigable Congressman spent two days in Auckland and Wellington undertaking what the American embassy called a 'comprehensive cataloguing' of New Zealand opinion among academics, journalists and politicians. He was told that New Zealanders saw their country as 'special'. They had little experience of the wider world and were not greatly interested. Hence arguments that New Zealand should play a part in collective security had no resonance. People saw ANZUS as a 'friendship treaty', a symbol for the whole relationship, and were upset by what they perceived as the US's unfriendly response. The anti-nuclear argument was clear and simple and sat well with the average New Zealander's desire to set a tone of moral leadership. Coupled with a small country's feeling of helplessness in a big world seemingly unable to control the spread of these terrifying weapons, New Zealanders believed they had taken one step back from the brink and hoped that others would follow their example.

He was given some straightforward political analysis by Malcolm Templeton, the Director of the Institute of Policy Studies at Victoria University in Wellington, who thought the government had underestimated the American determination over NCND. Lange had been dragged into the anti-nuclear cause further than he had intended, in large part by talking himself under pressure from the Left into a position from which he could not escape. He was now leading public opinion, playing on the deeply held public belief that nuclear weapons were uniquely bad and that he was striking a blow for disarmament and world peace. It was too late to expect that any American action could reverse this policy; suspending its defence commitment was all that was left.

Politicians from both sides of the House were agreed that the Left would not allow Lange to make any compromise. Sir Robert Muldoon did not think Lange could convince his party to make any changes and added that the issue was not a winning one for his National Party. Helen Clark of the Labour Left was more blunt. If Lange accepted a nuclear-capable ship there would be a major crisis, the harbour would be full of protesters and the party would split. ANZUS was now no more than a shell and breaking with it would be less damaging to the government than backing away from its commitment. Its supporters would abandon it at the next election; 'Lange knows that and is enough of a politician to recognize reality'.*

With this sobering introduction, Solarz shelved any talk of a Congressional resolution in his two-hour meeting with Lange and instead probed for any hints of a possible compromise. The Prime Minister said he did not see ANZUS as a nuclear alliance but if it had to be, New Zealand was better out of it. His country would certainly be destroyed in any all-out war – he accepted the nuclear winter theory then much discussed by those who felt that a nuclear war was virtually inevitable – but 'New Zealand was not in the business of being among the first to be hit'. It would, he said, be political suicide for him to renege on the legislation – he had gone out on a limb even to stall it for as long as he had.

Solarz came up with a suggestion on the most difficult point of the legislation. Clause 9 of the Bill required the Prime Minister to be satisfied that any visiting ship was not carrying nuclear weapons. He asked if it would help to shift the burden of proof so that the Prime Minister would be required to deny approval if he 'concluded' that a given ship was carrying nuclear weapons. Lange undertook to look at this, saying courteously that it was the most ingenious idea to come

---

* US embassy cable of 24 January 1986, State Department Papers.

across the Pacific, but Cleveland interjected to say that whichever way you looked at it a declaration by the Prime Minister was not compatible with NCND. It might not have fared any better from party scrutiny. The Solarz formula, whether intended or not, lowered the barrier for consent – if the Prime Minister was in doubt he could still approve a visit.*

When four Senators arrived three weeks later, Lange said that he was willing to listen to any reasonable proposals to allay the US's concern about NCND. He said that a careful study was being made of Solarz's suggestion and, more vaguely, that consideration was also being given to 'painting into the statute a broader range of strategic concerns'. He said he was not trying to twist the tail of the US or shrug off New Zealand's legitimate responsibilities for Western defence, but emphasised that it was impossible to talk seriously to Washington when his ambassador's access to top officials was restricted and he could not talk to Shultz. The Senators were not impressed by Lange's claim that he was willing to listen; they had hoped to hear some proposals from New Zealand. 'They were clearly sceptical of the sincerity of the Prime Minister by the time they left.'†

Outside the visiting season (at one point Lange said he had so many British callers he was thinking of hiring a butler), the diplomatic efforts went on. They were now being conducted in two separate channels. With Washington the issues raised in the 'Caygill process' were still to be resolved, the main ones being whether a programme of ship visits could be agreed in accordance with the policies of both governments, and if so when the first might take place. The other sticking point, the legislation, had fallen to London to handle. Since the Americans did not like even the idea of legislation, they felt more comfortable leaving detailed negotiations about the wording to the British who, they both agreed, had an easier and therefore more promising relationship with the New Zealanders. Both capitals

---

* Lange–Solarz meeting, 16 January 1986, PM 59/8/5 Part 7, MFAT, and FCO Papers.
† US embassy, 13 February 1986, State Department Papers.

kept in close touch during their negotiations and it was understood (though never admitted) that any British proposals on the legislation had been cleared with Washington and any breakthrough would solve the difficulties of both.

The Los Angeles meeting had ended with Caygill undertaking to send a reply to the points that Lilley had raised. Over two months went by before Wellington did so and its ebbing interest was apparent. The best reason Foreign Affairs could muster for continuing the negotiations was to demonstrate that any failure was not the result of any lack of effort or goodwill by New Zealand. It told the Prime Minister gloomily that the Americans were unlikely to summon up sufficient flexibility to allow a settlement.

Even so the Ministry's first draft for a reply was too accommodating for Lange who wrote on it: 'Need to revise. We should concede nothing.' He thought that, given the Americans' unresponsiveness, it would not be right to provide written answers to their questions to Caygill. Instead, and the distinction was rather mysterious, Rowling was to hand over another 'non-paper'. He did so in mid-February, explaining to Lilley that New Zealand was looking for a more forthcoming political signal. The redrafted paper raised the bar. Anything 'harder' than a FFG-7 could not be considered before the legislation was passed, but other proposals for a visit could be discussed from late 1986 on. But it declined to give a written response on nuclear propulsion. Caygill had made it clear that there was a measure of flexibility on this but the government was willing to discuss it further only 'if there is any sign of movement on the American side'.[*]

There for the time being the Washington exchanges rested. Any hopes of an accommodation on the legislation (Clause 11 of which prohibited nuclear-powered vessels) depended on the British discussions. After a month in his post, Cleveland gave his views on the most significant question: did Lange wish for a resolution of the dispute

---

[*] Cable to Washington embassy, 29 January 1986, PM 59/8/5 Part 7, MFAT.

or were his proposals simply a political smokescreen to cover his retreat?

He judged that 'the taproot of New Zealand attitudes these days is nationalism and national self-assertiveness'. After a rising tide of nationalism in Asia and even Australia, 'now we must contend with a more nationalistic New Zealand'. Misguided or not, New Zealanders were not just arguing with themselves about ship visits, they were wrestling with their souls about some basics: self-defence and the role they wanted to play in the world. It might be some time before they reached an answer.

He therefore saw little prospect of resolving the immediate problem. Legislation ruling out American naval visits would pass; the current political winds were blowing too strongly in that direction. 'We conclude that the chances of Lange's either making the concessions that would allow us to make port calls without the appearance of having compromised NCND or of mustering the political will to force a de facto modification of his government's policy are very slim indeed.' Any effort to find a compromise that would suit the US would be so obvious a climb-down and risk so much politically 'he just will not'.*

By then the British were making the running. The Foreign Office was hard at work on possible amendments to the legislation which Howe was to set out in a letter to Lange. The crucial difficulty was how to reconcile NCND with Clause 9 which required the Prime Minister to be 'satisfied' that a ship was not carrying nuclear weapons before approving its visit. If this could be overcome London felt that everything else could be managed or lived with. It was, however, very challenging to find a formula which was both legally sound and not 'absolute political suicide'. In January the lawyers went through 'sacks and sacks of redrafts' in the search for something that might be acceptable.

---

* US embassy cable, 18 February 1986, State Department Papers.

The chief obstacle was that the clause specified only one uncompromising basis for the Prime Minister's decision – whether he judged the ship to be nuclear-armed or not. It might blur the challenge to NCND, they felt, if further considerations could be added about which the Prime Minister had to satisfy himself, and the need to consider national security and strategic requirements seemed the most promising possibility. The lawyers were doubtful even about this but it was the principal amendment among a list of others put to the State Department that month.

The British ideas were the subject of intense inter-agency discussion in Washington and a 'substantial dialogue' developed through the American embassy in London. The British were well aware that the Americans 'remain deeply distrustful of Mr Lange, whom they accuse of deviousness during the ill-tempered exchanges of recent months'. Washington's main concern with the legislation was that others might imitate it and that pressure to do so would build in Australia. They were still apprehensive about the need for the Prime Minister to 'satisfy himself' at all but the British were hopeful that they could be persuaded to accept this if the right addition could be found. For all their doubts, the Americans were pleased that Britain was working on reformulations; the United States was not prepared to do so, and if they did it would look as if Lange was buckling under American pressure.[*]

All this work and transatlantic consultation came together in a letter which Howe sent to Lange at the end of January. He regretted that the Bill as currently drafted would not allow ships of the Royal Navy to visit. NCND was a global policy for Britain and could not be bent. A declaration by the Prime Minister would inevitably imply that a ship was *not* carrying nuclear weapons, and Britain would either have to comply or deliberately deceive. Neither option was acceptable. It was of the greatest importance to Britain to maintain

---

[*] NZHC, London, 17 January 1986, LON B106/4/1 Part 8, MFAT, and paper by Foreign Office Defence Department of 23 January 1986, FCO Papers.

the effectiveness of its forces worldwide, and he gently implied that if necessary it might have to sacrifice its long-standing defence relationship with New Zealand.

In the hope of avoiding this outcome he enclosed a list of possible amendments covering a number of difficulties with the Bill. On the main one he suggested a formula which might be added to the wording of Clause 9 to specify also that 'the Prime Minister shall have regard to all relevant information and advice covering the strategic and security interests of New Zealand and New Zealand's interest in the non-proliferation of nuclear weapons'. The amendments had been discussed with the United States and Howe implied that if British concerns could be met there would also be progress with the Americans, though they would still want to reach agreement on a programme for ship visits.

The letter was handed over by O'Leary in Wellington. He said that Britain would normally be reluctant to comment on other people's legislation and in this case would prefer no legislation, but the hope of solving the problem came first. Lange repeated as he did frequently that he did not wish to challenge NCND but 'I really find it hard to believe that the Soviets would regard our acceptance of individual ships, particularly British ships, as tantamount to identifying whether or not they were potential targets'.*

There was a tired and flat air about the discussion, with both sides simply repeating their positions. The High Commissioner judged that Lange would prefer the UK and US to shut up and was anxious to minimise these consequences of the anti-nuclear policy. A week later the Prime Minister sent a guarded reply saying he would study the comments and amendments and give a reply as soon as he could.

Two months went by without the promised response and in the end no reply was ever sent. There was little sign in Wellington of energy or even enthusiasm for negotiating a settlement. Any compromise

---

* Howe's message of 28 January 1986 is in PM 59/8/5 Part 7, MFAT, and O'Leary's account of the same date in the FCO Papers.

likely to be acceptable to Britain and the United States, or indeed any compromise at all, would almost certainly be rejected by the caucus and the party. The radical economic reforms being pushed through by the Finance Minister, Roger Douglas, were shrinking Labour's traditional voting base. Amid the upending of long-standing political assumptions the anti-nuclear policy stood out as one of Labour's few familiar landmarks, with correspondingly greater reluctance to see it overturned. The best that could be done was to keep some semblance of talks going to avoid the political embarrassment of acknowledging that membership of ANZUS could not be retained. A Foreign Affairs paper spelt this out frankly, urging that talks be spun out as long as possible to avoid a break and the legislation should not be passed before the end of the year at the earliest.[*]

The trouble with negotiating in slow motion – or possibly the advantage for those of a subtle turn of mind – was the vulnerability to other events. Harold Macmillan's dictum that the chief driver of public policy was 'events, dear boy' meant that the exchanges were hostage to other events as the weeks went by. Delay was tempting fate and fate duly obliged, in the unexpected shape of a British admiral and an air-force exercise no one had ever heard of before.

The British Government, like the American Administration, had been troubled that the case for ANZUS and collective security seemed to be failing for lack of any vigorous defence in New Zealand. The Left and the peace groups were energetic in lobbying against the country's links with the West but, apart from the retired generals, no one, not even the political Opposition, seemed to be making any comprehensive counter-arguments. They decided to send their CDS, Admiral Sir John Fieldhouse, to give a straightforward military message.

In New Zealand's hypersensitive mood it was not a success. Fieldhouse gave a clear and indeed simple view of the strategic situation, of the dangers of New Zealand's policy and the risk that it

---

[*] Foreign Affairs to PM, 10 March 1986, PM 59/8/5 Part 7, MFAT.

would 'give comfort to the Queen's potential enemies'. He opened a brisk fire as soon as he came over the horizon, telling a press conference: 'Let me make it quite clear that it will be extremely sad if we are required to break this relationship. And let me make it equally clear that it is not the British government that has changed its policy.'* The Foreign Office said he had done exactly what had been asked of him, delivering a strong message straight from the shoulder. Criticism by visitors, though, has never been popular in New Zealand and there was irritation that Fieldhouse had not only come to criticise but had done so in a very English accent.

Lange was uncomfortable with being talked at, especially by high-ranking officers indifferent to his charm. He bridled at being told 'You will pull a thread that unravels Western security', retorting that there was no evidence the fabric of Western security had even been puckered. He later described the interview as 'the most unpleasant half-hour of his time in office' and took his revenge by spreading a story that Fieldhouse had left his office, preceded by an aide carrying his hat on a silk cushion.†

Almost before the hat was back on the admiral's head another row blew up over an anti-submarine exercise called 'Fincastle 86'. This was a competition among maritime patrol aircraft (Orions in New Zealand's case) to locate a patrolling submarine. The New Zealand Air Force had won it on several occasions in the past and was to be host this year when, without consultation, the venue was shifted to Australia. The Australian and British defence chiefs were quick to blame each other, though it did seem that Fieldhouse had first suggested the change which had been warmly accepted by his Australian colleague. More to the point, it had been regarded as a purely military matter and neither foreign ministry had been consulted. Both were quick to apologise but Lange was angered by

---

* Press conference, 18 February 1986.
† Speaking to the Australian High Commissioner, 12 March, PM 59/8/5 Part 7, MFAT, and Vernon Wright interview, 13 January 1987, Lange Papers, Box 1, ANZ. The Fieldhouse visit was 14–19 February 1986.

the politically awkward implication that its defence partners were dropping New Zealand.

After the 'somewhat truculent' attitude of Fieldhouse and the Fincastle affair, the Prime Minister now chose to doubt the seriousness of the British and declined to reply to Howe's January letter. Instead he decided to wait for the next British visitor, Baroness Young, the junior Minister at the Foreign Office, who would arrive in the second week of April. This did not suggest that New Zealand felt any great urgency about seeking a settlement and Harland in London told Lady Young he was not sure the position was retrievable.

As time drifted by and July crept closer the Americans were becoming increasingly jumpy. Some like Laux at the National Security Council had given up on New Zealand. He thought that every possible formulation had been tried over the previous year and 'every time we had performed a stately dance, eventually returning to the point of seemingly irreconcilable differences from which we had started out'.[*] Even the State Department was losing heart. Armacost called in Rowling to say that time was passing and nothing had so far emerged from the 'Caygill process'. In particular there had been no evidence of the promised flexibility over nuclear propulsion. If New Zealand was serious, why could it not set a target for removing the propulsion ban? As New Zealand had done earlier, Washington now tightened its terms. Armacost seemed willing to let the other US concerns – the legislation and a first ship visit – rest with the British for the time being, but now said that unless the nuclear propulsion issue could be overcome there could be no normal port access for the United States.[†]

As the delay drifted on, small irritants brought increasing rumbles of concern. Lange's interviews with Swedish journalists and

---

[*] Laux to Wood, 10 March 1986.
[†] Armacost to Rowling, 24 March 1986, PM 50/6/4 Part 15, MFAT.

the Japanese newspaper *Asahi Shimbun* brought protests from Washington that he was encouraging the export of New Zealand's anti-nuclear policies. He told the Swedish reporters: 'We want to export our standpoint, we don't want to export our solution.' By an unfortunate coincidence the Swedish Government then sharpened its procedure for permitting naval visits, saying that public opinion had been roused by the New Zealand example.

Speaking to his Japanese interviewer, Lange said that New Zealand's policy on ship visits was 'stricter' than Japan's and he would have difficulty admitting an American ship coming directly from Japan. The implication was that the Japanese policy was insufficiently rigorous and the Gaimusho (Japan's Foreign Ministry) sought clarification. After yet another Japanese interview, Wolfowitz's successor, Gaston Sigur, reported from Tokyo that the Japanese 'dumped all over New Zealand . . . and revealed great sensitivity about the export of the anti-nuclear policy'.* The Japanese Government thereupon became 'too busy' to accept a visit by Lange.

These comments raised even more doubts about what the wayward Lange might say when he visited China at the end of March. His habit of reflecting to the media his feelings of the moment, a kind of spontaneous street theatre, had been the key to his domestic success but was far from being an advantage in foreign policy. The US was arranging a visit to Beijing by the Chief of Naval Operations which it was hoped would lead to a first ship visit and wanted no repetition of the Hu Yaobang incident the year before. Armacost did not mince words; if Lange said anything indiscreet in Beijing the bilateral process with New Zealand would be 'irretrievable'. Lange complained plaintively that he could scarcely sit mute if asked there for an account of New Zealand's policy. In this situation almost anything said to the press would be wrong, and it was.

---

* Sigur (in Tokyo) to Armacost, 7 April 1986, PM 50/6/4 Part 16, MFAT. The interview with the Swedish journalists and the *Asahi Shimbun* correspondent was 3 March 1986, and the reluctance to have a Lange visit, 28 March 1986, PM 50/6/4 Part 16, MFAT.

He told a press conference: 'What we have is a very firm position by China, which I did not elicit from them. [They] told me that they did not propose to have in China vessels carrying nuclear weapons from other countries.' This might have seemed harmless enough but the ground shook in Washington. Glassman telephoned the embassy twice on Easter Monday and Lilley said that if the discussions with the Chinese over naval visits broke down it would be hard not to blame New Zealand. The Chinese seemed embarrassed by the comment and took the unusual step of giving the Americans and Australians their view of what had happened. Lange, the briefers said, had not made a deep impression except that he had 'talked a lot'. The Chinese leaders had been taken aback by his extensive criticism of the United States which they felt was inappropriate in a visitor to another country.*

On his return, the Prime Minister found comfort in opening his mind to Lee Kuan Yew when they met at Rotorua. He recalled Lee's advice in October 1984 that he should use the honeymoon to tackle the hard domestic tasks and not be distracted by foreign policy issues, and said ruefully, 'the government had allowed itself to be distracted and the wisdom of Mr Lee's advice was apparent with hindsight'. He was pessimistic about ANZUS. When the anti-nuclear Bill had been tabled, the US had disengaged and spoken only through the media; he thought it was about to declare the alliance inoperable. This left him in a very difficult position. The morale of the armed forces was low and the cost of defence was going up. The public mood was unpredictable. 'It might decide that the risk posed by nuclear ships in New Zealand ports for a while was substantially less than the danger of being at odds with a major trading partner.'

The British had asked Lee to express concern to Lange about the risks New Zealand's policy posed to the region's security interests. He did so gently. Noting that Singapore and New Zealand

---

* Washington embassy, 29 March 1986, PM 111/3/3/1 Part 47, ANZ, and 250/11/18 Part 32, NAA. Chinese briefings given to the Australians in Beijing and Washington are in 221/1/4/4 Part 7, DFAT.

were comfortable with one another – 'the grain goes with us' – he commented that public moods could vary but legislation could not, except by amendment. Might it be better to leave things as they were rather than bring the dispute to a conclusion which was probably what the pressure groups wanted?*

He left it at that but gave a virtuoso demonstration of how to manage a press conference. He declined to comment on New Zealand's policy, saying: 'My immediate interest is not to put my foot in it.' He had listened to Lange with attention and was trying to figure out the consequences for Singapore. But as long as 'Australasia' had a defence umbrella with the United States, the other regional partnerships such as the Five Power Arrangements would be viable. He was not interested in asking if American ships in Singapore had nuclear weapons: 'I'm only interested in having the Seventh Fleet around.' When asked who was threatening Singapore he said: 'Nobody, because they're around.'

On his heels came Lady Young whose primary aim was 'to influence political and parliamentary opinion in New Zealand on the ships visit issue'.† She was warned by the British High Commissioner that 'Mr Lange is adept at evading logical argument. His forte is assertion and reiteration, not logical analysis.' Her talks would not therefore be easy and he cautioned against any false expectations of early success.‡ New Zealand officials were also losing confidence, one in London urging her to concentrate on Palmer (whom she had already met) – 'his personality might also be more conducive to a measured discussion than Mr Lange's flamboyance'.§

She spoke to the Institute of International Affairs to set out 'basic facts about the security of all of us', with the customary lack of effect except to note that the questions were 'naive', and met with

---

* Note of meeting by the New Zealand High Commissioner, Singapore, 5 April and *Dominion*, 7 April 1986.
† Unclassified review by the FCO, 26 April 1986, FCO Papers.
‡ Briefing by O'Leary, 27 March 1986, FCO Papers.
§ Stuart Prior talking to the Foreign Office, 13 February 1986, FCO Papers.

Labour backbenchers who surprised her by their reluctance to see New Zealand as part of the West and their readiness to walk away from ANZUS. An aide said they now understood the difficulties Lange was up against.*

The talks themselves went well. Despite Lange's ungallant crack to journalists that she had left her broomstick behind, Janet Young was felt to have taken a helpful rather than a hectoring approach. The Prime Minister again complained that he could not understand why the US would not talk to New Zealand, and said that he was not disposed to surrender the clause banning nuclear propulsion without more movement by the US and UK. Lady Young came up with a new idea, asking whether the 'China formula' being negotiated by Britain to allow the Royal Navy to visit Shanghai in July would work for New Zealand.

The China formula was a refinement of the standard 'don't ask, don't tell' approach of the Nordic and other anti-nuclear countries. Each side would state its own policy and neither would comment on the policy of the other. Lange said he liked it but would the US? When O'Flynn intervened to say that it might not be sellable to the New Zealand public, he retorted cheerfully that it would be 'a Chinese formula with New Zealand characteristics'. Lady Young asked for this in writing and the next day, before her departure for Australia, yet another 'non-paper' appeared.

It expressed appreciation for Britain's efforts and agreed that officials should meet to discuss the principal British concerns about the legislation – the Prime Minister's ability to decide on visiting ships (Clause 9) and the prohibition on nuclear propulsion (Clause 11). It also agreed that the Chinese formula might provide an acceptable wording for the public presentation of ship visits: 'Such a formula would make it clear that while each government would, if asked, state its own policy, neither would comment on the policy of the other

---

* 8 April 1986, LON B 106/4/1 Part 9, MFAT.

government.' She was authorised to discuss this initiative with the Australians, and with Weinberger who would also be in Canberra.*

This was promising and she felt she had achieved something. The Foreign Office was also pleased. The Americans had looked for Lady Young to take the temperature and might take heart because 'scorn and vitriol had not been poured on her'. The Australians, though, remained extremely sceptical. They had given up on New Zealand and were less concerned to hide it. After a good lunch in Brisbane, Hayden had spoken about ANZUS. His text said: 'The government strongly disagrees with New Zealand's policy. We understand the confusion it can cause.' Then with a grin he added, 'At times New Zealand is like the cross-eyed javelin thrower who doesn't win any medals, but keeps the crowd on its toes.' There were denials and a diplomatic flurry, but as with any contest of wit Lange had the last word. He said that the only thing Australia was known for was the boomerang and Hayden 'might have cause to reflect on this'.†

In Canberra, Lady Young described her talks with Labour MPs in Wellington as depressing; 'many of them appeared naive and unrealistic and some criticised the draft legislation for not going far enough'. She thought David Lange had 'nibbled' at her suggestion of the Chinese formula but was uncertain of New Zealand's real intentions.‡

The Australians were. They thought Lange was now simply playing for time in the hope that something might turn up. 'Whatever his original intentions, Mr Lange has become the prisoner of an influential and vocal movement, both inside and outside the Labour Party, which sees its objective of a nuclear-free New Zealand as within reach' and would not allow any weakening of the legislation.§ They did not believe that Lange could deliver his party even if he wanted to. The legislation would pass later in the year in a form unacceptable

---

* 9 April 1986, PM 59/8/5 Part 8, MFAT.
† Brisbane *Courier-Mail*, 21 February 1986, PM 111/3/3/1 Part 46, ANZ.
‡ Baroness Young, 10 April 1986, FCO Papers
§ AHC assessment of 11 March 1986, 370/1/20 Part 52, NAA.

to both the British and the United States; and the Americans would then say something about New Zealand's position in ANZUS. Hawke and Beazley preferred no agreement to a compromise which fudged the issues and allowed Lange to claim that he had got away with it, but they were no longer worried about the possible consequences for Australia. The Americans had reassured them that their ANZUS links would not be affected and there was now much less chance of any wave of ALP opinion supporting similar policies.*

Lee Kuan Yew, who also went on to Canberra, told Hawke that he had given up hope. He had originally thought that a solution would be found but did not think so now. That being so, it was important that both should 'pretend' that ANZUS still existed. If a three-sided triangle was not possible then a US/Australian and Australian/NZ alliance was much better than nothing. A two-sided ANZUS joining the US and Australia would ensure the continuance of American commitment to the security of the region.†

In the meantime the State Department was chewing its pencil over the China formula but did not like it. The Labour Party, which had just issued a public call for New Zealand to get out of ANZUS, did not either, regarding it as little different from the much-abused Japanese practice. In London the enterprising Harland asked the Chinese ambassador about ship visits. He said their policy was not as clear and as public as New Zealand's. China was glad to have visits but they should be arranged 'in a friendly way', by agreement between the two parties.‡

Later in the month Lange told Lady Young that he could not accept her proposal for talks in the very near future; he needed first to have a clear understanding from the Americans that the talks would have value for them. The Foreign Office found this a 'disappointment', becoming increasingly doubtful that they could work out a package acceptable to both sides. Talks at official level did finally get under

---

* BHC, Canberra, 26 March and 10 April 1986, FCO Papers.
† 18 April 1986, PM 111/3/3/1 Part 48, ANZ.
‡ Harland, 29 April 1986.

way in London a month later but lacking urgency and political impetus they achieved little.

The consequences of drift were underlined once again at the end of April. A Soviet nuclear power station at Chernobyl suffered an explosion and catastrophic meltdown as a result of a reckless test, and a cloud of radioactive dust spread over the western Ukraine and parts of Europe. As with the attack on *Rainbow Warrior* anti-nuclear feeling in New Zealand was once again inflamed. A huge and badly designed power station bore no resemblance to the small, tightly sealed maritime propulsion units of the US Navy but activists could now describe them as 'floating Chernobyls'. That this was scientific nonsense did not diminish the emotional response. Even vague promises of flexibility about accepting nuclear-propelled vessels were no longer possible and the government took them off the negotiating table.

Though not to be compared to the Chernobyl disaster, a gathering of the Labour Party then made matters worse. The course of the dispute had been punctuated by periodic addresses to its provincial branches but Lange's speech on 9 May to the Auckland Regional Labour Party brought something of a full stop. It managed to upset the whole of NATO. Half of it was devoted to foreign policy and made it clear that the Prime Minister, bored and exasperated by the failure to reach the settlement he had hoped for, had given up being conciliatory to New Zealand's allies and was conciliating only the party faithful. The text sounded as if it owed more to the sentiments of his speechwriter, Margaret Pope, but he delivered it with vigour.

New Zealand was no longer a client state, he said, and 'would not grovel before the French, bow to the Americans, nor genuflect to the British'. The British took a hit over the Fieldhouse visit – 'we are not a colony'. Then, in a tilt at NCND, he said that 'everyone knows' that the two Royal Navy ships going to China were not nuclear-armed. NATO too came under attack: 'It is outrageous that the defence of Western Europe is based on NATO's promise to blow up the world if the Russians attack them with overwhelming force. They [NATO] have no right to decide the fate of the rest of us.'

ANZUS was next: efforts to resolve the dispute had come unstuck because the US saw the alliance as part of the global projection of its power. 'If that is all there really is to ANZUS there is no point in New Zealand being in it.... We have talked to the United States on the nuclear ships issue almost to the limits of human endurance, but with no results.'

Finally there were some murky remarks about American activities in New Zealand which played on the paranoid convictions of some New Zealanders that the CIA was at work among them, actively destabilising the government and the currency – 'Do what we say, or you won't see your dollar again' in the words of one cartoon. He said that 'Americans have been active in Auckland and Wellington... trying to find out where the power really is in the Labour Party', adding even more murkily that the next question was what the Americans would do with this information.

Public reaction ranged from puzzlement to concern that he was signalling a sharp turn in the country's direction, towards the non-alignment that Margaret Wilson and the party advocated. One observer said 'Lange has lost his marbles'.[*] Sharp-eyed journalists thought that the customary excuse that he was placating party militants would no longer work; the offensive remarks were in the text and not 'the extemporaneous utterances so characteristic of past Lange performances'.[†] Even Margaret Wilson was baffled by the allegation about American probes into the Labour Party, saying that American embassy officials quite properly liked to talk to them from time to time.

The American embassy concluded that 'The speech, in our view, is clearly unacceptable'. So did Washington. Over the months the lights on the Washington switchboard had one by one flickered and gone out: first Weinberger, then Shultz, the Pentagon, the National Security Council and almost the whole Inter-Agency Group. Now

---

[*] Frank Corner, chairman of the Defence Committee of Enquiry.
[†] US embassy, 9 May 1986, State Department Papers.

even Lilley and Glassman gave up and the American switchboard went dark.

The members of NATO were also highly displeased that distant New Zealand could assail the nuclear deterrence on which their safety depended while being unwilling to carry even a small part of the burden itself. Canada, hitherto sympathetic towards New Zealand's difficulties but about to host a meeting of NATO Ministers, was concerned that New Zealand intended to export its anti-nuclear policy. Other observers were baffled by the timing. Lange would shortly leave on a tour of several governments in the EEC, the periodic round required of New Zealand Prime Ministers to plead for the continuance of the special arrangement which admitted New Zealand exports of lamb and dairy products into the Community. For butter alone shipments worth over $300 million were at stake. Almost all Community members were also members of NATO. Several like France, Belgium and Denmark were perennially keen to cut back on New Zealand farm access and the attack on NATO would make their task easier.

More surprising still, Lange had decided that on his tour of European capitals he would take time to speak at the annual congress of International Physicians for the Prevention of Nuclear War (IPPNW) in Cologne. The IPPNW was widely regarded as being under Soviet influence; its co-chairman was Brezhnev's doctor and, though many unpolitical and genuinely idealistic doctors belonged, it was never known to take positions contrary to the Soviet line. Why Lange agreed to speak to them is unknown. Perhaps, as now a world figure in the anti-nuclear movement, he hoped to repeat his Oxford Union triumph. The parallel certainly struck Chancellor Kohl and the German Government, who had their own domestic opposition to manage, and like Mrs Thatcher could not understand why a New Zealand Prime Minister would travel all that way to make trouble for them.

Lange assured those who were uneasy that he was going to 'unload on the Russians', and though he did not go as far as that, his speech was careful. He acknowledged that it was directed more to the US and Britain than to a group of doctors – 'of course it was' – and the journalists with him thought he was treading much more warily than at the time of the Oxford Union debate. He avoided any moral arguments about nuclear weapons, stressing instead that in New Zealand's situation they were simply not needed. A Foreign Office minute acknowledged this but did not think the speech (let alone the audience he chose to give it to) would persuade British Ministers that 'there is an orthodox alliance-minded man inside Mr Lange struggling to get out'.

In a less usual turn most of the criticism came from the Left. It was denounced from the floor by a New Zealand delegate, Dr Erich Geiringer, who said Lange was 'trying to dance at two weddings'.* At home critics on the Left noted the contrast between his Auckland speech on 9 May and his speech in Cologne which appeared to justify reliance on nuclear strategies. He had to be defended by Margaret Wilson who, in a slightly unhappy choice of phrase, said: 'It would be wrong to go stumbling around the world exhorting others to follow our example.'†

Even if he was relieved by Lange's caution, Chancellor Kohl said that he could not understand New Zealand's position. His government had taken painful decisions, like stationing cruise missiles and extending conscription, because Soviet troops were only six tank hours away from Bonn. Small steps were the only practicable way to make progress on détente and disarmament. He ended by noting, pointedly for a visitor concerned about trade access, that Germany felt Western security should not be divided between those countries assuming the responsibility for defence and those concerned only with finance and business.‡

Lange went on to lunch with Mrs Thatcher at Chequers and reported with relief to Palmer that 'altogether, it was not too bad a

---

* The *Press*, 2 June 1986.
† 3 June 1986, PM 50/6/4 Part 17, MFAT.
‡ Report by NZ embassy, Bonn, 5 June 1986, LON B 106/4/1 Part 11, MFAT.

meeting'. Although he claimed that she still addressed him as if he were one of the larger pre-war German rallies, she seemed to have accepted that there was little more that could be done. She was happy to have continued talks in London but firmly ruled out the China formula – China was not an ally and did not have a nuclear allergy. It was up to allies to help each other and neither Britain nor the US could accept an ally which refused 'safe-haven' for their ships.*

He said that New Zealand and Britain were 'groping their way towards a solution' but was doubtful whether the United States was willing to follow the same path. After *Buchanan* he sometimes felt that the US regarded him personally as the stumbling block to progress; he was ready to resign if it would help get a solution. Mrs Thatcher ignored this and repeated firmly that if New Zealand wanted visits it would have to make them possible. The next day Lange sent what was almost literally a bread-and-butter letter, thanking her for her frankness and expressing gratitude for her assurance of Britain's full support for butter access which is 'of enormous importance to us'.†

Sir Geoffrey Howe's mood was also sombre. Britain wanted to help and still saw scope for ingenuity in drafting. So did the Americans but they had less confidence in New Zealand and put more weight on the political pressures Lange faced. Time was running out to search for a solution. In spelling out the requirements, he sounded none too hopeful: 'Any solution would need the skill of Nelson in combining a well-controlled tongue with the ability, when appropriate, to turn a blind eye. A solution which safeguarded our "NCND" policy could be frustrated by ill-considered public statements.' Lange again offered to step aside if that would help. Howe said he still hoped that an agreement with Britain might be the first step in resolving the

---

* Lange to Palmer, 5 June 1986, PM 58/206/2, MFAT. The German rally reference is in the Vernon Wright interview of 5 December 1986, Lange Papers, Box 1, ANZ.
† Note of meeting by Charles Powell, 5 June 1986, FCO Papers.

dispute, but Britain could not do much more in the absence of more effort from New Zealand.*

In Washington the embassy reported 'a vague but imminent sense of foreboding'. After Lange's Auckland speech Shultz had said, 'Why are we still talking to these people?'† and the British account of Lange's talks suggested that there was nothing left to say. The discussions in London had offered nothing of substance and American disappointment was not helped by Lange telling the BBC that the Americans 'are going to rat on the treaty'. For some months it had been accepted that the deadline for a settlement was July or early August, when the truncated ANZUS Council (now officially a US–Australian Ministerial Meeting) would convene in San Francisco. It was expected that the US would then announce the suspension of its security obligations to New Zealand under the treaty. Now some in Washington were pushing for the US to take earlier action, without waiting for the San Francisco meeting.

There was, however, a last chance to avert or at least postpone the blow. Both Shultz and Lange would be at an ASEAN meeting in Manila at the end of June. Although he had been a little wary of a meeting in case Shultz chose to 'throw the bucket at him', Lange sent a message a week beforehand suggesting they use the opportunity to review the situation on ANZUS and ship visits. 'I know you are doubtful that any solution is possible. My view, as you know, has always been that the enactment of our nuclear legislation need not be a barrier to the resumption of ship visits.' Shultz was happy to agree.‡

Neither side saw much prospect of a breakthrough. Armacost sent Shultz, who was already on his way, a chilly set of recommendations for the meeting. 'Lange has had two years to make the adjustments he pledged to you ... He has expended no political capital on this issue, has played an opportunistic game, and has neither the disposition

---

* Report by NZHC, London, 9 June, LON B 106/4/1 Part 11, MFAT, and note of meeting, 9 June 1986, FCO Papers.
† Sigur to Rowling, 13 June 1986, PM 59/8/5 Part 8, MFAT.
‡ Lange to Shultz, 17 June 1986, PM 59/8/5 Part 8, MFAT.

nor the political capacity to make a satisfactory accommodation.' In view of these dilatory tactics, Armacost thought the price should go up. If the Prime Minister once again talked of an early ship visit, Shultz should insist on a cruiser or a nuclear-propelled vessel. And if this (predictably) failed, 'you should get our side of the dispute out again to the press in sadness rather than anger, without however announcing the suspension of defence obligations yet (given the sensitivities of Bob Hawke prior to his ALP convention in early July)'.*

Lange was equally pessimistic, telling a press conference that he did not believe it was now possible to negotiate wording for the legislation that would be acceptable to the US. Britain was still willing but the US was not. Since Australia was the more important member of the alliance Washington had no incentive to accommodate New Zealand. He thought the US would suspend its commitments at San Francisco though it could act sooner, but this would not leave New Zealand more vulnerable since he argued that ANZUS provided for a process of consultation rather than an automatic security guarantee. The American embassy read this as setting up the US for the blame if the talks broke down.†

They met in Manila on 27 June. The 35-minute discussion was businesslike and amiable, with both traversing their familiar arguments. Shultz began by expressing an interest in New Zealand's economic policies. Lange said their 1984 manifesto had been very general about economic policy and some would describe the government's current measures as 'not Labour Party economics'. After some talk about the government's moves to dismantle protection and open up the economy, Lange moved on to the anti-nuclear policy. The polls consistently showed a deep-rooted and overwhelming anti-nuclear disposition among New Zealanders. The *Rainbow Warrior* incident and more recently Chernobyl had both reinforced these feelings.

---

* Armacost to Shultz, 21 June 1986, State Department Papers.
† Press conference of 23 June 1986.

Consistent with Washington's renewed insistence on nuclear propulsion, Shultz spoke for ten minutes (he had brought a lengthy paper with him) on the safety record of US naval ships. Then, coming to the main point, he said that President Reagan hoped for drastic reductions in nuclear weapons but the nuclear deterrent and the ability to move ships where they were needed was as important for New Zealand as for the US. So NCND was vital and the US could not have different policies among its alliances. It was for New Zealand to decide where it stood, but he said he liked New Zealanders and admired their system of government and if there had to be a parting on this issue it should be as friends.

Lange equally courteously said he admired the integrity the US had shown in its dealings with New Zealand. New Zealand did not seek to challenge NCND and if presentation was the problem there would be no public rejection of any proposed visit. If it would help, his government could accept the China formula which the British had negotiated. The United States had been willing to accommodate other allies – Spain had just endorsed a non-nuclear policy in a referendum – and he asked why this or the Danish position could not apply to New Zealand.

The Secretary rejected the China formula as not workable for the United States and pointed out, not for the first or last time, that countries like Spain, Denmark and Norway had anti-nuclear policies but did not rule out ship visits. New Zealand wanted a way to accept or reject visits. Then, to the surprise of his hearers from both delegations, he added that New Zealand had to accept that from time to time there would inevitably be nuclear weapons aboard the occasional visiting ship. 'The chances were high there would be weapons aboard at one time or another. That was the reality. That is the way the US Navy arms its vessels, which are just platforms to carry the weapons around.'

He was making a statistical point, not that the United States wanted to put the weapons in New Zealand harbours but that the essence of NCND was that on some unforeseeable occasions (such as a warship coming off patrol in the Indian Ocean) the weapons would be there.

Nevertheless, such a frank admission caused a stir in the meeting, and disappeared entirely from the American record. The Prime Minister switched off and changed the subject to the South Pacific. New Zealand's defence policy was a regional one. It did not intend to rat on a treaty commitment but the outlook was bleak if military ties with the United States were to founder on the nuclear issue.

Shultz said merely that 'New Zealand would have to take a roll of the dice on that'. The country could always re-enter the treaty if its position changed, but in the meantime the United States would have to make it clear that it was relieved of the obligation to assist New Zealand. A statement along these lines would have to be made, probably after consulting the Australians at the meeting in San Francisco. He then fell into thought, perhaps musing on the possibility of making an earlier statement, and did not respond when Lange anxiously asked whether the United States would take any further steps on the bilateral relationship.

His final comments, however, gave no hint of any dramatic conclusion; he merely expressed a great regret that things had come to this – he would still like to go fishing in New Zealand.[*] It seemed though that, as the talk wandered on, the man Norrish saw as 'straightforward, warm and quick-tempered' had suddenly decided to get it over with. A break was inevitable and he saw no point in prolonging the uncertainty until August. The Prime Minister had no forewarning and was surprised. 'I was certainly just proposing to be very restrained and to leave the premises.'[†] They walked together to the door. Outside was a throng of reporters and TV cameras. Shultz stood at the doorway and then pronounced the requiem: 'We part company as friends, but we part company as far as the alliance is concerned.'

---

[*] There are accounts of the meeting in PM 58/206/2, PM 59/8/5 Part 8, MFAT and PM 111/3/3/1 Part 50, ANZ. Lange reported to Palmer in PM 50/6/4 Part 17, and Norrish gave additional details to the Japanese ambassador on 4 July, LON B 106/4/1 Part 11, MFAT. An American cable of 27 June 1987 summarised the press conference.
[†] Vernon Wright interview, 13 January 1987, Lange Papers, Box 1, ANZ and interview with Norrish, 26 October 2010.

Chapter Twelve
The End of the Argument

Parting as friends had been Shultz's hope all along, and 25 years later he was still anxious to emphasise his desire not to make an enemy of New Zealand.* But the dispute had dragged on at such length with recurrent outbursts of anger or disappointment on both sides that a considerable body of resentment had built up. Parting as friends turned out to be more difficult than it looked.†

There was considerable astonishment that Shultz had chosen to do it so abruptly. His doubts had been accumulating for months but the American embassy believed that he had finally 'got off the train' after Lange's speech to the Auckland Labour Party conference on 9 May. Even so, he had not mentioned the possibility to his staff or to the Australian Foreign Minister the previous evening. It was

---

* Interview with George P. Shultz, 2 November 2011.
† It might have been foreseen. Lord Castlereagh said in 1821: 'Alliances and Treaties anul'd, whilst amicable relations are preserved, does to the English Ear sound altogether Incomprehensible.' Castlereagh to his brother, Charles Stewart, 13 March 1821.

understood that in due course a statement would have to be made about the withdrawal of the American security commitment, but during the meeting with Lange he still seemed to be thinking that this would be done at the August gathering in San Francisco. However, as the two set out their positions the Secretary of State – once described by Lange as 'a man of implacable logic' – seems to have concluded that there was little left to talk about. He decided – 'to everyone's surprise, perhaps even his own', said Norrish – to end the wearisome and barren dialogue and tidy the issue away.

The Prime Minister was taken aback by Shultz's announcement, believing that diplomatic practice was always to telegraph a major punch before it was delivered. He made no immediate comment but claimed later that the issue had taken over the subsequent ASEAN press conference and gave a new impetus to Indonesia's talk of a nuclear-free zone in South East Asia.* This was straining the evidence; ANZUS took up only the opening minutes of a lengthy press gathering attended by all the Ministers in Manila.

It was nonetheless a very embarrassing moment for Lange, made more embarrassing by the coincidence that he had agreed to the repatriation of the only two French agents to be imprisoned after the *Rainbow Warrior* bombing, after promising that they would not be released during the term of his government. The Manila announcement marked the collapse of the main plank in his foreign policy. He had gambled or hoped that the nuclear ships ban would in the end be accepted by the United States and for two years had assured New Zealanders (who liked both the ban and the alliance) that their anti-nuclear stance was fully compatible with membership of ANZUS. Now this hope had been decisively rejected by Shultz who told the Australian Minister of Defence that he 'was tired of being strung along' by the New Zealanders.†

---

* Vernon Wright interview, 13 January 1987, Lange Papers, Box 1, ANZ.
† Beazley to the NZ High Commissioner in Canberra, 18 August 1986, PM 59/8/5 Part 8, MFAT.

It was not possible, even for the Prime Minister's quick mind, to pass this off as other than a setback. His first instinct, when he went on the offensive three days later in Bangkok, was to attack Shultz, departing from another diplomatic practice to give a critical account of what the Secretary had said in the meeting. Shultz had surprised his hearers (and the Australians too) by stating that over time some visiting vessel would be likely to have nuclear weapons on board; the whole point of NCND was that nobody could be sure whether the weapons were there or not. Lange said he found this 'chilling'; it revealed that the previous National Government had 'consistently misled New Zealand on nuclear ships'. And it had not proved possible to talk the differences through; the US had 'almost heroically refused to engage in negotiations or consultation – at each turn of the tide we have been met by statements of rejection'.[*]

Back home both his and Palmer's initial comments seemed flurried and indeed contradictory. They swivelled between an anxiety to claim that anyhow there was nothing much to ANZUS which provided only for consultation, and the assertion that the ANZUS treaty remained in force with New Zealand as a full member who could not be ejected. Palmer as Acting Prime Minister just before Lange's return told a press conference that to say there was a security guarantee was 'a considerable exaggeration'. In support of this assertion he quoted Weinberger's statement that the US would not commit its forces to combat unless its vital interests were at stake. But he notably failed to quote the Secretary of Defense's next sentence: 'Our interests of course include the vital interests of our allies.'[†]

Lange made the same points, but more vividly: 'A moron in a hurry could see that ANZUS was not a security guarantee, but just an agreement to consult.'[‡] Those in a hurry had perhaps only read the

---
[*] Press conference of 30 June 1986, State Department Papers.
[†] Speech by Weinberger of 28 November 1984, outlining six criteria for the US use of military force. See Robert J. Bresler, 'War and the American People', *USA Today* magazine, vol. 119, issue 2550, March 1991, p. 9, for the text of this speech.
[‡] Quoted in the *Dominion*, 7 July 1986. For those with more time the full text of the two articles stated: 'The Parties will consult together whenever in the opinion of any of them the

first of the operative articles which obliged the parties to consult if a *threat* arose in the Pacific. The next article declared that, if the threat became real, the parties would *act to meet the common danger* – an obligation which the New Zealand negotiator of the treaty, Sir Carl Berendsen, regarded as equivalent to that in the NATO treaty.

The Prime Minister went on once again to revive the claim that the US was willing to accommodate other allies with anti-nuclear policies, such as Denmark and Norway, but was unreasonably refusing to do so for New Zealand. But he also emphasised that the country's continued membership of ANZUS was not in doubt. It could only be amended with the agreement of all three parties and even then twelve months' notice was required. As a final bewildering touch, he added on 9 July that the relationship with the US 'has become much warmer since we became friends and not allies'. He was beginning to feel the strain of these gyrations. In mid-July the British High Commission picked up the first hint that he was tiring of the Foreign Affairs portfolio, causing a Foreign Office official to minute: 'The thought of Helen Clark fills me with dread.'[*]

Washington certainly did not think relations had become much warmer and was incensed by Lange's rather free-spoken accounts of the American position. His statement that the treaty contained only 'an obligation to consult' was described by the State Department as 'at variance with the facts', a comment which the *Dominion* thought came 'as close as a diplomat's mouthpiece to calling Mr Lange a liar'. To make the point doubly clear, the Department issued a formal statement confirming that 'it would fully and promptly fulfil its security requirements under ANZUS by both military and non-military means as best would meet the threat'. The American embassy attacked the comparison with Denmark and Norway, pointing out

---

territorial integrity, political independence or security of any of the Parties is threatened in the Pacific' (Article III); and 'Each Party recognizes that an armed attack in the Pacific Area on any of the Parties would be dangerous to its own peace and safety and declares that it would act to meet the common danger in accordance with its constitutional processes' (Article IV).

[*] Cable of 17 July 1986, FCO Papers.

once more that though they had anti-nuclear policies both accepted US naval visits without enquiring into their armament. American warships made thirteen visits to five Danish ports in 1985, including the battleship *Iowa* and the cruiser *Ticonderoga*. In the course of a NATO naval exercise Norway had an American aircraft carrier and other large warships in its fiords which were visited by Norwegian Ministers.*

The warm-tempered Shultz was angered by Lange's accounts of their Manila meeting, and possibly a little embarrassed by the frequent play made with his comment that it had to be accepted that visiting warships would occasionally carry nuclear weapons. He no doubt meant that over time this would be statistically likely, for NCND would be meaningless if it could be assumed that visiting ships were always conventionally armed. It was, though, a point never before publicly acknowledged and came as a surprise to the Australians, and no doubt to the Japanese and others. It was a frankness he never repeated.

At a White House reception for the diplomatic corps he pulled John Wood aside, visibly angry (he turned red in the face), and said that he and the Prime Minister had understood one another well enough at Manila, but Lange was now giving accounts of their meeting 'that I do not recognise and which is very, very distressing to me personally, and the United States'.†

This did not bode well for Lange's more considered response, that New Zealand–American relations would be the better for the break. He hoped that with the wreckage of the crash tidied away it would be possible to turn attention to 'the enormously important' wider relationship with America. Given this importance, the new policy he laid down was, as far as possible, to be 'business as usual'.

Washington was understandably wary but first there was public disquiet to weather. This was more a matter of press unease; polling

---

* Both statements from the *Dominion*, 4 July 1986.
† Interview with John Wood, 11 August 2011.

showed the public more concerned with the imposition of a new consumption tax (GST) and the America's Cup contest than the loss of the security guarantee. An American visitor noted a widespread view that the argument over the guarantee did not matter much because 'the US will defend New Zealand anyway'. This was Lange's own view. He told the Australians that if a crisis were to emerge, the 'chemistry' would begin to work and New Zealand would receive the assistance it always had from the US and Britain.[*]

There was, however, some resentment of what was seen as American sternness. Many New Zealanders felt that the US was unsympathetic and indeed peremptory in demanding that New Zealand either comply with its wishes or leave. A smaller group on the Left were delighted that the country's ties with America's global policing had been cut. W. P. Reeves in the *Dominion* welcomed 'Kissing Goodbye to America': 'Who will wish to be allied to a country locked into an ideological crusade harbouring the illusion of security through military superiority?'[†]

Editorial opinion, however, was scathing about the government's inability despite repeated protestations to maintain its treaty relationship with the United States. These protestations, said the *New Zealand Herald*, 'can now be seen for the sham they always were'. In an earlier leader it castigated the government for being naive in imagining that ANZUS would not be a casualty of its policy, and naive in talking about a substitute security partnership with Australia which after all relies for its own defence on the United States and 'accepts occasional calls by nuclear ships as a modest reciprocal courtesy'. It quoted with approval Shultz's claim that New Zealand's actions 'can only encourage those who hope to tear at the fabric of Western cooperation'.

The Christchurch *Press* worried that 'New Zealand has come close to isolation from all its former friends and allies in the Western

---

[*] Lt Col Jim Williams, the NZ desk officer at the Pentagon, PM 111/3/3/1 Part 56, ANZ. Lange's comment was made on 18 June 1986 to the AHC, 1628/25/7 Part 7, NAA.
[†] *Dominion*, 4 July 1986.

world' and saw it risking 'a lonely, exposed and intellectual isolation'. The Wellington *Evening Post* said that along with nuclear ships New Zealand had tossed out its special trading relationship with the US, its special access to American policy-makers, and its voice as a small, but valuable and respected, member of the Western system of alliances. The only dissenting editorial voice was that of the *Otago Daily Times* which saw the continuation of ANZUS as conditional on suppressing a policy which had been democratically approved and dancing to American requirements: 'For all the value of ANZUS that is rather too high a price to pay.'*

All in all, it was, as the American embassy observed, a bumpy week for the government. All governments have bad weeks and the embassy wisely did not make too much of it, saying it was too early to judge the effects. The press smelt blood but 'media interest in any one story is extremely short-lived here'. It went on to marvel at the way that Lange, when in trouble over the past two years, had been saved by foreign events – the *Rainbow Warrior* attack, the 'bellicosity from Anglo-allies', and even Chernobyl. It asked what could save him this time and gave a firm answer: Washington. Any attempt to force him to jettison the anti-nuclear legislation – 'anything that smacked of punishment rather than inevitable consequences sadly taken – would give Lange a heaven-sent escape from his troubles'.†

Before Wellington and Washington could work out their new relationship, defining what being a friend rather than an ally really meant, there was some unfinished business from the old relationship to be cleared up. Surprisingly, the British, even after the finality of Manila, were still interested in carrying on the technical talks aimed at finding acceptable wording in the proposed anti-nuclear legislation which would enable their ships to visit. When Howe suggested

---

* *New Zealand Herald*, 30 June, 13 and 15 August; *Otago Daily Times*, 11 August; *Evening Post* and *Press*, 13 August 1986.
† Despatch of 11 July 1986, State Department Papers.

another round, the Prime Minister's scribbled reaction was a vehement 'No! I am not going to be whipped on this one.'*

Palmer on a visit to London was left to convey this sentiment more tactfully. His instructions from the Prime Minister were to say that the government did not see any point in continuing the negotiations. The reality was that British ships would not visit while the American Administration maintained its position, and 'the climate created by Shultz' made it politically impossible to weaken the legislation; if anything, the pressure from the party was to toughen it. He told Lady Young at the Foreign Office that it was Shultz not New Zealand who had walked away. He thought that Australian and Japanese influence explained why the Administration had declined to reach an agreement with New Zealand, 'as they had been willing to do with other small allied countries'. Lady Young, calling this 'a most unhappy outcome', pressed him to think again about possible changes to the legislation before their next meeting. Palmer assured the Prime Minister that he had given her no encouragement 'to believe we could contemplate embarking upon that overgrown directionless track'.†

When they met again almost two weeks later Lady Young accepted that any hopes of compromise were over. She said sadly that ties with Britain would loosen a little as a result but said that London's real concern was that New Zealand might drift out of the Western camp and slide into non-alignment. Given that the direction of New Zealand's foreign policy was no longer clear, this was becoming a growing concern among its traditional friends, in Japan and ASEAN as well as Australia and the US. Palmer gave the first of many reassurances, telling Lady Young that his country would not be darting off in new directions and would remain firmly resistant to Soviet influence. He added, though, that this depended partly on American

---

* His comment on a MFAT note suggesting some possible redrafting, 9 July 1986, PM 59/8/5 Part 8, MFAT.
† Lange's instructions of 17 July are in PM 111/3/3/1 Part 54, ANZ, and Palmer's reports of 23 July and 4 August 1986 in LON B 106/4/1 Part 12, MFAT.

restraint. Any intemperate response might push New Zealand towards non-alignment.

He was thinking of the meeting in San Francisco on 11 August where the United States and Australia were expected to read New Zealand out of the alliance. In the event that occasion passed off quietly. The formal statement was stern. The US said it was 'suspending its security obligations to New Zealand under the ANZUS Treaty pending adequate corrective measures' and Australia said 'it disagreed completely with New Zealand policy on port and air access and expressed its understanding of the action which the United States had taken'. In their comments, however, both took a more conciliatory line. Shultz gave a polite account of the discussions over the previous two years: 'In the end New Zealand chose, as it has a right to do, basically to withdraw itself from the alliance by denying port access. And we're sorry about that. I miss New Zealand, and as I said after my meeting with Prime Minister Lange in Manila only a few weeks ago, we part as friends, but we part on security matters.' Hayden added his support, saying that the New Zealand Government's policy violated the long-standing principle of NCND: 'It's not a policy we accept; we've had the opportunity of adopting that policy, and we rejected it overwhelmingly as a party.'[*]

All this, as usual with international meetings, had been agreed behind the scenes and took up little of the conference's time. Most of the discussion, unprecedented in previous ANZUS meetings, was devoted to trade and an Australian attack on protectionist policies. They were wrathful over Washington's decision to sell surplus wheat to Russia and stockpiled sugar to China and expressed their resentment at some length, at the meeting and in the communiqué. As Hayden said ruefully at the press conference, sometimes it was better to be a friend than an ally.

There had been some inter-agency argument in Washington beforehand about the right line to take on New Zealand. The legal

---

[*] US cable of 23 August 1986, State Department Papers.

experts (sometimes a little inflexible in international relations) had argued that New Zealand had by its ban placed itself in 'material breach' of the treaty, and thus should be expelled from the alliance. Shultz, to the relief of the more pragmatic, 'took it away from the lawyers' and made a political rather than a legal decision, speaking not of membership of the treaty but only of 'the security obligations' of the US. Hayden and Beazley were insistent at the meeting that New Zealand's policy could not be cost-free, but they too were more comfortable with the decision not to expel New Zealand but simply to suspend its membership, leaving it free to return if it ever changed its mind.

They were helpful in another way. The only battle over the communiqué was their insistence on inserting the statement that 'Australia retains its traditional bilateral security relationship with New Zealand'.* The Americans were initially resistant on the grounds that this had nothing to do with ANZUS, but the Australians were responding to an appeal from Lange. With all his security eggs now in the Australian basket he was worried that the US might put some constraints on this. A few days before the meeting he asked for Hayden's help; 'New Zealand's bilateral relationship with Australia is considerably more important to us in every respect' and he hoped that nothing at San Francisco would cause it damage.†

Though he had some qualms about how to handle the situation, at home Lange dismissed the San Francisco decisions as a formality: 'in effect, nothing has changed', this had been the situation for the past two years. In the subsequent parliamentary debate he fell back on legal quibbling more reminiscent of his earlier days in court, arguing that ANZUS was not a security guarantee but only an agreement to consult; the treaty said nothing about port access so it was the US which was trying to rewrite it; and in fact it was the US which had walked away from the treaty. His irritability showed

---

* Cable by New Zealand High Commissioner, Canberra, 20 August 1986, PM 50/6/4 Part 17, MFAT.
† Lange to Hayden, 6 August 1986, PM 111/3/3/1 Part 52, ANZ.

when he referred at his press conference to the visit of the battleship *New Jersey* to Japan. Disclaiming any intention of commenting, he then did, saying, 'there can be few classes of vessel more likely to be nuclear-armed than the *New Jersey*'. This was gratuitous mischief-making and the American embassy did not report it for fear that Washington would 'go up like a rocket'.*

The San Francisco meeting attracted editorial rather than public interest. After months of American warnings the result brought little surprise. A *Herald* poll put ANZUS and the nuclear issue well down on the list of people's concerns: 26 per cent were worried about the economy, 25 per cent about unemployment, but only 3 per cent about ANZUS.† In any case, lingering embarrassment over the suspension was quickly overlaid by a greater embarrassment when the Defence Committee of Enquiry reported a week later.

The Committee had been set up the previous December to enquire into public views about defence and the ANZUS relationship. Its membership of five was headed by Frank Corner, a former Secretary of Foreign Affairs. He had apparently been suggested by Helen Clark who perhaps overlooked the sharpness of his mind and his lengthy experience in foreign policy going back to 1943.‡ The other members followed a more predictable pattern: a Maori major-general, Brian Poananga (who said he still held to his views as a 'geriatric general'); Diane Hunt, a Wellington planner and scientist; and Dr Kevin Clements, a sociology lecturer and peace activist. Announcing this mixture the Prime Minister said, to no one's surprise, that he expected the members to have differing views when they reported: 'It would have to be a report of such stupefying blandness that they could all agree on it.'§

The Committee called for submissions and had received over 500 by February, most expressing intense anti-nuclear feeling.

---

* 20 August 1986, PM 111/3/3/1 Part 52, ANZ.
† The poll was reported on 14 August 1986.
‡ Michael Bassett, *Working With David: Inside the Lange Cabinet*, Hodder Moa, 2008, p. 215.
§ Press statement of 6 December 1985.

That month Corner told Radio New Zealand that the majority saw New Zealand situated solely in the South Pacific among a group of small countries, a big change from a generation earlier. The idea, he said, that 'New Zealand's defence was bound up with protecting certain ideas, a certain kind of civilisation' did not come through in the submissions. Collective security under ANZUS was firmly rejected. Helen Clark, presenting the Labour Party's submission, said that members did not want ANZUS even if the alliance could accept a nuclear-free policy.*

Rather than rely wholly on self-selected submissions, the Committee undertook a comprehensive range of polling to seek to establish what most New Zealanders thought and took statistical advice on how to interpret the resulting figures. Its own discussions were predictably contentious. Corner told the Australians that the left-leaning members were refusing to consider contrary arguments as 'fascist'.† So the result when it came was a surprise to everyone. The Committee's report was unanimous and it concluded that by a small but clear majority New Zealanders would prefer to stay in ANZUS even if this meant accepting nuclear ship visits.

As expected, the polls showed the country to be deeply divided: 72 per cent wished to be in the alliance, but 73 per cent, many of them the same people, wished New Zealand to be nuclear-free. While different meanings could be (and had been) attached to the concept of a nuclear-free New Zealand, the government's was a ban on nuclear-armed or -powered vessels. The best-liked option would be membership of ANZUS without its nuclear obligations but the positions of the US and New Zealand did not permit this. When pressed to decide on what was on offer, 52 per cent of respondents favoured accepting ship visits in return for an operational ANZUS while 44 per cent preferred to withdraw from the alliance.

---

* Corner's radio interview was 21 February and Clark's comment to the Committee 24 April 1986.
† Talking to the AHC, 28 May 1986, 221/1/4/4 Part 11, DFAT.

It was clear from the polling that most New Zealanders did not wish to be neutral, non-aligned, or even the more mysterious 'semi-aligned' (Helen Clark's suggestion). But there was no consensus on a preferred defence policy: enhancing the security relationship with Australia was the only option left open – 'Hobson's choice' Corner called it. The Committee's parting shot was that enquiries of this sort should precede, not follow, major policy changes.[*]

When shown the report at the beginning of August, Lange was upset, coinciding as it did with New Zealand's suspension from ANZUS. As Ian Templeton, writing in the *Guardian*, said: 'The committee had sung in unison, and he did not like the tune.'[†] He delayed publishing the report pending 'clarification' and presented the Committee with detailed critiques prepared by John Henderson, the head of his office. But the Committee stood its ground and took its revenge by adding to its published report the 'distinctly sharp' exchanges with the Prime Minister's Office over the parts objected to, ranging from interpretation of the polling to the (literally) more academic charge that insufficient footnotes had been supplied for the historical background.

Lange's subsequent press conference was lengthy and ill-tempered. He described the Committee's basic recommendations – the need for an enhanced defence relationship with Australia and for a greater focus on New Zealand's own region, the South Pacific – as clear and perfectly valid. Regrettably, the Committee had also indulged in 'a series of speculative and totally unfactual pieces of reporting'. He attacked the poll results as invalid, clashing irritably with several questioners, and explained the continuing support for ANZUS as the result of New Zealanders having always seen it as a non-nuclear alliance.[‡]

The newspapers gave extensive coverage to the report. In a detailed commentary Roger Mackey, the *Evening Post*'s defence

---

[*] Report of the Defence Committee of Enquiry, 31 July 1986.
[†] The *Guardian*, 11 August 1986.
[‡] Press conference of 21 August 1986.

correspondent, concluded that New Zealand had an anti-nuclear policy 'but not much of a defence policy'. He thought it was difficult to argue that the policy had not been a net loss to the country. It had given hope to those who marched against the entry of American warships but on its own this would be an admission that the anti-nuclear policy was 'the most expensive form of middle-class psychotherapy yet practised in this country'. The Prime Minister conceded it had failed to diminish the world's nuclear arsenal; the only important effects had been to cut ties with New Zealand's largest ally and to begin to reduce the capabilities of the country's armed forces.[*]

Several editorials saw the polling as exposing the government's claimed mandate for its policy as a sham, and Lange's criticism of the methodology used was seen as carping. Opinion was more evenly divided over greater dependence on the Australian connection. The *Evening Post* saw this as a second-class option which left the country dependent on Australian goodwill, but the *Dominion* thought that a return to ANZUS would divide the whole country and was unacceptable. A closer relationship with Australia was full of uncertainties and perhaps costs but that was what life was like after ANZUS and New Zealanders would have to get used to it.[†]

While this excitement flared and faded, both the United States and New Zealand were thinking about their new relationship. Rowling called on Wolfowitz's successor, Gaston Sigur, to say that Humpty Dumpty had fallen and they now needed to pick up the pieces. He hoped that both sides could still do sensible things outside the alliance.[‡] This was a reasonable expectation; the mood in Washington was one of sorrow rather than anger. The sense of betrayal had come

---

[*] *Evening Post*, 30 August 1986.
[†] *Dominion*, 22 August 1986.
[‡] Report of 11 July 1986, PM 50/6/4 Part 18, MFAT. Humpty Dumpty was itself a piece of defence equipment – not an egg but a large gun mounted on the walls of Colchester when that town was being besieged by Parliamentary forces. When it was knocked to the ground and shattered, all the King's horses and men could not do much about it.

when the *Buchanan* was declined, and the subsequent events were seen by the Congress and public as the sadly inevitable consequences. The relationship went into a diplomatic limbo. The existing constraints remained in place but Shultz gave no guidance about any new measures. There was no open season on New Zealand; instead a feeling of leaving well alone for a while. A formal review was postponed until November and was cursory when it came, simply confirming that there would be no going back to 'business as usual' but adding nothing new.[*]

Rowling was told that the Administration had no intention of doing anything or of encouraging Congress to do so, though some adjustment would have to be made in military cooperation. This was confirmed when Rowling took soundings with Congressmen. Solarz called it 'worse than unfortunate, a tragedy' and Jim Leach thought it might be 'half a decade or a decade' before a working relationship on defence could be re-established. They confirmed that the Administration was not trying to activate the House and that, despite the usual calls for restrictive measures by one or two representatives from dairy districts, Congress was not inclined to take any action on trade.[†] The only Bill introduced was one cutting back on military sales and assistance to which the Administration gave lukewarm support as the least it could get away with. It passed the House but died in the Senate.

For all the fears and occasional stories of the abrupt cancellation of orders for luxuries like flowers and fresh raspberries, trade was not affected.[‡] The United States remained New Zealand's third-largest export market and the slight decline in trade for the 1986 year was due to a rise in the New Zealand dollar rather than to ANZUS. The weakening of New Zealand's ability to lobby against occasional outbursts of protectionist sentiment remained a worry. Four years earlier the

---

[*] The Inter-Agency Group met only briefly on 5 November and decided to make no moves to augment or change the existing 'rules of engagement'. PM 111/3/3/1 Part 54, ANZ.
[†] Talking to Rowling, 31 July 1986, PM 111/3/3/1 Part 51, ANZ.
[‡] Report by the Department of Trade and Industry, 23 September 1986, PM 194/1/1/1, MFAT.

Vice President, George H. W. Bush, had intervened to halt the sale on the world market of $US350 million worth of American butter which would have damaged New Zealand's returns, and two years later the Administration had stepped in to remove a legislative attempt to block the country's casein exports. This kind of influence had now gone but in practice the US Department of Agriculture continued to consult quietly on sales of butter and the irony, as Hayden noted, was that New Zealand suffered less from surplus disposals than Australia.

The one possible cause of friction was the American Antarctic base at Christchurch known as 'Deep Freeze'. US aircraft used it to support operations on the ice but also staged through it on a 'milk run' to the joint base at Pine Gap in Australia and on to the Indian Ocean. It might have been a prime target for anti-nuclear and anti-American protest but it was in Jim Anderton's electorate and jobs were at stake. The New Zealand Government was anxious not to disturb this arrangement: the draft legislation simply provided a blanket clearance for Deep Freeze aircraft. The Administration agreed, with Shultz saying that the existing arrangement was 'the right thing for the moment'.*

New Zealand's reluctance to see any change in Christchurch, however, gave one or two critics in Washington the opportunity to pull a few feathers from the kiwi for a change. The Navy was resentful of its treatment by New Zealand and the Secretary of the Navy, John Lehman, was for a time outspoken in calling for the base to be shifted to Tasmania. He was barely able to be held back when passing through Christchurch on his way to the ice but once in Australia called for a review of the base's location and muttered about economic sanctions as well. He was slapped down by Ambassador Cleveland who put out a crisp release saying that Lehman's view was personal and not Administration policy. This damped the issue down but it continued to grumble like a retreating storm on one or two occasions when Lange sailed a little too close to the NCND rocks

---

* Cable of 17 August 1986, LON B 106/4/1 Part 12, MFAT.

by assuring the public that the transiting aircraft were not carrying nuclear weapons.

Otherwise the tone in Washington was mainly one of regret – regret over the loss of the close personal contacts that had grown up over the years. Armitage said that above all he would miss the opportunities to discuss a wide range of issues with New Zealand representatives through which they had indirectly influenced American thinking. The relationship would no doubt improve over time but he 'did not see that situation coming back in the future'.[*] Jim Kelly of the National Security Council thought the New Zealand people had not been aware of how the close the relationship had been and therefore did not miss it when it was gone. New Zealand, he said, had been a full player – not large but full – in all the things that 'go on around this town'. The damage now was 'deep and long lasting'; things would never be quite the same again between New Zealand and the United States.[†]

Influence is notoriously difficult to trace, but Wellington's diplomats, regarded as clear-sighted and representing a small country with few interests to push, roamed in and out of offices all over Washington with privileged access almost everywhere in the huge bureaucracy. When issues were sharply fought between agencies, the view of a trusted ally could occasionally have unexpected leverage.[‡] A Pentagon official took issue with Shultz's statement that New Zealand's principal contribution to ANZUS was through port access. No one, he said, believed this. New Zealand's contribution was by being there, a valued member of the highest inner circle of American allies. He was not 'ecstatic' about contemplating a future where Australia was the only consultative partner in the Pacific.[§]

---

[*] Armitage to Rowling, 29 July 1986, PM 59/8/5 Part 8, MFAT.
[†] Conversation of 25 February 1987, reported in PM 50/6/4 Part 21, MFAT.
[‡] A random example would be the New Zealand protest against the Christmas bombing of Hanoi in 1971. In the battle for the President's ear, the State Department quietly thanked the embassy for strengthening its case.
[§] Williams to Murdoch, 28 August 1986, PM 50/6/4 Part 19, MFAT.

THE END OF THE ARGUMENT

In the grip of single-issue diplomacy, the New Zealand Government could not afford to be greatly concerned about its influence in Washington. With the argument over, Wellington made it clear that the anti-nuclear legislation would go ahead as originally drafted. There was a little anxiety over the consequences of the abrupt departure from the alliance.* When Armitage said that New Zealand's new defence relationship would be like Malaysia's, Wellington was offended, feeling that even as a non-ally New Zealand should have a distinctive position and not be ranked with other non-allies. The offence was briefly deepened when by an oversight New Zealand was invited to a briefing on arms control with the non-aligned and neutral group.

The touchiness reflected the fears of New Zealand's traditional friends that suspended from the alliance the country would drift towards non-alignment and that under pressure from the Left it would look with more sympathy on Soviet aims in the Pacific. Backed by a sizeable fleet using the former American base at Cam Ranh Bay, the Soviet Union was looking to expand its influence in the South Pacific through 'fishing boat diplomacy', agreements with island countries like Kiribati and Vanuatu to support its fish harvesting. Palmer therefore touched a sore spot during his visit to the United Kingdom in July when he contrasted the 'dogmatic and inflexible' regional fishing policy of the United States with that of the Russians who were prepared to pay for what they took.†

After Armitage warned in *Yomiuri* that the Russians were taking advantage of Lange's position to extend their presence in the South Pacific, senior Japanese officials felt it necessary to emphasise more than once the need for New Zealand to maintain Western solidarity and resist Soviet influence.‡ The British too were concerned, warning

---

* An unwary reference to the 'post-ANZUS era' in a Foreign Affairs briefing had to be hastily amended to reflect the official position that the alliance remained in force with New Zealand as a full member.
† Speech in Edinburgh, 23 July 1986.
‡ The interview was 10 July and the warnings were given on 18 July and again more formally on 22 August 1986, PM 50/6/4 Part 19, MFAT.

that the Americans would look closely for any signs of cosying up to the Russians, such as the drydocking facilities or Aeroflot landing rights for which Moscow frequently pressed, and 'would see red' if any of these were accepted.* It was only natural also for the Russians to wonder whether new opportunities were opening up and towards the end of August, Mikhail Kapitsa, the able Deputy Foreign Minister and Pacific specialist, made a 'private visit' to Wellington to assess the possibilities.

Despite the 'undisguised anti-Americanism'† still on display at the Labour Party conference the prospects were not promising. The Prime Minister, who regarded Soviet diplomacy in New Zealand as 'insensitive' and based on a curious misreading of the situation, was firmly opposed to any further links.‡ For lack of anything more substantial the International Department of the Soviet Communist Party tried its hand at some people-to-people diplomacy, inviting several influential members of the Labour Party for visits to the Soviet Union. The President of the party, Margaret Wilson, and the Associate Foreign Minister, Fran Wilde, were given a lavish welcome the following January. They were received by the Chairman of the Supreme Soviet and in a statement which showed signs of having been drafted for them praised the 'numerous peace initiatives of the Soviet Union' and hailed the important practical steps it had taken on nuclear tests and the South Pacific nuclear-free zone. Lange clamped down on further visits.

There were a few further ripples, but none could be attributed to Soviet influence. The decision to withdraw New Zealand's battalion from Singapore after eighteen years was if anything a belated acknowledgement of reality and the Singapore Government raised no objection. In a decision announced just before the party conference and clearly aimed at the lingering fears of nuclear war, the

---

* Foreign Office message, 1 August 1986, FCO Papers.
† In its report of 2 September the British High Commission added that all references to Britain were uniformly disparaging which the Foreign Office described as 'depressing'. FCO Papers.
‡ Lange to Cleveland, 23 December 1986, PM 111/3/3/1 Part 54, ANZ.

Prime Minister announced a Nuclear Impact Study to look at the consequences for New Zealand of a nuclear war in the northern hemisphere.* The study was by a pleasant irony funded from the compensation money paid by the French Government for the *Rainbow Warrior* affair and carried out by a team of five from the Planning Council. Its first report came to the unsurprising conclusion that the most important need was to avoid a nuclear war. It proposed extensive further study into something called 'southern trade', alternative sources of medicines, recycling lubricating oils, greater use of vegetable feed stocks, and the possible decentralisation of government. Lange had little interest in such survivalist thinking, especially after the peace movement ungratefully said the money could have been better spent on enquiring into South Pacific health, and the project was allowed to lapse.

By then it had become clear even to the worriers overseas that the country's foreign policy was not going to drift into the Red sunset. The Prime Minister's statements were quite categorical that, apart from the ANZUS break, New Zealand's foreign policy would be unchanged. Even a blip a year later, when a New Zealand delegate in Geneva made a speech attacking nuclear deterrence, caused only temporary alarm. The British delegate said it had little effect in Geneva 'where New Zealand carries little or no weight', except to draw favourable comment from the Soviet bloc. There was a flurry of messages, with the American embassy describing the speech in a testy cable as 'a specious argument for the self-indulgent, unrealistic and preachy strategic approach New Zealand is currently taking toward the world', but the fuss died away when it was realised that it was merely an overzealous pitch for election to the Committee on Disarmament.†

After San Francisco the government's main preoccupation was with plugging the gaps in defence and intelligence left by the loss

---

* He made the announcement 'with more than a hint of irony' according to the BHC, 29 August 1986, FCO Papers.
† Cable from British embassy, Geneva, of 23 July 1987 and from US embassy, Wellington, early August, FCO Papers.

of ANZUS access. Reviews of both were commissioned. The intelligence review led to the abolition of the Intelligence Council and the merger of its functions into a new position of Coordinator of Domestic and External Security, reflecting the government's passing interest in the concept of 'comprehensive security' which was hoped could cover all emergencies from trouble overseas to earthquakes and floods at home. It found itself almost immediately dealing with a coup in Fiji.

The defence review had much the harder task. The United States had for years underpinned the exercising, training and armament of the Defence Force. Relying on the Australians was very much a second-best since they themselves depended on the Americans for their doctrine, interoperability and weapons. Nonetheless it was the only substitute available and the greater financial and political costs, the Prime Minister said, just had to be accepted. The public did so with little protest; unexpectedly it was the Australians who showed more reluctance.

Henderson in the Prime Minister's Office was commissioned to prepare an 'interim review' in preparation for a defence White Paper but two deadlines for its completion passed while he wrestled with the complexities of the new relationship with Australia. The Americans were inclined to dismiss the new emphasis on the Anzac connection as 'a convenient figleaf to help disguise the fact that New Zealand's security foundation since World War II had come to an end' and the Australian High Commission in Wellington told them that Australia was not going to 'bend over backwards' to meet New Zealand's political needs. The American ambassador noted a contrast between ANZUS, in which the country had been one of two junior partners in a relationship that did not make large demands, and the new economic and now defence dependency on Australia. New Zealand, he thought, 'could drift into a far more dependent and uncomfortable relationship with its abrasive big cousins'.[*]

---

[*] US embassy to Washington, 4 November 1986, State Department Papers.

This was underlined a month later by a visit to Wellington by Hayden whose blunt comments rather shook the new hopes placed in the trans-Tasman relationship. The Australian military had told the Henderson review team that they would do what they could to help, provided there was no great increase in costs and no risk of jeopardising their own relations with the United States. Canberra felt that this 'cold shower' had not been absorbed in Wellington and Hayden was commissioned to deliver a firmer message, though even the Americans were surprised that he did so in public.

He made it clear that Australia could not replace the United States as a strategic partner. Even enhancing the bilateral security relationship would require significantly more spending by Australia which had gone about as far as it could, given the costs of conducting the defence relationship on a bilateral rather than trilateral basis. This did not go down well and led Corner to say that the country's defence policy had effectively been hijacked by a small group within the anti-nuclear movement. His Committee had seen an enhanced defence relationship with Australia as the only recourse left, but Hayden's statements had shown that there were real difficulties even with this.*

The White Paper came out the following February and as expected stressed regional self-reliance and closer ties with Australia and foreshadowed the move to 'comprehensive security' which appealed to the Left because it held that military threats were less likely to trouble New Zealand than eruptions or earthquakes. New Zealand would continue to meet its ANZUS obligations through conventional means, doing so by strengthening collective security in 'our part of the world', which Lange defined to the American ambassador as covering Polynesia to Tuvalu and Kiribati, revealing how much the country had narrowed its outlook on the world.

---

* The Hayden visit was 10–13 December 1986, PM 59/8/5 Part 9 and PM 50/6/4 Part 21, MFAT. Corner's statement was made in an interview on 12 December.

The paper received a lukewarm reception, doubts being widely expressed that funding would be available to support the new security policy and the equipment it would need.* Nor were the Australians mollified. Some months later the *Australian* noted tartly that New Zealand was able 'to export thousands of its unemployed and potentially unemployed to Australia while relying on this country to carry out its obligations in the defence of the region'.†

Corner called the White Paper the work of 'amateurs' and Lange was stung. He had been showing signs of strain from the end of the previous year. Behind the booming voice and jolliness there had never been a great self-confidence; early in his term he had said to Margaret Pope, 'I don't think I can do this job.'‡ He hated confrontation, and the strain of the long wrangle over ANZUS and of managing a Cabinet increasingly divided over economic reform began to tell. It showed over the turn of the year in the long and rambling interviews he gave to Vernon Wright for a projected book, with spiteful remarks about reputable New Zealanders and sad claims about the great press conferences he had given to packed audiences. Indeed an unknowing reader might have thought these were the reminiscences of an entertainer rather than a Prime Minister.§

Now his irritability burst out in public with an intemperate attack on both Corner and Jamieson. The Hoover Institute had organised a seminar in Washington, called 'The Red Orchestra', on Soviet influence in the South Pacific and listed both men as speakers. Lange told Wright: 'I am going to unload on the unsuspecting world the real role of Ewan Jamieson, the man commenting with lofty objectivity on our defence needs' and planned to announce this 'at a moment of maximum inconvenience to Uncle Ewan'.¶ In a press conference he lashed

---

* *Trans Tasman*, 5 March 1987.
† Quoted by BHC, Canberra, 20 August 1987, FCO Papers.
‡ *At the Turning Point: My Political Life with David Lange*, AM Publishing New Zealand, 2011, p. 93.
§ There are three lengthy interview transcripts, corrected by Lange himself, 5 December 1986, 13 January and 4 February 1987, Lange Papers, Box 1, ANZ.
¶ Vernon Wright interview, 4 February 1987, Lange Papers, Box 1, ANZ.

out at the seminar which he said was arranged by Washington, with the collusion of the Opposition in New Zealand, as a 'campaign to undermine New Zealand's defence policies'. He abused Corner as 'a sort of bard of Thorndon in search of a punchline' and Jamieson as 'pursuing his interests in selling armaments on behalf of United States missile manufacturers'.[*]

The bomb went off in the maker's hands. Corner and Jamieson turned out to be in Wellington, with no plans to go to Washington. The American embassy flatly rejected the Prime Minister's conspiracy accusations as 'extraordinary' and 'unbelievable'. Lange had to make a full public apology for his offensive and inaccurate remarks. He wrote to the ambassador rather lamely to say that he had been misquoted, an explanation that Cleveland politely but firmly said was not borne out by the transcript.

After that the relationship with America faded from sight. The passage of the anti-nuclear legislation at the beginning of June 1987 caused not even a ripple. The August General Election saw the government returned with only a 3 per cent swing against it. Lange was able with relief to hand over the Foreign Affairs portfolio to Russell Marshall and turn his attention to a reform of education. Marshall immediately and pointedly signalled a new approach, saying, 'I am not about the business of having our negotiations or discussions with the Americans constantly at the confrontational level' and that he had no desire to be 'aggressively promoting a particular New Zealand view around the world and getting offside with people'.[†]

The Prime Minister worked with enthusiasm at his new portfolio but the divisions in his Cabinet and party deepened after the election. The Labour Party conference in November should have been a celebration – Labour had not won a second term since 1938 – but it was not. Delegates worried instead about the government's economic and social policies which they belatedly felt betrayed the traditional

---

[*] Press conference of 2 March 1987, PM 111/3/3/1 Part 56, ANZ.
[†] Noted with approval and relief by the Foreign Office, 28 August 1987, FCO Papers.

roots of Labour's support. The British High Commission saw a party governing against its instincts. When Cleveland remarked to Lange that he seemed to be successful in running a government without a party, the Prime Minister said he had been doing that for three years, commenting that he was no longer the 'fat, fair-minded and benign' young politician of the late 1970s. He struck the ambassador as 'evidently weary' (and if more worldly-wise, still fat) and was preoccupied with the restlessness in the party and caucus.*

The ensuing year went by with Cabinet resignations and open feuding over economic policy. There was an autumnal tinge to the government. The ANZUS quarrel slipped from sight, to make a last and quite unexpected reappearance on Anzac Day in 1989.† The Prime Minister went to the United States for a week, the main purpose being to speak at Yale University. But for the speech it might have been something of a romp; as a journalist pointed out, the week started with him walking in Strawberry Fields in New York with Yoko Ono and ended with him rolling in the grass like a starlet in a photo for *Time* magazine.‡

The Yale lecture was on 'New Zealand Foreign Policy: The Nuclear Issue and Great-Power Small-State Relations' and it exploded a landmine under his weakened premiership. The speech drew in general on familiar material, except for a paragraph which said that 'as between the United States and New Zealand, the security alliance is dead'. If the present sterile situation continued for long New Zealand might formally withdraw from the ANZUS Council. This might not have seemed especially inflammatory. Shultz himself had said the two countries had parted company on security, and Lange had more than once hinted in public that there might be little point in New Zealand remaining a formal member of the alliance.§

---

* BHC report of 12 November 1987, FCO Papers, and Cleveland's despatch of 21 December 1987, State Department Papers.
† Anzac Day (25 April) has revered status as a day of remembrance for wartime losses in both New Zealand and Australia.
‡ John Goulter in the *Evening Post*, 29 April 1989.
§ Speaking to the Wellington Branch of the New Zealand Institute of International Affairs on

But in politics as in stand-up comedy timing is everything. Lange had not prepared the ground and reports of the speech reached New Zealand as people were attending Anzac Day services. The Minister of Police, speaking at a wreath-laying, was hissed. The public reaction was uniformly hostile. The *Press* called it 'The Next Step to Isolationism'; the *Auckland Star* 'Another Shot through the Foot'; and the *Dominion* declared 'Lange's tilt at ANZUS Backfires'. The *Christchurch Star* pointed to the government's 'ever-narrowing base of support' and the *Evening Post* concluded that 'Mr Lange's leadership deserves to be on the line'.*

Lange had distributed a number of copies of the speech in Wellington before he left but when everyone hastily checked their text the offending paragraph was not there. John Henderson had been despatched to Washington to brief the Americans two days before the speech. His message was reassuring and did not mention the possibility of a withdrawal of which he was presumably unaware. The additional paragraph seemed to have been added by Lange in New York just before he left for Yale. The delivery copy of his speech shows no sign of the interpolation.

His motives for the sudden decision were, as usual, unclear. Anderton had resigned from the Labour Party in protest at the government's free-market economic policies and set up New Labour which in an Orwellian way stood for old Labour policies. It was attracting a steady flow of defectors and shaking the loyalty of some in the caucus. Lange may have decided on a gamble, an appeal to the anti-nuclear cause to stem the losses and restore his waning popularity. The old magic, however, no longer worked. He had misjudged and even the peace groups were ungrateful, dismissing his statement as 'a hollow gesture designed to soften opposition to the [purchase of the] frigates'.

---

6 August 1987, he said that in the long run New Zealand was better off without an alliance relationship with the US.

* All these comments were on 26 and 27 April 1989.

When he moved on to Ottawa the next day he seems to have lost his composure. Richard Griffin of Radio New Zealand, travelling with him, said that no one had ever seen anything like it, 'and although the Prime Minister argues vehemently, it still doesn't convince I think even the people travelling with him'.* He alternated between denouncing the journalists for not telling the truth and saying that the comments on ANZUS were self-evident truths which should not have been a surprise to anyone. Disturbed by the reports of Cabinet dissatisfaction coming back from Wellington, he lashed out even in the middle of a press conference with Canadian journalists. 'A very strange overreaction' his own entourage thought as the Prime Minister ranted about malice and invention, powerful forces at work and 'a campaign of lies', declaring darkly that there were some people who would stop at nothing to have nuclear weapons back in New Zealand.†

He said that the speech had been discussed with Cabinet and all key Ministers had a copy 'well before it was delivered'. And, 'it was another lie that it was done without consultation with other countries' – both the US and Australia knew what was going to be said. None of this was true as far as the controversial paragraph was concerned. It had not been discussed or approved by Cabinet. In early March he had mused with some colleagues about the possibility of leaving ANZUS but a week later assured Cabinet that he would not do so.‡ Ministers therefore knew nothing of what he planned to say and the Foreign Minister was embarrassed to have dismissed the possibility of a withdrawal at a farewell dinner for the American ambassador the night before the speech.§ Both the Americans and the Australians denied that they had been given any advance warning; the Australians said they had only received a copy of the speech after it had been delivered.

---

* 28 April 1989.
† Wayne Mouat, also of Radio New Zealand, and Barry Soper, Independent Radio News.
‡ Michael Bassett, *Working With David*, pp. 472 & 478. David Caygill confirms the recollection.
§ Interview with Russell Marshall, 19 August 2011.

THE END OF THE ARGUMENT

Palmer told Parliament that Cabinet would not necessarily endorse the Prime Minister's 'suggestion'. The proposal directly contradicted the 1987 Defence White Paper which said 'the New Zealand government does not plan to give notice of intent to withdraw from the ANZUS Council'. Lange's popularity dropped further and the first poll after the speech suggested that 56 per cent of respondents wanted him replaced as Prime Minister.[*] More importantly, his Cabinet colleagues had lost their remaining confidence in him and critically Palmer, who had been the most loyal of lieutenants, walked away. It was the end of the line and three months later he resigned.

It would, however, have been untrue to life with Lange if the disaster had not also had a moment of comedy. In Ottawa, returning unexpectedly to his rooms in the government guest-house (guarded by the Royal Canadian Mounted Police), he found someone with a camera and tripod taking photographs in his bedroom. The Canadian Government explained hastily that the photographer was taking pictures for a future redecoration of the room, but it seemed odd that they had not waited until it was unoccupied or at least warned their guest. The Canadian Opposition said the explanation 'seems rather thin'. Nothing more was said and the affair remained murky. Yet it was somehow appropriate that David Lange's last journey as Prime Minister should end on the ambiguous note that had always marked his involvement in international affairs.[†]

---

[*] A Heylen poll in mid-May 1989.
[†] These last three paragraphs draw on material in the Lange Papers, Boxes 7, 9 and 10, ANZ.

Epilogue

Sir Walter Scott thought that 60 years had to pass before 'the record of political struggles mellows into history'. It is not a timescale possible for this history or for those still living whose recollections are an essential part of the story. His prediction is accurate though; after a quarter of a century the quarrel over New Zealand's participation in the ANZUS alliance has yet to mellow into history. Views are still sharply divided between those who see it as the worst mistake ever made in the country's foreign policy, and those who regard it as the dawn of true national independence. All the historian can do is to recount as dispassionately and accurately as possible the features of the dispute which have given rise to such opposed interpretations.

Whichever view is preferred, there is no doubt that the ANZUS quarrel marked a revolution in New Zealand's outlook on the world. The country turned away – or for a time showed an inclination to turn away – from the aims its foreign policy had followed since the Second World War: a close partnership with its wartime allies, the United States, Britain and Australia, in pursuit of a stable and non-Communist world order. This pattern was now seen by many younger members of the Labour Party as outmoded, perhaps even dangerous. New Zealand was felt to have been too long in thrall to the 'great powers' (a term which irritated even the former Prime Minister Norman Kirk), doing their bidding and pursuing their interests even at the cost of its own. It had fought obediently in 'other people's wars' where the benefit to New Zealand seemed far from clear, and it had supported imperialist adventures and opposed progressive movements in ways which were not the pattern of the future.

An American visitor in 1987 was bemused by this unfamiliar reading of New Zealand's history. He heard much about the country's real destiny being in the Pacific and not the English-speaking world and found these arguments difficult to understand. Nor did his reading of history confirm the assertions that New Zealand had been too willing to fight other people's wars for other people's interests. He sensed behind some of these remarks undertones of a withdrawal from the 'traditional concerns of the Western democracies'.* Others, like Frank Corner, Chair of the Defence Committee of Enquiry, did too. The thought, he said, that New Zealand had an interest in protecting certain ideas, a certain kind of civilisation, did not shine through in the submissions to his Committee.

The national psychology seemed to have sustained some blows which had shaken the faith of many in their traditional Western outlook. Britain's entry into the European Common Market in 1973 had a more profound effect on New Zealand than was apparent at the time. Many New Zealanders had shaped their outlook around an Anglocentric view of the world, as reliable partners of Britain in war and peace, in trade and diplomacy. The departure of Britain and Empire (which New Zealanders had enjoyed as opening wider vistas than life on three small islands) left the country feeling abandoned, deprived of a secure identity, a snail without a shell.

---

* Lt Col Jim Williams to Simon Murdoch in Washington, 23 March 1987, PM 111/3/3/1 Part 56, ANZ.

Europe called forth no such loyalty despite the sacrifices New Zealanders had made for it. It was unfamiliar, alien except as battlefields, its protectionism a standing threat to the country's trade and, in the form of French nuclear testing in the South Pacific, a source of growing anger.

It was also clear that the United States could not take Britain's place in the affection of New Zealanders, although it had been our help in ages past and might still be our hope in years to come. The ANZUS treaty of 1952 ensured that the close wartime partnership would continue; we welcomed our association with the world's most powerful democracy and the security it guaranteed for us. But the partnership had no deep roots. It was the experience only of governments and diplomats, and for all the gratitude of an older generation, New Zealanders never bonded to it emotionally.

A long association with Britain had accustomed New Zealanders to being treated with indulgence by a larger partner. In ANZUS they saw, not the security alliance that it was in American eyes, but a more general declaration of friendship and support, and were surprised and shocked that Washington did not extend the forbearance and tolerance that London had always shown.[*] So the dispute brought disillusion to many, not merely on the Left; and charges of bullying, 'heavying' and even of destabilising the government were a testimony to the sense of hurt that the Americans could treat the country in such an unfeeling way.

From all this – from the British departure, European indifference, and American lack of sympathy – grew a vague feeling that not just these countries but the West as a whole had let New Zealand down. The instinctive identification with Western attitudes and policies was shaken and disillusion focused on the weakest spot, its reliance on nuclear deterrence as a protection from the huge Soviet Army. Natural discomfort with the bleak doctrine of Mutually Assured Destruction

---

[*] Mrs Thatcher told Lee Kuan Yew over lunch on 8 April 1985 that 'the UK was prepared to be tolerant of New Zealand because of our long historical connection and to continue to help them in the EEC context' despite its deep disapproval of the ship visits policy. FCO Papers.

EPILOGUE

and assiduous playing on fears of a nuclear war led a growing number of New Zealanders to believe that association with the West might be more risky than going it alone. The Lange Government equivocated over nuclear deterrence but every time the finger of Western disapproval was lifted it reverted to an instinctive distaste.

What emerged for many younger people was the desire for an 'independent foreign policy' that would release the country from doing the bidding of the Western powers and unchain it from the yoke of nuclear deterrence. ANZUS had come to seem, to the Left at least, not a willing alliance to safeguard the country's freedom but compulsory participation in the arms race. In a government with so many lawyers at the top it seemed often to be viewed as a binding legal contract, with obligations that were enforceable in some unnamed court of law. ANZUS, it was claimed, had 'compelled' the country to intervene in Vietnam and might well compel it to join some other American adventure. It was a mortgage on New Zealand's ownership of its own, independent foreign policy.

The cry was a hope rather than a coherent policy and what the independent foreign policy meant was never fully spelt out. It lived on as a political slogan for over two decades, looking every year more and more like a new name for the old foreign policy. But in the 1980s, as demanded by Labour Party conferences, it was a code word for anti-Americanism. However enticing the dreams of being free and leading the world in anti-nuclearism, the independent foreign policy meant in practice opposition to American influence. Playing on fears of being a nuclear target alarmed a significant number of people and gave a small but dedicated anti-American group the chance to detach New Zealand from its alliance and for a time unsettle its customary pro-Western orientation.

The result was a bit flat. An independent foreign policy freed of its ANZUS ties turned out to mean concentrating on the island countries of the South Pacific, and spokespeople from the Prime Minister down stressed that henceforth New Zealand would be minding its backyard and developing its Pacific identity. David Lange defined the new area of interest as Polynesia, extending to Tuvalu and Kiribati and less certainly to Papua New Guinea.* Lowering its horizons to this extent represented a considerable loss of nerve by a country that had been one of the handful of victors in World War II and had played a significant part in establishing the United Nations.

The new emphasis on the South Pacific, however, was no more than a polite fiction. There were no major challenges in the region since decolonisation had been completed, and when a coup took place in Fiji in 1987 there was little that New Zealand could do about it. Revealingly, politicians and diplomats who carried the message of New Zealand's Pacific identity to foreign governments rarely confirmed their words by wanting a posting there. The stress on the South Pacific was a figleaf to cover a more fundamental withdrawal from the world. With the national consensus on foreign policy broken, New Zealand entered an isolationist phase.

Labour Party conferences in the 1980s lit bonfires of withdrawals from world affairs – not just from ANZUS, but from South East Asia, the Multilateral Force in the Sinai, from the American Antarctic base in Christchurch, from military and intelligence-gathering links, from the rapid deployment force, from using the rest of the Defence Force for other than relief work, from exercises with nuclear powers, from recognising the Philippines Government, and from buying frigates from Australia. Though it was claimed to be a more forward-looking view of the world, it looked more like a retreat. With a weakening economy and a weaker faith in the West, they and other New Zealanders found it increasingly uninviting to be asked to grapple with the complex calculations required for engagement with the outside world.

This showed most clearly in the Labour policy on ANZUS, adopted for the 1984 election. It called for a renegotiation of New Zealand's treaty links with the US and Australia, not only to accept its unconditional anti-nuclear stance but 'the acceptance of absolutely equal

---

* Talking to the American ambassador, 23 December 1986, PM 111/3/3/1 Part 54, ANZ.

EPILOGUE

partnership' and also 'an absolute guarantee of the complete integrity of New Zealand's sovereignty'.* This insistence showed a strange lack of confidence in the country's ability to hold its own in dealing even with friendly countries; others were called on to guarantee its absolute independence. It was a sign of how the treaty had become a focus for feelings of national inadequacy.

After the war the treaty had been seen as a reassuring acknowledgement that New Zealand and Australia did not stand alone, as they had in the anxious years of 1940–41. But by a strange irony the nuclear stalemate which so concerned many New Zealanders shifted the footing under this reassurance. While the country was under the American umbrella (and David Lange liked to say that New Zealanders accepted this but did not want to hold the handle) the risk of conventional attack in the Pacific was no longer conceivable. This raised questions about the treaty. If the threat of an invasion had lost its meaning, was there any point in a security guarantee from the Americans?

The Americans saw gloomily that they were at the wrong end of this upwelling of nationalism, indeed becoming the wall from which it rebounded. The embassy in Wellington thought that Kiwis, increasingly preoccupied by economic and social upheaval at home, had tried to put the blame on external influences, especially the United States. It noted that expressions of frustration often had the appearance of anti-Americanism but, apart from fringe groups, 'this is more a symptom of malaise than of malevolence'. Because the problems were essentially internal, there was not much Washington could do, except make it worse. 'Relations between the US and NZ will continue to be difficult and frustrating for some time to come' and the only course was to be patient.†

Patience was required because inevitably, in a dispute with a small democratic nation, they could see that they were going to be portrayed

---

* The Labour Party International Affairs Policy, June 1984.
† The embassy sums up, 11 September 1987, State Department Papers.

as bullies. New Zealand nationalists were outraged by the thought that they were being dictated to by Washington and commentators in the press and radio urged the necessity of not yielding to American pressure. It became ingrained and the resentment long outlived the dispute. Twenty years later Geoffrey Palmer still noted: 'I think the harder the U.S. pushed, the more rebellious New Zealanders became, including those of us in Cabinet. We felt offended that we were being instructed what to do in our own country.' Or, as Fran Wilde put it more succinctly, 'We thought, bugger you!'*

The excitement over attempts to push New Zealand around obscured the point that the country's freedom of action was not the issue. The Americans said several times that New Zealand as a sovereign nation was perfectly entitled to exclude nuclear or any other ships from its ports. The dispute was not over harbour access. It was over whether New Zealand could unilaterally redefine the nature of a three-member alliance and continue to be a full member. Despite Wellington's insistence on its right to be an ally, neither of the other two partners, the US and Australia, could agree to this new definition. They felt that it was for New Zealand either to continue to admit the ships of its American partner, as it had for many years, or to withdraw from an alliance whose requirements it no longer wished to accept. New Zealand declined to follow either course, a refusal to choose which its partners found exasperating.

The outcome of this swirl of nationalist resentments was the wreck of the country's long-standing position in the outside world. New Zealand, since 1942 one of the inner circle of allies in Washington, threw away access and influence with the world's most powerful nation that other and much larger countries could only dream of ever securing. If the purpose was to protest against the nuclear arms race and launch a global demand for a reduction in nuclear weapons then it failed. The world's stock of armaments

---

* Both quotations are taken from Amy L. Catalinac, 'Why New Zealand Took Itself out of ANZUS: Observing "Opposition for Autonomy" in Asymmetric Alliances', (2010) 6(3) *Foreign Policy Analysis*, p. 331.

EPILOGUE

was reduced only when the two superpowers reached a deal, and no other country, however anti-nuclear its sentiments, was prepared to lock out the US Navy.

Even in the South Pacific, the nominal centre of Wellington's new policy, only Vanuatu which had earlier declared itself nuclear-free stood with New Zealand; the rest continued to welcome American warships, including *Buchanan*. Indeed, taking fright at the possible drawbacks of 'being a light unto the nations', New Zealand itself backed away from being an anti-nuclear beacon. If anti-nuclear calls were added to its other exports, trade with Japan, the United States and Western Europe might well be imperilled. Instead the country, which had never possessed nuclear weapons, declared with some illogicality that nuclear disarmament was for itself alone. It was hard to see what this half-hearted stance achieved internationally. In the eyes of the foreign policy professionals the main result of the anti-nuclear campaign was that the country managed to exchange a seat at the top table in Washington for one on a bench in the corridor outside.

Other countries found it hard to credit that steady New Zealand, a country that had built its reputation on being reliable, 'a stout-hearted and generous people' who had held their nerve, in the words of Lee Kuan Yew, should be acting so out of character.[*] When they got over their surprise, most in South East Asia and elsewhere concluded that there was less to the dispute than met the eye. It was one of those quarrels that blow up in families, a passing storm of bad temper that could not disguise the close ties of language and outlook that continued to link the angry disputants. Like many New Zealanders (including David Lange), they did not doubt that the United States would come to the rescue if the country were ever to get into more serious trouble.

All the same, New Zealand's views counted for less around the Pacific basin, in Japan, the ASEAN countries and even the South

---

[*] Speech by Lee Kuan Yew, 4 April 1975.

Pacific. Those views had been listened to in capitals such as Beijing not just because they were the opinions of Wellington but because they were considered to reflect a closer knowledge of where Washington and Western policy in general might be heading. For countries in South East Asia, like Thailand, Malaysia and Singapore, the country's ANZUS connection had been a tripwire, helpfully if indirectly linking their own security to the United States. Speaking in Rotorua in 1986, Lee Kuan Yew gently underlined the extent of the change: the departure of New Zealand mattered less because Singapore would still have its link with ANZUS through Australia.[*]

As a result Australia loomed larger in the region and it loomed larger in New Zealand's foreign policy. Australia's own views were mixed. They were angry that New Zealand's actions might upset the treaty on which their own security depended. When Lange complained to the Australian High Commissioner that New Zealand was being made to sit in the dunce's corner, 'where it belongs' was the tart marginal comment in Canberra.[†] But there were compensations. Their professionals hankered for a more direct, bilateral relationship with the United States; they chafed that when out driving with their bigger friend their little sister always had to be in the back. The anti-nuclear policy gave them what they wanted, but at the price of additional expense and bother in managing a separate security relationship with the Kiwis.

There was a price for New Zealand too. As Lange foresaw, the move to a greater independence from America left his country much more reliant on Australia's goodwill. Its Defence Force became dependent on Australia for training and exercising, and Australian equipment was bought wherever possible. Intelligence now came largely across the Tasman, filtered to remove any American input. The new foreign policy in the South Pacific as elsewhere tended to follow Canberra's

---

[*] Press conference, 7 April 1986. In *Nuclear Free: The New Zealand Way*, Penguin Books, 1990, p. 118, David Lange says: 'Singapore put little value on the presence of our soldiers once we'd fallen out with the United States.'
[†] Minute on High Commissioner's report of 12 March 1986, 370/1/20 Part 52, NAA.

EPILOGUE

lead. New Zealand since the war had sat comfortably on a three-legged stool, able to juggle and balance the influence of the United States and Australia. Sitting on a two-legged stool required more effort and was less comfortable.

All this was important, but the changes in foreign policy were the manifestations and not the drivers of a deeper shift in national attitudes. Over the previous decade a comfortable national consensus had splintered into warring fragments, in angry arguments over economic policy, the environment, women's rights, the meaning of the Treaty of Waitangi and even that patriotic icon, rugby football. New Zealand's old image of itself had gone for good and something new and equally compelling was needed to take its place. An uneasy nationalism floated in the air, like gas in a mine, and ANZUS was the spark that touched it off. Foreign policy became the battleground in the war for a new national identity.

A significant minority was energised and it is significant minorities that bring change, though in the confusion of the 1980s the lasting changes were less in foreign than in economic policy – the last result the activists might have looked for. For them New Zealand was too traditional, too conservative, and too pro-American. An 'independent', less aligned status would be more appropriate for a genuinely liberated nation than being condemned forever to be a junior partner in the Western coalition.

For those who agreed, the quarrel with America signalled a break with an uncomfortable past and a new self-respect. The country would have a fresh national identity, 'clean, green and non-nuclear'. In taking on the United States it had stood up and spoken for itself. In the engaging way of small nations the point was frequently made that New Zealand had got itself noticed 'on the world stage'. Assertions of nationalism may betray an insecure identity but the powerful emotions aroused by the country's stand justified and ennobled the anti-nuclear policy for many people. So the ANZUS quarrel inaugurated a new national myth, that of a country determined to seek its own way in the world, and so became part of the new identity the country had been searching for. There were costs to be met, but who could quibble about the price of national pride?

To confirm this, a legend grew up in retrospect that the country had spoken as one in repudiating anti-nuclearism and the American alliance. Like most legends, it was not accurate. Even at the end of the dispute the polls consistently showed a narrow but clear majority in favour of accepting ship visits if that was the price of the treaty. Like most legends, though, it reflected a fundamental truth. Those who had worried about losing the security guarantee found that the world looked no different when it went. In the midst of the Long Peace such guarantees seemed to have lost their point. When nothing happened, either to New Zealand's trade or its security, the worries about the country's new stance faded as quickly as they had arisen. Instead life without the alliance became a new thread in the national tradition. New Zealanders declared themselves unshakably anti-nuclear and cherished this amid their other differences as a unifying cause to which everyone could rally.

At the height of the crisis in 1985 the US Secretary of Defense, Caspar Weinberger, gave offence to national feelings by saying cheerfully, 'We have lost New Zealand's address.' Great umbrage was taken by commentators and letter-writers, but once the risk of Japan and others being contaminated by the 'New Zealand infection' had faded, there was no reason why New Zealand should figure noticeably in America's address book. As an island nation remote from the world's trouble spots, of no strategic significance and with only a small share of international trade, there was little to distinguish it from a score of other small countries.

It is worth asking (though few New Zealanders did) why the United States did *not* lose the address, why it was troubled by the loss and persistently hoped that the relationship could be repaired. Because of the British relationship, New Zealanders had come to assume that they had a special standing in the world. It is less easy to explain why the Americans should have accepted the same point. But to an important extent they did. As the 1984 General Election got

EPILOGUE

under way, Wolfowitz worried that whatever New Zealand decided to do 'would have a long carry'.* It may be that, as in any marriage break-up, the warring couple had accumulated too much in common over the years. Even if divorced, they were still stuck with one another. They were both Pacific nations and had fought together in all the wars of the twentieth century. But none of these was the chief bond. The two found themselves more tightly linked because they spoke English and their societies, however disparate in size, wealth and traditions, had more in common with each other in institutions, politics, law and outlook than either had with most other countries.

Because of the world war and its aftermath a special community had grown up among the countries of the Anglosphere and New Zealand could not be left out – its address was there for everyone in Washington to see, written in English. If this bothered successive Administrations, it also meant that New Zealand could never be easy about the break. For all the surges of nationalism and anti-Americanism, the country found by experience that it could not manage without a comfortable relationship with America. Under several governments it spent the next 25 years trying to get back to roughly where it started – a clear sign both of the magnitude of the original mistake and the unavoidable need to set it right.

But there was a difference. The ship visits prohibition largely lost its point when the United States took all nuclear weapons off its surface vessels and the use of nuclear propulsion diminished greatly. Nonetheless the policy, enshrined in law, remained. It had become a distinctive flag of New Zealandness, marking out the country as firmly as hakas and gumboots, and in the absence of any threat there was no disposition to abandon it. Like those who would rather live together than accept the bonds of matrimony, New Zealanders turned out to prefer an informal partnership with the United States to the formality of an alliance.

---

* Wolfowitz to Wood, 29 June 1984, PM 59/8/5 Part 1, MFAT.

Select Bibliography

Andrew, Christopher and Oleg Gordievsky, *KGB: The Inside Story*, Hodder & Stoughton, 1990
Arbatov, Georgi and Willem Oltmans, *The Soviet Viewpoint*, Dodd, Mead & Company, 1983
Bassett, Michael, *Working With David: Inside the Lange Cabinet*, Hodder Moa, 2008
Bialer, Seweryn and Michael Mandelbaum, *The Global Rivals: The Soviet-American Contest for Supremacy*, Alfred A. Knopf, 1988
Boston, Jonathan and Martin Holland (eds), *The Fourth Labour Government: Radical Politics in New Zealand*, Auckland: Oxford University Press, 1987
Brinkley, Douglas (ed.), *The Reagan Diaries*, Harper Perennial, 2005
Camilleri, Joseph A., *ANZUS: Australia's Predicament in the Nuclear Age*, Westview Press, 1987
Clark, Margaret (ed.), *For the Record: Lange and the Fourth Labour Government*, Dunmore Press, 2005
Clements, Kevin, *Back from the Brink: The Creation of a Nuclear-Free New Zealand*, Allen & Unwin/Port Nicholson Press, 1988
Gaddis, John Lewis, *We Now Know: Rethinking Cold War History*, New York: Oxford University Press, 1997
——, *The Cold War*, Allen Lane, 2005
Garthoff, Raymond, *Détente and Confrontation: American-Soviet Relations from Nixon to Reagan*, The Brookings Institution, 1994
Gates, Robert M., *From the Shadows: The Ultimate Insider's Story of Five Presidents and How They Won the Cold War*, Simon & Schuster, 1996
Grant, David, *Man for All Seasons: The Life and Times of Ken Douglas*, Random House New Zealand, 2010
Hawke, Bob, *The Hawke Memoirs*, William Heinemann Australia, 1994
Hayden, Bill, *Hayden: An Autobiography*, Angus & Robertson, 1996
Hoffman, David E., *The Dead Hand: Reagan, Gorbachev and the Untold Story of the Cold War Arms Race*, Icon Books, 2011
James, Colin, *The Quiet Revolution: Turbulence and Transition in Contemporary New Zealand*, Allen & Unwin/Port Nicholson Press, 1986
Jamieson, Ewan, *Friend or Ally: New Zealand at Odds with its Past*, Brassey's Australia, 1990
Laidlaw, Chris, *Rights of Passage*, Hodder Moa Beckett, 1999
Lange, David, *Nuclear Free: The New Zealand Way*, Penguin Books, 1990
——, *My Life*, Penguin/Viking, 2005
McGibbon, Ian and John Crawford (eds), *Seeing Red: New Zealand, the Commonwealth and the Cold War, 1945-91*, New Zealand Military History Committee, 2012
Moon, Paul, *New Zealand in the Twentieth Century: The Nation, The People*, HarperCollins, 2011
Palmer, Geoffrey, and Matthew Palmer, *Bridled Power: New Zealand Government under MMP*, 3rd edition, Auckland: Oxford University Press, 1997
Pope, Margaret, *At the Turning Point: My Political Life with David Lange*, AM Publishing New Zealand, 2011
Pugh, Michael C., *The ANZUS Crisis, Nuclear Visiting and Deterrence*, Cambridge University Press, 1989
Richards, Raymond, *Palmer: The Parliamentary Years*, Canterbury University Press, 2010
Sheppard, Simon, *Broken Circle: The Decline and Fall of the Fourth Labour Government*, Publishing Solutions Limited, 1999
Smith, Ron, *Working Class Son: My Fight Against Capitalism and War - Memoirs of Ron Smith, A New Zealand Communist*, published by Ron Smith, 1994
Solomon, Richard H. and Nigel Quinney, *American Negotiating Behavior: Wheeler-Dealers, Legal Eagles, Bullies, and Preachers*, United States Institute of Peace, 2010
Wilson, A. C., *New Zealand and the Soviet Union, 1950-1991: A Brittle Relationship*, Victoria University Press, 2004
Wilson, Margaret, *Labour in Government, 1984-1987*, Allen & Unwin/Port Nicholson Press, 1989

Index

Abramowitz, Morton, xiv, xvii, 64, 144–5
Afghanistan, 154
Albania, 133–4
American Antarctic base, Christchurch ('Deep Freeze'), 60, 283, 300
American Samoa, 102, 104, 105
Amery, Julian, 167
Anderton, Jim, 21, 93, 100, 105, 200, 283, 293
Antarctica, 68; *see also* American Antarctic base, Christchurch
anti-Americanism, 8–9, 13, 16–17, 40, 46, 57, 60, 117, 143, 197, 202, 283, 286, 299, 301, 307
anti-nuclear countries, 69, 70, 73, 79, 101–2, 171, 256, 266, 271, 303
anti-nuclear movement, 8, 10, 18, 33–34, 42, 71, 72, 93, 99, 109, 112–13, 119, 122, 135, 176, 177, 201, 240, 259, 261, 289, 293, 299, 306; *see also* Campaign for Nuclear Disarmament; Coalition against Nuclear Warships (CANWAR); Nuclear Disarmament Party (Australia); Peace Movement Aotearoa; peace movements; protests: anti-nuclear
anti-nuclear policy (New Zealand), *see* Lange, David: THE NUCLEAR AND ANZUS ISSUES: and anti-nuclear policy; New Zealand: and anti-nuclear legislation; New Zealand: and anti-nuclear policy; New Zealand Nuclear Free Zone, Disarmament and Arms Control Act 1987; Nuclear Free New Zealand Bill
anti-nuclear policy, fears of export of, 70–72, 180, 243, 253, 261
anti-nuclear sentiment, in New Zealand, 66, 97, 126, 128, 186–7, 198, 217, 259, 265, 269, 278–9, 306
anti-submarine missiles (ASROCs), 86, 104, 110
ANZUS: alliance, ix–x, 1, 5–6, 8, 12, 13, 26, 31–32, 36, 45, 50, 54, 62, 66–67, 68, 77, 82, 83, 88, 94–95, 100, 112, 121, 127–8, 131, 132, 138, 143, 151, 193, 221, 250, 287–8, 296, 304; as bilateral relationship, 183; dispute, x–xi, xii, 19, 22, 24, 37–38, 47, 130, 136, 163, 171, 183, 269, 290, 296, 305–6; exercises, 81, 141, 181; New Zealand's suspension from, ix, 126, 147, 193, 242, 276–7, 280, 287; possible collapse and dissolution of, 83, 181, 190, 193, 225, 264–7; treaty, 1, 3–4, 8, 13–14, 26, 33, 42, 44, 52, 56, 58, 60, 67, 121, 125, 193, 270, 271, 276–7, 298; *see also* Australia: and ANZUS; Beyond ANZUS' conference 1984; China, and ANZUS; Great Britain: and ANZUS; Hawke, Bob, and ANZUS; Japan, and ANZUS; Lange, David: THE NUCLEAR AND ANZUS ISSUES: and ANZUS; Lee Kuan Yew, and ANZUS; New Zealand: and ANZUS; Palmer, Geoffrey, and ANZUS; press reactions: to ANZUS; ship visits, and ANZUS; Shultz, George, and ANZUS; Soviet Union, and ANZUS; television coverage of anti-nuclear and ANZUS issue; United States: and ANZUS
ANZUS Council, 30, 34–35, 79, 85, 149–50, 151, 171–5, 192, 264, 292, 295
apartheid, 18
Armacost, Michael, xiv, xvii, 75, 120, 143–4, 172, 203–4, 223, 252, 253, 264–5
Armitage, Richard, xiv, xvii, 23, 35, 60, 65, 68, 151, 189, 206, 208, 209–10, 212, 213, 285
arms control, 59, 134, 135–6, 163, 176, 179, 195, 285
'arms race', xi, 11, 13, 71, 123, 137, 158, 166, 299, 302
arms sales, 148, 282
Asahi Shimbun, 60, 253
ASEAN, 14; countries, x, 54, 134, 275, 303; meetings, 35, 179, 192, 264–5, 269
Auckland, 7, 19, 112; port of, 71, 87, 190
Auckland Chamber of Commerce, 235
Auckland Engineers' Union, 27
Auckland Regional Labour Party, David Lange's speech to, 259–60, 262, 264, 268
Australia: and ANZUS, x, 1, 3, 5–6, 31, 32, 33, 35, 36, 38, 41, 42, 45–49, 61, 62, 94–95, 130, 132, 138, 172–3, 193, 216–17, 219, 243, 257–8, 264, 276–7; and ASEAN, 54; and bilateral security arrangement with New Zealand, 258, 277; and China, 180; and David Lange, 29, 182–3, 240, 257–8, 294; and French nuclear testing, 37; and Great Britain, 17, 95, 131, 142, 219, 256–7; and intelligence community, 140, 143, 145–7; and joint installations in, 119; and military exercises, 181–2, 251–2; and NCND policy, 70, 142; and New Zealand, ix, 38, 45–48, 61, 62, 68, 94–96, 105, 130–2, 142, 146–7, 156, 168, 172–3, 181–2, 193, 240, 257–8, 275, 276, 283, 288–90, 294, 302, 304; and nuclear issue, 47–49, 56, 78, 132; and NZ/US dispute, 142, 156, 216–19, 220, 227; and port access, 38, 45; and Second World War, 2, 140, 296, 301; and security issues, x, 45–49, 56, 119, 120, 132, 138, 143, 258, 304; and ship visits, 46, 48–49, 57, 70, 94–95, 203, 217–18, 242, 273; and South Pacific Nuclear Free Zone Treaty, 197; and United States, 17, 31, 33, 47, 53, 70, 82, 121, 130–1, 132, 138, 142, 146–7, 183, 192–3, 203, 207, 217, 218–19, 258, 264, 272, 276, 283, 289, 304; and Western alliance, 120, 138; nationalism in, 17, 247

INDEX

Australian, 61, 132, 168, 290
Australian embassy, Washington, 43, 58n, 105
Australian High Commission, Wellington, 97, 182, 190, 288
Australian High Commissioner, Wellington, 31, 95, 304
Australian Labor Party (ALP) 49, 57, 78, 130, 172, 193, 218, 240, 243, 258, 265; *see also* Hawke, Bob, and Australian Labor Party
Australian Studies Center, Pennsylvania State University, 33
Avondale (trader ship), 97, 99, 102, 105

baby-boom generation, 15–16, 17, 19, 124
Bassett, Michael, xiii, xiv, xvi, 19, 108
Beazley, Kim, xv, xvii, 181–2, 203, 242, 258, 269, 277; and David Lange, 218
Beeby, Chris, 226
Belgium: and anti-nuclear movement in, 137; and New Zealand trade access to EEC, 261; and nuclear weapons in, 10–11, 135, 163, 176; and Western alliance, 120, 135, 136, 137
Berendsen, Sir Carl, 3, 271
Berlin, Isaiah, 101
'Beyond ANZUS' conference 1984, 27–28, 35
Biden, Joe, 121
Bjelke-Petersen, Joh, 132
Bradley, Tom, 153
Brentwood meeting, 148–53
British embassy, Washington, 57, 111–12, 140, 215
British Foreign Secretary, *see* Howe, Sir Geoffrey
British High Commission: Canberra, 95, 219; Wellington, 33, 96, 118, 197, 271, 292
British High Commissioner, Wellington, 33, 53, 54, 141, 163, 228, 242, 249, 255
British Labour Party, 55, 163, 169
British Minister of State for the Armed Forces, *see* Stanley, John
Buchanan, USS, xii, 97, 98, 147, 159, 171, 200, 202, 203, 303; and David Lange, 105, 107, 108–9, 110, 112–15, 126, 127, 128–9, 149, 263; and Geoffrey Palmer, 204–5, 220; and New Zealand's choice of, 86–87, 88–89, 102, 103–4, 110–11, 149; and United States request for visit by, 97, 110, 111–12, 116, 149; United States reaction to rejection of, 116–17, 121, 123, 127, 129–30, 138, 143, 144–5, 157, 174, 188–9, 192–4, 206, 207, 208, 230, 242, 255, 281–2
Buckley, William, 120
Bureau of Intelligence and Research (State Department), 144
Bush Administration (George H. W. Bush), 154
Bush, George H. W., 32, 154, 283
butter industry, New Zealand, and concessions, 32, 121, 162, 261, 263, 283
Bykov, Vladimir, 57

Cabinet processes, 62, 98, 107–8, 112–13, 116–17; *see also* Lange Cabinet
Caldicott, Helen, 18
Cam Ranh Bay, 152, 285
Campaign for Nuclear Disarmament, 229
Canada, 6, 52, 134, 135, 205, 294–5; and intelligence community, 140, 142–3, 145–6; and military exercises, 141, 181; and New Zealand, 134, 135, 142, 261
Canterbury Labour Party Council, 222, 227
Caribbean, 27
Carrington, Lord, 25
Carroll, Eugene, 92
casein industry, New Zealand, and concessions, 80, 121, 123, 283
Casey, William, 144
'Caygill process', 245, 252
Caygill, David, xiv, xvi, 204, 234–6, 237–8, 246
Center for Defense Information (US), 92
Central America, 27; *see also* Nicaragua
Chain, Major-General John, 68, 94
Chamberlain, Neville, 164
Cheney, Dick, 121
Chernobyl nuclear power station disaster, 259, 265, 274
Chief of Defence Staff (CDS) (GB), 250; *see also* Fieldhouse, Admiral Sir John
Chief of Defence Staff (CDS)(NZ), xii, xiv, 22, 73, 82, 103, 209, 199, 235; *see also* Jamieson, Ewan
'China formula', 256–7, 258, 263, 266
China, People's Republic of, 3–4; and ANZUS, 50; and Australia, 254; and David Lange, 253–4; and New Zealand's nuclear policy, 137, 180–1, 218; and Pacific security, 50; and ship visits, 180–1, 208, 218, 253–4, 256–7, 258, 259; and United States, 137, 189, 208; as threat, 54, 132, 134
CIA, 19, 96, 144, 260
CINCPAC (American Commander in Chief, Pacific), 31, 70, 82, 84, 150; *see also* Crowe, Admiral William
Clark, Helen, xiv, xvi, 30, 72n, 92–94, 100, 102, 197–8, 200, 244, 271, 278, 279, 280
Clements, Kevin, xiii, 93, 278
Cleveland, Paul, xiv, xvii, 30, 241–2, 245, 246–7, 283, 286, 288, 289, 291, 292, 294
Clinton, Bill, 121
Coalition against Nuclear Warships (CANWAR), 93, 109–10
Cohen, William, 121
Committee on Disarmament, 287
Commonwealth, 21, 45, 181, 183
Commonwealth Secretariat, 162
Commonwealth Secretary-General, 56, 137; *see also* Ramphal, Shridath
Communism, 3–5, 124, 286, 296
conspiracy theories, 19, 96, 260, 291; *see also* CIA

INDEX

Cook Islands, 56, 196
Cooper, Warren, 35
Coordinator of Domestic and External Security, 288; *see also* Hensley, Gerald
Corner, Frank, xvi, 260n, 278-80, 289, 290-1, 297; *see also* Defence Committee of Enquiry; Lange, David: As LEADER OF THE LABOUR PARTY AND PRIME MINISTER: and Frank Corner
Crowe, Admiral William, 31, 65, 70, 82-83, 84, 85-87, 89, 110-11, 118-19, 121, 149
cruise missiles, 10, 133, 135, 163, 262
Cuban missile crisis, 11
Czechoslovakia, 164

dairy industry, New Zealand, and concessions, 32, 80, 121, 261
Dam, Kenneth, 23, 147, 204
de Cuéllar, Pérez, 137
de Gaulle, General Charles, 1, 147
decolonisation, 5, 16, 300
'Deep Freeze', *see* American Antarctic base, Christchurch
Defence Committee of Enquiry, 260, 278-81, 289, 297; *see also* Corner, Frank
defence spending, New Zealand, 34, 67, 127, 175, 182, 188, 254, 288; *see also* frigates, purchase of
Defence White Paper 1987, 288, 289-90, 295
Denmark: and anti-nuclear policy, 69, 92, 101-2, 135-6, 186, 266, 271-2; and New Zealand, 135-6; and New Zealand trade access to EEC, 261; and ship visits, 7, 186, 266
deterrence, as a strategy, 70, 71, 72, 79, 84, 119, 163-4, 189, 207, 224, 261, 287, 298-9
DGSE, 191
Dhanabalan, Suppiah, 135
Digby, Kenelm, 169
disarmament, x, 3, 7, 8, 42, 49, 53, 71, 92, 137, 163, 244, 262, 303
Dominion, 114, 125-6, 270-1n, 271, 273, 281, 293
'don't ask, don't tell' approach, 73, 171, 256-7
Douglas, Roger, 28, 29, 30, 34, 122-3, 204, 250
Drew, Brigadier-General Philip, 230
Duff, Sir Anthony, 140

East Asia Pacific (EAP) division (State Department), 222, 236
Eckhart, Dennis, 20
economic retaliation and sanctions, 136-7, 306; American, 37-38, 63, 71, 80, 117, 120, 122-3, 123-5, 139, 151, 154-5, 156, 178, 195, 235, 242, 276, 282-3; Australian, 132; German, 262
environmental movement, 18, 100, 305
European Common Market, 16, 297
European Economic Community (EEC), 136, 162, 163, 170, 261

European Parliament, 136
Evening Post, 77, 162, 274, 280-1, 293
External Intelligence Bureau (EIB), 99, 103, 109-10

Falklands War, 19, 61, 141, 228
Falwell, Jerry, 160, 161, 162, 165, 167; *see also* Oxford Union debate
Federation of Labour, 21, 27
FFG-7s (Oliver Hazard Perry class frigates), 86, 103, 109, 111, 189, 196, 198, 200-1, 203-4, 237, 246
Fieldhouse, Admiral Sir John, xvii, 250-2, 259
Fiji: and ship visits, 56; coups in, 288, 300
'Fincastle 86', 251-2
First World War, 31
'fishing boat diplomacy', 285
Five Power Defence Arrangements, 60-61, 67, 134, 140, 146, 197, 255
Foreign Office (GB), 26, 52, 53, 61, 132-3, 156, 161, 162, 163, 169-70, 198, 199, 225, 228, 230-1, 238, 239, 246, 251, 252, 257, 258, 262, 271, 275
France, 15, 191; and New Zealand, 136; and New Zealand trade access to EEC, 162, 219, 261; and *Rainbow Warrior*, 125, 190-1, 219, 269, 287; and ship visits, 177
Francis, Tim, xvi, 117, 147, 149, 172, 205, 211, 212, 213
Fraser, Peter, 38, 219
free-market policies, x, 28, 60-61, 293
French Polynesia, 37
French nuclear tests in the Pacific, 7-8, 37, 191, 298
frigates, purchase of, 300

Galvin, Bernard, 122-3
Gandhi, Mrs Indira, 51
Gatt Subsidies Code, 151
Geiringer, Erich, 262
Geneva, arms control meetings in, 72, 94, 135, 167, 176, 225, 287
Genscher, Hans-Dietrich, 220-1
'geriatric generals', *see* Lange, David: As LEADER OF THE LABOUR PARTY AND PRIME MINISTER: and 'geriatric generals'
Germany, West, 12, 71, 170, 263; and New Zealand, x, 220-1, 261; and nuclear weapons in, 10-11; and Soviet Union, 136, 262; and Western alliance, 71, 120, 136, 220-1, 262
Glassman, Jon, xvii, 149, 152, 187, 222, 234, 236-7, 254, 261
Glenn, John, 121
Gordievsky, Oleg, 12
Graham, Billy, 160
Great Britain: and ANZUS, 5-6, 52-53, 54, 163, 250; and Australia, 4, 248, 256-7;

INDEX

and China, 263; and David Lange, 161–2, 163, 169, 262; and EEC, 16, 136, 162, 170, 263, 297; and intelligence community, 139–43, 145–6; and Iraq, 108; and military exercises, 141, 181; and New Zealand, 4, 16, 53–54, 133, 134, 136, 139–42, 164, 170, 183, 198–9, 219, 220, 228, 250–1, 262–3, 275, 286, 287; and NCND policy, 141, 170, 198, 248; and nuclear testing, 7; and nuclear weapons in, 10–11; and NZ/US dispute, 53–54, 132–3, 139–43, 199, 214, 220, 227–32, 238–9, 240, 245–6, 247–52, 254, 255–6, 258–9, 262–4, 265, 266, 274–5, 285–6; and *Rainbow Warrior*, 191; and Second World War, 2, 140, 159, 296; and security issues, 2–5, 133, 143, 198, 248–50, 285–6; and ship visits, 52–54, 96, 133, 146, 171, 198, 203, 209, 228–9, 230, 239–40, 255–6, 263, 275, 298; and Soviet Union, 285–6; and United States, 133, 140–2, 146, 198–9, 215, 230
Greece, 120
Greenham Common, 11
Greenpeace, 190; *see also Rainbow Warrior*
Griffin, Richard, 294
Gronslo, Mark, 166–7

Habib, Philip, 232–3
Harland, Bryce, xvi, 77, 223, 228–9, 238–9, 252, 258
Hawke, Bob, xi, xv, xvii, 22–23, 29, 41, 45–49, 82, 86, 96; and ANZUS, 47–48, 62–63, 94–95, 130–1, 132, 172–3, 196–7, 258; and Australian Labor Party, 48–49, 91, 130, 172–3, 218, 258, 265; and David Lange, 35–36, 45–49, 53, 94–95, 117, 142, 182–3, 196–7, 218; and Geoffrey Palmer, 47n; and letter to David Lange, 94–95, 96, 105, 109–10; and NZ/US dispute, 132, 172–3, 218–19, 258, 265; and United States, 35–36, 117, 130–1, 172–3, 196; *see also* Lange, David: On the International Stage: and Bob Hawke
Hayden, Bill, xvii, 29, 38, 41, 44n, 80, 88, 142, 193, 216–17, 219, 243, 257, 276, 277, 283, 289
Heenan, Peter, 148–9
Henderson, John, 205, 211–12, 280, 288–9, 293
Hensley, Gerald, xvi, 73, 76–77, 83, 87, 109, 110–11, 114, 143, 146–7, 149, 151, 153
Hitler, Adolf, 159
Holyoake Government, 6, 92–93n
Hong Kong, 2, 111
Hoover Institute, Washington, 290–1
House Agricultural Committee (US), 122
House Armed Services Committee (US), 92, 242
House Foreign Affairs Committee (US), 122
House Subcommittee on East Asia and the Pacific (US), 177–8, 242
Howe, Sir Geoffrey, xv, xvii, 140, 141, 163, 169, 216, 220, 223, 229–31, 232, 247, 248–9, 263–4, 274–5; and David Lange, 239, 252
Hu Yaobang, 180, 253
Hughes, John, 40
Hunt, Diane, 278

Illustrious, HMS, 198
India, and ship visits, 209, 218
Indian Ocean, 84, 266, 283
Indonesia, 5, 35, 269; and New Zealand, 134–5; as threat, 4, 132
Intelligence Council, 199, 235, 288
intelligence cooperation, 65, 125, 126, 139–40, 141–3, 144, 145–7, 148, 150, 153, 156, 170, 175, 181, 182, 185, 287–8, 220, 300, 304
Inter-Agency Group (US), 74, 88, 139, 143, 188, 203, 205, 206, 216, 222, 226, 231, 234, 248, 260, 276, 282n
International Physicians for the Prevention of Nuclear War (IPPNW), 94, 261
Iowa, USS, 272
Iraq war, 108
isolationism, 16, 31, 61, 68, 132, 141, 142, 154, 175, 182, 192, 199, 207–8, 221, 228, 273–4, 293, 300
Italy: and New Zealand, 136; and nuclear weapons in, 10; and ship visits, 177

Jackson, Keith, 124
Jamieson, Ewan, xiv, xvi, 22, 73, 82–83, 84, 85–88, 103–4, 106, 110–11, 114, 118–19, 198, 209, 214, 290–1; Lange, David: As Leader of the Labour Party and Prime Minister: and Ewan Jamieson
Japan, 2, 3, 23, 87; and anti-nuclear movement in, 49–52, 56, 60, 119, 134, 137, 253, 306; and ANZUS, 62, 138; and David Lange, 134, 253; and New Zealand, x, 49–52, 96, 253, 285, 303–4; and non-nuclear status, x, 49–50, 52, 134, 137; and Second World War, 2; and security issues, 3–4, 23, 49–50, 82, 86, 96, 119, 138, 171, 180–1, 189; and ship visits, 49, 50–52, 60, 70, 87, 119, 177, 180, 242, 253, 258, 272, 275, 278; and United States, 50–51, 70, 96, 120, 138, 171, 177
'Japanese formula', 50–51, 258
Joint Intelligence Committee (GB), 146

'Kangaroo 85', 181
Kapitsa, Mikhail, 286
Keating, Colin, 222, 223
Kelly, Jim, xiv, xvii, 284
Kennedy, Robert, 153
KGB, 11, 12, 56–57
King, Admiral Ernest, 2
Kinnock, Neil, 169
Kiribati, 56, 285, 289, 300
Kirk, Norman, 7, 297
Kirkpatrick, Jean, 137

INDEX

Knox, Jim, 152
Kohl, Chancellor Helmut, 261, 262
Korean War, 3; New Zealand involvement in, 68
Kos, Stephen, 166

Labor Government (Australia), 1–2, 38, 131; accusations of CIA removal of, 96
Labor Party (Australia), *see* Australian Labor Party (ALP)
Labour Government, 6, 13, 76, 92, 131; accusations of CIA removal of, 96; *see also* Cabinet processes; Lange Government; Rowling Government
Labour Party, xi, 9, 12–14, 15, 16, 19, 20–24, 75, 93, 95, 96, 102, 107–8, 114, 142, 144, 161, 163, 171, 293, 297, 299; and 1984 conference, 60–61, 71, 72; and 1984 election, 28, 33–34, 41, 57, 300–1, 306–7; and 1985 conference, 197, 199–200; and 1986 conference, 286; and 1987 conference, 291–2; and anti-Americanism, 117, 286, 299; and Baroness Young's visit, 255–6, 257; and Bill Rowling's 1983 memorandum for, 187; and visits to Soviet Union, 285–6; left wing of, x, xi, 6, 7, 12, 27, 28, 29, 30, 34, 42, 44, 46, 58, 59, 60, 61, 67, 70, 91–92, 93, 97, 99–102, 173, 192, 240, 243–4, 250, 262, 273, 285–6, 289, 296–8, 299; structure of, 142, 193; threats to unity of, 217, 244; *see also* Auckland Regional Labour Party; Canterbury Labour Party Council; Lange, David: As LEADER OF THE LABOUR PARTY AND PRIME MINISTER; Wellington Regional Labour Party
Labour Party Executive Council, 26, 100–2, 105
lamb industry, New Zealand, and concessions, 80, 121, 151, 162, 261
Lange Cabinet, 3, 21, 29, 37, 87, 88, 89, 93, 97, 98–99, 100, 103, 105, 106–7, 108–9, 110, 112–13, 114, 116, 117, 127, 131, 168, 182, 196, 200–1, 203, 204, 213–14, 218, 221, 235, 237, 290–1, 294–5, 302; papers, 87, 102–4, 128, 174–5
Lange Government, 15, 16, 100
Lange, David
  AS LEADER OF THE LABOUR PARTY AND PRIME MINISTER
    and 1984 election, 19–22, 28, 36; and 1987 election, 291; and Defence Committee of Enquiry, 280–1; and economic policies, 17; and education portfolio, 291; and Ewan Jamieson, 290–1; and foreign policy, 46, 55, 188, 269, 287; and Frank Corner, 290–1; and Geoffrey Palmer, 98, 99n, 203–4, 212, 262–3; and 'geriatric generals', 224; and Labour Party, xi, 13–14, 20, 22, 46, 75, 78, 79–80, 101, 198, 199, 227, 257, 259–60; and Mike Moore, 15n; and press conferences, xi, 43, 47, 55, 59–60, 65, 71, 75, 80, 88–89, 109, 111, 112–13, 126–7, 129, 154, 164, 168, 173, 191, 201, 224–5, 235, 253–4, 265, 269, 277–8, 280, 290–1, 294; and role of prime minister, 290, 295; and speech to Auckland Regional Labour Party, 259–60, 262, 264, 268; *see also* Muldoon, Robert, and David Lange; Palmer, Geoffrey, and David Lange; press reactions: to David Lange
  ON THE INTERNATIONAL STAGE
    and Australia, xi, 42, 49, 78, 131–2, 182–3, 195, 218, 223, 225, 257, 265, 273, 275, 277, 280, 294, 304–5; and Baroness Young, 161n, 255–6, 258; and Bob Hawke, 22–23, 29, 45–49, 173, 182–3; and China, 253–4; and George Shultz, 37–43, 63, 74, 75–76, 79–80, 91, 118, 120, 176, 179–80, 245, 264, 265–6, 270; and Great Britain, xi, 165, 183, 245, 259; and Japan, 50–51, 60, 253, 275; and Lee Kuan Yew, 55, 84, 135, 254–5; and Margaret Thatcher, 53–54, 162, 169–71, 262–3; and South East Asia, 54–55; and Soviet Union, 56–57, 59, 137, 160, 162, 164, 249, 261, 275, 286; and speech in California, 154–5, 156–7; and tripartite talks with Great Britain and United States, 232, 259; and United States, xi, 22–23, 31, 36–37, 38–43, 55, 62–65, 70–71, 78–86, 88, 91, 126–7, 128, 147–57, 163, 164, 172, 176, 179–80, 185–6, 192, 193–4, 195, 200–1, 222, 223, 225, 231, 233, 241, 245, 269–70, 272, 273, 275, 277–8, 292–3; and visit to Africa, 179, 182, 224; and visit to Australia, 182–3; and visit to EEC countries, 261–4; and visit to Manila for ASEAN meeting, 264, 265–6; and visit to Tokelau, 97–99, 104–5, 113; and Yale lecture tour 1989, 292–4; and Yasuhiro Nakasone, 51–52, 96; *see also* Australia: and David Lange; Beazley, Kim, and David Lange; Brentwood meeting; China, and David Lange; Great Britain: and David Lange; Hawke, Bob, and David Lange; Hawke, Bob, and letter to David Lange; Howe, Sir Geoffrey, and David Lange; Japan, and David Lange; Lange, David: AS LEADER OF THE LABOUR PARTY AND PRIME MINISTER: and press conferences; Lee Kuan Yew, and David Lange; Muldoon, Robert, and David Lange; Shultz, George, and David Lange; Thatcher, Margaret, and David Lange; United Nations General Assembly, David Lange at; United States: and David Lange; Wolfowitz, Paul, and David Lange
  THE NUCLEAR AND ANZUS ISSUES
    and anti-nuclear policy, 46, 64, 70, 74–75, 85, 88, 141, 191–2, 195, 201, 243–4, 249; and anti-nuclear stance, xi, 7, 30–31, 33, 34,

313

INDEX

38–44, 47–49, 50, 52, 66, 71–72, 73, 222–3, 256, 265–6; and ANZUS, xi, xii, 13, 22, 23–24, 33, 36, 39, 42, 43–44, 45, 47, 50, 57, 59, 60, 62, 63–64, 66–67, 78, 87, 94, 126–7, 129, 133, 147–8, 164, 172, 183–4, 186, 195, 222–3, 225, 244, 254, 260, 264, 265, 269, 270–1, 277–8, 280, 287, 290, 292–4, 294, 299; and NCND policy, 69–70, 79, 81, 84, 197, 247, 249, 270, 283–4; and *Rainbow Warrior*, 191, 225; and security issues, 50–51, 115, 163–4, 289; and ship visits, xi, 22, 29, 33, 39–44, 47, 48, 60, 70, 87–89, 91, 94, 95, 97–98, 103, 104–5, 107–11, 113–15, 126–7, 128–9, 131, 145, 147, 149, 151–2, 170–1, 176, 198–200, 202, 209–10, 223, 237–8, 240, 241, 247, 253, 260, 264, 269; as anti-nuclear celebrity, 58, 157, 158, 224, 243–4, 261; *see also Buchanan*, USS, and David Lange; Nobel Peace Prize; Oxford Union debate

Lange, Naomi, 106
Larocque, Admiral, 125
Laux, David, xiv, xvii, 30, 36, 208, 252
Leach, Jim, 178, 282
Leask, Derek, xiv, 165n, 167
Lee Kuan Yew, 4, 55, 84, 298; and ANZUS, 258, 304; and David Lange, 135, 181, 254–5; and New Zealand, 181, 303–4; and United States, 14, 55; *see also* Lange, David: ON THE INTERNATIONAL STAGE: and Lee Kuan Yew
Lehman, John, 283
Libya, 133–4
Lilley, James, xvii, 188–9, 216, 233–5, 236–8, 246, 254, 261
Lugar, Senator, 120–1

Mackey, Roger, 280–1
Macmillan, Harold, 250
Mahathir Mohamad, 54, 135
Malaya, 2, 4–5
Malaysia, 4, 5, 54; and New Zealand, 54, 61, 134, 135, 304; and United States, 285, 304
Mao Zedong, 4, 5
Maori renaissance, 18–19
Marsden Point oil refinery, 84
Marshall, Russell, xiv, xvi, 20, 21, 107, 161–2, 201, 291, 294
Massé, Marcel, 146
McIntosh, Sir Alister, 5
McLay, Jim, 34, 157
McLean, Denis, xiv, xvi, 73, 83, 118
McMahon, John, 144
media, *see* press; press reactions; radio coverage of anti-nuclear issue; television coverage of anti-nuclear and ANZUS issues
military exchanges and exercises, 141, 150–1, 181–2, 185, 238, 250, 251, 272

Molesworth demonstrations (GB), 133
Molinari, Guy, 121–2
Moore, Mike, xii, xiv, xvi, 15, 20, 29, 31, 33, 107, 109, 113, 114, 161, 168, 204; *see also* Lange, David: AS LEADER OF THE LABOUR PARTY AND PRIME MINISTER: and Mike Moore
Muldoon Government, 36–37, 118, 149–50, 270
Muldoon, Robert, 9, 17, 33–34, 52, 108, 155, 208; and 1984 election, 25, 27–28, 31, 33, 35; and David Lange, 244
Mulroney, Brian, 135
Murdoch, Simon, xiv, xvi, 143, 212
Mururoa, 7–8, 191
Mussolini, Benito, 159
Mutual Security Treaty (Japan and the US), 49–51, 180–1
Mutually Assured Destruction, 7, 71, 298–9
MX missile, 130–1

Nakasone, Yasuhiro, 51–52, 53, 96; *see also* Lange, David: ON THE INTERNATIONAL STAGE: and Yasuhiro Nakasone
National Government, *see* Holyoake Government; Muldoon Government
National Party, 27–28, 34, 193, 244
National Security Council (US), xiv, 30, 37, 43, 65, 74, 119–20, 143, 144, 208, 231, 252, 260, 284
nationalism, ix–x, 16–17, 124, 176, 227; *see also* Australia: nationalism in; New Zealand: nationalism in
NATO, 2–3, 10, 96, 133, 136, 148, 160, 163–4, 170–1, 259; member countries, 69–70, 92, 93, 135, 138, 148, 171, 218, 261; military exercises, 11, 272; treaty, 3, 271
'neither-confirm-nor-deny' policy (NCND), 65, 69–70, 73–74, 79, 81, 84, 85, 87, 88, 101, 111, 127, 141, 142, 148, 157, 170–1, 180, 185–6, 198, 199, 201, 202, 203, 209, 215, 218, 227, 233, 235, 237, 238, 239, 243, 245, 247–9, 259, 263, 266, 270, 272, 276, 283
Netherlands: and anti-nuclear movement in, 137; and nuclear weapons in, 10–11, 135, 163, 176; and ship visits, 177; and Western alliance, 120, 135, 137
neutrality, 2, 10, 34, 173–4, 185, 197, 207, 280, 285
New Jersey, USS, 278
New Labour Party, 293
New York Times, 187, 194
New Zealand: and alliance obligations, 75, 76–77, 100, 164, 279–80, 296, 300–3; and anti-nuclear legislation, 27, 30–31, 93, 109, 191–4, 196–7, 198, 199–203, 208, 210, 213–14, 216–19, 220, 222, 226, 229, 231–40, 242, 244–6, 247–9, 250, 252, 254, 255–8, 264–5, 274–5, 283, 285, 291; and anti-nuclear policy, x, xi, xiii, 8, 13, 17, 21, 26, 27, 29–31,

INDEX

33–34, 39–40, 42–44, 46, 48, 55–57, 61, 64, 66–67, 69, 71–72, 73, 75, 83–84, 92–93, 95, 99–102, 106, 124, 132, 137, 154, 155, 168, 180, 186–7, 190, 191–2, 193, 201, 205–6, 207, 217, 221, 225, 228, 235, 240, 249–50, 252–3, 257, 265, 279, 281, 299–300, 303; and ANZUS, ix, x, 1, 3, 5–6, 12–14, 23–24, 26–27, 32, 38, 39–40, 43–44, 54, 58–59, 60–61, 62–63, 66, 67, 77, 78, 81, 83–84, 88–89, 93, 97, 115, 123, 125–7, 128, 134, 143, 147, 149, 151, 153, 155, 170, 173–5, 181, 184, 185, 186–90, 195, 197–8, 207, 208, 211–12, 217, 221, 222–3, 225–6, 227, 243, 244, 250, 256, 258, 269, 271, 273, 278–9, 280, 289, 292, 296, 298, 299–301, 303, 304, 305–6; and ASEAN, 54, 275; and Australia, ix, 27, 30–31, 42, 52, 97, 100, 129, 174, 175, 182–3, 195, 207, 251–2, 273, 275, 279, 280–1, 288, 289, 296, 302, 304–5; and China, 180; and economic policy and reforms, 16–17, 28, 29, 30–31, 34, 60, 61, 78, 100, 240, 250, 265, 290, 291–2, 293, 305; and foreign policy, ix, xiii, 8–9, 15–17, 26, 28–29, 31, 39–40, 55–56, 60–61, 90, 106–7, 173–5, 221, 255–6, 259–60, 275–6, 285–6, 287, 296–7, 299–301, 304–5; and French nuclear testing, 37; and Great Britain, 4, 17, 19, 52–53, 61, 76, 170, 171, 183, 189, 239, 251–2, 263, 275, 296, 297, 298, 306; and Japan, 50–52, 96, 180–1, 275; and Second World War, 296, 301; and ship visits, 29–31, 39–40, 91–93, 171, 185, 188, 190, 191, 196, 197–8, 199–200, 221, 240, 253, 279; and South Pacific, 189, 195, 197, 224, 267, 279, 280, 299–300, 303–4; and Soviet Union, 12, 13, 27, 56, 58, 93, 112, 188, 275, 285–6, 298; and United States, ix, 4, 6, 13, 15, 17, 19, 56, 58, 62, 73, 74, 78–79, 82–84, 91–93, 100–2, 106, 112, 123–6, 129, 134, 142–5, 170, 175, 183, 189, 190–1, 200–1, 205–7, 211–12, 216–17, 221, 223, 229–30, 232, 239, 243, 259–60, 263, 272–3, 275–6, 281–2, 285–6, 291, 296–8, 300–1, 302–3, 305–6; and Western alliance, 12, 54, 55, 57, 71, 102, 115, 137, 153, 163–4, 174–5, 176, 183, 296, 298; nationalism in, ix–x, 16–17, 96, 109, 112, 123–4, 130, 143, 152, 173, 195, 227, 247, 301–2, 305–6, 307
New Zealand embassy: Moscow, 137; Tokyo, 51; Washington, xiin, xiv, 39, 64, 65, 68, 77–78n, 116–17, 123, 129, 138, 143, 150–1, 171, 190, 202, 205–6, 211–12, 214, 216, 223, 236, 254, 264
New Zealand Herald, 62, 111n, 124, 273, 278
New Zealand High Commission: Canberra, 95, 173; London, 161–3, 164, 167–8, 170
New Zealand High Commissioner, London, 171, 228
New Zealand Institute of International Affairs, 255, 292–3n

New Zealand Nuclear Free Zone, Disarmament and Arms Control Act 1987: Australian attitudes to, 193, 217, 219, 240, 257–8; British attitudes to, 199, 220, 229, 239, 245–6, 247–9, 250, 274, 275; New Zealand steps towards, 93, 109, 191–2, 193–4, 198, 199, 200–1, 208, 214, 233, 235, 238, 244–5, 249–50, 256–7, 265, 275, 283, 285, 291; US attitudes to, 191, 192, 196–7, 202, 203, 208, 210, 214, 216, 218, 222, 231, 233–4, 236, 238, 239–40, 242–6, 247, 248, 252, 283
New Zealand Party, 34
New Zealand Planning Council, 287
Nicaragua, 61, 152, 197
Nobel Peace Prize, 46, 93–94
non-alignment, 143, 174, 188, 197, 228, 260, 275–6, 280, 285
Norrish, Merwyn, xiv, xvi, 16, 20, 35, 36, 39, 63, 73, 74–76, 82, 83, 84, 87, 88, 89–90, 97, 103, 110–11, 174, 184, 187–8, 189–90, 192, 214, 223n, 267, 269
Norway, 136; and anti-nuclear policy, 69, 92, 96, 186, 266, 271–2; and nuclear weapons in, 7–8, 79; and ship visits, 7, 177, 186, 266, 272
'Norwegian formula', 40, 79
nuclear-armed and nuclear-capable distinction, 101–2
nuclear-armed and nuclear-powered distinction, 26, 73, 180, 279
Nuclear Disarmament Party (Australia), 132
Nuclear Free New Zealand Bill, 27, 30–31
Nuclear Impact Study (Planning Council), 287
Nuclear Non-Proliferation Treaty, 8, 50, 72
nuclear-propelled warships (NPWs), 9, 32, 67, 73–74, 179–80, 235
nuclear propulsion, 6, 9, 21, 23, 30, 63, 73–74, 92–93, 196, 203, 236, 237, 246, 252, 256, 259, 265, 266, 307
nuclear tests, in the Pacific, 7–8, 26
Nuclear Weapons-free Zone conference 1984, 62

O'Brien, Gerald, 96
Office of the US Trade Representative (USTR), 123
O'Flynn, Frank, xvi, 58, 60, 76–77, 78, 83, 105, 144, 180, 192, 256; *see also* Shultz, George, and Frank O'Flynn
O'Leary, Terence, xvii, 141, 163, 230–1, 249
Oliver Hazard Perry class frigates, *see* FFG-7s
Otago Daily Times, 274
Oxford Union debate, xiv, xv, 115, 147–8, 156–7, 158–60, 184, 199, 261, 262; agreeing to the motion, 160–3; lead-up, 163–5; preparation of speech, 164–5; speeches, 166–7; the responses, 168–71

INDEX

Pacific Fleet (US), 2
Palmer, Geoffrey, xiv, xvi, 29, 30–31, 41, 47, 59, 96, 302; and ANZUS, 147, 174–5, 216–18, 227, 270; and David Lange, 216–17, 221, 223, 227, 295; and press conferences, 211, 235, 270; and UN General Assembly, 219; and United States mission 1985, 190–1, 192, 196, 198–214, 215, 216–18, 219–20, 221, 222, 224, 226, 227, 229–30, 231, 233, 234; and visit to Germany 1985, 220–1; and visit to London 1985, 214, 219–20; and visit to London 1986, 275–6, 285; as Acting Prime Minister, 62, 97–99, 100–1, 102–5, 106–7, 108, 110, 113, 114, 270; as Deputy Prime Minister, 28, 57, 87, 156, 158, 168, 173, 174–5, 199, 221, 224, 237–8, 255, 262, 295; *see also* Buchanan, USS, and Geoffrey Palmer; Dam, Kenneth; Hawke, Bob, and Geoffrey Palmer; Lange, David: As LEADER OF THE LABOUR PARTY AND PRIME MINISTER: and Geoffrey Palmer; Shultz, George, and Geoffrey Palmer; United Nations General Assembly, Geoffrey Palmer at; Wolfowitz, Paul, and Geoffrey Palmer's visit
Papua New Guinea, 56, 189, 300
peace movement, xiii, 11, 12, 91–92, 100, 105, 109, 111, 112, 132, 133–4, 169, 201–2, 208, 250, 287, 293
Peace Movement Aotearoa, 93
peacekeeping responsibilities, New Zealand, 67
Pearl Harbor, 2, 87
Pentagon, xiv, 23, 35, 37, 74, 92, 133, 141, 150–1, 188, 209, 220, 231, 236, 260, 284
Pershing II missiles, 10, 163
Philby, Kim, 57
Philippines, 5, 61, 82, 300
Pine Gap, Australia, 283
Poananga, Brian, 278
Poindexter, Admiral John, 144
polls, opinion, 9, 44, 58–59, 66, 113, 125–6, 132, 172, 186–7, 224–6, 265, 272–3, 278, 279–81, 295, 306
Pope, Jeremy, 162, 163
Pope, Margaret, xiv, xvi, 114, 129, 149, 154, 164–5, 184, 186, 259, 290
port access, 37–38, 45, 47, 49, 63, 64, 69, 82, 85, 88, 122, 127, 131, 139, 145, 150, 172, 176, 177, 178–9, 188, 194, 197, 200, 203, 207–9, 215, 217, 226, 231, 232, 233, 234, 235, 236–8, 241, 252, 276, 277, 284
Powell, Charles, 171
Prebble, Richard, xiv, xvi, 27, 29, 30–31, 40–41, 104, 106–7, 113, 114, 204
Press, 62–63, 225, 273–4
press: Australian, 45, 48, 183; British, 168, 280; Chinese, 137; Japanese, 51; Soviet, 57; United States, 41, 152–3, 154

press reactions: to ANZUS, 62–63, 77, 132, 225–6, 272–4, 278, 280–1, 293–4; to David Lange, 48, 224, 293; to nuclear issue, 111–12, 137, 149, 151, 180, 191, 278, 280–1, 302; to Oxford Union debate, 161, 167–9; to United States, 273–4, 302; *see also* radio coverage of anti-nuclear issue; television coverage of ANZUS issue
protectionism, 123, 265, 276, 282–3, 298
protests: anti-American, 283; anti-Australian, 181–2; anti-nuclear, 7, 11–12, 61–62, 93–94, 112, 126, 136, 201, 244, 283, 302–3

radio coverage of anti-nuclear issue, 93
Radio Moscow, 223
Radio New Zealand, 63, 279, 294
Rainbow Warrior, 125, 190–1, 219, 225, 259, 265, 269, 274, 287
Ramphal, Shridath, 56, 137
Reagan Administration, xii, 11, 32, 37–38, 43, 49, 63, 74–75, 80, 112, 116, 117, 118, 120–5, 128, 129–30, 138, 139, 140, 141, 145, 147–8, 149, 150, 151, 153–6, 157, 160, 172, 177–8, 189, 196, 202, 204, 207, 210, 211, 214, 218, 223, 232–5, 238, 242–3, 250, 275, 282–4, 307; view of in New Zealand, 206, 226, 232, 233, 235, 236–7
Reagan, Ronald, xvii, 23, 37, 47, 52, 84, 112, 118, 121, 117, 139, 141–2, 143, 144, 146, 147, 148, 160, 163, 178, 225, 266
Reeves, Sir Paul, 242
Reeves, W. P., 273
Richardson, Ken, 165
Rowling Government, 6
Rowling, Bill, 9–10, 13, 26, 32, 127, 187; as ambassador to United States, xi, xvi, 13, 62, 90, 97, 117, 127–8, 129–30, 139, 147, 149, 151, 177–8, 179, 180–1, 190, 196, 201, 203, 206, 212, 213, 216, 223, 233, 234, 237, 246, 252, 281–2
Roy, Stapleton, xii
Royal Navy, 52, 53, 69, 170, 198, 201, 203, 220, 230, 248, 256, 259
Royal New Zealand Air Force, 36, 251
Royal New Zealand Navy, 81, 97
Royal Society, 74
Rudd, Roland, xv, 160, 161, 165, 166–8; *see also* Oxford Union debate
Rusk, Dean, 4

Samoa, 97; and ship visits, 56; *see also* American Samoa
Schroeder, Pat, 92
Sea Eagle, 81, 86, 99, 103, 135
Second World War, ix, 2, 140, 159, 224, 288, 296, 300, 301, 307
Select Committee on Foreign Affairs and Trade, 92

INDEX

Senate, US, 121, 147, 179, 282
Senate Armed Services Committee, 121
Senate Foreign Relations Committee, 120
Shadbolt, Tim, 28
ship visits, xiii, 6, 8, 9–10, 12, 36, 46, 47–49, 67–69, 71, 73–75, 96, 117, 119–20, 136, 137, 148, 157, 188, 306; American requests for, 32–33, 40, 64–65, 79–81, 84–87, 88–90, 91, 93, 94–96, 97, 99–103, 105, 111–13, 117, 119, 154, 186–7, 203–4; and ANZUS, 13, 31, 32, 33, 46, 49, 67, 81, 216–17, 221; banning of, 6, 9, 53, 116, 118, 124, 126, 127, 149, 151–2, 155, 170, 191, 196–7, 200–1, 229, 302, 307; negotiations for, 82–83, 91, 149, 178, 188–90, 196–211, 216, 222, 230, 232, 234–8, 240, 244–7, 249, 252, 264–7; opposition to, 58–59, 67, 91–93, 96, 126, 185, 186–7, 201–2, 279; United States responses to New Zealand's banning of, 138, 148, 155, 178, 188–90, 230; *see also* Lange, David: THE NUCLEAR AND ANZUS ISSUES: and ship visits and ship visits
Shultz, George, xii, xiv, xvii, 30, 47, 74, 77, 82, 85, 92, 94, 105, 119, 120, 130, 147, 148, 233, 236; and American Antarctic base, Christchurch, 283; and ANZUS, 38, 194, 284; and Australia, 35–36, 142, 172–3, 192–4; and David Lange, 37–43, 47, 75–76, 78–81, 82, 91, 118, 120, 210, 264–7, 272, 276; and Frank O'Flynn, 52, 58, 180, 192; and Geoffrey Palmer, 192, 202, 203–4, 211–13, 214, 215–17, 220, 222, 231; and Great Britain, 140, 141–2, 223, 231–2, 239; and NCND policy, 69–70, 81, 215, 239, 272; and New Zealand, 37–43, 47, 68, 117–18, 140, 141–2, 194–5, 210, 211, 216, 222, 223, 227, 231–2, 237, 239, 240, 242, 260, 264–7, 268–9, 273, 275, 276–7, 282–3, 284, 292; and renewed talks with New Zealand, 232–2, 236–7, 240; *see also* Lange, David: ON THE INTERNATIONAL STAGE: and George Shultz
Sigur, Gaston, xvii, 253, 281
Sinai, New Zealand observer force in, 61, 67, 175, 197, 300
Singapore, 4–5, 17; and New Zealand, 19, 54–55, 135, 167, 181, 254–5, 304; and New Zealand battalion in, 54, 60–61, 67, 134–5, 164, 175, 181, 197, 286, 304n; and ship visits, 177, 255
Social Credit Party, 34
Socialist Unity Party, 58
Solarz, Stephen, 13, 122, 177–8, 189, 242–5, 282
Somare, Michael, 56
South Africa, 18
South East Asia nuclear-free zone, 269
South East Asia, security of, 1, 4, 5, 14, 15, 26, 54–55, 67, 134–5, 181, 188, 197, 300, 303–4
South Pacific Forum, 48, 196–7

South Pacific Nuclear Free Zone and Treaty, 26, 48–49, 178, 197, 286
South Pacific security, 67, 68, 71, 73–74, 75, 80–81, 87, 137, 152, 154–5, 174–6, 177, 189, 195, 267, 285–6, 290
Soviet Communist Party, International Department, 286
Soviet Navy, 133–4
Soviet Union, 136, 160–1, 261; and ANZUS, 136–7; and arms control, 72, 134; and arms race, 11; and Australia, 12, 56, 57; and invasion of Afghanistan, 154; and New Zealand, 12, 13, 23, 56–58, 96, 136–7, 223, 286, 287; and South Pacific, 46, 50, 137, 150, 188, 285–6, 290; and United States, 3, 11, 57–58, 94, 133–4; and Western Alliance, 12, 23; as superpower, 13, 132, 303; as threat, 8, 10–11, 46, 53, 58, 93, 112, 119, 132, 133–4, 136, 137, 150, 152, 195, 262, 298
Spain: and anti-nuclear policy, 69, 92, 101–2, 266; and ship visits, 266
Springbok tour protests, 126
Stanley, John, xvii, 198–200, 214, 220
State Department, xii, xiii, xiv, 37, 40, 42, 63, 64, 65, 68, 74, 82, 92, 96, 111–12, 117, 119–20, 143, 144, 148, 149, 154, 177, 179, 180, 185–6, 187–9, 190, 192, 197, 202, 206, 210–11, 216, 223, 226, 227–8, 231, 234–5, 236, 239, 240, 248, 252, 258, 271–2, 284; *see also* Bureau of Intelligence and Research; East Asia Pacific (EAP) division; Inter-Agency Group
Steinlager beer, 122, 132
Sweden, and ship visits, 253
Sydney Morning Herald, 62, 132, 142, 168–9

Tangimoana defence station, 61–62
Tashkent, 152
Tass, 57, 96, 137
Teare, Richard, xiv, xvii, 76–77, 83, 89, 119
television coverage of anti-nuclear and ANZUS issues, 93, 124–5
Templeton, Ian, 48, 280
Templeton, Malcolm, xiii, 243–4
Terrorism Committee, 191
Texas, USS, 179–80
Thailand, 5, 54, 134, 304
Thatcher, Margaret, xvii, 52–54, 140, 141–2, 159, 162, 171, 181, 199, 228–9, 298; and David Lange, 53–54, 169–70, 171, 229, 261, 262–3; and ship visits, 228–9, 263, 298n; *see also* Lange, David: ON THE INTERNATIONAL STAGE: and Margaret Thatcher
The Times, 161, 169
'Think Big', 28
Thompson, Mervyn, 19
Three Mile Island nuclear power station, 9
Ticonderoga, USS, 272

317

INDEX

'Tiger Balm' exercise, 181
Time magazine, 163, 292
Tokelau, xiv, 97–98, 99, 105, 113, 114
Tonga, and ship visits, 56
Topping, Seymour, 186–7
trade: with Europe, 298, 303; with Great Britain; with Japan, 303; with United States, 63, 71, 80, 122–3, 139, 179, 226, 235, 282–3, 303
trade unions, 20, and anti-nuclear issue, 100, 152
Truman Administration, 2–3
Truxtun, USS, 9–10, 126
Tuvalu, 48, 56, 289, 300

United Nations, 2, 4, 51, 53, 84, 137, 219, 231, 300
United Nations General Assembly, 43, 48, 75–76; David Lange at, 62; Geoffrey Palmer at, 190, 216–17, 219
United States: and alliance relationship with New Zealand, 68–69, 82–86, 92, 125, 186, 192–5, 232–4, 239–40, 253, 264–7, 276, 285, 296; and ANZUS, 1–5, 13, 31–32, 36–38, 39, 78, 94, 121–2, 125, 128, 147, 171–5, 177–9, 186, 188–90, 193, 239, 240, 242–3, 258, 271–2, 276, 284, 287–8; and Australia, 2, 3–4, 5, 32, 41, 43, 53, 69, 82, 86, 117, 121, 130–1, 145, 148, 172–3, 178, 189, 192, 242, 248, 267, 268, 269, 270, 284, 288; and China, 137, 180–1, 208, 253–4, 276; and David Lange, 42, 44, 57, 59–60, 74–76, 82–83, 110, 112, 145, 162, 176–7, 187, 196, 202–3, 222–3, 240, 252–3, 264, 271, 294; and Great Britain, 53, 120, 146, 189, 196; and Japan, 69–70, 82, 86, 119–20, 145, 189, 253, 306; and New Zealand, ix–x, xi, 2, 3–4, 5, 6, 31–32, 33, 37, 40–41, 43, 50, 53, 58–64, 65, 66, 68–69, 73–81, 85, 110–12, 117–23, 138, 139, 140, 141–2, 145–6, 147–57, 172–3, 176–9, 180–1, 185–6, 187–9, 190, 191–3, 195–6, 202, 207–11, 212–14, 222, 223, 226–8, 230, 231–4, 238, 242–3, 246–7, 252–3, 254, 260–1, 264–7, 274–5, 276–7, 281–4, 298, 301–2, 303, 306–7; and security issues, 2–3, 7, 27, 38, 50, 68–69, 120, 132–4, 145, 185, 189, 194–5, 207–8, 213, 217, 239; and Soviet Union, 10–11, 94, 119, 194–5, 207–8, 276; and Western alliance, 10, 119, 189; as superpower, 13, 58, 124–5, 132, 303; missile testing by, 130–1
United States Congress, 37, 63, 80, 121, 122, 123, 125, 139, 156, 177, 179, 189, 192, 193, 242–4, 282
United States Department of Agriculture, 283
United States embassy: London, 53, 248; Wellington, 6, 10, 22–23, 26, 30, 43, 60, 61, 84–85, 89, 97, 150, 151, 195, 204, 234, 243, 260, 265, 268, 271–2, 274, 278, 287, 291, 301

United States Information Agency, 58, 125–6
United States Navy, 68, 69, 81, 86–87, 89, 92, 110, 114, 125, 134, 195, 200–1, 202, 203, 236, 259, 266, 283, 303
United States Seventh Fleet, 50, 119, 255
University of Canterbury, 17, 18, 124
University of Chicago, 205
University of Otago Foreign Policy School, 183–4

Vanuatu, 56, 185, 285, 303
Vietnam, 54, 61, 133, 206
Vietnam War, 1, 5–6, 7, 8, 9, 14, 38; Australian involvement in, 5–6; New Zealand involvement in, 5–6, 68, 299; opposition to, 6, 14, 92
Vietnamese Workers' Party, 5
Vintiner, Ross, xiv, xvi, 97, 104–6, 158, 160

Walding, Joe, xvi, 171, 229
Walker, Simon, 29
Washington Post, 92n, 112, 154
Watergate, 9
Watson, Peter, xv, 154
weapons: conventional, 66, 67, 170; nuclear, 6, 10–11, 49
Weinberger, Caspar, xvii, 65, 68, 117–18, 126, 159, 209, 210, 257, 260, 270, 306
Weiss, Cora, 92, 178
Wellington Regional Labour Party, 195
Western alliance, 12, 23, 59, 78, 94, 102, 120, 122, 160, 163–4, 183, 194–5, 220–1
Wilde, Fran, xvi, 93, 100, 197–8, 201, 286, 302
Wilson, Jeya, 160
Wilson, Margaret, xiv, xvi, 13, 15, 28, 30, 51, 61, 93, 100, 102, 107, 161, 204, 260, 262, 286
Woerner, Manfred, 221
Wolfowitz, Paul, xiv, xvii, 50, 148, 151, 205, 216, 253, 281; and David Lange, 31, 38–39, 40–41, 231; and Geoffrey Palmer's visit, 206, 207–9, 213–14; and New Zealand, 31–33, 35, 64, 74–75, 79, 82, 122, 127, 128, 130–1, 139, 177, 178–9, 180–1, 189, 192, 196, 203, 213–14, 222, 224, 227, 231, 307
Wood, John, xiv, xvi, 77, 116–17, 190, 212, 272
wool industry, New Zealand, and concessions, 121
World Peace Council, 96
Wright, Vernon, 290

Yomiuri, 285
Young, Baroness Janet, xvii, 161, 252, 255–7, 258, 275; *see also* Labour Party, and Baroness Young's visit; Lange, David: ON THE INTERNATIONAL STAGE: and Baroness Young